Better Homes and Gardens®

9x13

THE PAN THAT CAN

MORE THAN 370 FAMILY FAVORITES
TO FIT AMERICA'S MOST POPULAR PAN

MEREDITH® BOOKS
DES MOINES, IOWA

9X13: THE PAN THAT CAN

Editor: Lois White
Contributing Project Editor: Spectrum Communication
  Services, Inc.
Contributing Writer: Virginia Nemmers
Graphic Designer: Chad Jewell
Copy Chief: Doug Kouma
Copy Editor: Kevin Cox
Publishing Operations Manager: Karen Schirm
Edit and Design Production Coordinator: Mary Lee Gavin
Editorial Assistant: Sheri Cord
Book Production Managers: Marjorie J. Schenkelberg,
  Mark Weaver
Imaging Center Operator: Tony Jungweber
Contributing Copy Editor: Jane Burns
Contributing Proofreaders: Stephanie Boeding,
  Nicole Clausing, Maria Duryee
Contributing Indexer: Elizabeth T. Parsons
Test Kitchen Director: Lynn Blanchard
Test Kitchen Product Supervisor: Marilyn Cornelius
Test Kitchen Culinary Specialists: Juliana Hale, Maryellyn
  Krantz, Jill Moberly, Colleen Weeden, Lori Wilson
Test Kitchen Nutrition Specialists: Elizabeth Burt, R.D.,L.
  D.; Laura Marzen, R.D., L.D.

Meredith® Books
Editorial Director: John Riha
Managing Editor: Kathleen Armentrout
Deputy Editor: Jennifer Darling
Brand Manager: Janell Pittman
Group Editor: Jan Miller
Senior Associate Design Director: Mick Schnepf

Director, Marketing and Publicity: Amy Nichols
Executive Director, Sales: Ken Zagor
Director, Operations: George A. Susral
Director, Production: Douglas M. Johnston
Business Director: Janice Croat

Vice President and General Manager, SIM: Jeff Myers

Better Homes and Gardens® Magazine
Editor in Chief: Gayle Goodson Butler
Deputy Editor, Food and Entertaining: Nancy Hopkins

Meredith Publishing Group
President: Jack Griffin
Executive Vice President: Doug Olson

Meredith Corporation
Chairman of the Board: William T. Kerr
President and Chief Executive Officer: Stephen M. Lacy

In Memoriam: E. T. Meredith III (1933–2003)

All of us at Meredith® Books are dedicated to providing you
with the information and ideas you need to create delicious
foods. We welcome your comments and suggestions. Write to
us at: Meredith Books, Cookbook Editorial Department, 1716
Locust St., Des Moines, IA 50309-3023.

Our Better Homes and Gardens® Test Kitchen seal on the back
cover of this book assures you that every recipe in *9x13: The Pan
That Can* has been tested in the Better Homes and Gardens Test
Kitchen. This means that each recipe is practical and reliable,
and meets our high standards of taste appeal. We guarantee your
satisfaction with this book for as long as you own it.

TABLE OF CONTENTS

INTRODUCING AMERICA'S FAVORITE PAN—THE 9×13

At first glance, devoting an entire cookbook to a single pan might seem too narrow a focus. But it makes perfect sense when you consider that almost every household in the country has at least one 9x13 pan, and that—without a doubt—it is the most versatile vessel in the kitchen.

In this book, you'll find recipes for everything from classics such as German Chocolate Cake and Creamy Chicken Enchiladas to fun, updated flavors such as Greek-Style Lasagna and Fennel-Lime-Crusted Beef Tenderloin. No other pan is so versatile.

As with many inventions, the creation of the 9x13 pan was part stroke of brilliance, part serendipity.

It began with the collaboration of Jesse and Bessie Littleton. In 1912 Jesse, a physics instructor at the University of Michigan, joined the staff of Corning Glass Works in Corning, New York. Scientists at Corning had just developed a heat-resistant glass for railroad lanterns. The glass wouldn't shatter when cold rain or snow hit it.

Jesse thought this heat-resistant glass might make good cookware. He reasoned that while metal reflects heat, glass absorbs it. He cut the bottom off a large heat-resistant glass jar and brought it home to his wife, Bessie, who baked a cake in the improvised pan. Jesse brought the cake to work the next day for his colleagues to sample. They were impressed.

While scientists worked to improve the glass at Corning, Bessie did her own experimenting. She made a number of other recipes in her new dish and found that the cooking time was shorter than in her metal or earthenware pans, that food didn't stick (which made cleanup easier), that there was no residual smell or taste once the pan was washed, and that she could more easily monitor the food as it cooked in the clear glass to know when it was perfectly done.

In 1915 Corning introduced a line of new glass ovenware called Pyrex®, or "fire glass" (from the Greek "pyro" for fire and the "ex" from the branded name of the heat-resistant glass, Nonex). By 1920 the line included a rectangular dish with dimensions of $8\frac{1}{8} \times 12\frac{5}{8} \times 2$ inches—close to today's standard.

The pan proved so popular that by the 1930s, recipes were specifically calling for a 9x13 pan. A 1937 edition of the *Better Homes and Gardens® Cook Book* featured a recipe for Meringue-Topped Spice Cake that instructed cooks to "pour into a greased 9-by-13-inch pan." (You'll find an updated version of this popular snack cake on page 300.)

As American cooks became more familiar and innovative with the 9x13, they moved beyond cakes to bars and brownies and eventually to roasting meats and making one-dish dinners such as chicken potpie, chicken and rice casserole, and pork chop bakes. Handles were added to the pan in 1949 to make it easier to transport from the oven to the table.

Through the years Pyrex tinkered with the exact dimensions of its rectangular baking dish—expanding and contracting it slightly—until 1987, when the company settled on the 9x13 standard. Other manufacturers now make the pan in aluminum— uncoated, anodized, and nonstick— stainless steel, porcelain enamel-coated cast iron, ceramic, and copper.

From its beginning the 9x13 pan has made baking easier and more successful for American cooks. And while the pan has undergone a few changes over the years, its impact remains the same.

DID YOU KNOW?

- Not all manufacturers make this rectangular baking dish with the exacting 9x13 dimensions. Measure yours (or one you're considering buying) to be sure.

- A 9x13x2-inch pan has a volume of 3 quarts, so you can use it to make any recipe that calls for a 3-quart casserole. Because of the pan's shallow depth, food will cook faster and more evenly than in a deeper dish.

- A 9x13x2-inch pan is almost twice the size of an 8-inch square pan, so you can easily double most recipes for bars, brownies, and corn bread.

- The 9x13 pan is one of the top 20 items sold by bakeware maker Wilton, and the 9x13 glass baking dish is the No. 1-selling item of Pyrex glassware. Since the 1950s more than 50 million 9x13 pans have been purchased.

5

PAN PRIMER
HOW TO CHOOSE THE RIGHT PAN AND MAKE IT WORK

It goes by many names: that rectangular pan, your lasagna dish, the 3-quart casserole, Mom's favorite cake pan, and that one you always make the layered salad in for the neighborhood potluck. With endless uses, the 9x13 is the No. 1 pan or dish working in kitchens across America.

Many cooks received their first pan or dish as a bridal shower gift. Others bought theirs when they spotted a great cake or casserole and continue to use the pan on a regular basis.

Whether you're choosing bakeware for a new kitchen or you've been relying on your trusty old pans for years, check out the current selection of 9x13s and discover more exciting uses for them.

WHICH 9x13 IS FOR YOU?

Having the right pan or dish opens a world of possibilities for foods you can make—everything from savory roasts and lasagnas to gelatin salads and casseroles to cakes, cobblers, and bars. Today the variety of materials

the pans are made of is enough to make your head spin: glass, aluminum, plastic, even silicone; with nonstick finishes and without; with racks or with ridges. A rule of thumb when selecting pans or dishes: Choose according to the types of recipes you plan to prepare. Here are examples of recipes you'll find in this book.

Tomato-based recipes: If you're fond of making lasagna or red-sauced casseroles, glass bakeware is best. Baking pans made of aluminum, iron, or tin can react with acidic ingredients such as tomatoes or lemons, causing the foods to discolor. Nonstick pans may work, as long as you use serving utensils that won't scratch the surface.

No-bake bars, gelatin salads, and freezer desserts: Sturdy plastic containers will give you the best storage results. Choose a container that has an airtight seal that can store food at room temperature, in

the fridge, or in the freezer. Avoid choosing lighter plastic containers because they have a tendency to bend or fold when full.

Bars, brownies, and cakes: Dark or dull finish pans (tin, nonstick, or glass) absorb heat, which produces nice, even browning. Shiny finishes such as steel or stainless reflect heat, causing cakes to have thin, golden crusts.

Numerous 9×13 pans, available with removable roasting racks, can do double duty. With the rack it's a roasting pan; without, it's great for baking. You can also fashion your own roasting pan by inserting a roasting rack into a 9×13 pan or dish. Or if you are roasting meat and vegetables together, line the pan or dish with foil, add the vegetables, and roast the meat on top, letting the juices run down into the vegetables. Just be sure the meat or poultry sits at least ¾ inch above the bottom of the pan to prevent the roast from stewing in the pan juices.

MORE POINTERS FOR THE PAN

PAN COMPARISON

Glass or Stoneware

+
- Nonreactive surface
- Retains heat well
- Good for tomato-based casseroles such as lasagna, and citrus-sauced poultry or fish
- Rims/handles make it easy to grab with oven mitts for oven-to-table serving
- Clear glass makes it easy to monitor browning
- Nice for showing off beauty of gelatin or layered salads
- Some come with lids
- Dishwasher safe

−
- Breakable
- Cannot withstand sudden temperature change
- Unsafe for stovetop or broiler
- Some stoneware dishes require initial seasoning and cannot go in the dishwasher

Metal

+
- Good for roasting meats and poultry; cleans up easily
- Helps promote even cooking
- Can be used on stovetop
- Many pans come with lids
- Pans travel well and won't break
- Pans with handles are easier to remove from oven

−
- Less sturdy pans show wear over time and may need to be replaced more frequently.
- Can't use knives or forks, and other pointed items may damage the surface
- Some pans are not dishwasher safe

Plastic

+
- Good for no-bake recipes, refrigerator salads, or freezer desserts
- Good for storing cakes and cookies
- Good for toting
- Most are dishwasher safe

−
- Not for baking
- Sharp utensils damage surface

MORE POINTERS FOR THE PAN

SAFE TOTING

Choose a pan or dish with a tight-fitting lid. Pack cold foods in an insulated cooler with ice packs. Insulated casserole carriers are great for transporting hot dishes. You can also wrap a tightly covered dish of hot food in layers of newspaper or towels and transport it in an insulated carrier. Fill gaps around the food container with crumpled newspaper or towels to prevent shifting or spills.

SERVING SAVVY

Nonmetal spoons or spatulas are great serving utensils when using nonstick pans because they won't scratch or damage the surface. If you're looking for a quick way to get bars out of a pan without using a knife or spatula, line the pan with foil. After baking, grab the foil ends and lift the bars out of the pan before cutting. This way your pans won't become damaged by knife cuts and cleanup will be easier.

LEFTOVERS AND FREEZING

Whether you have one serving of a hot dish left or are dividing a casserole for another meal, here are a few things to keep in mind:

- It is best to refrigerate leftovers immediately after you have finished eating. Never let perishable foods cool at room temperature.
- Divide cooked foods into small portions in shallow containers. Place in refrigerator to chill. Then, if freezing, move food to the freezer.
- If you are freezing an entire dish before or after baking, always use freezer-to-oven dishes lined with foil. Cover them with plastic freezer wrap or with foil. When frozen, lift out the foil-lined food and place it in a storage container or freezer bag or wrap it in additional foil and return to the freezer. Be sure to label and date the food.

SLICK WAY TO GREASE A 9×13

When a recipe calls for greasing a pan or dish, dip a ball of waxed paper in shortening and wipe the pan with a light coating. Or use a light coating of nonstick cooking spray.

BAKING BARS AND BROWNIES

Lining the 9×13 pan with foil makes removing bars from the pan easier. Foil also helps keep pans from being damaged from knife cuts and makes cleanup easier. Just shape the foil over the outside of the pan, extending it over the edges about 1 inch, then place the shaped foil inside the pan. If your recipe calls for a greased pan, grease the foil inside the pan (or choose no-stick foil). Bake and cool the bars as usual, then grasp the extra foil at the edges to pull the uncut bars out of the pan.

WHEN TO USE A PAN, WHEN TO USE A DISH

Most of the recipes in this book call for a 9×13 pan or dish interchangeably. But when a recipe specifies one or the other, you'll want to choose accordingly in order to get the best results. Silicone pans are another alternative for using in the microwave, oven, and freezer. Follow the manufacturer's directions when using silcone pans.

BREAKFAST STRATAS AND EGG DISHES

After a week of on-the-go breakfasts, slow down and enjoy the most important meal of the day on the weekend. With these make-ahead and oven-ready dishes, you can sleep in or read the morning paper, even if you're serving brunch or treating your family. Nothing says you have to save these for the weekend.

MAKE-AHEAD EGGS BENEDICT

How can you possibly make eggs Benedict for a crowd? Prepare this clever recipe that has all the original's flavor with none of the last-minute preparation.

Prep: 25 minutes   **Chill:** 4 to 24 hours   **Bake:** 25 minutes   **Oven:** 350°F

- 8 **eggs**
- 4 **English muffins, split**
- 8 **slices Canadian-style bacon**
- 1 **recipe Mock Hollandaise Sauce**
- **Paprika (optional)**

1 Lightly grease a large skillet. Half-fill the skillet with water. Bring water to boiling; reduce heat to simmering (bubbles should begin to break the surface of the water). Break one of the eggs into a measuring cup. Holding the lip of the cup as close to the water as possible, carefully slide egg into simmering water. Repeat with remaining eggs, allowing each egg an equal amount of space.

2 Simmer eggs, uncovered, for 3 to 5 minutes or until the whites are completely set and yolks begin to thicken but are not hard. Using a slotted spoon, remove eggs to a plate.

3 Meanwhile, place muffin halves, cut sides up, on a baking sheet. Broil 3 to 4 inches from the heat about 2 minutes or until toasted.

4 Grease a 9×13-inch baking pan or baking dish. Place muffin halves in prepared pan or dish. Top each muffin half with a slice of Canadian-style bacon and one cooked egg. Cover and chill for at least 4 hours or up to 24 hours. Prepare Mock Hollandaise Sauce; cover and chill for up to 24 hours.

5 To serve, preheat oven to 350°F. Spoon Mock Hollandaise Sauce over eggs. Bake, covered, about 25 minutes or until heated through. If desired, sprinkle with paprika.

Makes 8 servings.

Nutrition Facts per serving: 366 cal., 27 g total fat (7 g sat. fat), 241 mg chol., 692 mg sodium, 15 g carbo., 1 g fiber, 15 g pro.

Mock Hollandaise Sauce:
In a small bowl stir together ¾ cup dairy sour cream, ¾ cup mayonnaise or salad dressing, 1 tablespoon lemon juice, and 1½ teaspoons yellow mustard. If desired, thin with a little milk. Makes 1½ cups.

Salmon Benedict:
Prepare as directed, except omit the Canadian-style bacon and use 8 ounces thinly sliced smoked salmon (lox style) and stir 2 tablespoons drained capers into the Mock Hollandaise Sauce. Do not use the paprika.

Nutrition Facts per serving: 357 cal., 27 g total fat (7 g sat. fat), 234 mg chol., 964 mg sodium, 15 g carbo., 1 g fiber, 14 g pro.

Crab Benedict:
Prepare as directed, except omit the Canadian-style bacon and use two 6½-ounce cans crabmeat, drained, flaked, and cartilage removed.

Nutrition Facts per serving: 369 cal., 26 g total fat (7 g sat. fat), 268 mg chol., 487 mg sodium, 15 g carbo., 1 g fiber, 19 g pro.

Mushroom Benedict:
Prepare as directed, except before cooking eggs, in a large skillet melt ¼ cup butter. Add 4 cups sliced fresh mushrooms. Cook and stir until mushrooms are tender. Continue as directed, except use the mushrooms instead of the Canadian-style bacon and sprinkle with 2 tablespoons snipped fresh basil instead of the paprika.

Nutrition Facts per serving: 385 cal., 31 g total fat (10 g sat. fat), 243 mg chol., 377 mg sodium, 16 g carbo., 1 g fiber, 11 g pro.

OVEN OMELET

OVEN-STYLE EGG

It's the easiest way to make omelets for a crowd. This oven method lets you vary the fillings to suit your family's tastes.

Prep: 20 minutes **Bake:** 15 minutes **Oven:** 400°F

Nonstick cooking spray

10	eggs
¼	cup water
½	teaspoon salt
⅛	teaspoon white pepper or black pepper
1	recipe Ham and Vegetable Filling or Tomato-Basil Filling
1	cup shredded cheddar cheese, Swiss cheese, mozzarella cheese, or Monterey Jack cheese (4 ounces)

1. Lightly coat a 9×13-inch baking pan or baking dish with nonstick cooking spray; set aside. Preheat oven to 400°F. In a large bowl whisk together eggs, the water, salt, and pepper until combined but not frothy.

2. Pour egg mixture into the prepared pan or dish. Bake about 15 minutes or until egg mixture is set but still has a glossy surface.

3. Meanwhile, prepare Ham and Vegetable Filling or Tomato-Basil Filling. Cut the baked egg mixture into six "omelets." Using a wide metal spatula, remove each omelet. Invert omelets onto warm serving plates. Sprinkle omelets with shredded cheese.

4. Divide Ham and Vegetable Filling or Tomato-Basil Filling among omelets, spooning the filling over half of each omelet. Fold the other half of each omelet over the filled half, forming a triangle or a rectangle; press lightly. Serve the omelets immediately.

Makes 6 servings.

Nutrition Facts per serving with Ham and Vegetable Filling: 263 cal., 19 g total fat (7 g sat. fat), 385 mg chol., 732 mg sodium, 4 g carbo., 1 g fiber, 20 g pro.

11

Ham and Vegetable Filling: *In a large skillet heat 1 tablespoon cooking oil over medium-high heat. Add 2 cups of your favorite chopped vegetables (such as broccoli, zucchini, and/or sweet peppers); cook and stir for 3 to 4 minutes or until crisp-tender. Add 1 cup diced cooked ham (about 5 ounces); heat through. Makes 2 cups.*

Tomato-Basil Filling: *In a medium skillet heat 1 teaspoon olive oil over medium heat. Add 2 cups chopped plum tomatoes; cook and stir for 2 to 3 minutes or until heated through. Remove from heat. Stir in 1 tablespoon snipped fresh basil. Makes 1¼ cups. Nutrition Facts per serving with Tomato-Basil Filling: 213 cal., 15 g total fat (7 g sat. fat), 372 mg chol., 431 mg sodium, 3 g carbo., 1 g fiber, 17 g pro.*

OVEN-STYLE EGGS AND HAM

Scrambled eggs, ham, and vegetables in a creamy cheese sauce—if anything can make you look forward to getting out of bed on a weekend morning, this is it. Toasted English muffins are easy serve-alongs.

Prep: 30 minutes   **Chill:** 4 to 24 hours   **Bake:** 45 minutes   **Oven:** 350°F

- 5 eggs
- ⅛ teaspoon salt
- 2 tablespoons butter or margarine
- 1 tablespoon all-purpose flour
- ⅛ teaspoon black pepper
- ¾ cup milk
- ¾ cup cut-up process Swiss cheese (3 ounces)
- 1 teaspoon yellow mustard
- 1 16-ounce package desired loose-pack frozen vegetable mix (such as corn, broccoli, and red sweet peppers)
- 3 ounces cooked ham, cut into bite-size strips (about ½ cup)
- ¼ cup shredded process Swiss cheese (1 ounce)

1 In a medium bowl whisk together eggs and salt. In a 10-inch skillet melt 1 tablespoon of the butter over medium heat; pour in egg mixture. Cook, without stirring, until mixture begins to set on the bottom and around the edge.

2 With a spatula or large spoon, lift and fold the partially cooked eggs so that the uncooked portion flows underneath. Continue cooking over medium heat for 2 to 3 minutes or until eggs are cooked through but are still glossy and moist. Immediately remove from heat; set aside.

3 For sauce, in a large saucepan melt the remaining 1 tablespoon butter over medium heat. Stir in flour and pepper. Add milk all at once. Cook and stir until mixture is thickened and bubbly. Add the ¾ cup cheese and the mustard, stirring until cheese melts.

4 Stir in vegetables and ham; gently fold in cooked eggs. Transfer mixture to an ungreased 9×13-inch baking pan or baking dish. Cover and chill for at least 4 hours or up to 24 hours.

5 Preheat oven to 350°F. Bake, covered, for 45 to 50 minutes or until heated through, gently stirring after 15 minutes. Gently stir again before serving. Sprinkle with the ¼ cup cheese.

Makes 6 servings.

Nutrition Facts per serving: 262 cal., 15 g total fat (8 g sat. fat), 214 mg chol., 386 mg sodium, 14 g carbo., 2 g fiber, 16 g pro.

ALL-IN-ONE BREAKFAST

All it takes is six ingredients to deliver an impressive breakfast entrée. Serve this with fresh fruit and coffee cake warm from the oven.

Prep: 25 minutes   **Chill:** 4 to 24 hours   **Bake:** 35 minutes   **Stand:** 10 minutes   **Oven:** 375°F

- 6   English muffins, split
- 1   pound bulk pork sausage
- 12 eggs
- 1   8-ounce carton dairy sour cream
- 1   4-ounce can chopped green chile peppers
- 1   cup shredded cheddar cheese (4 ounces)

1 Grease a 9×13-inch baking pan or baking dish. Arrange English muffins in prepared pan or dish, overlapping as necessary; set aside.

2 In a large skillet cook sausage until cooked through, using a wooden spoon to break up sausage as it cooks; drain off fat.

3 In a large bowl beat eggs lightly with a whisk until combined. Add the sausage, sour cream, and chile peppers; whisk until combined. Pour egg mixture evenly over muffins in pan or dish. Press down lightly with a rubber spatula or the back of a large spoon to moisten all of the muffins. Sprinkle with cheese. Cover and chill for at least 4 hours or up to 24 hours.

4 Preheat oven to 375°F. Bake, uncovered, for 35 to 40 minutes or until a knife inserted near the center comes out clean (170°F). Let stand for 10 minutes before serving.

Makes 12 servings.

Nutrition Facts per serving: 334 cal., 23 g total fat (9 g sat. fat), 257 mg chol., 554 mg sodium, 15 g carbo., 1 g fiber, 17 g pro.

13

HERBED EGG-CHEESE CASSEROLE

Remember this dish in the spring if you have a refrigerator full of hard-cooked Easter eggs. But don't feel you have to wait until then!

Prep: 20 minutes **Bake:** 25 minutes **Oven:** 350°F

POTLUCK ● FAVORITE

14

- ¼ cup butter or margarine
- ¼ cup all-purpose flour
- ¾ teaspoon dried Italian seasoning, crushed
- 1 12-ounce can (1½ cups) evaporated milk or 1⅓ cups half-and-half or light cream
- ⅔ cup milk
- 2 cups shredded sharp cheddar cheese (8 ounces)
- 18 hard-cooked eggs, thinly sliced
- 8 ounces bacon, crisp-cooked, drained, and crumbled
- ¼ cup snipped fresh parsley
- 1 cup fine dry bread crumbs
- ¼ cup butter or margarine, melted

1 Grease a 9×13-inch baking pan or baking dish; set aside. Preheat oven to 350°F. In a medium saucepan melt ¼ cup butter over medium heat. Stir in flour and Italian seasoning. Stir in evaporated milk and milk all at once. Cook and stir until thickened and bubbly. Cook and stir for 1 minute more. Remove from heat. Slowly add shredded cheddar cheese, stirring after each addition until cheese is melted. Set aside.

2 Layer half of the hard-cooked eggs, half of the bacon, and half of the parsley in prepared pan or dish. Pour half of the cheese mixture evenly over egg mixture. Repeat layers.

3 In a small bowl stir together bread crumbs and ¼ cup melted butter. Sprinkle crumb mixture over layers in pan or dish.

4 Bake casserole, uncovered, for 25 to 30 minutes or until heated through.

Makes 12 servings.

Nutrition Facts per serving: 384 cal., 28 g total fat (14 g sat. fat), 374 mg chol., 471 mg sodium, 13 g carbo., 0 g fiber, 20 g pro.

SPINACH BREAKFAST CASSEROLE

Spinach and carrots add colorful nutrients to this all-time overnight favorite. For variety substitute frozen kale or chopped broccoli for spinach.

Prep: 30 minutes **Chill:** 8 to 24 hours **Bake:** 55 minutes **Stand:** 10 minutes **Oven:** 325°F

4 cups seasoned croutons (about 7 ounces)

1 pound bulk pork sausage, cooked and well drained

1 10-ounce package frozen chopped spinach, thawed and well drained

½ cup coarsely shredded carrot

4 eggs, beaten

2 cups milk

1 10¾-ounce can condensed cream of mushroom soup

1 cup shredded cheddar cheese (4 ounces)

1 cup shredded Monterey Jack cheese (4 ounces)

1 4-ounce can (drained weight) sliced mushrooms, drained

¼ teaspoon dry mustard

Shredded cheddar and/or Monterey Jack cheese (optional)

1 Spread croutons evenly in an ungreased 9×13-inch baking pan or baking dish. Spread sausage evenly over croutons. Sprinkle spinach and carrot evenly over sausage.

2 In a medium bowl stir together eggs, milk, cream of mushroom soup, the 1 cup cheddar cheese, the 1 cup Monterey Jack cheese, the mushrooms, and the dry mustard until well mixed. Pour egg mixture evenly over ingredients in pan or dish. Press down lightly with a rubber spatula or the back of a large spoon to moisten all of the croutons. Cover and chill for at least 8 hours or up to 24 hours.

3 Preheat oven to 325°F. Bake, uncovered, for 45 minutes. If desired, sprinkle with additional cheese. Bake about 10 minutes more or until edges are bubbly and center is heated through. Let stand for 10 minutes before serving.

Makes 12 servings.

Nutrition Facts per serving: 346 cal., 24 g total fat (10 g sat. fat), 115 mg chol., 754 mg sodium, 15 g carbo., 2 g fiber, 15 g pro.

CHEESE AND MUSHROOM EGG CASSEROLE

A classic combination of mushrooms and cheese
gets dressed up for a special family breakfast
or a company brunch.

Prep: 25 minutes **Bake:** 20 minutes **Oven:** 350°F

16 eggs

1 cup milk

2 tablespoons butter or margarine

3 cups sliced fresh mushrooms

½ cup thinly sliced green onions

1 10¾-ounce can condensed cream of broccoli soup or cream of asparagus soup

¼ cup milk

1 cup shredded Monterey Jack cheese (4 ounces)

¼ cup grated Parmesan cheese

1 Grease a 9×13-inch baking pan or baking dish; set aside. Preheat oven to 350°F.

2 For scrambled eggs, in a large bowl beat together eggs and the 1 cup milk with a rotary beater. In a 12-inch nonstick skillet melt 1 tablespoon of the butter over medium heat. Add half of the egg mixture. Cook over medium heat, without stirring, until mixture begins to set on the bottom and around the edge. Using a large spoon, lift and fold the partially cooked egg mixture so the uncooked portion flows underneath. Continue cooking until egg mixture is cooked through but is still glossy and moist. Remove from heat immediately.

3 Transfer scrambled eggs to prepared pan or dish. Repeat to scramble the remaining eggs in the remaining 1 tablespoon butter; remove from heat immediately. Transfer to the pan or dish.

4 In the same nonstick skillet cook mushrooms and green onions until tender. Stir in cream of broccoli soup and the ¼ cup milk. Stir in Monterey Jack cheese and Parmesan cheese. Spread soup mixture over eggs in pan or dish.

5 Bake, covered, about 20 minutes or until heated through.

Makes 10 servings.

Nutrition Facts per serving: 239 cal., 17 g total fat (8 g sat. fat), 361 mg chol., 435 mg sodium, 6 g carbo., 1 g fiber, 16 g pro.

HEARTY POTATO AND SAUSAGE CASSEROLE

Herbs, onions, and cheese spruce up sliced potatoes and sausage. This dish makes a great partner for scrambled eggs. Add fruit and cinnamon rolls to round out the meal.

Prep: 30 minutes **Cook:** 12 minutes **Bake:** 20 minutes **Oven:** 350°F

- 3 large long white potatoes (about 1½ pounds), peeled and cut into ¼-inch-thick slices (about 5 cups)
- 3 tablespoons butter or margarine
- 2 cups chopped onion
- 1 tablespoon dried parsley flakes, crushed
- ½ teaspoon garlic salt
- ½ teaspoon black pepper
- ½ teaspoon dried thyme, crushed
- ½ teaspoon dried sage, crushed
- ¼ teaspoon dried rosemary, crushed
- 1 pound bulk pork sausage
- 2 cups shredded Swiss cheese (8 ounces) or 8 ounces sliced Swiss cheese

1 In a covered large saucepan cook potatoes in lightly salted boiling water for 12 to 15 minutes or just until tender. Drain well.

2 Preheat oven to 350°F. In a large heavy skillet melt butter over medium-high heat. Add potatoes and onion; cook until potatoes are lightly browned, turning often. Add parsley flakes, garlic salt, pepper, thyme, sage, and rosemary; toss lightly. Spoon mixture into an ungreased 9×13-inch baking pan or baking dish.

3 In the same skillet cook sausage over medium-low heat until cooked through, using a wooden spoon to break up sausage as it cooks; drain off fat. Spread the cooked sausage over potato mixture. Sprinkle evenly with shredded cheese or arrange cheese slices over the sausage.

4 Bake casserole, uncovered, for 20 to 25 minutes or until heated through.

Makes 8 servings.

Nutrition Facts per serving: 423 cal., 29 g total fat (13 g sat. fat), 76 mg chol., 549 mg sodium, 24 g carbo., 2 g fiber, 16 g pro.

SOUTHWESTERN POTATO BREAKFAST BAKE

Bring on the mariachi band! Tomatoes and green chile peppers give this hearty dish a definite sunny flavor. Serve it with salsa, warmed tortillas, and an orange-avocado salad.

Prep: 25 minutes **Bake:** 30 minutes **Stand:** 10 minutes **Oven:** 375°F

Nonstick cooking spray

- 5 cups frozen shredded hash brown potatoes (half of a 30-ounce package)
- ¼ teaspoon seasoned salt
- 1 large onion, chopped
- 1 tablespoon olive oil
- 2 14½-ounce cans diced tomatoes and green chile peppers, undrained
- 1 teaspoon chili powder
- ½ teaspoon seasoned salt
- ¼ teaspoon black pepper
- 8 eggs
- ⅓ cup milk
- 1 cup shredded Mexican cheese blend (4 ounces)

1 Lightly coat a 9×13-inch baking pan or baking dish with nonstick cooking spray. Preheat oven to 375°F. Arrange potatoes evenly in prepared pan or dish; sprinkle with the ¼ teaspoon seasoned salt. Set aside.

2 In a large skillet cook onion in hot oil until tender. Stir in undrained tomatoes, chili powder, the ½ teaspoon seasoned salt, and the black pepper. Bring to boiling; reduce heat. Simmer, uncovered, for 10 minutes, stirring occasionally. Spoon over potatoes in pan or dish.

3 In a large bowl whisk together eggs and milk; pour evenly over mixture in pan or dish. Sprinkle with shredded cheese.

4 Bake, uncovered, for 30 to 35 minutes or until a knife inserted near the center comes out clean (170°F). Let stand for 10 minutes before serving.

Makes 8 servings.

Nutrition Facts per serving: 221 cal., 11 g total fat (5 g sat. fat), 225 mg chol., 635 mg sodium, 17 g carbo., 3 g fiber, 13 g pro.

HAM-ASPARAGUS STRATA

Enjoy this delicious dish any time of year

by using fresh or frozen asparagus or broccoli

depending on the season.

Prep: 25 minutes   **Chill:** 2 to 24 hours   **Bake:** 1 hour   **Stand:** 10 minutes   **Oven:** 325°F

- **6** English muffins, torn or cut into bite-size pieces (about 6 cups)
- **3** cups cubed cooked ham or chicken (about 1 pound)
- **1** 9-ounce package frozen cut asparagus or frozen cut broccoli, thawed and well drained, or 2 cups cooked cut-up fresh asparagus or broccoli
- **9** slices process Swiss cheese, torn (6 ounces)
- **6** eggs
- **⅓** cup dairy sour cream
- **1¾** cups milk
- **¼** cup finely chopped onion
- **2** tablespoons Dijon-style mustard
- **¼** teaspoon black pepper

1 Grease a 9×13-inch baking pan or baking dish. Arrange half of the English muffin pieces in the prepared pan or dish. Top with ham, asparagus, and cheese. Top with the remaining English muffin pieces.

2 In a large bowl whisk together eggs and sour cream. Stir in milk, onion, mustard, and pepper. Pour egg mixture evenly over ingredients in pan or dish. Press down lightly with a rubber spatula or the back of a large spoon to moisten all of the muffin pieces. Cover and chill for at least 2 hours or up to 24 hours.

3 Preheat oven to 325°F. Bake, uncovered, for 60 to 70 minutes or until a knife inserted near the center comes out clean (170°F) (the top will appear moist but will set up during standing). Let stand for 10 minutes before serving.

Makes 9 servings.

Nutrition Facts per serving: 334 cal., 15 g total fat (7 g sat. fat), 192 mg chol., 1,287 mg sodium, 22 g carbo., 2 g fiber, 25 g pro.

19

CANADIAN BACON AND SWISS STRATA

The dry white wine in this
do-ahead recipe gives the
strata a pleasant, subtle flavor.

Prep: 20 minutes   **Chill:** 2 to 24 hours   **Bake:** 50 minutes   **Stand:** 10 minutes   **Oven:** 325°F

- 8 ounces firm-texture whole wheat bread, cut into 1-inch cubes (6 cups)
- 1 4-ounce can (drained weight) sliced mushrooms, drained
- ½ cup sliced green onions
- ½ cup chopped Canadian-style bacon
- 1¼ cups shredded Swiss cheese (5 ounces)
- 4 eggs, beaten
- 4 egg whites
- 1¾ cups milk
- 1 cup cream-style cottage cheese
- ½ cup dry white wine or reduced-sodium chicken broth
- 2 tablespoons Dijon-style mustard
- ¼ teaspoon salt
- ¼ teaspoon black pepper
- ⅛ teaspoon cayenne pepper
- ⅓ cup grated Parmesan cheese
- 2 tablespoons toasted wheat germ

1 Grease a 9×13-inch baking pan or baking dish. Place bread cubes in prepared pan or dish. Top with mushrooms, green onions, and Canadian-style bacon. Sprinkle with Swiss cheese.

2 In a large bowl whisk together eggs, egg whites, milk, cottage cheese, wine, mustard, salt, black pepper, and cayenne pepper. Pour egg mixture evenly over ingredients in baking pan or dish. Press down lightly with a rubber spatula or the back of a large spoon to moisten all of the bread. Cover and chill for at least 2 hours or up to 24 hours.

3 Preheat oven to 325°F. Bake, uncovered, for 40 minutes. In a small bowl stir together Parmesan cheese and toasted wheat germ; sprinkle over strata.

4 Bake about 10 minutes more or until a knife inserted near the center comes out clean (170°F) and top is golden brown. Let stand for 10 minutes before serving.

Makes 10 servings.

Nutrition Facts per serving: 243 cal., 11 g total fat (5 g sat. fat), 113 mg chol., 646 mg sodium, 17 g carbo., 2 g fiber, 19 g pro.

SPICY SICILIAN STRATA

Who says you can't have pizza for breakfast? Kids will love this winning dish loaded with favorite pizza toppings and a few good-for-you extras.

Prep: 40 minutes **Chill:** 2 to 24 hours **Bake:** 40 minutes **Stand:** 10 minutes **Oven:** 350°F

- 1 8-ounce loaf French bread, cut into 1-inch cubes (10 cups)
- 1 3½-ounce package sliced pepperoni, coarsely chopped
- ½ cup pepperoncini salad peppers, drained, stemmed, and chopped
- 1 10-ounce package frozen chopped spinach, thawed and well drained
- ½ cup oil-pack dried tomatoes, drained and chopped
- 1 8-ounce package shredded Italian blend cheese (2 cups)
- 6 eggs, slightly beaten
- 3 cups milk
- 2 teaspoons dried Italian seasoning, crushed
- ¼ teaspoon salt
- ⅛ teaspoon cayenne pepper
- ¼ cup grated Parmesan cheese

1 Preheat oven to 350°F. Place bread cubes in a 10×15-inch baking pan. Bake, uncovered, for 10 minutes, stirring once.

2 Grease a 9×13-inch baking pan or baking dish. Arrange half of the bread cubes evenly in prepared pan or dish. Top with half of the pepperoni, half of the pepperoncini peppers, all of the spinach, and all of the tomatoes. Sprinkle with 1 cup of the Italian blend cheese. Repeat layers with the remaining bread, the remaining pepperoni, the remaining pepperoncini peppers, and the remaining Italian blend cheese.

3 In a large bowl whisk together eggs, milk, Italian seasoning, salt, and cayenne pepper. Slowly pour egg mixture evenly over layers in dish. Press down lightly with a rubber spatula or the back of a large spoon to moisten all of the bread. Sprinkle with Parmesan cheese. Cover and chill for at least 2 hours or up to 24 hours.

4 Preheat oven to 350°F. Bake, uncovered, for 40 to 45 minutes or until a knife inserted near the center comes out clean (170°F). Let stand for 10 minutes before serving.

Makes 10 to 12 servings.

Nutrition Facts per serving: 290 cal., 16 g total fat (7 g sat. fat), 162 mg chol., 811 mg sodium, 18 g carbo., 2 g fiber, 18 g pro.

CHICKEN MUSHROOM STRATA

This dish, like other stratas, is perfect for entertaining. You can get it oven-ready up to 24 hours in advance, easing the last-minute time crunch when you're serving a crowd.

Prep: 25 minutes **Chill:** 2 to 24 hours **Bake:** 45 minutes **Stand:** 10 minutes **Oven:** 325°F

- 2 5½-ounce packages (about 6 cups) large croutons
- 2½ cups chopped cooked chicken or turkey (about 12 ounces)
- 1 4-ounce can (drained weight) sliced mushrooms, drained
- ½ cup sliced green onions
- 1½ cups shredded Colby and Monterey Jack cheese or cheddar cheese (6 ounces)
- 5 eggs
- 1 10¾-ounce can condensed cream of chicken soup or cream of mushroom soup
- 1½ cups milk
- 1 tablespoon Dijon-style mustard
- ¼ teaspoon black pepper

1 Grease a 9×13-inch baking pan or baking dish. Place croutons in prepared pan or dish. Layer chicken, mushrooms, and green onions over croutons; sprinkle with cheese.

2 In a large bowl whisk together eggs, cream of chicken soup, milk, mustard, and pepper. Pour egg mixture evenly over layers in the pan or dish. Press down lightly with a rubber spatula or the back of a large spoon to moisten all of the croutons. Cover and chill for at least 2 hours or up to 24 hours.

3 Preheat oven to 325°F. Bake, uncovered, about 45 minutes or until a knife inserted near the center comes out clean (170°F). Let stand for 10 minutes before serving.

Makes 10 to 12 servings.

Nutrition Facts per serving: 355 cal., 15 g total fat (7 g sat. fat), 158 mg chol., 722 mg sodium, 29 g carbo., 2 g fiber, 23 g pro.

BAKED DENVER STRATA

An old favorite, the Denver omelet, is revitalized in this trendy one-dish meal. Complete with veggies, cheese, meat, and eggs, this new version adds English muffins to the mix to create a complete and convenient breakfast dish.

Prep: 25 minutes **Chill:** 2 to 24 hours **Bake:** 45 minutes **Stand:** 10 minutes **Oven:** 350°F

6	English muffins, split and quartered
9	eggs
1	cup milk
1	4-ounce can diced green chile peppers, drained
¼	teaspoon salt
¼	teaspoon black pepper
1	cup diced cooked ham (about 5 ounces)
1	7-ounce jar roasted red sweet peppers, drained and cut into strips (about 1 cup)
½	cup finely chopped green onions
1	2½-ounce can sliced pitted ripe olives, drained
1½	cups shredded provolone cheese (6 ounces)
½	cup shredded cheddar cheese (2 ounces)

1 Grease a 9×13-inch baking pan or baking dish. Arrange English muffin quarters in a single layer in prepared pan or dish; set aside.

2 In a large bowl whisk together eggs, milk, chile peppers, salt, and black pepper. Pour egg mixture evenly over muffin quarters. Press down lightly with a rubber spatula or the back of a large spoon to moisten all of the muffins. Sprinkle with ham, roasted sweet peppers, green onions, and olives. Sprinkle with provolone cheese and cheddar cheese. Cover and chill for at least 2 hours or up to 24 hours.

3 Preheat oven to 350°F. Bake, uncovered, about 45 minutes or until a knife inserted near the center comes out clean (170°F). Let stand for 10 minutes before serving.

Makes 10 to 12 servings.

Nutrition Facts per serving: 279 cal., 14 g total fat (6 g sat. fat), 218 mg chol., 744 mg sodium, 20 g carbo., 2 g fiber, 18 g pro.

REUBEN BREAKFAST STRATA

Attention Reuben sandwich lovers! Now you can have your favorite flavors for breakfast—or any time of the day, for that matter—in one dish with this easy strata. Make it up to 24 hours ahead and chill until ready to bake.

Prep: 20 minutes **Chill:** 2 to 24 hours **Bake:** 40 minutes **Stand:** 10 minutes **Oven:** 350°F

- 8 slices rye bread, cubed (6 cups)
- 12 ounces sliced deli corned beef, chopped
- 1½ cups shredded Swiss cheese (6 ounces)
- 8 eggs, beaten
- 1¼ cups milk
- ½ cup bottled Thousand Island salad dressing
- ½ teaspoon salt
- ½ teaspoon caraway seeds
- ½ teaspoon dry mustard

1 Grease a 9×13-inch baking pan or baking dish; set aside. In a large bowl combine bread cubes, corned beef, and 1 cup of the cheese. Spread bread mixture evenly in prepared pan or dish.

2 In a medium bowl whisk together eggs, milk, salad dressing, salt, caraway seeds, and dry mustard. Pour egg mixture evenly over bread mixture in pan or dish. Press down lightly with a rubber spatula or the back of a large spoon to moisten all of the bread. Cover and chill for at least 2 hours or up to 24 hours.

3 Preheat oven to 350°F. Sprinkle the remaining ½ cup cheese over egg mixture in pan or dish. Bake, uncovered, for 40 to 45 minutes or until a knife inserted near the center comes out clean (170°F). Let stand for 10 minutes before serving.

Makes 6 servings.

Nutrition Facts per serving: 561 cal., 35 g total fat (12 g sat. fat), 373 mg chol., 1,469 mg sodium, 28 g carbo., 3 g fiber, 32 g pro.

LOX-STYLE STRATA

The take-out favorite bagels with cream cheese
and lox finds its way to your breakfast table
via this delicious do-ahead recipe.

Prep: 30 minutes   **Chill:** 4 to 24 hours   **Bake:** 45 minutes   **Stand:** 10 minutes   **Oven:** 350°F

- **4** to 6 plain bagels, cut into bite-size pieces (8 cups)
- **1** 3-ounce package thinly sliced smoked salmon (lox-style), cut into small pieces
- **2** 3-ounce packages cream cheese, cut into ½-inch pieces
- **¼** cup finely chopped red onion
- **4** teaspoons dried chives, crushed
- **8** eggs, beaten
- **2** cups milk
- **1** cup cream-style cottage cheese
- **½** teaspoon dried dill, crushed
- **¼** teaspoon black pepper

1 Lightly grease a 9×13-inch baking pan or baking dish. Arrange half of the bagel pieces in prepared pan or dish. Top with salmon, cream cheese, red onion, and chives. Spread the remaining bagel pieces over the salmon mixture.

2 In a large bowl whisk together eggs, milk, cottage cheese, dill, and pepper. Pour egg mixture evenly over ingredients in pan or dish. Press down lightly with a rubber spatula or the back of a large spoon to moisten all of the bagels. Cover and chill for at least 4 hours or up to 24 hours.

3 Preheat oven to 350°F. Bake, uncovered, for 45 to 50 minutes or until a knife inserted near the center comes out clean (170°F) and the edges are puffed and golden. Let stand for 10 minutes before serving.

Makes 12 servings.

Nutrition Facts per serving: 212 cal., 11 g total fat (5 g sat. fat), 164 mg chol., 447 mg sodium, 16 g carbo., 1 g fiber, 13 g pro.

APPLE-ALMOND CINNAMON STRATA

Here are all the flavors of a great apple crisp in a breakfast dish! Try peach or cherry pie filling too, or make one of each for a buffet.

Prep: 20 minutes **Chill:** 2 to 24 hours **Bake:** 50 minutes **Stand:** 15 minutes **Oven:** 325°F

1 1-pound loaf cinnamon-raisin bread, cut into 1-inch pieces

8 eggs, slightly beaten

2 cups milk

¼ teaspoon salt

¼ teaspoon almond extract

1 21-ounce can apple pie filling

½ cup slivered almonds, toasted

Powdered sugar

1 Grease a 9×13-inch baking pan or baking dish. Place bread pieces in prepared pan or dish; set aside.

2 In a large bowl whisk together eggs, milk, salt, and almond extract. Stir in apple pie filling and half of the almonds. Pour egg mixture evenly over the bread pieces in the pan or dish. Press down lightly with a rubber spatula or the back of a large spoon to moisten all of the bread. Sprinkle with the remaining almonds. Cover and chill for at least 2 hours or up to 24 hours.

3 Preheat oven to 325°F. Bake, uncovered, about 50 minutes or until a knife inserted near the center comes out clean (170°F). Let stand for 15 minutes before serving. Sift powdered sugar over.

Makes 8 servings.

Nutrition Facts per serving: 387 cal., 13 g total fat (3 g sat. fat), 216 mg chol., 422 mg sodium, 55 g carbo., 4 g fiber, 15 g pro.

SAUSAGE BREAD PUDDING

The aroma of these savory Italian ingredients is sure to wake up the sleepyheads in your family. Use half sweet, half spicy sausage for extra kick.

Prep: 35 minutes **Bake:** 40 minutes **Stand:** 10 minutes **Oven:** 350°F

- 1 pound sweet Italian sausage (remove casings, if present)
- 1 medium onion, chopped
- 2 cloves garlic, minced
- ⅓ cup purchased basil pesto
- Nonstick cooking spray
- 6 cups dry white or wheat bread cubes*
- 1 cup shredded provolone or cheddar cheese (4 ounces)
- 2½ cups milk
- 1 10¾-ounce can condensed cream of mushroom soup
- 4 eggs
- ¼ teaspoon salt
- ⅛ teaspoon black pepper

1 In a large skillet cook sausage, onion, and garlic until sausage is cooked through, using a wooden spoon to break up sausage as it cooks; drain off fat. Stir pesto into sausage mixture; set aside.

2 Meanwhile, lightly coat a 9×13-inch baking pan or baking dish with nonstick cooking spray. Preheat oven to 350°F. Spread half of the bread cubes evenly in prepared pan or dish. Top evenly with the sausage-pesto mixture and the cheese. Top with the remaining bread cubes.

3 In a large bowl whisk together milk, cream of mushroom soup, eggs, salt, and pepper. Pour egg mixture evenly over ingredients in pan or dish. Press down lightly with a rubber spatula or the back of a large spoon to moisten all of the bread.

4 Bake, uncovered, for 40 to 45 minutes or until a knife inserted in the center comes out clean (170°F). Let stand for 10 minutes before serving.

Makes 8 servings.

Nutrition Facts per serving: 507 cal., 35 g total fat (11 g sat. fat), 168 mg chol., 1,184 mg sodium, 24 g carbo., 1 g fiber, 22 g pro.

*Test Kitchen Tip: For 6 cups dry bread cubes, use about 9 slices of bread. To dry, spread cubes evenly in a shallow baking pan. Preheat oven to 300°F. Bake bread cubes for 10 to 15 minutes or until dry, stirring twice; cool. (Or let bread stand, loosely covered, at room temperature for at least 8 hours or up to 12 hours.)

CORN, SAGE, AND TOASTED CORN BREAD PUDDING

This flavorful combination of sage-seasoned mushrooms, corn, corn bread, onion, and eggs bakes up brown and puffy.

Prep: 35 minutes   **Bake:** 50 minutes   **Stand:** 10 minutes   **Oven:** 350°F

- 8 cups cubed corn bread*
- 2 tablespoons butter
- 4 cups sliced fresh mushrooms (cremini, stemmed shiitake, oyster, or button)
- 1 medium onion, chopped
- 2 cloves garlic, minced
- 2 cups fresh corn kernels (4 ears) or loose-pack frozen whole kernel corn, thawed
- 3 tablespoons snipped fresh sage or 1 tablespoon dried leaf sage, crushed
- 5 eggs
- 2¾ cups milk
- ½ teaspoon salt
- ¼ teaspoon black pepper

1 Preheat oven to 350°F. Spread cubed corn bread in a 10×15-inch baking pan. Bake, uncovered, about 15 minutes or until lightly toasted, stirring once. Cool slightly.

2 Meanwhile, grease a 9×13-inch baking pan or baking dish; set aside. In an extra-large skillet melt butter over medium heat. Add mushrooms, onion, and garlic; cook until mushrooms and onion are tender. Add corn and sage; cook for 2 minutes more. Remove from heat. Gently stir in toasted corn bread cubes. Transfer mixture to prepared pan or dish.

3 In a medium bowl whisk together eggs, milk, salt, and pepper. Pour egg mixture evenly over corn bread mixture. Press down lightly with a rubber spatula or the back of a large spoon to moisten all of the corn bread.

4 Bake, covered, for 30 minutes. Uncover; bake for 20 to 30 minutes more or until pudding is browned and puffed and a knife inserted near the center comes out clean (170°F). Cool for 10 minutes before serving.

Makes 12 servings.

Nutrition Facts per serving: 299 cal., 13 g total fat (2 g sat. fat), 125 mg chol., 492 mg sodium, 39 g carbo., 1 g fiber, 10 g pro.

---

*Test Kichen Tip: *For the corn bread, grease two 8×8-inch baking pans. Preheat oven to 400°F. Prepare two 8-ounce packages corn muffin mix. Pour batter into prepared pans. Bake for 20 minutes. Cool in pans on wire racks. Let stand overnight before cubing.*

Make-Ahead Directions: *Prepare as directed through step 3. Cover and chill for up to 24 hours. Bake as directed in step 4.*

MORNING PECAN CASSEROLE

A crunchy, pralinelike layer tops this easy, make-ahead brunch dish. The recipe features pieces of sausage patties in a raisin-bread strata.

Prep: 25 minutes   **Chill:** 8 to 24 hours   **Bake:** 45 minutes   **Stand:** 15 minutes   **Oven:** 350°F

- 1 7-ounce package brown-and-serve sausage patties
- 12 slices raisin bread, cubed (about 8 cups)
- 6 eggs
- 3 cups milk
- 1 teaspoon vanilla
- ¼ teaspoon ground nutmeg
- ¼ teaspoon ground cinnamon
- 1 cup coarsely chopped pecans
- ½ cup packed brown sugar
- ¼ cup butter, softened
- 2 tablespoons pure maple syrup or maple-flavored syrup

1 Lightly grease a 9×13-inch baking pan or baking dish; set aside. Brown the sausage patties according to package directions. Cut sausage patties into bite-size pieces. Spread bread cubes evenly in prepared pan or dish. Top with sausage pieces.

2 In a large bowl whisk together eggs, milk, vanilla, nutmeg, and cinnamon. Pour egg mixture evenly over bread and sausage. Press down lightly with a rubber spatula or the back of a large spoon to moisten all of the bread. Cover and chill for at least 8 hours or up to 24 hours.

3 Preheat oven to 350°F. For topping, in a small bowl combine pecans, brown sugar, butter, and syrup. Drop by teaspoonfuls over top of egg mixture.

4 Bake, uncovered, for 45 to 50 minutes or until a knife inserted near the center comes out clean (170°F). Let stand for 15 minutes before serving.

Makes 10 servings.

Nutrition Facts per serving: 408 cal., 24 g total fat (7 g sat. fat), 162 mg chol., 386 mg sodium, 36 g carbo., 2 g fiber, 14 g pro.

ORANGE BLINTZ CASSEROLE

Blintzes are a Jewish-American favorite. This one-dish wonder makes preparing them easy by combining the classic ingredients into easy-pour layers.

Prep: 25 minutes   **Bake:** 45 minutes   **Cool:** 30 minutes   **Oven:** 350°F

6	eggs
2	egg whites
1½	cups dairy sour cream
2	teaspoons finely shredded orange peel
½	cup orange juice
¼	cup butter, softened
1	cup all-purpose flour
½	cup sugar
2	teaspoons baking powder
2	cups cream-style cottage cheese
1	8-ounce package cream cheese, softened
2	egg yolks
2	tablespoons sugar
2	teaspoons vanilla
½	cup orange marmalade, melted

1 Grease a 9×13-inch baking pan or baking dish; set aside. Preheat oven to 350°F. For batter, in a blender or food processor combine eggs, egg whites, sour cream, orange peel, orange juice, and butter. Cover; blend or process until smooth. Add flour, sugar, and baking powder. Cover; blend or process until smooth. Transfer to a medium bowl; set aside. Rinse blender or food processor.

2 For filling, in the blender or food processor combine cottage cheese, cream cheese, egg yolks, sugar, and vanilla. Cover; blend or process until smooth.

3 Pour about 2 cups of the batter into prepared pan or dish. Spoon filling evenly over batter in pan or dish. Using a table knife, swirl filling into batter. Pour the remaining batter evenly over mixture in pan or dish.

4 Bake, uncovered, about 45 minutes or until puffed and lightly golden brown. Cool on a wire rack for 30 minutes before serving (edges may fall during cooling). Drizzle with melted marmalade.

Makes 12 to 15 servings.

Nutrition Facts per serving: 357 cal., 21 g total fat (12 g sat. fat), 221 mg chol., 325 mg sodium, 30 g carbo., 0 g fiber, 12 g pro.

RICH AMARETTO BRIOCHE BAKE

A splash of amaretto adds amazing almond flavor to this elegant dish. If you can't find brioche, a French bread rich with butter and eggs, substitute challah or a sweet egg bread.

Prep: 20 minutes   **Chill:** 4 to 24 hours   **Bake:** 40 minutes   **Stand:** 15 minutes   **Oven:** 350°F

- ⅓ cup butter
- ¼ cup amaretto
- 1 cup packed brown sugar
- 2 tablespoons light-color corn syrup
- 1 12-ounce loaf brioche or other sweet bread, cut into 9 slices
- 4 eggs, beaten
- 2 cups half-and-half, light cream, or milk
- 1½ teaspoons vanilla
- ½ teaspoon salt
- ¼ teaspoon ground nutmeg or cardamom

1 Lightly grease a 9×13-inch baking pan or baking dish; set aside. In a medium saucepan combine butter, amaretto, brown sugar, and corn syrup; cook and stir until boiling. Boil, uncovered, for 1 minute. Pour into prepared pan or dish.

2 Arrange bread slices over brown sugar mixture. In a medium bowl whisk together eggs, half-and-half, vanilla, salt, and nutmeg. Pour egg mixture evenly over bread. Press down lightly with a rubber spatula or the back of a large spoon to moisten all of the bread. Cover and chill for at least 4 hours or up to 24 hours.

3 Preheat oven to 350°F. Bake, uncovered, for 40 to 45 minutes or until top is brown and a knife inserted near the center comes out clean (170°F). Let stand for 15 minutes before serving.

Makes 8 servings.

Nutrition Facts per serving: 483 cal., 23 g total fat (10 g sat. fat), 189 mg chol., 450 mg sodium, 57 g carbo., 1 g fiber, 9 g pro.

TROPICAL BREAKFAST AMBROSIA

Island fruits and nuts are a natural combination. When heated, they become even more sublime and a perfect accompaniment to muffins or scones.

Prep: 25 minutes   **Bake:** 30 minutes   **Oven:** 350°F

- 1 medium fresh pineapple, peeled, cored, and cut into bite-size pieces (about 4½ cups)
- 1 11-ounce can mandarin oranges, drained
- 1 medium mango, peeled, seeded, and cut into ½-inch pieces
- 1 cup frozen unsweetened pitted dark sweet cherries, thawed
- 2 tablespoons amaretto (optional)
- 2 medium bananas, cut into ½-inch-thick slices
- 1 cup flaked coconut
- ½ cup chopped macadamia nuts or sliced almonds

1 Preheat oven to 350°F. In a large bowl combine pineapple, mandarin oranges, mango, cherries, and, if desired, amaretto. Spoon pineapple mixture into an ungreased 9×13-inch baking pan or baking dish.

2 Bake, uncovered, for 15 minutes. Stir in bananas. Sprinkle with coconut and macadamia nuts. Bake about 15 minutes more or until fruit is heated through and coconut and nuts are golden brown. Serve warm, spooning some of the liquid in the pan or dish over fruit.

Makes 8 to 10 servings.

Nutrition Facts per serving: 241 cal., 12 g total fat (6 g sat. fat), 0 mg chol., 71 mg sodium, 36 g carbo., 5 g fiber, 3 g pro.

COFFEE CAKES, FRENCH TOAST, AND ROLLS

The aromas of cinnamon and brown sugar signal something special is baking for breakfast. And you're making it. From French toast to old-fashioned cinnamon rolls, with additions like blueberries or apples, pecans, and cream cheese, this chapter is loaded with delicious from-the-oven options that make mornings special.

RHUBARB-STRAWBERRY COFFEE CAKE

A favorite combo for springtime pies, strawberry and rhubarb add their fresh flavors to this streusel-topped coffee-time delight.

Prep: 35 minutes **Bake:** 40 minutes **Oven:** 350°F (baking pan) or 325°F (baking dish)

- 1 recipe Rhubarb Filling
- 3 cups all-purpose flour
- 1 cup sugar
- 1 teaspoon baking soda
- 1 teaspoon baking powder
- 1 teaspoon salt
- 1 cup butter
- 2 eggs, slightly beaten
- 1 cup buttermilk or sour milk*
- 1 teaspoon vanilla
- ½ cup sugar
- ½ cup all-purpose flour
- ¼ cup butter

1 Prepare Rhubarb Filling; set aside to cool.

2 Grease a 9×13-inch baking pan or baking dish. Preheat oven to 350°F if using a baking pan or 325°F if using a baking dish. In a large bowl stir together the 3 cups flour, the 1 cup sugar, the baking soda, baking powder, and salt. Using a pastry blender, cut in the 1 cup butter until mixture resembles fine crumbs. In a small bowl combine eggs, buttermilk, and vanilla; add to flour mixture. Stir to moisten.

3 Spread half of the batter evenly in prepared pan or dish. Spread cooled Rhubarb Filling evenly over batter in pan or dish. Spoon remaining batter in small mounds over filling. In a small bowl combine the ½ cup sugar and the ½ cup flour. Using a pastry blender, cut in the ¼ cup butter until mixture resembles fine crumbs.

4 Sprinkle crumb mixture over batter in pan or dish. Bake for 40 to 45 minutes or until golden brown. Serve warm.

Makes 15 servings.

Nutrition Facts per serving: 418 cal., 17 g total fat (10 g sat. fat), 70 mg chol., 393 mg sodium, 64 g carbo., 2 g fiber, 3 g pro.

Rhubarb Filling: *In a medium saucepan combine 3 cups fresh rhubarb or one 16-ounce package frozen unsweetened sliced rhubarb and 4 cups hulled fresh strawberries or one 16-ounce package frozen unsweetened whole strawberries, thawed and halved. Cover; cook fruit for 5 minutes. Stir in 2 tablespoons lemon juice. In a small bowl combine 1 cup sugar and ⅓ cup cornstarch; add to rhubarb mixture. Cook and stir for 4 to 5 minutes or until thickened and bubbly; cool.*

---

*Test Kitchen Tip: *To make 1 cup sour milk, place 1 tablespoon lemon juice or vinegar in a glass measuring cup. Add enough milk to make 1 cup total liquid; stir. Let stand for 5 minutes before using.*

CRANBERRY-PECAN COFFEE CAKE

Here's a festive cake for holiday time. Ruby cranberry sauce and pecans turn a basic batter into something you'll look forward to again and again.

Prep: 25 minutes **Bake:** 40 minutes **Oven:** 350°F (baking pan) or 325°F (baking dish)

- 1 **cup butter, softened**
- 1 **cup granulated sugar**
- ½ **teaspoon almond extract or vanilla**
- 2 **eggs**
- 2 **cups self-rising flour***
- 1 **8-ounce carton dairy sour cream**
- 1 **16-ounce can whole cranberry sauce**
- ½ **cup chopped pecans**
- 1 **cup powdered sugar**
- 2 **tablespoons milk**
- ½ **teaspoon vanilla**

1 Grease a 9×13-inch baking pan or baking dish; set aside. Preheat oven to 350°F if using a baking pan or 325°F if using a baking dish.

2 In a large bowl beat butter with an electric mixer on medium to high speed for 30 seconds. Add granulated sugar and almond extract; beat until combined. Add eggs, one at a time, beating well after each addition. Alternately add flour and sour cream to beaten mixture, beating on low speed after each addition just until combined. Spread batter evenly into prepared pan or dish. Spread cranberry sauce over batter. Sprinkle with pecans.

3 Bake about 40 minutes or until a toothpick inserted near center comes out clean. Cool in pan or dish on a wire rack.

4 Meanwhile, in a small bowl combine powdered sugar, milk, and vanilla. Drizzle over the warm coffee cake. Serve warm.

Makes 10 to 12 servings.

Nutrition Facts per serving: 549 cal., 30 g total fat (16 g sat. fat), 105 mg chol., 555 mg sodium, 68 g carbo., 2 g fiber, 5 g pro.

*Test Kitchen Tip: *If you can't find self-rising flour, substitute 2 cups all-purpose flour plus 2 teaspoons baking powder, 1 teaspoon salt, and ½ teaspoon baking soda.*

APRICOT COFFEE CAKE

Cream cheese in the batter
keeps this coffee cake extra moist. Peaches
would work as well as apricots.

Prep: 25 minutes **Bake:** 35 minutes **Oven:** 350°F (baking pan) or 325°F (baking dish)

- 1¾ cups all-purpose flour
- 1 teaspoon baking powder
- ½ teaspoon baking soda
- ¼ teaspoon salt
- 1 8-ounce package cream cheese, softened
- ½ cup butter, softened
- 1¼ cups granulated sugar
- 2 eggs, slightly beaten
- 1 teaspoon almond extract or vanilla
- ¼ cup milk
- ½ cup all-purpose flour
- ½ cup packed brown sugar
- 2 teaspoons ground cinnamon
- ¼ cup butter
- ½ cup chopped walnuts or almonds
- 1 24- to 26-ounce jar apricot halves, drained and halved to get quarters

1 Grease and flour a 9×13-inch baking pan or baking dish; set aside. Preheat oven to 350°F if using a baking pan or 325°F if using a baking dish. In a medium bowl stir together the 1¾ cups flour, the baking powder, baking soda, and salt; set aside.

2 In a large bowl combine cream cheese and the ½ cup butter; beat with an electric mixer on medium speed for 30 seconds. Add granulated sugar. Beat on medium to high speed until light and fluffy. Add eggs and almond extract; beat well. Alternately add flour mixture and milk to beaten mixture, beating until smooth after each addition.

3 Spread batter evenly into prepared pan or dish. Bake for 25 to 30 minutes or until top is lightly browned. Meanwhile, in a small bowl combine the ½ cup flour, the brown sugar, and ground cinnamon. Using a pastry blender, cut in the ¼ cup butter until mixture resembles coarse crumbs. Stir in walnuts. Carefully arrange quartered apricots atop cake. Sprinkle nut mixture over apricots and cake.

4 Bake for 10 to 15 minutes more or until a toothpick inserted near the center comes out clean. Serve coffee cake warm.

Makes 12 to 15 servings.

Nutrition Facts per serving: 445 cal., 22 g total fat (12 g sat. fat), 87 mg chol., 279 mg sodium, 57 g carbo., 2 g fiber, 4 g pro.

LEMON CREAM-FILLED COFFEE CAKE

A filling that's reminiscent of lemon cheesecake makes this coffee cake taste as heavenly as it sounds. It's just the right cake for midmorning coffees and get-togethers.

Prep: 25 minutes **Bake:** 45 minutes **Cool:** 45 minutes **Oven:** 350°F (baking pan) or 325°F (baking dish)

- 1 **8-ounce package cream cheese, softened**
- ¼ **cup sugar**
- 1 **8-ounce carton lemon yogurt**
- 1½ **teaspoons finely shredded lemon peel**
- 3 **cups all-purpose flour**
- 1 **cup sugar**
- 1 **tablespoon baking powder**
- ¼ **teaspoon salt**
- ¼ **teaspoon ground nutmeg or mace**
- 1 **cup butter**
- 2 **eggs, slightly beaten**
- 1 **cup milk**
- ½ **teaspoon almond extract**
- ½ **cup sugar**
- ½ **cup all-purpose flour**
- ¼ **cup butter**
- ½ **cup chopped pecans or sliced almonds**

1 Grease a 9×13-inch baking pan or baking dish; set aside. Preheat oven to 350°F if using a baking pan or 325°F if using a baking dish.

2 In a medium bowl beat cream cheese with an electric mixer on medium speed until fluffy. Beat in the ¼ cup sugar; fold in lemon yogurt and lemon peel. Set aside.

3 In a large bowl stir together the 3 cups flour, the 1 cup sugar, the baking powder, salt, and nutmeg or mace. Using a pastry blender, cut in the 1 cup butter until mixture resembles fine crumbs. In a small bowl combine eggs, milk, and almond extract. Add egg mixture to flour mixture, stirring until combined. Spread half of the batter evenly in prepared pan or dish.

4 Spoon the cream cheese mixture evenly over the batter in the pan or dish. Spoon the remaining batter in small mounds over the cream cheese mixture, spreading out batter as much as possible.

5 In a medium bowl combine the ½ cup sugar and the ½ cup flour. Using a pastry blender, cut in the ¼ cup butter until mixture resembles coarse crumbs. Stir in nuts. Sprinkle nut mixture over batter in pan.

6 Bake for 45 to 50 minutes or until golden brown and a toothpick inserted in dough mounds comes out clean (do not test in filling). Cool in pan or dish on a wire rack for at least 45 minutes before serving. Cover and store in the refrigerator within 2 hours.

Makes 12 servings.

Nutrition Facts per serving: 559 cal., 32 g total fat (18 g sat. fat), 114 mg chol., 447 mg sodium, 61 g carbo., 1 g fiber, 8 g pro.

BUTTERMILK COFFEE CAKE

Everyone will love this coffee cake—it's definitely worth adding to your repertoire. Serve the cake warm with scrambled eggs and fruit.

Prep: 30 minutes **Bake:** 35 minutes **Oven:** 350°F (baking pan) or 325°F (baking dish)

- 2½ cups all-purpose flour
- 1½ cups packed brown sugar
- ½ teaspoon salt
- ⅔ cup butter
- 2 teaspoons baking powder
- ½ teaspoon baking soda
- ½ teaspoon ground cinnamon
- ½ teaspoon ground nutmeg
- 2 eggs, beaten
- 1⅓ cups buttermilk or sour milk*
- ½ cup chopped pecans, walnuts, or almonds

1 Grease the bottom and ½ inch up the sides of a 9×13-inch baking pan or baking dish; set aside. Preheat oven to 350°F if using a baking pan or 325°F if using a baking dish. In a large bowl combine flour, brown sugar, and salt. Using a pastry blender, cut in butter until mixture resembles coarse crumbs; set aside ½ cup of the crumb mixture. Stir baking powder, baking soda, cinnamon, and nutmeg into the remaining crumb mixture.

2 In a medium bowl combine eggs and buttermilk. Add egg mixture all at once to cinnamon mixture, stirring just until moistened. Spoon batter evenly into prepared pan or dish. In a small bowl stir together the reserved ½ cup crumb mixture and the nuts; sprinkle over batter.

3 Bake for 35 to 40 minutes or until a toothpick inserted near the center comes out clean. Serve coffee cake warm.

Makes 18 servings.

Nutrition Facts per serving: 228 cal., 10 g total fat (4 g sat. fat), 43 mg chol., 212 mg sodium, 31 g carbo., 1 g fiber, 3 g pro.

*Test Kitchen Tip: *To make 1⅓ cups sour milk, place 4 teaspoons lemon juice or vinegar in a 2-cup glass measuring cup. Add enough milk to make 1⅓ cups total liquid; stir. Let stand for 5 minutes before using.*

MANGO COFFEE CAKE

A fresh tropical flavor makes this cake a great choice for morning coffee and equally tasty with whipped cream as dessert.

Prep: 25 minutes **Bake:** 40 minutes **Oven:** 350°F (baking pan) or 325°F (baking dish)

2	cups all-purpose flour
2	cups sugar
1½	teaspoons baking powder
½	teaspoon baking soda
½	teaspoon ground nutmeg
¼	teaspoon salt
½	cup butter
1	cup buttermilk or sour milk*
2	eggs, beaten
1	teaspoon vanilla
3	cups coarsely chopped, seeded, and peeled mangoes (about 3)
⅓	cup sugar
¾	teaspoon ground cinnamon
	Sweetened whipped cream

1 Grease a 9×13-inch baking pan or baking dish; set aside. Preheat oven to 350°F if using a baking pan or 325°F if using a baking dish. In a large bowl combine flour, the 2 cups sugar, the baking powder, baking soda, nutmeg, and salt. Using a pastry blender, cut in butter until mixture resembles coarse crumbs.

2 In a small bowl combine buttermilk, eggs, and vanilla. Add to flour mixture all at once; stir just until moistened. Fold in mangoes. Spread evenly in prepared pan or dish. In another small bowl combine the ⅓ cup sugar and the cinnamon. Sprinkle evenly over batter.

3 Bake for 40 to 45 minutes or until a toothpick inserted near center comes out clean, breaking crust slightly when inserting pick. (Mango pieces will sink to bottom of coffee cake.) Cool slightly. Serve warm with sweetened whipped cream.

Makes 12 to 16 servings.

Nutrition Facts per serving: 387 cal., 15 g total fat (8 g sat. fat), 78 mg chol., 229 mg sodium, 61 g carbo., 1 g fiber, 4 g pro.

***Test Kitchen Tip:** To make 1 cup sour milk, place 1 tablespoon lemon juice or vinegar in a glass measuring cup. Add enough milk to make 1 cup total liquid; stir. Let stand for 5 minutes before using.*

CREAM CHEESE-BERRY COFFEE CAKE

A swirl of raspberry jam winds through this cake that's kept extra moist with the addition of cream cheese. Try substituting blueberry or strawberry jam.

Prep: 20 minutes **Bake:** 30 minutes **Cool:** 30 minutes **Oven:** 350°F (baking pan) or 325°F (baking dish)

- 1 8-ounce package cream cheese or reduced-fat cream cheese (Neufchâtel), softened
- 1 cup granulated sugar
- ½ cup butter, softened
- 1¾ cups all-purpose flour
- 2 eggs
- ¼ cup milk
- 1 teaspoon baking powder
- ½ teaspoon baking soda
- ½ teaspoon vanilla
- ¼ teaspoon salt
- ½ cup seedless red raspberry jam
-     Powdered sugar

1 Grease 9×13-inch baking pan or baking dish; set aside. Preheat oven to 350°F if using a baking pan or 325°F if using a baking dish.

2 In large bowl combine cream cheese, granulated sugar, and butter; beat with an electric mixer on medium speed until smooth. Add ¾ cup of the flour, the eggs, milk, baking powder, baking soda, vanilla, and salt. Beat about 1 minute or until combined. Add the remaining 1 cup flour, beating on low speed just until combined. Spread batter evenly in prepared pan or dish. In small bowl stir jam with a spoon until nearly smooth. Spoon jam in 8 to 10 mounds on top of batter in pan or dish. Using thin spatula or knife, swirl jam into batter.

3 Bake for 30 to 35 minutes or until toothpick inserted into cake portion near center comes out clean. Cool cake in pan or dish on wire rack about 30 minutes. Dust with powdered sugar. Serve warm.

Makes 24 servings.

Nutrition Facts per serving: 158 cal., 8 g total fat (4 g sat. fat), 39 mg chol., 127 mg sodium, 20 g carbo., 0 g fiber, 2 g pro.

RICOTTA COFFEE CAKE

A cinnamon-laced wheat germ-and-nut topper
lends just the right crunch to this coffee cake, and
ricotta cheese adds richness.

Prep: 25 minutes **Bake:** 35 minutes **Oven:** 350°F (baking pan) or 325°F (baking dish)

- 3 cups all-purpose flour
- 1½ teaspoons baking powder
- 1½ teaspoons baking soda
- 1 teaspoon salt
- 1 cup butter, softened
- 1¼ cups granulated sugar
- 3 eggs
- 1 15-ounce carton ricotta cheese
- ¾ cup chopped nuts
- ½ cup packed dark brown sugar
- 2 tablespoons toasted wheat germ
- 1 tablespoon ground cinnamon
- 1 teaspoon ground nutmeg

1 Grease bottom and ½ inch up sides of a 9×13-inch baking pan or baking dish; set aside. Preheat oven to 350°F if using a baking pan or 325°F if using a baking dish.

2 In a large bowl combine flour, baking powder, baking soda, and salt; set aside. In a large bowl beat butter with an electric mixer on medium speed for 30 seconds. Add granulated sugar; beat until combined. Add eggs, one at a time, beating well after each addition. Beat in ricotta cheese. Beat in as much of the flour mixture as you can with the mixer. Using a wooden spoon, stir in any remaining flour mixture. Spread batter evenly in prepared pan or dish. In a small bowl combine nuts, brown sugar, wheat germ, cinnamon, and nutmeg. Sprinkle evenly over batter in pan or dish.

3 Bake for 35 to 40 minutes or until a toothpick inserted near the center comes out clean. Cool slightly in pan or dish on a wire rack. Serve warm.

Makes 15 servings.

Nutrition Facts per serving: 397 cal., 22 g total fat (10 g sat. fat), 91 mg chol., 438 mg sodium, 43 g carbo., 1 g fiber, 8 g pro.

Make-Ahead Directions: *Prepare coffee cake as directed through step 2. Cover and chill for at least 8 hours or up to 24 hours. Uncover coffee cake. Bake as directed in step 3.*

PEANUT BUTTER AND CORNMEAL COFFEE CAKE

Calling all PB lovers. This peanutty cake studded with raisins and topped with a peanut and cornmeal streusel is made just for you.

Prep: 25 minutes **Bake:** 30 minutes **Oven:** 375°F (baking pan) or 350°F (baking dish)

- ½ cup packed brown sugar
- ¼ cup all-purpose flour
- ¼ cup yellow cornmeal
- ¼ cup peanut butter
- 2 tablespoons butter, melted
- 1 cup packed brown sugar
- ½ cup peanut butter
- ¼ cup shortening
- 2 eggs
- 1½ cups all-purpose flour
- ¼ cup yellow cornmeal
- 2 teaspoons baking powder
- ½ teaspoon baking soda
- ¼ teaspoon salt
- 1 cup buttermilk or sour milk*
- ½ cup golden raisins or dried cherries or cranberries

1 Grease a 9×13-inch baking pan or baking dish; set aside. Preheat oven to 375°F if using a baking pan or 350°F if using a baking dish. In a medium bowl stir together the ½ cup brown sugar, the ¼ cup flour, ¼ cup cornmeal, the ¼ cup peanut butter, and the melted butter until crumbly. Set aside.

2 In a large bowl combine the 1 cup brown sugar, the ½ cup peanut butter, and the shortening; beat with an electric mixer on medium speed until combined. Add eggs, one at a time, beating after each addition until combined.

3 In a medium bowl combine the 1½ cups flour, ¼ cup cornmeal, the baking powder, baking soda, and salt. Alternately add flour mixture and buttermilk to beaten mixture, beating after each addition until combined. Stir in raisins. Spread batter evenly in prepared pan or dish. Sprinkle with crumb mixture.

4 Bake for 30 to 35 minutes or until a toothpick inserted off center comes out clean. Cool in pan or dish on wire rack.

Makes 16 servings.

Nutrition Facts per serving: 289 cal., 12 g total fat (3 g sat. fat), 31 mg chol., 231 mg sodium, 42 g carbo., 2 g fiber, 6 g pro.

*Test Kitchen Tip: *To make 1 cup sour milk, place 1 tablespoon lemon juice or vinegar in a glass measuring cup. Add enough milk to make 1 cup total liquid; stir. Let stand for 5 minutes before using.*

BLUEBERRY BUCKLE

This homey New England favorite bursts with nutritious blueberries and is drizzled with a lemony glaze. Use fresh berries when in season, though frozen work fine too.

Prep: 25 minutes **Bake:** 40 minutes **Broil:** 1 minute **Oven:** 350°F

1½	cups fresh or frozen blueberries
1½	cups fresh or frozen raspberries
1¼	cups sugar
⅓	cup butter, softened
2	eggs
½	cup buttermilk or sour milk*
2¼	cups all-purpose flour
1	tablespoon baking powder
¼	teaspoon salt
3	tablespoons butter
⅓	cup sugar
4	teaspoons orange juice

1 If using frozen berries, thaw and drain. Grease a 9×13-inch baking pan; set aside. Preheat oven to 350°F.

2 In a medium bowl combine the 1¼ cups sugar, the ⅓ cup butter, and the eggs. Beat with an electric mixer on medium speed until smooth. Continue beating while gradually adding the buttermilk.

3 In a small bowl stir together flour, baking powder, and salt. Add the flour mixture to the butter mixture, mixing well. Gently fold in berries.

4 Spread batter evenly into prepared pan. Bake about 40 minutes or until a toothpick inserted near the center comes out clean. Remove from oven; set pan on a wire rack. Turn oven to broil.

5 Meanwhile, for glaze, in a small saucepan melt the 3 tablespoons butter over low heat. Stir in the ⅓ cup sugar and the orange juice. Cook and stir until the mixture is bubbly. Remove from heat.

6 Pour the glaze evenly over the hot cake. Broil cake 3 inches from heat for 1 to 2 minutes or until the glaze is bubbly. Watch carefully to avoid overbrowning. Serve warm.

Makes 18 servings.

Nutrition Facts per serving: 196 cal., 6 g total fat (4 g sat. fat), 38 mg chol., 146 mg sodium, 33 g carbo., 1 g fiber, 2 g pro.

__Test Kitchen Tip:__ To make ½ cup sour milk, place 1½ teaspoons lemon juice or vinegar in a glass measuring cup. Add enough milk to make ½ cup total liquid; stir. Let stand for 5 minutes before using.

PECAN STREUSEL COFFEE CAKE

How sweet it is! Coffee cake mix
makes this delicious cake a cinch to prepare.
Sour cream makes it extra moist.

Prep: 20 minutes   **Bake:** 35 minutes   **Oven:** 350°F (baking pan) or 325°F (baking dish)

- 1 cup chopped pecans
- ⅔ cup packed brown sugar
- 2 tablespoons butter, melted
- 1½ teaspoons ground cinnamon
- 1 26½-ounce package cinnamon streusel coffee cake mix
- ½ cup dairy sour cream

1 Grease and flour a 9×13-inch baking pan or baking dish; set aside. Preheat oven to 350°F if using a baking pan or 325°F if using a baking dish. For topping, in a small bowl stir together pecans, brown sugar, melted butter, and cinnamon.

2 Prepare coffee cake mix according to the package directions, except stir sour cream into prepared batter. Spread half (about 3 cups) of the batter evenly in the prepared pan or dish. Sprinkle batter with the streusel mix from the package of coffee cake mix. Carefully spread the remaining batter over. Sprinkle with the topping.

3 Bake for 35 to 40 minutes or until a toothpick inserted near center comes out clean. Cool slightly in pan or dish on a wire rack.

4 Meanwhile, prepare glaze from the coffee cake mix according to package directions. Drizzle glaze over warm coffee cake. Serve warm.

Makes 15 servings.

Nutrition Facts per serving: 395 cal., 20 g total fat (5 g sat. fat), 50 mg chol., 248 mg sodium, 50 g carbo., 1 g fiber, 4 g pro.

FRENCH TOAST WITH PEARS

A hint of rosemary flavors pears that are layered with Brie for an elegant breakfast or brunch entrée. Freeze the Brie for 15 minutes for easy slicing.

Prep: 35 minutes **Chill:** 1 to 24 hours **Bake:** 40 minutes **Stand:** 10 minutes **Oven:** 375°F

- 2 **tablespoons butter**
- 3 **medium pears, peeled, cored, and thinly sliced**
- 2 **tablespoons packed brown sugar**
- ½ **teaspoon snipped fresh rosemary**
- 14 **to 16 ½-inch-thick slices French bread (about 1 loaf)**
- 8 **ounces Brie cheese, rind removed and cheese thinly sliced**
- 2 **tablespoons butter, melted**
- 3 **tablespoons granulated sugar**
- 1 **teaspoon ground cinnamon**
- 2½ **cups milk**
- 3 **eggs**
- 1 **tablespoon vanilla**
- ¼ **teaspoon salt**

  Warm maple syrup, fresh berries and honey, or cranberry conserve

1 Grease a 9×13-inch baking pan or baking dish; set aside. In a large skillet melt 2 tablespoons butter over medium heat. Add pears, brown sugar, and rosemary; cook for 4 to 5 minutes or just until pears are tender. Arrange half of the bread slices in a single layer in prepared pan or dish. Spoon pear mixture over; arrange Brie on bread slices. Top each stack with a bread slice. Brush bread with 2 tablespoons melted butter.

2 In a small bowl combine granulated sugar and cinnamon; sprinkle evenly over bread. In a medium bowl whisk together milk, eggs, vanilla, and salt. Slowly pour egg mixture over bread slices. Press lightly with a rubber spatula or the back of a large spoon to moisten bread. Cover; chill for at least 1 hour or up to 24 hours.

3 Preheat oven to 375°F. Bake, uncovered, for 40 to 45 minutes or until edges are puffed and golden brown. Let stand for 10 minutes before serving. Serve warm with maple syrup, berries and honey, or cranberry conserve.

Makes 8 servings.

Nutrition Facts per serving (without toppings): 405 cal., 19 g total fat (10 g sat. fat), 130 mg chol., 623 mg sodium, 44 g carbo., 3 g fiber, 15 g pro.

CARAMEL-PECAN FRENCH TOAST

One favorite becomes another when everything that makes caramel-pecan rolls so yummy shows up in this one-dish, do-ahead wonder.

Prep: 20 minutes   **Chill:** 2 to 24 hours   **Bake:** 30 minutes   **Stand:** 10 minutes   **Oven:** 350°F

- 1 cup packed brown sugar
- ½ cup butter
- 2 tablespoons light-color corn syrup
- 1 cup chopped pecans
- 36 to 40 ½-inch-thick slices baguette-style French bread (about two 8-ounce baguette loaves) or eighteen ½-inch-thick slices regular French bread
- 6 eggs, beaten
- 1½ cups milk
- 1 teaspoon vanilla
- 1 tablespoon granulated sugar
- 1½ teaspoons ground cinnamon
- ¼ teaspoon ground nutmeg

1 In a medium saucepan stir together brown sugar, butter, and corn syrup; cook and stir until the butter is melted and brown sugar is dissolved. Pour into a 9×13-inch baking pan or baking dish. Sprinkle with half of the pecans.

2 Arrange half of the bread slices in a single layer in pan or dish. Sprinkle with the remaining pecans; top with the remaining bread slices.

3 In a medium bowl stir together eggs, milk, and vanilla. Slowly pour egg mixture over bread. Press lightly with a rubber spatula or the back of a large spoon to moisten the bread.

4 In a small bowl stir together granulated sugar, cinnamon, and nutmeg; sprinkle over bread. Cover and chill for at least 2 hours or up to 24 hours.

5 Preheat oven to 350°F. Bake, uncovered, for 30 to 40 minutes or until lightly browned. Let stand for 10 minutes before serving. To serve, remove individual servings with wide spatula and invert onto serving plates.

Makes 9 servings.

Nutrition Facts per serving: 499 cal., 25 g total fat (9 g sat. fat), 174 mg chol., 494 mg sodium, 59 g carbo., 3 g fiber, 11 g pro.

BAKED BLUEBERRY PECAN FRENCH TOAST
WITH BLUEBERRY SYRUP

> Good-for-you blueberries double up to give the breakfast crowd a whole new reason to get out of bed.

Prep: 30 minutes   **Chill:** 8 to 24 hours   **Bake:** 35 minutes   **Stand:** 10 minutes   **Oven:** 350°F

Butter

- 12 ounces Italian bread, cut into 8 slices (each about 1 inch thick)
- 5 eggs, beaten
- 2½ cups milk, half-and-half, or light cream
- ⅔ cup packed brown sugar
- 1 teaspoon vanilla
- ½ teaspoon ground nutmeg
- 2 cups fresh blueberries
- 1 cup coarsely chopped pecans
- ¼ cup packed brown sugar
- ¼ cup butter, melted
- 1 cup fresh blueberries
- ½ cup pure maple syrup
- 1 tablespoon lemon juice

1 Butter a 9×13-inch baking pan or baking dish. Arrange bread slices in prepared pan or dish, overlapping if necessary.

2 In a large bowl combine eggs, milk, the ⅔ cup brown sugar, the vanilla, and nutmeg. Slowly pour egg mixture evenly over bread. Press lightly with a rubber spatula or the back of a large spoon to moisten bread. Cover; chill for at least 8 hours or up to 24 hours.

3 Preheat oven to 350°F. Evenly sprinkle the 2 cups blueberries and the chopped pecans over bread mixture. In a small bowl stir together the ¼ cup brown sugar and the ¼ cup melted butter. Drizzle butter mixture over chopped pecans.

4 Bake, uncovered, for 35 to 40 minutes or until a knife inserted near center comes out clean. Let stand for 10 minutes before serving.

5 Meanwhile, for blueberry syrup, in a small saucepan combine the 1 cup blueberries and the maple syrup; cook and stir over medium heat about 3 minutes or until blueberries have burst. Pour syrup through a sieve into heatproof pitcher, pressing juice out of blueberries. Stir in lemon juice. Serve with the baked French toast.

Makes 8 to 10 servings.

Nutrition Facts per serving: 535 cal., 22 g total fat (7 g sat. fat), 155 mg chol., 404 mg sodium, 75 g carbo., 4 g fiber, 12 g pro.

47

Make-Ahead Directions: *The blueberry syrup may be made up to 1 day ahead, covered, and chilled. Reheat before serving.*

BAKED FRENCH TOAST WITH BERRIES
AND STREUSEL TOPPING

This one's for lovers of blueberries and strawberries. And best of all, you can make it one day and bake it the next.

Prep: 20 minutes **Chill:** 2 to 24 hours **Bake:** 25 minutes **Stand:** 5 minutes **Oven:** 350°F

- 1 8-ounce loaf or ½ of a 1-pound loaf French bread, cut into ¾-inch-thick slices
- 4 eggs, beaten
- 2 cups milk
- ¼ cup granulated sugar
- 1 tablespoon vanilla
- ⅔ cup all-purpose flour
- ⅓ cup packed brown sugar
- ½ teaspoon ground cinnamon
- ¼ cup butter
- 1 cup fresh or frozen blueberries
- 1 cup quartered fresh strawberries

  Whipped cream (optional)

1 Lightly grease a 9×13-inch baking pan or baking dish. Arrange bread slices in prepared pan or dish.

2 In a large bowl stir together eggs, milk, granulated sugar, and vanilla. Slowly pour over bread. Press lightly with a rubber spatula or the back of a large spoon to moisten bread. Cover; chill for at least 2 hours or up to 24 hours.

3 In a small bowl combine flour, brown sugar, and cinnamon. Using a pastry blender, cut in butter until mixture resembles coarse crumbs. Cover; chill for up to 24 hours.

4 Preheat oven to 350°F. Sprinkle blueberries over bread; sprinkle flour mixture over blueberries. Bake, uncovered, for 25 to 30 minutes or until a knife inserted near the center comes out clean. Let stand for 5 minutes; cut into squares. Top with strawberries. If desired, serve with whipped cream.

Makes 8 servings.

Nutrition Facts per serving: 312 cal., 11 g total fat (5 g sat. fat), 127 mg chol., 302 mg sodium, 44 g carbo., 2 g fiber, 9 g pro.

RASPBERRY-ALMOND FRENCH TOAST BAKE

> Mmmm. Fresh raspberries combine with almonds to top French toast for this impressive do-ahead breakfast meal.

Prep: 30 minutes   **Chill:** 8 to 24 hours   **Bake:** 40 minutes   **Stand:** 10 minutes   **Oven:** 350°F

12	ounces Italian bread, cut into 8 slices (each about 1 inch thick)
5	eggs
2½	cups half-and-half or light cream
⅔	cup packed brown sugar
1	teaspoon vanilla
½	teaspoon ground nutmeg
2	cups fresh blueberries and/or raspberries
1	cup sliced almonds, lightly toasted
¼	cup packed brown sugar
¼	cup butter, melted

1 Lightly grease a 9×13-inch baking pan or baking dish; set aside. Arrange bread slices in prepared pan or dish, overlapping as necessary to make bread fit.

2 In a large bowl whisk together eggs, half-and-half, the ⅔ cup brown sugar, the vanilla, and nutmeg. Carefully pour over bread in dish. Press lightly with a rubber spatula or the back of a large spoon to moisten bread. Cover and chill for at least 8 hours or up to 24 hours.*

3 Preheat oven to 350°F. Sprinkle berries and almonds over bread mixture. In a small bowl combine the ¼ cup brown sugar and the melted butter. Drizzle over fruit.

4 Bake, uncovered, about 40 minutes or until bubbly around edges and center is set. Let stand for 10 minutes before serving.

Makes 8 servings.

Nutrition Facts per serving: 525 cal., 28 g total fat (10 g sat. fat), 176 mg chol., 377 mg sodium, 57 g carbo., 5 g fiber, 14 g pro.

*Test Kitchen Tip: *If using a dense Italian bread, turn slices over once halfway through chilling.*

BEST-EVER CINNAMON ROLLS

A cinnamon, raisin, and pecan filling makes these rolls rise and shine above the rest. Toast the pecans to bring out their flavor. (Pictured on the cover and page 111.)

Prep: 1 hour   **Rise:** 2¼ hours   **Bake:** 25 minutes   **Cool:** 5 minutes   **Oven:** 375°F

POTLUCK ● FAVORITE
50

- 4½ to 5 cups all-purpose flour
- 1 package active dry yeast
- 1 cup milk
- ⅓ cup butter
- ⅓ cup granulated sugar
- ½ teaspoon salt
- 3 eggs
- ¾ cup packed brown sugar
- ¼ cup all-purpose flour
- 1 tablespoon ground cinnamon
- ½ cup butter
- ½ cup golden raisins
- ½ cup chopped pecans, toasted if desired
- 1 recipe Powdered Sugar Icing (see recipe, page 331)

1 In a large bowl combine 2¼ cups of the flour and the yeast; set aside. In a small saucepan combine milk, the ⅓ cup butter, the granulated sugar, and salt; heat and stir just until warm (120°F to 130°F) and butter is almost melted. Add to flour mixture. Add eggs. Beat with an electric mixer on low speed for 30 seconds, scraping side of bowl constantly. Beat on high speed for 3 minutes. Using a wooden spoon, stir in as much of the remaining 2¼ to 2¾ cups flour as you can.

2 Turn out dough onto a lightly floured surface. Knead in enough of the remaining flour to make a moderately soft dough that is smooth and elastic (3 to 5 minutes total). Shape into a ball. Place in a greased bowl, turning once to grease the surface. Cover; let rise in a warm place until double in size (1½ to 1¾ hours).

3 Punch down dough. Turn out onto a lightly floured surface. Cover and let rest for 10 minutes. Meanwhile, lightly grease a 9×13-inch baking pan or baking dish; set aside.

4 For filling, in a small bowl combine brown sugar, the ¼ cup flour, and the cinnamon. Using a pastry blender, cut in the ½ cup butter until crumbly.

5 Roll out dough into a 12×18-inch rectangle. Sprinkle filling over dough; top with raisins and pecans. Starting from a long side, roll up dough rectangle into a spiral. Press seam to seal. Cut spiral into 12 equal pieces. Arrange slices, cut sides up, in prepared pan or dish.

6 Loosely cover; let dough rise in a warm place until nearly double in size (about 45 minutes).

7 Preheat oven to 375°F. Break any surface bubbles with a greased toothpick. Bake for 25 to 30 minutes or until golden brown. Cool in pan or dish on a wire rack for 5 minutes. Carefully invert cinnamon rolls onto a wire rack; remove pan or dish. Cool slightly. Invert again onto a serving platter. Drizzle with Powdered Sugar Icing. Serve warm.

Makes 12 rolls.

Nutrition Facts per roll: 500 cal., 18 g total fat (9 g sat. fat), 89 mg chol., 222 mg sodium, 77 g carbo., 2 g fiber, 4 g pro.

ZESTY ORANGE CINNAMON ROLLS

Two icings, one orange and one almond, are drizzled on top to add a fresh twist to this perennial favorite.

Prep: 55 minutes **Rise:** 2¼ hours **Bake:** 30 minutes **Cool:** 10 minutes **Oven:** 350°F

- 1 medium potato, peeled and quartered
- 1 package active dry yeast
- ¼ cup warm water (105°F to 115°F)
- ½ cup granulated sugar
- ⅓ cup butter, softened
- 1 egg
- 1½ teaspoons salt
- 5¼ to 5¾ cups all-purpose flour
- ½ cup butter, softened
- ⅔ cup granulated sugar
- 1 tablespoon ground cinnamon
- 2 cups powdered sugar
- 1 teaspoon finely shredded orange peel
  Orange juice
- ½ teaspoon vanilla
  Milk
- ¼ teaspoon almond extract

1 In a covered small saucepan cook potato in a small amount of boiling lightly salted water for 20 to 25 minutes or until tender; drain, reserving 1 cup cooking liquid. Mash potato; measure ½ cup (discard any remaining potato). Cool to 120°F to 130°F (about 15 minutes).

2 Stir yeast into the ¼ cup warm water. Let stand for 5 minutes. In a large bowl combine the reserved cooking liquid, the mashed potato, the ½ cup granulated sugar, the ⅓ cup butter, the egg, and salt. Stir in the yeast mixture. Beat with an electric mixer on low to medium speed for 30 seconds. Add 2 cups of the flour; beat on high speed for 2 minutes. Using a wooden spoon, stir in as much of the remaining flour as you can.

3 Turn out dough onto a floured surface. Knead in enough of the remaining flour to make a moderately stiff dough that is smooth and elastic (6 to 8 minutes total). Shape dough into a ball. Place the dough in a lightly greased bowl; turn once to grease the surface. Cover; let rise in warm place until double in size (about 1½ hours). Punch down dough. Turn dough out onto a lightly floured surface. Cover; let rest for 10 minutes. Lightly grease a 9×13-inch baking pan or baking dish; set aside.

4 Roll dough to an 8×14-inch rectangle. Spread the ½ cup softened butter over the dough. In a bowl combine the ⅔ cup granulated sugar and the cinnamon; sprinkle over dough. Starting from a long side, roll up rectangle into a spiral. Pinch seam to seal. Cut into 12 equal pieces. Place pieces, cut sides down, in prepared pan or dish. Cover and let rise in a warm place until nearly double in size (about 45 minutes).

5 Meanwhile, preheat oven to 350°F. Bake for 30 to 35 minutes or until golden brown. Cool in pan or dish on a wire rack for 10 minutes. Carefully invert rolls onto a wire rack; remove pan or dish. Cool slightly. Invert again onto a serving platter.

6 For orange icing, mix 1 cup of the powdered sugar, the orange peel, 1 tablespoon orange juice, and vanilla. Stir in orange juice, 1 teaspoon at a time, to make icing of drizzling consistency. For almond icing, mix the remaining 1 cup powdered sugar, 1 tablespoon milk, and the almond extract. Stir in milk, 1 teaspoon at a time, to make icing of drizzling consistency. Drizzle rolls with icings.

Makes 12 jumbo rolls.

Nutrition Facts per jumbo roll: 462 cal., 14 g total fat (9 g sat. fat), 54 mg chol., 436 mg sodium, 77 g carbo., 2 g fiber, 7 g pro.

CREAMY CARAMEL-PECAN ROLLS

These gooey, gorgeous rolls are shaped from frozen dough. Your family will never guess how easy they are to make.

Prep: 25 minutes **Rise:** 1 hour **Bake:** 25 minutes **Stand:** 5 minutes **Oven:** 375°F (baking pan) or 350°F (baking dish)

- 1¼ **cups powdered sugar**
- ⅓ **cup whipping cream**
- 1 **cup coarsely chopped pecans**
- ½ **cup packed brown sugar**
- 1 **tablespoon ground cinnamon**
- 2 **16-ounce loaves frozen white bread dough or sweet roll dough, thawed**
- 3 **tablespoons butter or margarine, melted**
- ¾ **cup raisins (optional)**

1 Generously grease a 9×13-inch baking pan or baking dish. Line with parchment paper or nonstick foil; set aside. For topping, in a small bowl stir together powdered sugar and whipping cream; pour evenly into prepared pan or dish and spread gently. Sprinkle pecans evenly over whipping cream mixture.

2 In another small bowl stir together brown sugar and cinnamon; set aside. On a lightly floured surface, roll each loaf of dough into an 8×12-inch rectangle, stopping occasionally to let dough relax, if necessary. Brush each dough rectangle with melted butter; sprinkle with brown sugar-cinnamon mixture. If desired, sprinkle with raisins.

3 Starting from a short side, roll up each dough rectangle into a spiral. Press seams to seal. Cut each spiral into eight pieces; place pieces, cut sides down, on topping in pan or dish.

4 Cover; let rise in a warm place until nearly double (about 1 hour). Preheat oven to 375°F for baking pan or 350°F for baking dish. Break any surface bubbles with a greased toothpick.

5 Bake for 25 to 30 minutes or until rolls are golden brown and sound hollow when gently tapped. If necessary to prevent overbrowning, cover rolls with foil for the last 10 minutes of baking.

6 Cool in pan or dish on a wire rack for 5 minutes. Loosen edges and carefully invert rolls onto a serving platter. Remove parchment paper or foil. Spoon any nut mixture that remained in pan or dish over rolls. Serve warm.

Makes 16 rolls.

Nutrition Facts per roll: 309 cal., 13 g total fat (5 g sat. fat), 45 mg chol., 122 mg sodium, 45 g carbo., 2 g fiber, 5 g pro.

Make-Ahead Directions: *Prepare as directed through step 3. Cover with oiled waxed paper, then with plastic wrap. Chill for at least 2 hours or up to 24 hours. Let rolls stand, covered, at room temperature for 1 hour. Preheat oven to 375°F for baking pan or 350°F for baking dish. Uncover. Bake and serve as directed in steps 5 and 6.*

APPLE HARVEST CINNAMON ROLLS

Big, beautiful rolls warm cool fall mornings with a triple dose of apples and the irresistible aroma of cinnamon. Chill dough up to 24 hours before baking.

Prep: 45 minutes **Rise:** 1¼ hours **Bake:** 35 minutes **Cool:** 10 minutes **Oven:** 350°F

- 6 to 6½ cups all-purpose flour
- 2 packages active dry yeast
- 2 cups milk
- ¼ cup granulated sugar
- ¼ cup butter or margarine
- 1½ teaspoons salt
- 1 egg
- 1 cup packed brown sugar
- ½ cup butter or margarine, melted
- 2 teaspoons ground cinnamon
- 2 cups chopped, peeled apple
- ¾ cup apple butter
- 1 cup powdered sugar
- ¼ teaspoon ground cinnamon
- Apple juice

Make-Ahead Directions:

Prepare as directed through step 4. Cover with oiled waxed paper, then with plastic wrap. Chill in the refrigerator for at least 2 hours or up to 24 hours. Let pan or dish of rolls stand, covered, at room temperature for 20 minutes. Uncover and break any surface bubbles with a greased toothpick. Bake and glaze as directed in steps 6 and 7.

1 In a large bowl stir together 3 cups of the flour and the yeast; set aside. In a medium saucepan combine milk, granulated sugar, the ¼ cup butter, and the salt; heat and stir until warm (120°F to 130°F) and butter is almost melted. Add to flour mixture. Add egg. Beat with an electric mixer on low to medium speed for 30 seconds, scraping side of the bowl. Beat on high speed for 3 minutes. Using a wooden spoon, stir in as much of the remaining flour as you can.

2 Turn out dough onto a lightly floured surface. Knead in enough of the remaining flour to make a moderately soft dough that is smooth and elastic (3 to 5 minutes total). Shape dough into a ball. Place dough in a lightly greased bowl, turning once to grease the surface. Cover and let rise in a warm place until double in size (45 to 60 minutes).

3 For filling, in a medium bowl combine brown sugar, the ½ cup melted butter, and the 2 teaspoons cinnamon. Stir in chopped apple and apple butter. Set aside.

4 Punch down dough. Turn out dough onto a lightly floured surface. Divide dough in half. Cover and let rest for 10 minutes. Grease a 9×13-inch baking pan or baking dish. Roll each half of the dough into a 12×16-inch rectangle. Spread half of the filling evenly over each dough rectangle to within 1 inch of the short sides. Starting from a short side, roll up each rectangle into a spiral. Pinch seams to seal. Cut each spiral into 2-inch-wide slices. Place slices, cut sides down, in prepared pan or dish.

5 Cover pan or dish and let rolls rise in a warm place until nearly double in size (30 to 40 minutes).

6 Preheat oven to 350°F. Bake for 35 to 40 minutes or until golden brown. If necessary to prevent overbrowning, cover with foil for the last 15 minutes of baking. Cool in pan or dish on a wire rack for 10 minutes. Carefully invert rolls onto a wire rack; remove pan or dish. Cool slightly. Invert again onto a serving platter.

7 Meanwhile, for glaze, in a small bowl combine powdered sugar and the ¼ teaspoon cinnamon. Add 1 tablespoon apple juice. Stir in enough additional apple juice, 1 teaspoon at a time, to make glaze of drizzling consistency. Drizzle glaze over rolls. Serve warm.

Makes 12 rolls.

Nutrition Facts per roll: 582 cal., 14 g total fat (8 g sat. fat), 51 mg chol., 431 mg sodium, 108 g carbo., 3 g fiber, 9 g pro.

DREAMY CINNAMON BREAKFAST ROLLS

No one will ever suspect these rolls are made with cake mix! Walnuts and brown sugar combine for the delicious crunchy top.

Prep: 30 minutes **Rise:** 1 hour **Chill:** 8 to 24 hours **Bake:** 25 minutes **Stand:** 40 minutes **Oven:** 350°F

- 1 package 2-layer-size French vanilla cake mix
- 5½ to 6 cups all-purpose flour
- 2 packages active dry yeast
- 1 teaspoon salt
- 2½ cups warm water (120°F to 130°F)
- ¼ cup butter, softened
- ¾ cup granulated sugar
- 1 tablespoon ground cinnamon
- 1⅓ cups packed brown sugar
- 1 cup butter
- 2 tablespoons light-color corn syrup
- 1½ cups chopped walnuts

1 In a large bowl combine the dry cake mix, 2 cups of the flour, the yeast, and salt. Add the warm water; beat with an electric mixer on low speed until combined, scraping side of bowl constantly. Beat on high speed for 3 minutes.

2 Stir in as much of the remaining flour as you can with a wooden spoon. Turn out dough onto a floured surface. Knead in enough of the remaining flour to make a smooth dough (about 3 minutes total; dough will still be slightly sticky). Place dough in a large greased bowl. Cover and let rise in a warm place until double in size (about 1 hour).

3 Punch down dough. Turn out onto a well-floured surface. Divide dough in half. Cover; let stand for 10 minutes. Roll each dough portion into a 9×16-inch rectangle.

4 Spread each dough rectangle with half of the ¼ cup butter. In a small bowl combine granulated sugar and cinnamon; sprinkle over buttered dough rectangles. Starting from a long side, roll up each dough rectangle into a spiral. Pinch seams to seal. Cut each spiral into 16 equal pieces (32 total).

5 In a medium saucepan combine the brown sugar, the 1 cup butter, and the corn syrup. Bring to boiling. Remove from heat. Divide mixture between two 9×13-inch baking pans or baking dishes.

6 Sprinkle walnuts evenly into pans or dishes. Place half of the dough slices, cut sides down, into each pan or dish. Cover and chill for at least 8 hours or up to 24 hours.

7 Let pans or dishes of rolls stand at room temperature for 30 minutes. Meanwhile, preheat oven to 350°F. Bake, uncovered, about 25 minutes or until golden brown. Let cool in pans or dishes on wire racks for 10 minutes. Turn out onto foil. Serve warm or cool.

Makes 32 rolls.

Nutrition Facts per roll: 298 cal., 13 g total fat (0 g sat. fat), 21 mg chol., 258 mg sodium, 43 g carbo., 1 g fiber, 4 g pro.

Make-Ahead Directions: *Prepare and bake as directed. Cool completely. Cover and store at room temperature for up to 8 hours or wrap and freeze for up to 3 months. Thaw rolls, if frozen, before serving.*

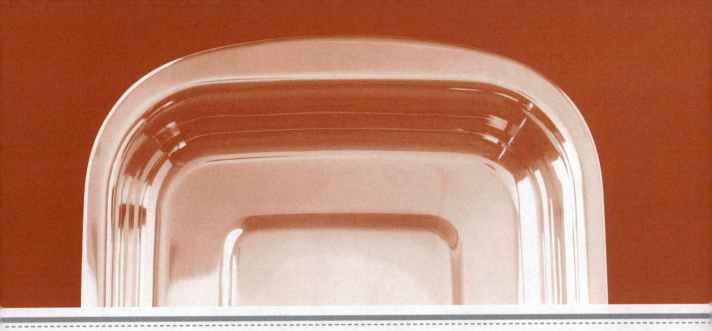

LASAGNAS

Down-home, spruced up, with meat, without noodles. Lasagna can take on many tempting and tantalizing tastes as shown in these 21 recipes. Some have familiar ingredients, some break the mold. One thing is for sure: They are all as comforting as ever.

LASAGNA

Here's the mother of all others. This is the classic dish we grew up loving and the one you'll fall back on time and time again.

Prep: 30 minutes **Cook:** 15 minutes **Bake:** 30 minutes **Stand:** 10 minutes **Oven:** 375°F

- 9   dried lasagna noodles
- 1   pound bulk Italian or pork sausage or ground beef
- 1   cup chopped onion
- 2   cloves garlic, minced
- 1   14½-ounce can diced tomatoes, undrained
- 1   8-ounce can tomato sauce
- 1   tablespoon dried Italian seasoning, crushed
- 1   teaspoon fennel seeds, crushed (optional)
- ¼   teaspoon black pepper
- 1   egg, slightly beaten
- 1   15-ounce carton ricotta cheese or 2 cups cream-style cottage cheese, drained
- ¼   cup grated Parmesan cheese
- 2   cups shredded mozzarella cheese (8 ounces)
      Grated Parmesan cheese (optional)

1 Preheat oven to 375°F. Cook lasagna noodles according to package directions; drain well. Rinse with cold water; drain well. Place lasagna noodles in a single layer on a sheet of foil; set aside.

2 For sauce, in a large skillet cook sausage, onion, and garlic until meat is cooked through, using a wooden spoon to break up meat as it cooks; drain off fat. Stir undrained tomatoes, tomato sauce, Italian seasoning, fennel seeds (if desired), and pepper into meat mixture. Bring to boiling; reduce heat. Cover; simmer for 15 minutes, stirring occasionally.

3 For filling, in a medium bowl combine egg, ricotta, and the ¼ cup Parmesan cheese; set aside.

4 Spread about ¼ cup of the sauce over the bottom of an ungreased 9×13-inch baking dish. Place three of the cooked lasagna noodles on the sauce in the dish. Spread with one-third of the filling. Top with one-third of the remaining meat sauce and one-third of the mozzarella cheese. Repeat layers two more times, starting with noodles and ending with mozzarella cheese; make sure the top layer of noodles is completely covered with meat sauce. If desired, sprinkle with additional Parmesan cheese.

5 Bake, uncovered, for 30 to 35 minutes or until heated through. Let stand for 10 minutes before serving.

Makes 12 servings.

Nutrition Facts per serving: 335 cal., 21 g total fat (10 g sat. fat), 78 mg chol., 623 mg sodium, 19 g carbo., 2 g fiber, 18 g pro.

Quick Lasagna: *Substitute 9 no-boil lasagna noodles for the regular lasagna noodles and skip cooking the lasagna noodles. Omit the tomatoes, tomato sauce, Italian seasoning, fennel seeds, and black pepper. For sauce, stir one 26-ounce jar tomato-base pasta sauce into the browned meat mixture. Do not simmer. Continue as directed in steps 3 through 5, except cover tightly with foil before baking. Nutrition Facts per serving: 334 cal., 20 g total fat (11 g sat.fat), 87 mg chol., 714 mg sodium, 18 g carbo., 2 g fiber, 21 g pro.*

Make-Ahead Directions:
Prepare as directed through step 4. Cover with plastic wrap; chill for up to 24 hours. Preheat oven to 375°F. Remove plastic wrap and cover with foil. Bake for 40 minutes. Uncover; bake about 20 minutes more or until heated through. Let stand for 10 minutes before serving.

MEATY LASAGNA BOLOGNESE

Named after Bologna, Italy, Bolognese sauce is loaded with meat. Here it's layered with traditional fillings for a hearty meat-lover's dish.

Prep: 45 minutes **Bake:** 50 minutes **Stand:** 15 minutes **Oven:** 375°F

- 1 pound lean ground beef
- 8 ounces bulk Italian sausage
- 4 ounces pancetta or bacon, cut up
- 1 large onion, chopped
- 2 medium carrots, chopped
- 2 stalks celery, chopped
- 3 cloves garlic, minced
- 1 cup whole milk or half-and-half
- ½ cup dry white wine
- ½ cup chicken broth
- 1 cup canned crushed tomatoes
- 2 tablespoons tomato paste
- 1 tablespoon snipped fresh sage
- 1 tablespoon snipped fresh flat-leaf parsley
- ½ teaspoon black pepper
- ¼ teaspoon salt
- ¼ teaspoon crushed red pepper
- 2 cups shredded mozzarella cheese (8 ounces)
- 1 cup finely shredded Parmesan cheese (4 ounces)
- 12 no-boil lasagna noodles
- 1 10-ounce container refrigerated Alfredo pasta sauce

1 For meat sauce, in a Dutch oven cook ground beef, sausage, pancetta, onion, carrots, celery, and garlic over medium-high heat until meat is cooked through, using a wooden spoon to break up meat as it cooks; drain off fat.

2 Stir in milk. Simmer, uncovered, until milk is nearly evaporated. Stir in wine and broth. Simmer, uncovered, until liquid is nearly evaporated. Stir in crushed tomatoes, tomato paste, sage, parsley, black pepper, salt, and crushed red pepper. In a medium bowl combine mozzarella cheese and Parmesan cheese.

3 Preheat oven to 375°F. Spread one-third of the meat sauce in an ungreased 9×13-inch baking dish. Sprinkle with one-fourth of the cheese mixture. Top with four of the uncooked lasagna noodles. Repeat layers two more times, starting with meat sauce and ending with noodles. Spread the Alfredo sauce evenly over the noodles. Cover tightly with foil.

4 Bake for 40 minutes. Uncover; sprinkle with the remaining cheese mixture. Bake lasagna about 10 minutes more or until heated through and noodles are tender when pierced with a fork. Let stand for 15 minutes before serving.

Makes 9 or 10 servings.

Nutrition Facts per serving: 631 cal., 38 g total fat (17 g sat. fat), 95 mg chol., 1,157 mg sodium, 38 g carbo., 1 g fiber, 32 g pro.

RED PEPPER LASAGNA

Prep: 35 minutes   **Cook:** 20 minutes   **Bake:** 35 minutes   **Stand:** 20 minutes   **Oven:** 350°F

- 2 **7-ounce jars roasted red sweet peppers, drained**
- 1 **tablespoon olive oil**
- 1 **28-ounce can crushed tomatoes, undrained**
- 2 **tablespoons dried basil, crushed**
- 4 **cloves garlic, minced**
- ¾ **teaspoon black pepper**
- ½ **teaspoon salt**
- 8 **ounces sweet or hot bulk Italian sausage, cooked and drained (optional)**
- ⅓ **cup butter or margarine**
- ⅓ **cup all-purpose flour**
- ½ **teaspoon salt**
- ½ **teaspoon ground nutmeg**
- 3 **cups milk**
- 12 **no-boil lasagna noodles**
- 1¼ **cups shredded Parmesan cheese (5 ounces)**

1 Cut roasted red sweet peppers into thin strips. In a large saucepan heat oil over medium heat. Add roasted red peppers; cook for 1 minute. Stir in undrained tomatoes, basil, garlic, black pepper, and ½ teaspoon salt. Bring to boiling; reduce heat. Simmer, uncovered, for 20 minutes, stirring often. Set aside to cool. If desired, stir in sausage.

2 For béchamel sauce, in a medium saucepan melt butter over medium heat. Stir in flour, ½ teaspoon salt, and the nutmeg until smooth. Add milk all at once. Cook and stir until thickened and bubbly. Set aside to cool.

3 Grease a 9×13-inch baking dish. Preheat oven to 350°F. Arrange three of the uncooked lasagna noodles in prepared dish. Spread about 1 cup of the red pepper mixture over the noodles. Top with ¾ cup of the béchamel sauce, spreading evenly; sprinkle with ¼ cup of the Parmesan cheese. Repeat layers three more times, starting with noodles and ending with Parmesan cheese; make sure the top layer of noodles is completely covered with sauce. Sprinkle with the remaining ¼ cup Parmesan cheese.

4 Bake, uncovered, for 35 to 40 minutes or until bubbly, noodles are tender when pierced with a fork, and lasagna is light brown on top. Let stand for 20 minutes before serving.

Makes 8 servings.

Nutrition Facts per serving: 753 cal., 44 g total fat (24 g sat. fat), 109 mg chol., 2,137 mg sodium, 45 g carbo., 3 g fiber, 45 g pro.

Make-Ahead Directions: *Prepare as directed through step 3. Cover with plastic wrap; chill for up to 24 hours. Preheat oven to 350°F. Remove plastic wrap and cover with foil. Bake for 30 minutes. Uncover; bake for 15 to 25 minutes more or until bubbly.*

LASAGNA BLANCA

No tomatoes in sight, this version features a white sauce and noodles that are rolled into spirals for easy serving. (Pictured on page 98.)

Prep: 1 hour **Bake:** 35 minutes **Stand:** 10 minutes **Oven:** 350°F

12	dried lasagna noodles
1	pound spicy bulk pork sausage
½	cup chopped green onions
½	cup chopped fresh mushrooms
1½	cups shredded cheddar or Monterey Jack cheese (6 ounces)
1	cup cream-style cottage cheese
½	of an 8-ounce package cream cheese, softened and cut up
½	teaspoon garlic powder
⅛	teaspoon black pepper
1	tablespoon butter or margarine
1	tablespoon all-purpose flour
⅛	teaspoon dried tarragon, crushed
⅛	teaspoon black pepper
1	cup milk

1 Cook lasagna noodles according to package directions; drain well. Rinse with cold water; drain well. Place lasagna noodles in a single layer on a sheet of foil; set aside. Meanwhile, in a large skillet cook sausage, green onions, and mushrooms until sausage is cooked through, using a wooden spoon to break up sausage as it cooks; drain off fat. Set aside.

2 For filling, in a medium bowl combine ½ cup of the cheddar cheese, the cottage cheese, cream cheese, garlic powder, and ⅛ teaspoon pepper; set aside.

3 Grease a 9×13-inch baking pan or baking dish; set aside. Preheat oven to 350°F. Spread filling evenly over cooked noodles. Sprinkle sausage mixture on top. Roll up each noodle into a spiral. Place lasagna roll-ups, seam sides down, in the prepared pan or dish; set aside.

4 For tarragon sauce, in a small saucepan melt butter over medium heat. Stir in flour, tarragon, and ⅛ teaspoon pepper. Add milk all at once. Cook and stir until slightly thickened and bubbly. Remove from heat. Stir in ½ cup of the cheddar cheese. Pour the tarragon sauce over the lasagna roll-ups in pan or dish.

5 Bake, covered, for 25 minutes. Uncover; sprinkle with the remaining ½ cup cheddar cheese. Bake, uncovered, about 10 minutes more or until heated through. Let stand for 10 minutes before serving.

Makes 12 servings.

Nutrition Facts per serving: 317 cal., 17 g total fat (9 g sat. fat), 54 mg chol., 378 mg sodium, 21 g carbo., 1 g fiber, 17 g pro.

Make-Ahead Directions: *Prepare as directed through step 4. Cover with foil; chill for up to 24 hours. Preheat oven to 350°F. Bake, covered, for 40 minutes. Uncover; sprinkle with the remaining ½ cup cheddar cheese. Bake, uncovered, about 10 minutes more or until heated through.*

HAM AND CHEESE LASAGNA

You love ham and cheese together in a sandwich. Now pair the favorite combo with mushrooms for a creamy and comforting lasagna.

Prep: 35 minutes **Cook:** 25 minutes **Bake:** 50 minutes **Stand:** 20 minutes **Oven:** 350°F

- 2 tablespoons olive oil
- 1 large onion, chopped
- 4 stalks celery, thinly sliced
- 4 carrots, chopped
- 2 cloves garlic, minced
- 3 cups sliced fresh mushrooms
- 2 cups cubed cooked ham (about 10 ounces)
- 2 cups whipping cream
- 1 14½-ounce can diced tomatoes with basil, garlic, and oregano, undrained
- ½ cup water
- ¼ cup dry red wine
- Salt
- Black pepper
- 1½ cups shredded Swiss cheese (6 ounces)
- 1 cup grated Parmesan cheese
- 12 no-boil lasagna noodles

1 Preheat oven to 350°F. For sauce, in a 12-inch skillet or Dutch oven heat oil over medium heat. Add onion, celery, carrots, and garlic; cook and stir about 10 minutes or just until vegetables are tender. Add mushrooms and ham. Cook for 10 minutes, stirring occasionally. Stir in whipping cream, undrained tomatoes, the water, and wine. Bring to boiling; reduce heat. Simmer, uncovered, for 5 minutes. Season to taste with salt and black pepper.

2 In a medium bowl combine cheeses. Spoon 1½ cups of the sauce into an ungreased 9×13-inch baking dish. Sprinkle with ⅔ cup of the cheese mixture. Top with four uncooked lasagna noodles. Repeat layers two more times, starting with sauce and ending with noodles. Spoon the remaining sauce over, making sure the top layer of noodles is completely covered with sauce. Sprinkle with the remaining cheese mixture. Cover tightly with foil.

3 Bake about 50 minutes or until heated through and noodles are tender when pierced with a fork. Let stand for 20 minutes before serving.

Makes 12 servings.

Nutrition Facts per serving: 376 cal., 25 g total fat (14 g sat. fat), 86 mg chol., 671 mg sodium, 22 g carbo., 2 g fiber, 15 g pro.

CREOLE LASAGNA

This robust Louisiana-style dish combines sausage and beef with traditional lasagna ingredients. Andouille, a spicy smoked sausage, is perfect in it.

Prep: 35 minutes **Bake:** 30 minutes **Stand:** 10 minutes **Oven:** 350°F

- 9 dried lasagna noodles
- 8 ounces cooked andouille sausage or smoked pork sausage links, halved lengthwise and sliced
- 8 ounces lean ground beef
- ½ cup chopped celery
- ⅓ cup chopped green sweet pepper
- ⅓ cup chopped onion
- 2 cloves garlic, minced
- 1½ cups water
- 1 6-ounce can tomato paste
- 2 teaspoons sugar
- ¼ teaspoon cayenne pepper
- 8 ounces sliced mozzarella cheese
- ⅓ cup finely shredded Parmesan cheese

1 Lightly grease a 9×13-inch baking dish; set aside. Preheat oven to 350°F. Cook lasagna noodles according to package directions; drain well. Rinse with cold water; drain well. Place lasagna noodles in a single layer on a sheet of foil; set aside.

2 Meanwhile, for meat sauce, in a large saucepan cook sausage over medium-high heat until brown, stirring frequently. Remove sausage from saucepan. In the same saucepan cook ground beef, celery, sweet pepper, onion, and garlic until meat is cooked through, using a wooden spoon to break up meat as it cooks; drain off fat. Stir sausage, the water, tomato paste, sugar, and cayenne pepper into ground beef mixture. Bring to boiling; reduce heat. Cover; simmer for 15 minutes.

3 Arrange three of the cooked lasagna noodles in the prepared dish. Top with one-third of the meat sauce, one-third of the mozzarella cheese, and one-third of the Parmesan cheese. Repeat layers two more times, except set aside the last one-third of the mozzarella and Parmesan cheeses.

4 Bake, covered, for 20 minutes. Uncover; top with the remaining mozzarella and Parmesan cheeses. Bake, uncovered, for 10 minutes more. Let lasagna stand for 10 minutes before serving.

Makes 8 servings.

Nutrition Facts per serving: 381 cal., 19 g total fat (9 g sat. fat), 54 mg chol., 494 mg sodium, 29 g carbo., 1 g fiber, 22 g pro.

GREEK-STYLE LASAGNA

Reminiscent of pastitsio, a traditional Greek dish, this lasagna gets a Mediterranean flavor with lamb, feta cheese, and a touch of cinnamon.

Prep: 45 minutes   **Bake:** 35 minutes   **Stand:** 10 minutes   **Oven:** 350°F

- 9   **dried lasagna noodles**
- 1   **pound ground lamb or ground beef**
- 1   **medium onion, chopped**
- 2   **cloves garlic, minced**
- 1   **8-ounce can tomato sauce**
- ¼   **cup dry red wine or beef broth**
- 1   **teaspoon dried oregano, crushed**
- ¼   **teaspoon ground cinnamon**
- 1   **egg, beaten**
- 3   **tablespoons butter or margarine**
- 3   **tablespoons all-purpose flour**
- ¼   **teaspoon black pepper**
- 1¾   **cups milk**
- ½   **cup grated Parmesan cheese**
- 2   **eggs, beaten**
- 1   **2¼-ounce can sliced pitted ripe olives, drained**
- 8   **ounces feta cheese, crumbled (2 cups)**
- 1   **cup shredded white cheddar cheese (4 ounces)**

1 Preheat oven to 350°F. Cook lasagna noodles according to package directions; drain well. Rinse with cold water; drain well. Place lasagna noodles in a single layer on a sheet of foil; set aside.

2 Meanwhile, for meat sauce, in a large skillet cook ground meat, onion, and garlic until meat is cooked through, using a wooden spoon to break up meat as it cooks; drain off fat. Stir tomato sauce, wine, oregano, and cinnamon into meat mixture. Bring to boiling; reduce heat. Simmer, uncovered, for 10 minutes. Gradually stir hot meat mixture into the one beaten egg; set aside.

3 For cheese sauce, in a medium saucepan melt butter over medium heat; stir in flour and pepper. Add milk all at once. Cook and stir until thickened and bubbly; cook and stir for 1 minute more. Stir in ¼ cup of the Parmesan cheese; set aside. In a small bowl stir together the two eggs and the remaining ¼ cup Parmesan cheese; set aside.

4 Spread about 2 tablespoons of the cheese sauce evenly in an ungreased 9×13-inch baking dish. Place three of the cooked lasagna noodles on the sauce in dish. Spread with one-third of the meat sauce, one-third of the remaining cheese sauce, and one-third of the olives. Drizzle with one-third of the egg-Parmesan mixture; sprinkle with one-third of the feta cheese and one-third of the cheddar cheese. Repeat layers two more times, starting with noodles and ending with cheddar cheese.

5 Bake, uncovered, for 35 to 40 minutes or until heated through. Let lasagna stand for 10 minutes before serving.

Makes 12 servings.

Nutrition Facts per serving: 372 cal., 22 g total fat (12 g sat. fat), 128 mg chol., 588 mg sodium, 21 g carbo., 1 g fiber, 21 g pro.

CAJUN CHICKEN LASAGNA

With a nod to New Orleans, classic Cajun flavorings and spicy andouille sausage provide kick. Smoked pork sausage would be a good substitute.

Prep: 45 minutes **Bake:** 1 hour **Stand:** 15 minutes **Oven:** 350°F

- Nonstick cooking spray
- 16 dried lasagna noodles
- 1 pound cooked andouille sausage or smoked pork sausage, quartered lengthwise and sliced
- 1 pound skinless, boneless chicken breasts, cut into ¾-inch pieces
- 2 to 3 teaspoons Cajun seasoning
- 1 teaspoon dried sage, crushed
- ½ cup chopped onion
- ½ cup chopped celery
- ¼ cup chopped green sweet pepper
- 6 cloves garlic, minced
- 2 10-ounce containers refrigerated Alfredo pasta sauce
- ½ cup grated Parmesan cheese
- 1½ cups shredded mozzarella cheese (6 ounces)

1 Lightly coat a 9×13-inch baking pan or baking dish with nonstick cooking spray; set aside. Preheat oven to 350°F. Cook lasagna noodles according to package directions; drain well. Rinse with cold water; drain well. Place lasagna noodles in a single layer on a sheet of foil; set aside.

2 In a large bowl combine sausage, chicken, Cajun seasoning, and sage. In a large skillet cook and stir chicken mixture about 8 minutes or until chicken is no longer pink. Using a slotted spoon, remove chicken mixture from skillet, reserving drippings in skillet. Set chicken mixture aside. In the same skillet cook onion, celery, sweet pepper, and garlic in drippings until vegetables are tender. Return chicken mixture to skillet; stir in half of the Alfredo sauce and the Parmesan cheese.

3 Arrange four of the cooked lasagna noodles in prepared pan or dish, cutting as necessary to fit.

Spread with one-third of the chicken-vegetable mixture. Sprinkle with one-third of the mozzarella cheese. Repeat layers two more times, starting with noodles and ending with cheese. Top with the remaining cooked lasagna noodles. Carefully spread remaining Alfredo sauce over.

4 Bake, covered, about 1 hour or until heated through. Let stand for 15 to 20 minutes before serving.

Makes 12 servings.

Nutrition Facts per serving: 507 cal., 31 g total fat (7 g sat. fat), 83 mg chol., 938 mg sodium, 27 g carbo., 1 g fiber, 29 g pro.

CHICKEN AND VEGETABLE LASAGNA

This layered entrée—featuring chicken, spinach, carrots, and tomatoes—is a delicious alternative to beef or sausage lasagna.

Prep: 30 minutes   **Cook:** 15 minutes   **Bake:** 40 minutes   **Stand:** 10 minutes   **Oven:** 350°F

- 1 15-ounce carton ricotta cheese
- 1 10-ounce package frozen chopped spinach, thawed and well drained
- 1 egg, slightly beaten
- 2 teaspoons dried Italian seasoning, crushed
- 1 pound skinless, boneless chicken breasts, cut into ½-inch pieces
- 3 cups sliced fresh mushrooms
- ½ cup chopped onion
- 1 tablespoon olive oil
- 2 14½-ounce cans diced tomatoes, undrained
- 1 8-ounce can tomato sauce
- 2 cups shredded carrots
- ½ teaspoon black pepper
- Nonstick cooking spray
- 9 dried lasagna noodles
- 2 cups shredded mozzarella cheese (8 ounces)

1 For cheese filling, in a small bowl combine ricotta cheese, spinach, egg, and half of the Italian seasoning. Cover and chill until ready to assemble lasagna.

2 For sauce, in a large skillet cook chicken, mushrooms, onion, and the remaining Italian seasoning in hot oil for 4 to 5 minutes or until chicken is no longer pink. Stir in undrained tomatoes, tomato sauce, carrots, and pepper. Bring to boiling; reduce heat. Simmer, uncovered, about 15 minutes or until mixture is slightly thickened, stirring occasionally.

3 Meanwhile, lightly coat a 9×13-inch baking dish with nonstick cooking spray; set aside. Preheat oven to 350°F. Cook the lasagna noodles according to package directions; drain well. Rinse with cold water; drain well.

4 Place three of the cooked lasagna noodles in prepared dish. Spread half of the cheese filling over the noodles. Spread one-third of the sauce over the cheese filling. Sprinkle with one-fourth of the mozzarella cheese. Repeat layers once more. Top with the remaining noodles. Spoon the remaining sauce over the top. Sprinkle with the remaining mozzarella cheese.

5 Bake, covered, for 35 minutes. Uncover; bake for 5 to 10 minutes more or until cheese is bubbly. Let stand for 10 minutes before serving.

Makes 8 to 10 servings.

Nutrition Facts per serving: 400 cal., 16 g total fat (8 g sat. fat), 102 mg chol., 552 mg sodium, 31 g carbo., 4 g fiber, 33 g pro.

CHICKEN CAESAR LASAGNA

Lasagna gets a tasty remake with whole wheat noodles, spinach, chicken, and a creamy white sauce instead of a tomato sauce.

Prep: 35 minutes **Bake:** 50 minutes **Stand:** 15 minutes **Oven:** 325°F

Nonstick cooking spray

9 dried whole wheat or regular lasagna noodles

2 10-ounce containers refrigerated light Alfredo pasta sauce

3 tablespoons lemon juice

½ teaspoon cracked black pepper

3 cups chopped cooked chicken breast*

1 10-ounce package frozen chopped spinach, thawed and well drained

1 cup bottled roasted red sweet peppers, drained and chopped

¾ cup shredded Italian blend cheese (3 ounces)

1 Lightly coat a 9×13-inch baking pan or baking dish with nonstick cooking spray; set aside. Preheat oven to 325°F. Cook lasagna noodles according to package directions; drain well. Rinse with cold water; drain well. Place lasagna noodles in a single layer on a sheet of foil; set aside. Meanwhile, in a large bowl combine Alfredo sauce, lemon juice, and black pepper. Stir in cooked chicken, spinach, and roasted red peppers.

2 Arrange three of the cooked lasagna noodles in prepared pan or dish. Top with one-third of the chicken mixture. Repeat layers two more times.

3 Bake, covered, for 45 to 55 minutes or until heated through. Uncover; sprinkle with cheese. Bake, uncovered, about 5 minutes more or until cheese is melted. Let stand for 15 minutes before serving.

Makes 9 servings.

Nutrition Facts per serving: 268 cal., 10 g total fat (6 g sat. fat), 68 mg chol., 557 mg sodium, 20 g carbo., 2 g fiber, 24 g pro.

65

***Test Kitchen Tip:** For chopped cooked chicken, season 2 pounds skinless, boneless chicken breasts with ¼ teaspoon salt and ⅛ teaspoon black pepper. In a large skillet heat 1 tablespoon olive oil over medium-high heat. Reduce heat to medium. Add chicken. Cook, uncovered, for 8 to 12 minutes or until no longer pink, turning halfway through cooking. Cool chicken slightly before chopping.*

SMOKED SALMON LASAGNA

Six cheeses, a splash of sherry,
and smoked salmon give this grown-up
lasagna its distinctive flavor.

Prep: 50 minutes **Bake:** 50 minutes **Stand:** 15 minutes **Oven:** 375°F

- 12 dried lasagna noodles
- ⅓ cup butter or margarine
- ⅓ cup all-purpose flour
- 4 cups milk
- ½ teaspoon salt
- ½ teaspoon black pepper
- ¼ cup finely shredded Parmesan cheese (1 ounce)
- ¼ cup shredded Swiss cheese (1 ounce)
- 2 tablespoons dry sherry
- 1½ cups finely shredded Romano cheese (6 ounces)
- 1 cup shredded mozzarella cheese (4 ounces)
- 1 cup shredded provolone cheese (4 ounces)
- ½ cup shredded cheddar cheese (2 ounces)
- 3 large plum tomatoes, peeled, seeded, chopped, and drained
- 1 6-ounce jar (drained weight) sliced mushrooms, drained
- 8 ounces smoked salmon, flaked, with skin and bones removed

1 Lightly grease a 9×13-inch baking dish; set aside. Preheat oven to 375°F. Cook lasagna noodles according to package directions; drain well. Rinse with cold water; drain well. Place lasagna noodles in a single layer on a piece of foil; set aside.

2 Meanwhile, for sherry sauce, in a medium saucepan melt butter over low heat. Add flour; cook and stir for 4 minutes. (Be careful not to let flour brown.) Gradually whisk in milk, salt, and pepper. Cook and stir until slightly thickened and bubbly. Reduce heat; stir in Parmesan cheese, Swiss cheese, and sherry. Cook and stir until cheeses are melted.

3 In a medium bowl combine Romano, mozzarella, provolone, and cheddar cheeses.

4 Sprinkle one-fourth of the cheese mixture evenly in the prepared dish. Layer with four of the cooked lasagna noodles, one-third of the sherry sauce, half of the tomatoes, half of the mushrooms, half of the salmon, and another one-fourth of the cheese mixture. Repeat layers once more, starting with noodles and ending with cheese mixture. Top with the remaining noodles, the remaining sherry sauce, and the remaining cheese mixture.

5 Bake, uncovered, for 50 to 55 minutes or until edges are bubbly and top is lightly browned. Let stand for 15 minutes before serving.

Makes 12 servings.

Nutrition Facts per serving: 371 cal., 19 g total fat (11 g sat. fat), 59 mg chol., 748 mg sodium, 27 g carbo., 1 g fiber, 22 g pro.

SEAFOOD LASAGNA

Crabmeat and shrimp dress up
this elegant dish. Serve a simple green
salad with it as a special dinner for guests.

Prep: 40 minutes **Bake:** 45 minutes **Stand:** 10 minutes **Oven:** 350°F

- 8 dried lasagna noodles
- 1 cup chopped onion
- 2 tablespoons butter or margarine
- 1 3-ounce package cream cheese, softened and cut up
- 1 12-ounce carton cream-style cottage cheese
- 1 egg, beaten
- 2 teaspoons dried basil, crushed
- ¼ teaspoon salt
- ⅛ teaspoon black pepper
- 2 10¾-ounce cans condensed cream of mushroom soup
- ⅓ cup milk
- 12 ounces cooked, peeled and deveined shrimp, halved lengthwise
- 1 6½-ounce can crabmeat, drained, flaked, and cartilage removed
- ¼ cup finely shredded Parmesan cheese (1 ounce)

1 Grease a 9×13-inch baking pan or baking dish; set aside. Preheat oven to 350°F. Cook lasagna noodles according to package directions; drain well. Rinse with cold water; drain well. Place lasagna noodles in a single layer on a piece of foil; set aside.

2 In a medium skillet cook onion in hot butter until tender. Remove from heat. Add cream cheese; stir until melted. Stir in cottage cheese, egg, basil, salt, and pepper; set aside. In a large bowl combine cream of mushroom soup and milk; stir in shrimp and crabmeat.

3 Arrange four of the cooked lasagna noodles in prepared pan or dish. Spread half of the cheese mixture over noodles. Spread half of the shrimp mixture over cheese layer. Repeat layers once more, starting with noodles and ending with shrimp mixture. Sprinkle with Parmesan cheese.

4 Bake, uncovered, about 45 minutes or until heated through. Let lasagna stand for 10 to 15 minutes before serving.

Makes 12 servings.

Nutrition Facts per serving: 243 cal., 11 g total fat (5 g sat. fat), 112 mg chol., 720 mg sodium, 18 g carbo., 1 g fiber, 17 g pro.

67

GARDEN VEGETABLE LASAGNA

Roasting brings out the earthy flavors of the vegetables that pack this delicious nonmeat lasagna with lots of pizzazz.

Prep: 30 minutes **Broil:** 12 minutes **Bake:** 50 minutes **Stand:** 10 minutes **Oven:** 375°F

- 12 dried lasagna noodles
- 4 cups zucchini cut into bite-size pieces
- 2½ cups thinly sliced carrots
- 2 cups fresh mushrooms, halved
- 1½ cups coarsely chopped red and/or green sweet pepper
- ¼ cup olive oil
- 1 tablespoon dried Italian seasoning, crushed
- ½ teaspoon salt
- ½ teaspoon black pepper
- 1 12-ounce carton cream-style cottage cheese
- 1 egg, beaten
- ½ cup grated Parmesan cheese
- 1 26-ounce jar marinara sauce
- 3 cups shredded mozzarella cheese (12 ounces)

1 Cook lasagna noodles according to package directions; drain well. Rinse with cold water; drain well. Place lasagna noodles in a single layer on a piece of foil; set aside.

2 Meanwhile, preheat broiler. In a very large bowl combine zucchini, carrots, mushrooms, and sweet pepper. Drizzle vegetables with oil; sprinkle with Italian seasoning, salt, and black pepper. Toss well to combine. Place vegetable mixture in a shallow roasting pan.

3 Broil vegetables 5 to 6 inches from heat for 6 minutes. Stir vegetables and broil for 6 to 8 minutes more or until light brown and tender. Set vegetables aside.

4 In a medium bowl combine cottage cheese, egg, and ¼ cup of the Parmesan cheese; set aside.

5 Grease a 9×13-inch baking dish. Reduce oven temperature to 375°F. Spoon one-third of the marinara sauce evenly into the prepared dish. Layer four of the cooked lasagna noodles on top of the sauce. Top with half of the roasted vegetables, one-third of the marinara sauce, and one-third of the mozzarella cheese. Add four more lasagna noodles, all of the cottage cheese mixture, and one-third of the mozzarella cheese. Add the remaining four noodles, the remaining vegetables, the remaining marinara sauce, and the remaining mozzarella cheese. Sprinkle with the remaining ¼ cup Parmesan cheese.

6 Bake, covered, for 30 minutes. Uncover; bake about 20 minutes more or until heated through. Let stand for 10 minutes before serving.

Makes 9 servings.

Nutrition Facts per serving: 420 cal., 21 g total fat (8 g sat. fat), 3 mg chol., 1,020 mg sodium, 37 g carbo., 3 g fiber, 22 g pro.

STEAMED VEGETABLE LASAGNA

This veggie-filled lasagna is great after those summer trips to the farmer's market, where you can get the crisp ingredients fresh off the trucks straight from the farm.

Prep: 45 minutes **Bake:** 45 minutes **Stand:** 10 minutes **Oven:** 375°F

- 9 dried lasagna noodles
- 6 cups broccoli florets
- 1 large red sweet pepper, seeded and cut into bite-size strips
- 1¼ cups sliced zucchini (1 medium)
- 1¼ cups sliced yellow summer squash (1 medium)
- 2 eggs, beaten
- 1 16-ounce carton low-fat cottage cheese
- 1 15-ounce carton light ricotta cheese
- 2½ tablespoons dried basil, crushed
- 2 teaspoons dried thyme, crushed
- 3 cloves garlic, minced
- ½ teaspoon salt
- ¼ teaspoon black pepper
- ¼ teaspoon bottled hot pepper sauce
- 3 cups shredded mozzarella cheese (12 ounces)

1 Cook lasagna noodles according to package directions; drain well. Rinse with cold water; drain well. Place lasagna noodles in a single layer on a piece of foil; set aside.

2 Meanwhile, place a steamer basket in a Dutch oven. Add water to just below the bottom of the steamer basket. Bring water to boiling. Add broccoli, sweet pepper, zucchini, and yellow squash. Reduce heat; cover and steam for 6 to 8 minutes or until vegetables are crisp-tender. Remove from heat.

3 Grease a 9×13-inch baking pan or baking dish; set aside. Preheat oven to 375°F. In a medium bowl combine eggs, low-fat cottage cheese, light ricotta cheese, basil, thyme, garlic, salt, black pepper, and hot pepper sauce.

4 Arrange three of the cooked lasagna noodles in prepared pan or dish. Spread with one-third of the ricotta cheese mixture. Top with one-third of the vegetable mixture and 1 cup of the shredded mozzarella cheese. Repeat layers two more times, starting with noodles and ending with mozzarella cheese.

5 Bake, covered, for 45 to 50 minutes or until heated through. Uncover; let stand for 10 minutes before serving.

Makes 8 to 10 servings.

Nutrition Facts per serving: 388 cal., 15 g total fat (8 g sat. fat), 101 mg chol., 683 mg sodium, 32 g carbo., 4 g fiber, 32 g pro.

69

Make-Ahead Directions: *Prepare as directed through step 4. Cover with foil; chill for up to 24 hours. Preheat oven to 375°F. Bake, covered, for 55 to 65 minutes or until heated through. Uncover; let stand for 10 minutes before serving.*

THREE-CHEESE LASAGNA

Three cheers for the three cheeses!
This delightful vegetarian lasagna features eggplant
and a sprinkling of fresh basil.

Prep: 30 minutes **Roast:** 30 minutes **Bake:** 35 minutes **Stand:** 15 minutes **Oven:** 450°F/375°F

- 2 **medium eggplants (2 pounds total), chopped (11 cups)**
- 2 **large red onions, halved crosswise and thickly sliced**
- 2 **cloves garlic, minced**
- ½ **cup snipped fresh basil**
- ¼ **cup olive oil**
- 12 **dried lasagna noodles**
- 2 **cups finely shredded Swiss cheese (8 ounces)**
- 1 **15-ounce carton ricotta cheese**
- 12 **ounces soft goat cheese (chèvre)**
- 1 **cup whipping cream**
- 2 **eggs**
- ½ **teaspoon salt**
- ½ **teaspoon black pepper**
- ¼ **teaspoon crushed red pepper**
- ½ **cup coarsely snipped or torn fresh basil**
- 2 **teaspoons finely shredded lemon peel**

1 Preheat oven to 450°F. In a roasting pan combine chopped eggplant, red onions, and garlic. Add ½ cup snipped basil and the oil; toss to coat. Roast, uncovered, for 30 to 35 minutes or until vegetables are very tender, stirring once; set aside.

2 Meanwhile, cook lasagna noodles according to package directions; drain well. Rinse with cold water; drain well. Place lasagna noodles in a single layer on a piece of foil; set aside.

3 For filling, in a food processor* combine 1½ cups of the Swiss cheese, the ricotta cheese, goat cheese, whipping cream, eggs, salt, black pepper, and crushed red pepper. Cover and process just until combined.

4 Reduce oven temperature to 375°F. Spoon one-third of the eggplant mixture evenly into an ungreased 9×13-inch baking pan or baking dish. Top with four cooked lasagna noodles and one-third of the filling. Repeat layers two more times, starting with eggplant mixture and ending with filling. Sprinkle with the remaining ½ cup Swiss cheese. Cover with nonstick foil.

5 Bake for 20 minutes. Uncover; bake for 15 to 20 minutes more or until heated through. Let stand for 15 minutes before serving. Sprinkle with ½ cup coarsely snipped or torn basil and the lemon peel.

Makes 12 servings.

Nutrition Facts per serving: 445 cal., 29 g total fat (16 g sat. fat), 111 mg chol., 290 mg sodium, 27 g carbo., 3 g fiber, 20 g pro.

Make-Ahead Directions: *Prepare as directed through step 4. Cover with foil; chill for up to 24 hours. Preheat oven to 375°F. Bake, covered, for 40 minutes. Uncover; bake for 20 to 25 minutes more or until heated through. Let stand for 15 minutes before serving. Top as directed.*

*Test Kitchen Tip: *If you do not have a food processor, combine filling ingredients in a large bowl. Beat with an electric mixer on low speed until combined.*

CREAMY WHITE ARTICHOKE LASAGNA

Layers of artichokes, noodles, and a
ricotta-Parmesan mixture meld with the flavors
of pine nuts and basil.

Prep: 50 minutes **Bake:** 35 minutes **Stand:** 15 minutes **Oven:** 350°F

- 9 dried lasagna noodles
- 3 tablespoons olive oil
- 2 9-ounce packages frozen artichoke hearts, thawed and halved
- ½ cup pine nuts
- 4 cloves garlic, minced
- 1 15-ounce carton ricotta cheese
- 1 cup finely shredded Parmesan cheese (4 ounces)
- 1 cup snipped fresh basil
- 1 egg
- ¾ teaspoon salt
- 1 cup chicken broth or vegetable broth
- ¼ cup all-purpose flour
- 2 cups half-and-half or light cream
- 1 cup shredded mozzarella cheese (4 ounces)

1 Preheat oven to 350°F. Cook lasagna noodles according to package directions; drain well. Rinse with cold water; drain well. Place lasagna noodles in a single layer on a sheet of foil; set aside.

2 In a large saucepan heat 2 tablespoons of the oil over medium heat. Add artichokes, pine nuts, and half of the garlic. Cook for 2 to 3 minutes or until artichokes are tender, stirring frequently. Transfer to the large bowl. Stir in ricotta cheese, ½ cup of the Parmesan cheese, ½ cup of the basil, the egg, and salt.

3 For sauce, in a small bowl combine broth and flour. In the same saucepan heat the remaining 1 tablespoon oil over medium heat. Add the remaining garlic; cook and stir until garlic is tender. Stir in flour mixture and half-and-half. Cook and stir until mixture is thickened and bubbly. Remove from heat. Stir in the remaining ½ cup basil.

4 In a small bowl combine mozzarella cheese and the remaining ½ cup Parmesan cheese.

5 Spread about 1 cup of the sauce evenly in an ungreased 9×13-inch baking pan or baking dish. Arrange three of the cooked lasagna noodles over the sauce in the pan or dish. Spread with one-third of the artichoke mixture and one-third of the remaining sauce. Sprinkle with ½ cup of the mozzarella cheese mixture. Repeat layers two more times, starting with noodles and ending with mozzarella cheese mixture.

6 Bake, uncovered, for 35 to 40 minutes or until edges are bubbly and top is lightly browned. Let stand for 15 minutes before serving.

Makes 12 servings.

Nutrition Facts per serving: 350 cal., 21 g total fat (`10 g sat. fat), 64 mg chol., 470 mg sodium, 25 g carbo., 3 g fiber, 16 g pro.

BROCCOLI LASAGNA

What a great way to pack in extra nutrients.
Meatless lasagna with broccoli and roasted
red peppers is destined to be a new family favorite.

Prep: 45 minutes **Bake:** 30 minutes **Stand:** 10 minutes **Oven:** 425°F

Nonstick cooking spray

2 **bunches broccoli, trimmed and cut up (about 8 cups)**

12 **dried lasagna noodles**

1 **15-ounce carton ricotta cheese**

¼ **cup grated Parmesan cheese**

1 **egg, slightly beaten**

2 **tablespoons snipped fresh parsley**

1 **12-ounce jar roasted red sweet peppers, drained**

¼ **cup butter or margarine**

¼ **cup all-purpose flour**

2 **cloves garlic, minced**

3 **cups milk**

½ **teaspoon salt**

½ **teaspoon dried basil, crushed**

¼ **teaspoon black pepper**

2 **cups shredded Monterey Jack cheese (8 ounces)**

3 **tablespoons grated Parmesan cheese**

1 Lightly coat a 9×13-inch baking pan or baking dish with nonstick cooking spray; set aside. Preheat oven to 425°F. Place a steamer basket in a 4-quart Dutch oven. Add enough water to come just below the bottom of the steamer basket; bring to boiling. Add broccoli. Cover and reduce heat. Steam for 4 to 5 minutes or until broccoli is crisp-tender.

2 Meanwhile, cook lasagna noodles according to package directions; drain well. Rinse with cold water; drain well. Place lasagna noodles in a single layer on a sheet of foil; set aside. In a small bowl stir together ricotta cheese, the ¼ cup Parmesan cheese, the egg, and parsley; set aside.

3 For sauce, place roasted red peppers in a blender or food processor; cover and blend or process until almost smooth. Set aside. In a large skillet melt butter over medium heat. Stir in flour and garlic. Cook and stir for 1 minute. Gradually add milk and pureed peppers. Cook and stir until thickened and bubbly. Stir in salt, basil, and black pepper.

4 Spread ¾ cup of the sauce in prepared pan or dish. Arrange three of the cooked lasagna noodles over sauce. Carefully spread one-third of the ricotta mixture over noodles. Top with one-third of the broccoli and sprinkle with ½ cup of the Monterey Jack cheese. Repeat layers two more times, starting with sauce and ending with cheese. Top with the remaining cooked lasagna noodles. Spoon remaining sauce over.

5 Bake, covered, for 20 minutes. Uncover; sprinkle with the remaining ½ cup Monterey Jack cheese and the 3 tablespoons Parmesan cheese. Bake, uncovered, about 10 minutes more or until heated through. Let stand for 10 minutes before serving.

Makes 10 servings.

Nutrition Facts per serving: 406 cal., 21 g total fat (13 g sat. fat), 84 mg chol., 460 mg sodium, 34 g carbo., 3 g fiber, 21 g pro.

BUTTERNUT SQUASH LASAGNA

Roasted squash takes the place of meat in this lasagna that has autumn written all over it, but it's one you'll definitely want to make in winter too.

Prep: 30 minutes **Roast:** 25 minutes **Bake:** 50 minutes **Stand:** 10 minutes **Oven:** 425°F/375°F

- 3 **pounds butternut squash,** peeled, seeded, and cut into ¼- to ½-inch-thick slices
- 3 **tablespoons olive oil**
- ½ **teaspoon salt**
- ¼ **cup butter or margarine**
- 6 **cloves garlic, minced**
- ¼ **cup all-purpose flour**
- ½ **teaspoon salt**
- 4 **cups milk**
- 1 **tablespoon snipped fresh rosemary**
- 9 **no-boil lasagna noodles**
- 1⅓ **cups finely shredded Parmesan cheese**
- 1 **cup whipping cream**

1 Lightly grease a 10×15-inch baking pan. Preheat oven to 425°F. Place squash, oil, and ½ teaspoon salt in the prepared baking pan; toss gently to coat. Spread in an even layer. Roast, uncovered, for 25 to 30 minutes or until squash is tender, stirring once. Reduce oven temperature to 375°F.

2 Meanwhile, for sauce, in a large saucepan melt butter over medium heat. Add garlic; cook and stir for 1 minute. Stir in flour and ½ teaspoon salt. Gradually stir in milk. Cook and stir until thickened and bubbly. Stir in the roasted squash and rosemary.

3 Lightly grease a 9×13-inch baking pan or baking dish. Spread about 1 cup of the sauce evenly in the prepared pan or dish. Layer three of the uncooked noodles in pan or dish. Spread with one-third of the remaining sauce. Sprinkle with ⅛ cup of the Parmesan cheese. Repeat layers two more times, starting with noodles and ending with cheese. Pour whipping cream evenly over layers in pan or dish. Sprinkle with the remaining ⅛ cup Parmesan cheese. Cover tightly with foil.

4 Bake for 40 minutes. Uncover and bake about 10 minutes more or until edges are bubbly, noodles are tender when pierced with a fork, and top is lightly browned. Let stand for 10 minutes before serving.

Makes 8 to 10 servings.

Nutrition Facts per serving: 525 cal., 29 g total fat (15 g sat. fat), 76 mg chol., 628 mg sodium, 53 g carbo., 4 g fiber, 16 g pro.

Make-Ahead Directions: *Prepare as directed through step 3. Cover with foil; chill for up to 24 hours. Preheat oven to 375°F. Bake, covered, for 45 minutes. Uncover; bake for 10 to 15 minutes more or until edges are bubbly and top is lightly browned. Let stand for 10 minutes before serving.*

BLACK BEAN LASAGNA

An Italian favorite goes south of the border with the addition of black beans, cilantro, and Monterey Jack cheese.

Prep: 45 minutes **Bake:** 35 minutes **Stand:** 10 minutes **Oven:** 350°F

- 9 dried lasagna noodles
- 2 15-ounce cans black beans, rinsed and drained
- 1 egg, beaten
- 1 12-ounce carton cream-style cottage cheese
- 1 8-ounce package cream cheese, cut into cubes and softened
- 1½ cups shredded Monterey Jack cheese (6 ounces)
- 1 tablespoon cooking oil
- 1 cup chopped onion
- ¾ cup chopped green sweet pepper
- 2 cloves garlic, minced
- 1 15-ounce can Italian-style tomato sauce
- 4 teaspoons dried cilantro, crushed
- 1 teaspoon ground cumin
- Coarsely chopped tomato

1 Lightly grease a 9×13-inch baking dish; set aside. Preheat oven to 350°F. Cook lasagna noodles according to package directions; drain well. Rinse with cold water; drain well. Place lasagna noodles in a single layer on a sheet of foil; set aside.

2 In a small bowl use a potato masher to mash one can of the black beans; set aside. In a medium bowl combine egg, cottage cheese, cream cheese, and 1 cup of the Monterey Jack cheese; set aside.

3 In a large skillet heat oil over medium-high heat. Add onion, sweet pepper, and garlic; cook and stir until tender. Stir in mashed beans, the remaining can of whole beans, the tomato sauce, cilantro, and cumin; heat through.

4 Arrange three of the cooked lasagna noodles in prepared dish. Top with one-third of the bean mixture. Spoon half of the cheese mixture over bean mixture. Repeat layers once more, starting with noodles and ending with cheese mixture. Top with the remaining cooked noodles and the remaining bean mixture.

5 Bake, covered, for 35 to 40 minutes or until heated through. Uncover; sprinkle with the remaining ½ cup Monterey Jack cheese. Let stand, uncovered, for 10 minutes. Sprinkle with chopped tomato before serving.

Makes 8 servings.

Nutrition Facts per serving: 456 cal., 22 g total fat (12 g sat. fat), 83 mg chol., 857 mg sodium, 46 g carbo., 8 g fiber, 25 g pro.

CHEESE-STUFFED RAVIOLI LASAGNA

**What's this recipe doing here? It's too good to leave out.
Cheese ravioli, tomatoes, and a meat sauce are layered like
lasagna for a super-easy, so-good dinner.**

Prep: 20 minutes **Bake:** 45 minutes **Stand:** 10 minutes **Oven:** 375°F

2	24- to 26-ounce jars pasta sauce with tomato and basil
12	ounces bulk Italian sausage
2	cups chopped tomatoes
1	15-ounce carton ricotta cheese
½	cup milk
½	teaspoon fennel seeds
¼	teaspoon ground nutmeg
2	9-ounce packages refrigerated light cheese-filled ravioli
1½	cups shredded part-skim mozzarella cheese (6 ounces)
	Shredded Parmesan cheese (optional)
	Snipped fresh parsley (optional)

1 Preheat oven to 375°F. Spread about ½ cup of the pasta sauce in the bottom of an ungreased 9×13-inch baking dish. Set the remaining pasta sauce aside.

2 In a 12-inch skillet cook sausage over medium-high heat until cooked through, using a wooden spoon to break up sausage as it cooks; drain off fat. Stir the remaining pasta sauce and the chopped tomatoes into cooked sausage; set aside. In a medium bowl combine ricotta cheese, milk, fennel seeds, and nutmeg; set aside.

3 Layer half of the uncooked ravioli over pasta sauce in baking dish. Spoon half of the sausage mixture over ravioli in dish; sprinkle with half of the mozzarella cheese. Top with the remaining ravioli; spoon ricotta mixture over ravioli and top with the remaining meat sauce.*

4 Bake, covered, for 30 minutes. Uncover; sprinkle with the remaining mozzarella cheese. Bake, uncovered, about 15 minutes more or until heated through and ravioli is cooked. Let stand for 10 minutes before serving. If desired, top with Parmesan cheese and parsley.

Makes 10 servings.

Nutrition Facts per serving: 456 cal., 23 g total fat (10 g sat. fat), 80 mg chol., 1,275 mg sodium, 42 g carbo., 5 g fiber, 24 g pro.

---

*Test Kitchen Tip: *Make sure all of the ravioli is covered by the meat sauce to prevent the edges of the ravioli from getting dry and crisp.*

SAUSAGE AND POTATO LASAGNA

Potatoes substitute for noodles,
and spinach adds color to give this version of lasagna
a homey, rustic flavor.

Prep: 25 minutes **Bake:** 35 minutes **Stand:** 10 minutes **Oven:** 350°F

- 1 **pound bulk Italian sausage or bulk pork sausage**
- 2 **cups thinly sliced fresh mushrooms**
- ½ **cup chopped onion**
- 2 **cloves garlic, minced**
- 1 **tablespoon all-purpose flour**
- ½ **teaspoon salt**
- ¼ **teaspoon white pepper**
- ¼ **teaspoon ground nutmeg**
- 1 **cup milk**
- 1 **15-ounce carton ricotta cheese**
- 1 **10-ounce package frozen chopped spinach, thawed and well drained**
- ½ **cup grated Parmesan cheese**
- 1 **egg, slightly beaten**
- 1 **20-ounce package (4 cups) refrigerated sliced potatoes***
- 2 **cups shredded mozzarella cheese (8 ounces)**

1 Grease a 9×13-inch baking pan or baking dish. Preheat oven to 350°F. In a large skillet cook sausage, mushrooms, onion, and garlic over medium heat until sausage is cooked through, using a wooden spoon to break up sausage as it cooks; drain off fat. Stir flour, salt, white pepper, and nutmeg into sausage mixture in skillet. Add milk all at once. Cook and stir until mixture is thickened and bubbly; set aside.

2 In a medium bowl combine ricotta cheese, spinach, Parmesan cheese, and egg.

3 Spread half of the potatoes in prepared pan or dish. Layer half of the spinach mixture and half of the sausage mixture on top. Sprinkle with 1 cup of the mozzarella cheese. Repeat with the remaining potatoes, the remaining spinach mixture, and the remaining sausage mixture.

4 Bake, covered, for 25 minutes. Uncover; sprinkle with the remaining 1 cup mozzarella cheese. Bake about 10 minutes more or until cheese is melted and mixture is bubbly around edges. Let stand for 10 minutes before serving.

Makes 8 servings.

Nutrition Facts per serving: 462 cal., 27 g total fat (14 g sat. fat), 116 mg chol., 888 mg sodium, 22 g carbo., 2 g fiber, 28 g pro.

*Test Kitchen Tip: *If you prefer to use fresh potatoes, in a covered large saucepan cook 4 cups sliced potatoes in a small amount of lightly salted boiling water for 5 minutes. Drain well before using.*

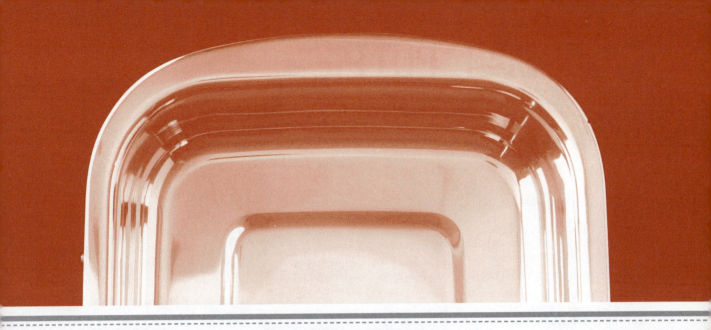

CASSEROLES

They satisfy hungry families, travel to potlucks, and soothe friends with homey flavors, and they are easy to make. Casseroles have become indispensable. Now the only problem is which one to make first!

EASY BEEF POTPIE

Using prepared pastry, refrigerated potatoes, and frozen veggies makes preparation a snap for this family favorite.

Prep: 20 minutes **Bake:** 18 minutes **Stand:** 10 minutes **Oven:** 400°F

½ of a 15-ounce package rolled refrigerated unbaked piecrust (1 crust)

1½ pounds lean ground beef

2 cups refrigerated diced potatoes with onions or loose-pack frozen diced hash brown potatoes with onions and peppers

2 cups loose-pack frozen mixed vegetables

1 15-ounce can Italian-style or regular tomato sauce

1 14½-ounce can Italian-style stewed tomatoes, undrained

2 teaspoons sesame seeds

1 Preheat oven to 400°F. Let refrigerated piecrust stand according to package directions. Meanwhile, in a large skillet cook ground beef over medium heat until cooked through, using a wooden spoon to break up meat as it cooks; drain off fat. Stir potatoes, mixed vegetables, tomato sauce, and undrained tomatoes into meat mixture. Bring to boiling; remove from heat. Spoon into an ungreased 9×13-inch baking dish.

2 Unfold piecrust; cut into eight wedges. Place half of the wedges, with points toward center, along one long side of the dish, overlapping wedges slightly at the base. Repeat with the remaining pastry wedges on the opposite side. Sprinkle with sesame seeds.

3 Bake, uncovered, for 18 to 20 minutes or until the pastry is golden brown. Let stand for 10 minutes before serving.

Makes 8 servings.

Nutrition Facts per serving: 342 cal., 16 g total fat (6 g sat. fat), 59 mg chol., 669 mg sodium, 32 g carbo., 3 g fiber, 19 g pro.

EASY SHEPHERD'S PIE

This hearty dish tops savory beef
with creamy mashed potatoes and bakes
to a delectable finish.

Prep: 30 minutes **Bake:** 25 minutes **Oven:** 425°F

- 2 pounds ground beef
- ¼ cup all-purpose flour
- 1 envelope (½ of a 2-ounce package) onion soup mix
- 1 10¾-ounce can condensed cream of mushroom soup
- 1 8-ounce carton dairy sour cream
- ¾ cup water
- 1 tablespoon ketchup
- 1½ cups water
- ¼ cup butter or margarine
- ½ teaspoon salt
- 2 cups packaged instant mashed potato flakes
- ½ cup milk
- 2 eggs, beaten
- 1 cup all-purpose flour
- 2 teaspoons baking powder

1 Preheat oven to 425°F. In an extra-large skillet cook ground beef until cooked through, using a wooden spoon to break up meat as it cooks; drain off fat. Stir the ¼ cup flour and the dry onion soup mix into meat. Stir in cream of mushroom soup, sour cream, the ¾ cup water, and the ketchup. Cook until heated through, stirring occasionally.

2 Meanwhile, in a medium saucepan combine the 1½ cups water, the butter, and salt; bring to boiling. Remove from heat. Add dry potato flakes and milk, stirring until combined. Stir in eggs, the 1 cup flour, and the baking powder.

3 Spoon meat mixture into an ungreased 9×13-inch baking pan or baking dish; spoon potato mixture in mounds on top of meat mixture. Bake, uncovered, about 25 minutes or until the potatoes are golden brown on top.

Makes 8 servings.

Nutrition Facts per serving: 558 cal., 36 g total fat (16 g sat. fat), 831 mg chol., 831 mg sodium, 30 g carbo., 1 g fiber, 27 g pro.

HAMBURGER, POTATO, AND BEAN CASSEROLE

Lovingly referred to as simply "the hotdish" in some parts of the country, this quintessential casserole is hometown cooking at its best and will surely warm your soul.

Prep: 30 minutes **Bake:** 55 minutes **Stand:** 10 minutes **Oven:** 350°F

- 1 pound lean ground beef
- 1 10¾-ounce can condensed golden mushroom soup
- ½ cup milk
- 1 teaspoon garlic salt
- ½ teaspoon black pepper
- 3 medium potatoes, peeled if desired, halved lengthwise, and cut into ¼-inch-thick slices
- 1 medium onion, halved and sliced
- 1 15½-ounce can dark red kidney beans, rinsed and drained
- 1 4-ounce can (drained weight) sliced mushrooms, drained
- 1 cup shredded cheddar cheese (4 ounces)

1 Preheat oven to 350°F. In a large skillet cook ground beef over medium heat until cooked through, using a wooden spoon to break up meat as it cooks; drain off fat. Set meat aside.

2 In a medium bowl combine golden mushroom soup, milk, garlic salt, and pepper; spread ⅓ cup of the soup mixture in an ungreased 9×13-inch baking pan or baking dish. Top with half of the potato slices, half of the onion slices, half of the beans, half of the beef, and half of the mushrooms. Drizzle with half of the remaining soup mixture. Repeat layers, starting with potato slices and ending with soup mixture.

3 Bake, covered, for 55 to 60 minutes or until potatoes are tender. Sprinkle with cheddar cheese. Let stand for 10 minutes before serving.

Makes 6 servings.

Nutrition Facts per serving: 364 cal., 15 g total fat (7 g sat. fat), 70 mg chol., 903 mg sodium, 32 g carbo., 6 g fiber, 27 g pro.

ITALIAN CRESCENT CASSEROLE

Break through the top crust of this inviting pie—made easy with crescent rolls—and you'll be rewarded with the rich aroma of tomatoes, beef, and cheese.

Prep: 25 minutes   **Bake:** 20 minutes   **Oven:** 375°F

- 2 pounds lean ground beef
- ½ cup chopped onion
- 2 cups bottled spaghetti sauce or tomato-base pasta sauce
- 3 cups shredded mozzarella cheese or Monterey Jack cheese (12 ounces)
- 1 8-ounce carton dairy sour cream
- 1 8-ounce package (8) refrigerated crescent rolls
- 2 tablespoons butter or margarine, melted
- ½ cup grated Parmesan cheese

1 Preheat oven to 375°F. In a 12-inch skillet cook ground beef and onion until meat is cooked through, using a wooden spoon to break up meat as it cooks; drain off fat. Stir spaghetti sauce into meat mixture; heat through. Spread meat mixture in an ungreased 9×13-inch baking dish.

2 Meanwhile, in a medium bowl combine mozzarella cheese and sour cream; spoon over meat mixture in baking dish.

3 Unroll crescent rolls, but do not separate into triangles. On a lightly floured surface, press dough edges together and roll out slightly to fit baking dish. Place dough over the cheese-sour cream layer. Brush with melted butter and sprinkle with Parmesan cheese. Bake, uncovered, for 20 to 25 minutes or until top is deep golden brown.

Makes 12 servings.

Nutrition Facts per serving: 360 cal., 23 g total fat (11 g sat. fat), 81 mg chol., 593 mg sodium, 14 g carbo., 0 g fiber, 25 g pro.

EGGPLANT AND BEEF CASSEROLE

Eggplant, ground beef, green sweet pepper, tomato sauce, and Italian blend cheese join forces in this delicious dinner-in-a-dish.

Prep: 50 minutes **Bake:** 30 minutes **Stand:** 10 minutes **Oven:** 350°F

- ¾ cup milk
- 1 egg, beaten
- ¾ cup all-purpose flour
- ½ teaspoon salt
- ¼ teaspoon black pepper
- 1 1½-pound eggplant, peeled and cut into ½-inch-thick slices
- 3 tablespoons cooking oil
- 1 pound lean ground beef
- 1 cup chopped green sweet pepper
- ¾ cup chopped onion
- 1 15-ounce can tomato sauce
- 1 8-ounce can tomato sauce
- 1½ teaspoons dried Italian seasoning, crushed
- 2 cups shredded Italian blend cheese (8 ounces)

1 Grease a 9×13-inch baking dish; set aside. In a small bowl combine milk and egg. In a shallow dish combine flour, salt, and pepper.

2 Dip eggplant slices into egg mixture; coat with flour mixture. In a 12-inch skillet heat oil over medium heat. Add several of the eggplant slices; cook about 4 minutes or until golden brown, turning once. Repeat with remaining eggplant slices, adding more oil if necessary. Drain on paper towels.

3 Preheat oven to 350°F. In a large skillet cook ground beef, sweet pepper, and onion until meat is cooked through, using a wooden spoon to break up meat as it cooks; drain off fat. Stir tomato sauce and Italian seasoning into meat mixture.

4 Arrange half of the eggplant slices in the prepared baking dish, cutting slices to fit. Spread with half of the meat mixture; sprinkle with half of the cheese. Repeat layers once more.

5 Bake, covered, for 20 minutes. Uncover and bake for 10 to 15 minutes more or until heated through. Let casserole stand for 10 minutes before serving.

Makes 8 servings.

Nutrition Facts per serving: 340 cal., 19 g total fat (7 g sat. fat), 84 mg chol., 796 mg sodium, 23 g carbo., 4 g fiber, 22 g pro.

BEAN AND BEEF ENCHILADA CASSEROLE

Think of this hearty casserole as comfort food with a south-of-the-border twist. It is a perfect choice for a potluck meal. (Pictured on page 108.)

Prep: 35 minutes **Bake:** 40 minutes **Oven:** 350°F

12	ounces lean ground beef
¾	cup chopped onion
1½	teaspoons chili powder
¾	teaspoon ground cumin
2	15-ounce cans pinto beans, rinsed and drained
2	4-ounce cans diced green chile peppers
1½	cups dairy sour cream
3	tablespoons all-purpose flour
½	teaspoon garlic powder
12	6-inch corn tortillas
2	10-ounce cans enchilada sauce
1	cup shredded cheddar cheese (4 ounces)
	Red sweet pepper strips (optional)

1 Lightly grease a 9×13-inch baking dish; set aside. Preheat oven to 350°F. In a large skillet cook the ground beef and onion until meat is cooked through, using a wooden spoon to break up meat as it cooks; drain off fat. Stir chili powder and cumin into meat mixture; cook and stir for 1 minute more. Stir pinto beans and undrained chile peppers into meat mixture; set aside. In a small bowl stir together sour cream, flour, and garlic powder; set aside.

2 Place half of the tortillas in the prepared baking dish, cutting to fit and overlapping as necessary. Top with half of the meat mixture, half of the enchilada sauce, and half of the sour cream mixture. Repeat layers once more.

3 Bake, covered, for 35 to 40 minutes or until heated through. Uncover and sprinkle with cheese. Bake, uncovered, about 5 minutes more or until cheese is melted.

4 If desired, garnish individual servings with red pepper strips.

Makes 12 servings.

Nutrition Facts per serving: 304 cal., 14 g total fat (7 g sat. fat), 38 mg chol., 682 mg sodium, 32 g carbo., 6 g fiber, 15 g pro.

BEEFY RAVIOLI BAKE

Cheese ravioli is the pasta of choice for this quick-fix casserole that has a top layer of melted cheese and a sure way of satisfying.

Prep: 20 minutes **Bake:** 20 minutes **Oven:** 375°F

- 2 9-ounce packages refrigerated 4-cheese ravioli
- 1½ pounds ground beef
- 1 large onion, chopped
- 6 cloves garlic, minced
- 1 14-ounce can diced tomatoes, undrained
- 1 10¾-ounce can condensed tomato soup
- 1 teaspoon dried basil, crushed
- 1 teaspoon dried oregano, crushed
- 1½ cups shredded mozzarella cheese (6 ounces)
- ½ cup finely shredded Parmesan cheese (2 ounces)

1 Preheat oven to 375°F. Cook ravioli according to package directions; drain and keep warm.

2 Meanwhile, in a large skillet cook ground beef, onion, and garlic until meat is cooked through, using a wooden spoon to break up meat as it cooks; drain off fat. Stir undrained tomatoes, tomato soup, basil, and oregano into meat mixture in skillet. Gently stir in cooked ravioli. Spread meat-ravioli mixture into an ungreased 9×13-inch baking dish. Sprinkle with mozzarella cheese and Parmesan cheese.

3 Bake, uncovered, about 20 minutes or until casserole is heated through.

Makes 8 to 10 servings.

Nutrition Facts per serving: 503 cal., 20 g total fat (9 g sat. fat), 113 mg chol., 854 mg sodium, 40 g carbo., 3 g fiber, 40 g pro.

CHEESEBURGER AND FRIES CASSEROLE

Forget going to the drive-through.
This recipe is so quick to prepare, you can
enjoy your burger and fries at home.

Prep: 15 minutes **Bake:** 45 minutes **Oven:** 350°F

- 2 pounds lean ground beef
- 1 10¾-ounce can condensed golden mushroom soup
- 1 10¾-ounce can condensed cheddar cheese soup
- 1 20-ounce package frozen fried crinkle-cut potatoes
- Toppings (such as ketchup, pickles, mustard, and chopped tomato) (optional)

1 Preheat oven to 350°F. In a large skillet cook ground beef, half at a time, until cooked through, using a wooden spoon to break up meat as it cooks; drain off fat. Spoon cooked meat into an ungreased 9×13-inch baking pan or baking dish.

2 In a medium bowl combine golden mushroom soup and cheddar cheese soup. Spread over the meat in pan or dish. Sprinkle frozen potatoes over. Bake, uncovered, for 45 to 55 minutes or until the potatoes are golden brown. If desired, serve with toppings.

Makes 8 to 10 servings.

Nutrition Facts per serving: 348 cal., 18 g total fat (6 g sat. fat), 78 mg chol., 654 mg sodium, 24 g carbo., 2 g fiber, 24 g pro.

GUADALUPE BEEF PIE

Like things a little spicier? Just add a can of green chile peppers or substitute Monterey Jack cheese with jalapeño chile peppers for the cheddar cheese.

Prep: 30 minutes **Bake:** 30 minutes **Oven:** 375°F

- 2¼ cups packaged biscuit mix
- ½ cup cold water
- 1 pound ground beef
- 1 8-ounce carton dairy sour cream
- 1 cup shredded cheddar cheese (4 ounces)
- ⅔ cup mayonnaise or salad dressing
- 2 tablespoons chopped onion
- 2 medium tomatoes, thinly sliced
- ¾ cup chopped green sweet pepper
  Paprika

1 | Grease a 9×13-inch baking pan or baking dish; set aside. Preheat oven to 375°F. For crust, in a medium bowl combine biscuit mix and the cold water, stirring with a fork until biscuit mix is moistened and a soft dough has formed. Press mixture into the bottom and ½ inch up the sides of prepared pan or dish. Bake about 12 minutes or until lightly browned.

2 | Meanwhile, in a large skillet cook ground beef over medium heat until cooked through, using a wooden spoon to break up meat as it cooks; drain off fat. Set aside. In a medium bowl combine sour cream, cheddar cheese, mayonnaise, and onion. Set aside.

3 | Sprinkle cooked ground beef over baked crust. Arrange tomato slices over beef and sprinkle with sweet pepper. Spread sour cream mixture evenly over top. Sprinkle with paprika.

4 | Bake, uncovered, about 30 minutes or until casserole is bubbly around edges.

Makes 8 to 10 servings.

Nutrition Facts per serving: 561 cal., 43 g total fat (15 g sat. fat), 75 mg chol., 653 mg sodium, 26 g carbo., 1 g fiber, 17 g pro.

PASTITSIO

Pastitsio (pah-STEET-see-oh) is a Greek-style pasta casserole made with a white sauce. A bit of cinnamon is typical—and provides an enticing flavor.

Prep: 20 minutes **Cook:** 30 minutes **Bake:** 30 minutes **Stand:** 15 minutes **Oven:** 350°F

- 1 pound lean ground beef
- 1 cup chopped onion
- 1 8-ounce can tomato sauce
- ¼ cup dry white wine, beef broth, or water
- ⅛ teaspoon ground cinnamon
- 8 ounces dried penne pasta
- ¾ cup milk
- 2 eggs, slightly beaten
- ¼ cup butter or margarine
- 2 tablespoons all-purpose flour
- ¼ teaspoon salt
- ⅛ teaspoon black pepper
- 1½ cups milk
- 2 eggs, slightly beaten
- 1 cup shredded Kefalotiri, kasseri, or Romano cheese* (4 ounces)

1 For meat sauce, in a large skillet cook ground beef and onion until meat is cooked through, using a wooden spoon to break up meat as it cooks; drain off fat. Stir tomato sauce, wine, and cinnamon into meat mixture. Bring to boiling; reduce heat. Simmer for 30 minutes, stirring occasionally.

2 Meanwhile, cook pasta according to package directions. Drain; rinse and drain well. In a large bowl toss cooked pasta with the ¾ cup milk, 2 eggs, and half of the butter. Set pasta mixture aside.

3 For cream sauce, in a small saucepan melt the remaining butter over medium heat. Stir in flour, salt, and pepper until smooth. Gradually add the 1½ cups milk. Cook and stir until mixture is thickened and bubbly. Gradually stir hot mixture into 2 eggs. Set aside.

4 Grease a 9×13-inch baking dish. Preheat oven to 350°F. Spread half of the pasta mixture in the prepared dish. Top with the meat sauce. Sprinkle with one-third of the cheese. Top with the remaining pasta mixture; sprinkle with another one-third of the cheese. Pour cream sauce evenly over all; sprinkle with the remaining cheese.

5 Bake, covered, for 20 minutes. Uncover and bake for 10 to 15 minutes more or until a knife inserted in center comes out clean. Let stand for 15 minutes before serving.

Makes 8 servings.

Nutrition Facts per serving: 431 cal., 23 g total fat (12 g sat. fat), 178 mg chol., 537 mg sodium, 30 g carbo., 2 g fiber, 23 g pro.

*Test Kitchen Note: *Kefalotiri and kasseri cheeses are both hard cheeses widely used in Greek cooking. They have sharp, salty flavors that are quite similar to Romano cheese, which you may find more readily in your supermarket. You can also substitute grated Parmesan cheese.*

POP-UP PIZZA CASSEROLE

Kids will love this upside-down pizza with filling on the bottom and a puffed biscuitlike top. If you want, use 2 cups leftover spaghetti sauce instead of the tomato sauce, water, and sauce mix.

Prep: 30 minutes **Bake:** 25 minutes **Oven:** 400°F

- 1½ pounds ground beef
- 1 cup chopped onion
- 1 cup chopped green sweet pepper
- 1 clove garlic, minced
- 1 1½-ounce envelope spaghetti sauce mix
- ½ teaspoon dried oregano, crushed
- 1 15-ounce can tomato sauce
- ½ cup water
- 1 cup milk
- 2 eggs
- 1 tablespoon cooking oil
- 1 cup all-purpose flour
- ½ teaspoon salt
- 1 cup shredded mozzarella cheese (4 ounces)
- ¼ cup grated Parmesan cheese

1. Preheat oven to 400°F. In a large skillet cook ground beef over medium heat until cooked through, using a wooden spoon to break up meat as it cooks; drain off fat. Stir onion, sweet pepper, garlic, dry spaghetti sauce mix, and oregano into meat. Add tomato sauce and the water. Cook and stir until boiling; reduce heat. Cover; simmer for 10 minutes.

2. Meanwhile, in a medium bowl beat milk, eggs, and oil with an electric mixer on medium speed for 1 minute. Add flour and salt; beat for 2 minutes more.

3. Transfer hot beef mixture to an ungreased 9×13-inch baking dish. Sprinkle with mozzarella cheese. Pour egg mixture evenly over top. Sprinkle with Parmesan cheese.

4. Bake, uncovered, for 25 to 30 minutes or until puffed and golden brown. Serve immediately.

Makes 9 servings.

Nutrition Facts per serving: 392 cal., 24 g total fat (10 g sat. fat), 119 mg chol., 896 mg sodium, 22 g carbo., 2 g fiber, 22 g pro.

SPAGHETTI BAKE

Mama mia! Spaghetti gets layered with a savory sauce and cheese. Nothing could be easier or as satisfying on a busy night.

Prep: 30 minutes   **Bake:** 30 minutes   **Oven:** 350°F

- 12 ounces dried spaghetti
- 1 pound lean ground beef
- 1 cup chopped onion
- 1 cup chopped green sweet pepper
- 1 28-ounce can diced tomatoes, undrained
- 1 4-ounce can (drained weight) sliced mushrooms, drained
- 1 2¼-ounce can sliced pitted ripe olives, drained
- 1½ teaspoons dried oregano, crushed
- 2 cups shredded cheddar cheese (8 ounces)
- 1 10¾-ounce can condensed cream of mushroom soup
- ¼ cup water
- ¼ cup grated Parmesan cheese

1 Grease a 9×13-inch baking dish; set aside. Preheat oven to 350°F. Cook spaghetti according to package directions; drain well. Return to pan.

2 Meanwhile, in a large skillet cook ground beef, onion, and sweet pepper until meat is cooked through, using a wooden spoon to break up meat as it cooks; drain off fat. Stir undrained tomatoes, mushrooms, olives, and oregano into meat mixture. Bring to boiling; reduce heat. Simmer, uncovered, for 10 minutes.

3 Spread half of the cooked spaghetti in prepared dish. Top with half of the meat mixture and half of the cheddar cheese. Repeat layers once more.

4 In a medium bowl combine cream of mushroom soup and the water; spread over layers in baking dish. Sprinkle with Parmesan cheese. Bake, uncovered, about 30 minutes or until heated through.

Makes 8 servings.

Nutrition Facts per serving: 498 cal., 24 g total fat (11 g sat. fat), 73 mg chol., 788 mg sodium, 44 g carbo., 3 g fiber, 25 g pro.

DOUBLE-CRUST PIZZA CASSEROLE

It's like stuffed pizza in a rectangular dish. Loaded with two kinds of meat and a spicy tomato sauce, this is sure to keep hungry teens happy.

Prep: 25 minutes **Bake:** 35 minutes **Stand:** 5 minutes **Oven:** 425°F

- 3 cups all-purpose flour
- 3 cups packaged instant mashed potatoes
- 2 cups milk
- ½ cup butter, melted
- 1 pound lean ground beef
- ¾ pound bulk Italian sausage
- 1 cup coarsely chopped onion
- 1 8-ounce can tomato sauce
- 1 6-ounce can Italian-style tomato paste
- ½ of a 1.3- to 1.5-ounce package sloppy joe seasoning mix (about 2 tablespoons)
- 1 2¼-ounce can sliced ripe olives, drained (optional)
- 1 cup shredded mozzarella cheese (4 ounces)
- 1 tablespoon yellow cornmeal

1 Preheat oven to 425°F. For crust dough, in a large bowl combine flour, dry instant mashed potatoes, milk, and butter; set aside. (Mixture will stiffen somewhat as it stands.)

2 For filling, in a large skillet cook ground beef, sausage, and onion over medium heat until meat is cooked through, using a wooden spoon to break up meat as it cooks; drain off fat. Stir tomato sauce, tomato paste, and dry seasoning mix into meat mixture. If desired, stir in olives.

3 Using floured fingers, press half of the dough over the bottom and about 1½ inches up the sides of an ungreased 9×13-inch baking dish. Spread filling over crust; sprinkle with cheese. Between two large sheets of waxed paper, roll remaining dough to an 11×15-inch rectangle; remove top sheet of waxed paper and invert rolled dough over filling. Remove waxed paper. Trim edges as necessary. Turn edges of the top crust under and seal to the bottom crust. Sprinkle with cornmeal.

4 Bake, uncovered, about 35 minutes or until heated through and crust is golden brown. Let stand for 5 minutes before serving.

Makes 12 servings.

Nutrition Facts per serving: 456 cal., 23 g total fat (10 g sat. fat), 76 mg chol., 708 mg sodium, 41 g carbo., 2 g fiber, 19 g pro.

REUBEN SANDWICH CASSEROLE

Classic Reuben sandwich fixings—sauerkraut, Swiss cheese, and corned beef—are layered with seasonings and croutons in this tasty casserole.

Prep: 20 minutes   **Bake:** 35 minutes   **Oven:** 375°F

- 1 32-ounce jar sauerkraut, rinsed and drained
- ½ cup chopped onion
- 4 teaspoons dried parsley flakes, crushed
- 2 teaspoons caraway seeds
- 4 cups shredded Swiss cheese (1 pound)
- 1⅓ cups bottled Thousand Island salad dressing
- 12 ounces thinly sliced cooked corned beef, coarsely chopped
- 6 slices rye bread, cut into ½-inch cubes
- ¼ cup butter or margarine, melted

1 Preheat oven to 375°F. In a large bowl combine drained sauerkraut, onion, dried parsley, and caraway seeds. Spread sauerkraut mixture evenly into an ungreased 9×13-inch baking pan or baking dish.

2 Top with half of the cheese, half of the salad dressing, and all of the corned beef. Top with the remaining salad dressing and the remaining cheese.

3 In a large bowl toss bread cubes with melted butter to coat. Sprinkle bread cubes over casserole.

4 Bake, uncovered, about 35 minutes or until heated through and bread cubes are browned.

Makes 8 to 10 servings.

Nutrition Facts per serving: 596 cal., 45 g total fat (18 g sat. fat), 120 mg chol., 3,872 mg sodium, 22 g carbo., 10 g fiber, 26 g pro.

MEATBALL AND POLENTA CASSEROLE

Tubes of prepared polenta, an Italian version of cooked cornmeal, can be found in the refrigerated or produce section of large supermarkets. Here it's used in place of pasta for a flavorful change of pace.

Prep: 20 minutes   **Bake:** 45 minutes   **Stand:** 5 minutes   **Oven:** 350°F

- 1 16-ounce package refrigerated polenta
- 2 16-ounce packages Italian-style frozen cooked meatballs
- 1 10¾-ounce can condensed golden mushroom soup
- ¾ cup water
- 1 4-ounce jar (drained weight) sliced mushrooms, drained
- 1 teaspoon dried Italian seasoning, crushed
- ¼ teaspoon garlic powder
- ⅛ teaspoon black pepper
- ½ cup shredded Parmesan cheese (2 ounces)

1 Grease a 9×13-inch baking pan or baking dish; set aside. Preheat oven to 350°F. Cut polenta crosswise into 12 slices. Arrange polenta slices in prepared pan or dish. Arrange meatballs on polenta. In a medium bowl combine golden mushroom soup, the water, mushrooms, Italian seasoning, garlic powder, and pepper. Pour evenly over meatballs.

2 Bake, uncovered, about 45 minutes or until heated through. Sprinkle with shredded Parmesan cheese. Let stand for 5 minutes before serving.

Makes 8 servings.

Nutrition Facts per serving: 551 cal., 35 g total fat (18 g sat. fat), 98 mg chol., 1,963 mg sodium, 22 g carbo., 6 g fiber, 34 g pro.

CREAMY MEATBALL CASSEROLE

There are just a handful of easy ingredients, so you can quickly toss this comforting casserole together after work. Then you can sit and relax while it bakes.

Prep: 15 minutes **Bake:** 1 hour **Oven:** 350°F

- 1 10¾-ounce can condensed cream of mushroom soup or cream of onion soup
- 1 cup milk
- ½ cup dairy sour cream
- ½ teaspoon salt
- ⅛ teaspoon black pepper
- 32 frozen cooked meatballs (½ ounce each)
- 1 20-ounce package refrigerated red-skinned potato wedges
- 1 16-ounce package loose-pack frozen stir-fry vegetables (any combination)

1 Preheat oven to 350°F. In a large bowl stir together cream of mushroom soup, milk, sour cream, salt, and pepper. Stir in meatballs, potato wedges, and vegetables. Spoon into an ungreased 9×13-inch baking pan or baking dish.

2 Bake, covered, about 1 hour or until heated through.

Makes 6 servings.

Nutrition Facts per serving: 423 cal., 28 g total fat (12 g sat. fat), 37 mg chol., 1,291 mg sodium, 28 g carbo., 6 g fiber, 17 g pro.

CHEESY ITALIAN MEATBALL CASSEROLE

Baked pasta is a surefire crowd pleaser, especially when it's partnered with Italian meatballs, tangy pasta sauce, and luscious cheeses.

Prep: 25 minutes **Bake:** 45 minutes **Oven:** 350°F

- 16 ounces dried cut ziti or penne pasta
- 1 26-ounce jar tomato-base pasta sauce
- 1 16-ounce package Italian-style frozen cooked meatballs, thawed
- 1 15-ounce can Italian-style tomato sauce
- 1 15-ounce carton ricotta cheese
- ½ cup grated Parmesan cheese
- 2 cups shredded mozzarella cheese (8 ounces)

1 Preheat oven to 350°F. Cook pasta according to package directions; drain well. Return to hot pan. Stir in pasta sauce, meatballs, and tomato sauce. Spoon into an ungreased 9×13-inch baking dish. Bake, covered, for 30 minutes.

2 Meanwhile, in a small bowl combine ricotta cheese and Parmesan cheese. Uncover pasta mixture and spoon ricotta mixture in mounds over pasta mixture. Cover loosely; bake about 10 minutes more or until heated through. Uncover and top with mozzarella cheese. Bake, uncovered, for 5 minutes more.

Makes 8 to 10 servings.

Nutrition Facts per serving: 611 cal., 28 g total fat (14 g sat. fat), 86 mg chol., 1,441 mg sodium, 57 g carbo., 7 g fiber, 33 g pro.

ZUCCHINI PORK CHOP SUPPER

Two layers of herb-seasoned croutons and a layer of creamy zucchini with juicy pork chops on top—this one-dish meal is so simple but oh so good.

Prep: 30 minutes   **Bake:** 50 minutes   **Oven:** 350°F

- 1   14-ounce package (about 9½ cups) herb-seasoned stuffing croutons
- ¼   cup butter or margarine, melted
- 4   cups coarsely chopped zucchini
- 1   10¾-ounce can condensed cream of celery soup
- 1   8-ounce carton light dairy sour cream
- ¾   cup milk
- ½   cup shredded carrot
- 1   tablespoon snipped fresh parsley or 1 teaspoon dried parsley flakes
- ¼   to ½ teaspoon black pepper
- 6   bone-in pork loin chops, cut ¾ inch thick (about 2¼ pounds total)

1 Grease a 9×13-inch baking pan or baking dish; set aside. Preheat oven to 350°F. In a large bowl stir together 7½ cups of the stuffing croutons and the melted butter. Spread half of the buttered croutons in prepared pan or dish.

2 In another large bowl stir together zucchini, cream of celery soup, light sour cream, ½ cup of the milk, the carrot, parsley, and pepper. Spoon over buttered croutons in baking pan or dish. Sprinkle the remaining buttered croutons on top of the zucchini mixture.

3 Coarsely crush the remaining stuffing croutons; place in a shallow dish. Place the remaining ¼ cup milk in another shallow dish. Trim fat from chops. Dip chops into milk, then into crushed croutons, turning to coat.

4 Place chops on top of the mixture in baking dish. Sprinkle with any remaining crushed croutons.

5 Bake, uncovered, for 50 to 60 minutes or until chops are done and juices run clear (160°F).

Makes 6 servings.

Nutrition Facts per serving: 639 cal., 24 g total fat (10 g sat. fat), 130 mg chol., 1,417 mg sodium, 57 g carbo., 4 g fiber, 46 g pro.

PORK CHOP CASSEROLE

Pork chops baked with crunchy onions and rich gravy are sublime served over hot cooked noodles. A simple tossed salad completes the hearty meal.

Prep: 25 minutes **Bake:** 30 minutes **Oven:** 350°F

- 8   boneless pork loin chops, cut about ¾ inch thick (about 2 pounds total)
- ⅓   cup all-purpose flour
- ¼   teaspoon salt
- ¼   teaspoon black pepper
- 2   tablespoons cooking oil
- 1   10¾-ounce can condensed cream of mushroom soup
- ⅔   cup chicken broth
- ½   cup dairy sour cream
- ½   teaspoon ground ginger
- ½   teaspoon dried rosemary, crushed
- 1   2.8-ounce can french-fried onions
    Hot cooked noodles

1 Preheat oven to 350°F. Trim fat from the pork chops. In a shallow dish combine flour, salt, and pepper. Dip pork chops in flour mixture, turning to coat.

2 In a large skillet cook chops, half at a time, in hot oil until browned, turning to brown on all sides. Remove from heat.

3 For sauce, in a medium bowl stir together cream of mushroom soup, broth, sour cream, ginger, and rosemary. Stir in half of the french-fried onions. Pour sauce into an ungreased 9×13-inch baking pan or baking dish. Top with browned chops.

4 Bake, covered, for 25 minutes. Uncover and sprinkle with the remaining french-fried onions. Bake for 5 to 10 minutes more or until pork chops are tender and juices run clear (160°F). Serve with cooked noodles.

Makes 8 servings.

Nutrition Facts per serving: 411 cal., 19 g total fat (5 g sat. fat), 95 mg chol., 536 mg sodium, 31 g carbo., 1 g fiber, 28 g pro.

97

HAM BALLS IN BARBECUE
SAUCE page 185

99

100

CANDY BAR COOKIE BARS
page 328

101

MUSTARD-MAPLE PORK ROAST page 173

103

104

ROSEMARY ROASTED

CARROT AND ZUCCHINI BARS

page 334

106

107

BEAN
AND BEEF
ENCHILADA
CASSEROLE
page 83

108

109

**CREAMY CHICKEN-
BROCCOLI BAKE**
page 131

112

PINEAPPLE CAKE
page 312

PORK CHOP AND RICE BAKE

Not much tastes as satisfying as browned chops baked on top of seasoned rice and mushrooms. Mmmm.

Prep: 25 minutes   **Bake:** 35 minutes   **Stand:** 10 minutes   **Oven:** 375°F

4   bone-in pork rib chops, cut ½ inch thick (about 2 pounds total)

1   tablespoon cooking oil
    Black pepper

1   small onion, thinly sliced and separated into rings

1   10¾-ounce can condensed cream of mushroom with roasted garlic soup

¾   cup water

½   cup dry white wine

¾   cup long grain rice

1   4-ounce can (drained weight) sliced mushrooms, drained

1   teaspoon Worcestershire sauce

¼   teaspoon dried thyme, crushed

2   tablespoons snipped fresh parsley

1 Preheat oven to 375°F. In a 12-inch skillet cook chops in hot oil until browned, turning to brown all sides. Remove chops from skillet, reserving drippings. Season chops with pepper; set aside.

2 In the same skillet cook onion in the reserved drippings until tender; set aside. In a large bowl combine cream of mushroom with roasted garlic soup, the water, and wine; stir in uncooked rice, mushrooms, Worcestershire sauce, and thyme. Spoon into an ungreased 9×13-inch baking pan or baking dish. Top with browned pork chops; spoon cooked onion over.

3 Bake, covered, for 35 to 40 minutes or until rice is done and chops are tender and juices run clear (160°F). Let stand, covered, for 10 minutes before serving. Sprinkle with parsley.

Makes 4 servings.

Nutrition Facts per serving: 602 cal., 22 g total fat (7 g sat. fat), 124 mg chol., 735 mg sodium, 36 g carbo., 2 g fiber, 55 g pro.

PORK CHOPS WITH SCALLOPED POTATOES

This old-fashioned duo goes together easier than ever with refrigerated potatoes and canned soup. It's a sure way to please fans of meat and potatoes.

Prep: 20 minutes **Bake:** 40 minutes **Oven:** 350°F

- 1 10¾-ounce can condensed cream of celery soup
- 1 cup milk
- 3 green onions, sliced
- 4 slices American cheese (4 ounces), torn
- 1 20-ounce package refrigerated diced potatoes with onions
- 4 cooked smoked pork chops (1½ to 2 pounds total)
- ⅛ teaspoon black pepper
- 2 tablespoons snipped fresh chives

1 Preheat oven to 350°F. In a medium saucepan combine cream of celery soup, milk, and green onions. Heat through over medium heat. Stir in cheese; cook and stir until cheese is melted. Remove from heat; set aside.

2 Arrange potatoes in a single layer in an ungreased 9×13-inch baking pan or baking dish. Place pork chops on top of potatoes. Sprinkle chops with pepper. Pour soup mixture evenly over chops and potatoes.

3 Bake, covered, about 40 minutes or until heated through. Sprinkle with snipped chives just before serving.

Makes 4 servings.

Nutrition Facts per serving: 541 cal., 23 g total fat (11 g sat. fat), 123 mg chol., 3,226 mg sodium, 39 g carbo., 4 g fiber, 43 g pro.

SOUTHWEST SPAGHETTI PIE

This dish is a little Italian, a little Mexican, and a whole lot of oohs and aahs. Cooked spaghetti forms the crust for a spicy meat and cheese topping.

Prep: 40 minutes **Bake:** 10 minutes **Stand:** 5 minutes **Oven:** 425°F

Butter

8	ounces dried spaghetti
½	cup milk
1	egg
1	pound ground pork
1	cup chopped onion
¾	cup chopped green sweet pepper
1	clove garlic, minced
1	tablespoon chili powder
½	teaspoon salt
½	teaspoon ground cumin
½	teaspoon dried oregano, crushed
¼	teaspoon black pepper
1	15-ounce can tomato sauce
1	cup shredded Monterey Jack cheese with jalapeño chile peppers (4 ounces)
1	cup shredded cheddar cheese (4 ounces)

1 Butter a 9×13-inch baking dish; set aside. Preheat oven to 425°F. Cook spaghetti according to package directions; drain well. Return to pan. In a small bowl combine milk and egg; stir into hot pasta. Transfer to prepared dish (there will be some liquid). Using a rubber spatula or the back of a large spoon, press spaghetti mixture into an even layer.

2 In a large skillet cook pork, onion, sweet pepper, and garlic until meat is cooked through, using a wooden spoon to break up meat as it cooks; drain off fat. Stir chili powder, salt, cumin, oregano, and black pepper into meat mixture. Cook and stir for 2 minutes. Stir in tomato sauce. Bring to boiling; reduce heat. Simmer, uncovered, for 2 minutes more. Spoon over pasta in baking dish. Sprinkle with cheeses.

3 Bake, uncovered, about 10 minutes or until bubbly around the edges. Let stand for 5 minutes before serving.

Makes 8 servings.

Nutrition Facts per serving: 330 cal., 15 g total fat (8 g sat. fat), 84 mg chol., 621 mg sodium, 29 g carbo., 2 g fiber, 20 g pro.

ITALIAN PENNE BAKE

This has everything that makes a great pasta dish—mushrooms, pepperoni, sweet peppers, and lots of cheese. It's sure to be an instant potluck favorite.

Prep: 30 minutes   **Bake:** 30 minutes   **Oven:** 350°F

Nonstick cooking spray

3   cups dried penne pasta

1   cup sliced fresh mushrooms

1   cup quartered thinly sliced onion

2   medium green and/or red sweet peppers, seeded and cut into thin bite-size strips

6   ounces sliced pepperoni or Canadian-style bacon, cut up

6   cloves garlic, minced

1   tablespoon olive oil or cooking oil

1   26- to 29-ounce jar (3 cups) marinara sauce

1¼ cups shredded Italian blend cheese (5 ounces)

1 Lightly coat a 9×13-inch baking dish with nonstick cooking spray; set aside. Preheat oven to 350°F. Cook pasta according to package directions; drain well. Return pasta to pan. Meanwhile, in a large skillet cook and stir mushrooms, onion, sweet peppers, pepperoni, and garlic in hot oil for 3 minutes. Add vegetable mixture and marinara sauce to pasta; toss to coat. Spoon pasta mixture into prepared baking dish.

2 Bake, covered, about 25 minutes or until heated through. Uncover and sprinkle with cheese. Bake about 5 minutes more or until cheese is melted.

Makes 8 servings.

Nutrition Facts per serving: 373 cal., 17 g total fat (6 g sat. fat), 27 mg chol., 905 mg sodium, 40 g carbo., 3 g fiber, 16 g pro.

HAM AND CHEESE MACARONI

The ultimate comfort food gets a flavor boost with broccoli, ham, and red sweet pepper. And you thought it couldn't get any better.

Prep: 30 minutes **Bake:** 35 minutes **Oven:** 350°F

- 1½ cups dried elbow macaroni
- 3 cups broccoli florets
- 1½ cups coarsely chopped red sweet pepper
- 1½ cups cubed cooked ham (about 8 ounces)
- 1½ cups milk
- 4½ teaspoons cornstarch
- ¼ teaspoon black pepper
- 1½ cups cubed American cheese (6 ounces)
- 1 cup soft bread crumbs
- 1 tablespoon butter or margarine, melted

1. Preheat oven to 350°F. Cook macaroni according to package directions, adding broccoli and sweet pepper for the last 2 minutes of cooking; drain. In a very large bowl combine macaroni mixture and ham; set aside.

2. For sauce, in a small saucepan stir together milk, cornstarch, and black pepper. Cook and stir until thickened and bubbly. Add American cheese; stir until melted. Stir sauce into macaroni mixture. Spoon into an ungreased 9×13-inch baking pan or baking dish.

3. Bake, covered, for 20 minutes. In a small bowl combine bread crumbs and butter. Uncover casserole; sprinkle with bread crumb mixture. Bake about 15 minutes more or until bubbly and crumbs are lightly browned.

Makes 6 servings.

Nutrition Facts per serving: 373 cal., 16 g total fat (9 g sat. fat), 58 mg chol., 1,036 mg sodium, 35 g carbo., 3 g fiber, 22 g pro.

HAM AND POTATOES AU GRATIN

Generations have grown up on this hearty entrée. The spinach not only adds colorful flavor but also a good dose of iron.

POTLUCK ● FAVORITE

Prep: 30 minutes   **Bake:** 30 minutes   **Stand:** 10 minutes   **Oven:** 350°F

- 3 tablespoons butter or margarine
- 3 tablespoons all-purpose flour
- 1¾ cups milk
- 2 eggs, slightly beaten
- 1½ cups shredded cheddar cheese (6 ounces)
- 1 tablespoon Dijon-style mustard
- ¼ teaspoon black pepper
- 2 tablespoons olive oil or cooking oil
- 2 small onions, thinly sliced
- 1 10-ounce package frozen chopped spinach, thawed and well drained
- 12 ounces cooked ham, cut into thin bite-size strips
- 1 20-ounce package refrigerated shredded hash brown potatoes
- ¼ cup grated Parmesan cheese

1 Preheat oven to 350°F. In a medium saucepan melt butter over medium heat; stir in flour. Add milk all at once. Cook and stir until thickened and bubbly. Cook and stir for 1 minute more. Remove from heat. Stir 1 cup of the hot mixture into eggs; return egg mixture to saucepan. Stir in cheddar cheese, mustard, and pepper until cheese melts. Set aside.

2 In a large skillet heat oil over medium heat . Add onions; cook until tender. Stir in spinach; set aside.

3 Spread half of the ham in an ungreased 9×13-inch baking pan or baking dish. Sprinkle half of the hash browns over ham. Spoon half of the cheese mixture over hash browns. Spoon the spinach mixture over cheese mixture in pan or dish. Repeat layers with the remaining ham, the remaining hash browns, and the remaining cheese mixture. Sprinkle with Parmesan cheese.

4 Bake, uncovered, about 30 minutes or until heated through. Let stand for 10 minutes before serving.

Makes 8 servings.

Nutrition Facts per serving: 371 cal., 22 g total fat (10 g sat. fat), 118 mg chol., 940 mg sodium, 24 g carbo., 3 g fiber, 20 g pro.

WHITE BEAN AND SAUSAGE RIGATONI

This hearty and comforting dish gets extra nutrients from spinach and a generous amount of fiber from beans.

Prep: 25 minutes **Bake:** 30 minutes **Oven:** 375°F

- 8 ounces dried rigatoni pasta
- 8 ounces cooked kielbasa or other smoked cooked sausage
- ½ of a 6-ounce can Italian-style tomato paste (⅓ cup)
- ¼ cup dry red wine or reduced-sodium chicken broth
- 1 10-ounce package frozen chopped spinach, thawed and well drained
- 2 14½-ounce cans diced tomatoes with basil, oregano, and garlic, undrained
- 1 15-ounce can Great Northern beans, rinsed and drained
- ⅓ cup shredded or grated Parmesan cheese

1 Preheat oven to 375°F. Cook pasta according to package directions; drain. Return to pan. Cut kielbasa in half lengthwise and then into bias slices; set aside. In a small bowl combine tomato paste and wine.

2 Add kielbasa, spinach, undrained tomatoes, beans, and tomato paste mixture to the cooked pasta; mix well. Transfer to an ungreased 9×13-inch baking dish.

3 Bake, covered, about 25 minutes or until heated through. Uncover; sprinkle with Parmesan cheese. Bake, uncovered, about 5 minutes more or until cheese is melted.

Makes 6 servings.

Nutrition Facts per serving: 564 cal., 20 g total fat (11 g sat. fat), 48 mg chol., 1,706 mg sodium, 62 g carbo., 7 g fiber, 30 g pro.

BAKED CAVATELLI

You can't beat the spicy flavor that Italian sausage gives to pasta. Choose mild or spicy or mix them to your liking in this crowd-pleasing dish.

- 1 **pound dried cavatelli pasta or wagon wheel macaroni (about 3½ cups)**
- 1 **pound uncooked Italian sausage links, cut into ½-inch-thick slices, or lean ground beef**
- 1¼ **cups chopped onion**
- 3 **cloves garlic, minced**
- 2 **26-ounce jars tomato-base pasta sauce**
- 1½ **cups shredded mozzarella cheese (6 ounces)**
- ¼ **teaspoon black pepper**

1 Preheat oven to 375°F. Cook pasta according to package directions. Drain; set aside.

2 In a large skillet cook sausage, onion, and garlic until sausage is cooked through; drain off fat. Remove from skillet.

3 In a very large bowl stir together pasta sauce, 1 cup of the mozzarella cheese, and the pepper. Add the cooked pasta and the drained sausage mixture. Stir gently to combine. Spoon the mixture into an ungreased 9×13-inch baking dish.

4 Bake, covered, for 30 to 35 minutes or until heated through. Uncover; sprinkle with the remaining ½ cup mozzarella cheese. Bake, uncovered, about 5 minutes more or until cheese is melted. Let stand for 10 minutes before serving.

Makes 8 servings.

Nutrition Facts per serving: 547 cal., 24 g total fat (9 g sat. fat), 57 mg chol., 1,130 mg sodium, 59 g carbo., 5 g fiber, 24 g pro.

ZUCCHINI-SAUSAGE CASSEROLE

When there's a nip in the air and an abundance of zucchini, this is the recipe you'll want. Stuffing mix creates the easy—and tasty—bottom and top layers.

Prep: 25 minutes **Bake:** 30 minutes **Oven:** 350°F

Nonstick cooking spray
1 **pound bulk pork sausage**
4 **medium zucchini**
1 **10¾-ounce can condensed cream of chicken soup**
1 **8-ounce carton dairy sour cream**
4 **cups chicken-flavor stuffing mix**
⅓ **cup butter or margarine, melted**

1 Lightly coat a 9×13-inch baking pan or baking dish with nonstick cooking spray; set aside. Preheat oven to 350°F. In a 12-inch skillet cook sausage until cooked through, using a wooden spoon to break up sausage as it cooks; drain off fat. Return sausage to skillet.

2 Meanwhile, quarter zucchini lengthwise; cut each quarter crosswise into ½-inch-thick slices. Add zucchini to sausage in skillet.

3 In a small bowl combine cream of chicken soup and sour cream; stir into sausage-zucchini mixture. Set aside. In a large bowl combine stuffing mix and melted butter.

4 Spoon half of the stuffing mixture into prepared pan or dish. Spread sausage-zucchini mixture over stuffing. Spoon remaining stuffing evenly over the top.

5 Bake, covered, about 30 minutes or until heated through.

Makes 8 to 10 servings.

Nutrition Facts per serving: 487 cal., 34 g total fat (16 g sat. fat), 70 mg chol., 1,128 mg sodium, 28 g carbo., 2 g fiber, 14 g pro.

CHEESY SAUSAGE AND RICE BAKE

Surprise! Crispy rice cereal is mixed with rice, then layered with pork and cheese in this comforting dish. More cereal on top adds crunch.

Prep: 25 minutes   **Bake:** 45 minutes   **Stand:** 10 minutes   **Oven:** 325°F

- 2   pounds mild and/or spicy bulk pork sausage
- ½   cup chopped onion
- 6   cups crisp rice cereal
- 1½   cups cooked rice*
- 2   cups shredded cheddar cheese (8 ounces)
- 6   eggs
- 2   10¾-ounce cans reduced-fat and reduced-sodium condensed cream of celery soup
- ½   cup milk
- 1   tablespoon butter or margarine, melted

1 Grease a 9×13-inch baking pan or baking dish; set aside. Preheat oven to 325°F. In a 12-inch skillet cook sausage and onion until sausage is cooked through, using a wooden spoon to break up sausage as it cooks; drain off fat. Set aside.

2 Meanwhile, in a large bowl combine 5 cups of the cereal and the cooked rice. Spread rice mixture evenly in prepared pan or dish. Spoon sausage mixture over rice mixture. Sprinkle with cheddar cheese.

3 In a medium bowl whisk together eggs, cream of celery soup, and milk until combined. Pour egg mixture evenly over layers in pan or dish. Press down lightly with a rubber spatula or the back of a large spoon to moisten all the rice mixture. In a small bowl toss the remaining 1 cup cereal with the melted butter; sprinkle over the top.

4 Bake, uncovered, for 45 to 50 minutes or until bubbly and golden brown. Let stand for 10 minutes before serving.

Makes 12 servings.

Nutrition Facts per serving: 490 cal., 33 g total fat (14 g sat. fat), 175 mg chol., 872 mg sodium, 24 g carbo., 0 g fiber, 19 g pro.

---

*Test Kitchen Tip: *For 1½ cups cooked rice, in a medium saucepan combine 1 cup water and ½ cup uncooked long grain rice. Bring to boiling; reduce heat. Simmer, covered, for 15 to 18 minutes or until rice is tender.*

CREAMY CABBAGE AND SAUSAGE

This classic combination is perfect to serve on cool nights. Sour cream and American cheese give the dish its creamy texture.

Prep: 35 minutes **Bake:** 20 minutes **Oven:** 375°F

1½	pounds bulk pork sausage
¾	cup chopped onion
10	cups coarsely chopped cabbage
1½	cups dairy sour cream
1½	cups shredded American cheese (6 ounces)
¼	teaspoon salt
¼	teaspoon black pepper
1½	cups soft bread crumbs
2	tablespoons butter or margarine, melted

1 Preheat oven to 375°F. In a Dutch oven cook sausage and onion over medium-high heat until sausage is cooked through, using a wooden spoon to break up sausage as it cooks; drain off fat. Stir coarsely chopped cabbage into sausage mixture. Cook, covered, over medium heat about 10 minutes or until cabbage is crisp-tender, stirring occasionally. Drain off any liquid.

2 Stir sour cream, cheese, salt, and pepper into sausage-cabbage mixture. Spoon into an ungreased 9×13-inch baking pan or baking dish.

3 In a small bowl combine bread crumbs and melted butter; sprinkle over sausage mixture. Bake, uncovered, about 20 minutes or until bread crumbs are golden brown.

Makes 8 servings.

Nutrition Facts per serving: 520 cal., 42 g total fat (21 g sat. fat), 93 mg chol., 902 mg sodium, 12 g carbo., 2 g fiber, 18 g pro.

BAKED RIGATONI WITH SAUSAGE

This is it—the pasta dish that is so simple and so good you can't help but fix it time and time again. Even kids will eat the broccoli in this!

Prep: 30 minutes   **Bake:** 20 minutes   **Oven:** 375°F

12 ounces dried rigatoni pasta (about 4½ cups)

4 cups broccoli florets

12 ounces bulk hot Italian sausage

½ cup finely chopped onion

1 26- to 32-ounce jar marinara sauce

1 8-ounce package shredded part-skim mozzarella cheese (2 cups)

2 tablespoons grated Parmesan cheese

1 Lightly grease a 9×13-inch baking dish; set aside. Preheat oven to 375°F. Cook pasta according to package directions, adding broccoli for the last 2 minutes of cooking; drain. Return to pan.

2 Meanwhile, for meat sauce, in a large skillet cook sausage and onion over medium heat until sausage is cooked through, using a wooden spoon to break up sausage as it cooks; drain off fat. Stir marinara sauce into sausage mixture; heat through. Stir meat sauce, mozzarella cheese, and Parmesan cheese into the cooked pasta. Transfer to prepared dish.

3 Bake, covered, for 20 to 25 minutes or until casserole is heated through.

Makes 6 servings.

Nutrition Facts per serving: 581 cal., 24 g total fat (10 g sat. fat), 64 mg chol., 1,134 mg sodium, 58 g carbo., 5 g fiber, 29 g pro.

ITALIAN POLENTA CASSEROLE

Layers of polenta that are rich with cheese surround Italian sausage. Use mild or spicy sausage to suit your taste.

Prep: 45 minutes **Bake:** 20 minutes **Oven:** 400°F

- 2½ cups chicken broth
- 3 tablespoons butter or margarine
- 2 cups milk
- 1½ cups quick-cooking polenta mix
- 1 3-ounce package cream cheese, cut up
- 1 cup shredded mozzarella cheese or provolone cheese (4 ounces)
- ½ cup finely shredded Parmesan cheese (2 ounces)
- 12 ounces mild or spicy bulk Italian sausage
- 1 cup fresh mushrooms, quartered
- 1 medium onion, cut into thin wedges
- 2 cloves garlic, minced
- 2 cups bottled tomato-base pasta sauce

1 Lightly grease a 9×13-inch baking dish; set aside. In a large saucepan bring broth and butter to boiling. Meanwhile, in a medium bowl stir together milk and polenta mix. Add polenta mixture to boiling broth. Cook and stir until bubbly; cook and stir for 3 to 5 minutes more or until very thick. Remove from heat. Stir in cream cheese, ¾ cup of the mozzarella cheese, and ¼ cup of the Parmesan cheese. Spread two-thirds of the polenta mixture in prepared dish; set aside.

2 Preheat oven to 400°F. In a large skillet cook sausage, mushrooms, onion, and garlic until meat is cooked through, using a wooden spoon to break up sausage as it cooks; drain off fat. Stir pasta sauce into sausage mixture; heat through. Spoon sausage mixture over polenta in dish, spreading evenly. Dollop remaining polenta atop sausage mixture and sprinkle with the remaining ¼ cup mozzarella cheese and the remaining ¼ cup Parmesan cheese.

3 Bake, uncovered, about 20 minutes or until heated through and top is light brown.

Makes 8 servings.

Nutrition Facts per serving: 583 cal., 34 g total fat (18 g sat. fat), 92 mg chol., 1,933 mg sodium, 37 g carbo., 4 g fiber, 31 g pro.

SUNDAY CHICKEN-RICE BAKE

The name says Sunday but you're going to want to enjoy this delectable dish other days too. It's so easy, it's the perfect any day meal.

Prep: 20 minutes **Bake:** 55 minutes **Oven:** 375°F

Nonstick cooking spray

1   10¾-ounce can condensed cream of chicken soup

1   cup milk

½   cup water

1   4-ounce can (drained weight) sliced mushrooms, drained

1   10-ounce package frozen peas and carrots, thawed

1   6.2-ounce package lemon and herb flavored rice

2½   pounds meaty chicken pieces (breast halves, thighs, and drumsticks), skinned

1 Coat a 9×13-inch baking pan or baking dish with nonstick cooking spray; set aside. Preheat oven to 375°F. In a large bowl stir together cream of chicken soup, milk, the water, and mushrooms. Remove ½ cup of the soup mixture; set aside. Stir vegetables and uncooked rice into the remaining soup mixture.

2 Spoon rice mixture into prepared pan or dish; top with chicken pieces. Pour the reserved ½ cup soup mixture over chicken.

3 Cover tightly with foil. Bake for 55 to 60 minutes or until chicken is no longer pink (170°F for breasts; 180°F for thighs and drumsticks) and rice is tender.

Makes 4 to 6 servings.

Nutrition Facts per serving: 545 cal., 16 g total fat (5 g sat. fat), 126 mg chol., 1,178 mg sodium, 52 g carbo., 4 g fiber, 47 g pro.

SPICY CHICKEN AND RICE BAKE

This Mexicali casserole includes black beans and corn. Adjust the cayenne pepper, adding more or less for the hotness you like. (Pictured on page 100.)

Prep: 25 minutes **Bake:** 55 minutes **Oven:** 375°F

- 1 tablespoon cooking oil
- ½ cup chopped onion
- ½ cup chopped green sweet pepper
- 2 cloves garlic, minced
- 1 15-ounce can black beans, rinsed and drained
- 1 14½-ounce can diced tomatoes, undrained
- 1 cup tomato juice
- 1 cup loose-pack frozen whole kernel corn
- ⅔ cup long grain rice
- 1 teaspoon chili powder
- ½ teaspoon salt
- ⅛ to ¼ teaspoon cayenne pepper
- 3 pounds meaty chicken pieces (small breast halves, thighs, and drumsticks)
   Salt
   Black pepper
   Paprika

1 Preheat oven to 375°F. In a large saucepan heat oil over medium heat. Add onion, sweet pepper, and garlic. Cook and stir until vegetables are tender. Stir in black beans, undrained tomatoes, tomato juice, corn, uncooked rice, chili powder, salt, and cayenne pepper. Bring to boiling. Transfer rice mixture to an ungreased 9×13-inch baking dish.

2 Arrange chicken pieces on top of the rice mixture. Sprinkle chicken lightly with salt, black pepper, and paprika.

3 Cover tightly with foil. Bake for 55 to 60 minutes or until chicken is no longer pink (170°F for breasts; 180°F for thighs and drumsticks) and rice is tender.

Makes 6 servings.

Nutrition Facts per serving: 446 cal., 15 g total fat (4 g sat. fat), 104 mg chol., 854 mg sodium, 39 g carbo., 6 g fiber, 40 g pro.

SAUCY CHICKEN DELIGHT

Sometimes all you want is a satisfying, uncomplicated dish to warm and nourish the family after a busy day. This is that kind of meal.

Prep: 20 minutes **Bake:** 45 minutes **Oven:** 350°F

2½ to 3 pounds meaty chicken pieces (breast halves, thighs, and drumsticks)

1 teaspoon paprika

½ teaspoon salt

Dash black pepper

2 tablespoons cooking oil

1 14-ounce jar (1½ cups) spaghetti sauce

1 10¾-ounce can condensed cream of chicken soup

1 4-ounce can (drained weight) sliced mushrooms, drained

Hot cooked noodles

1 Preheat oven to 350°F. If desired, skin chicken. In a small bowl combine paprika, salt, and pepper. Sprinkle paprika mixture evenly over chicken pieces.

2 In a 12-inch skillet brown chicken in hot oil, turning to brown evenly. Place chicken in an ungreased 9×13-inch baking dish. In a medium bowl combine spaghetti sauce, cream of chicken soup, and mushrooms. Pour soup mixture evenly over chicken.

3 Bake, covered, for 45 to 55 minutes or until chicken is no longer pink (170°F for breasts; 180°F for thighs and drumsticks). Serve chicken and soup mixture over hot cooked noodles.

Makes 4 to 6 servings.

Nutrition Facts per serving: 679 cal., 31 g total fat (8 g sat. fat), 175 mg chol., 1,551 mg sodium, 50 g carbo., 5 g fiber, 52 g pro.

CHICKEN PAPRIKASH

In this traditional Hungarian dish, chicken bakes on top of vegetables and noodles flavored with bacon and paprika. The tangy sour cream gravy adds richness and extraordinary flavor.

Prep: 30 minutes   **Bake:** 35 minutes   **Oven:** 375°F

- 4 cups dried medium noodles
- 3 slices bacon, chopped
- 1 cup chopped onion
- 1 cup chopped carrot
- 1 cup chopped celery
- 1 teaspoon paprika
- ½ teaspoon finely shredded lemon peel
- ¼ teaspoon salt
- ⅛ teaspoon black pepper
- 1 8-ounce carton dairy sour cream
- ⅓ cup all-purpose flour
- 1¾ cups milk
- 6 skinless, boneless chicken breast halves (about 2 pounds total)
  Salt
  Black pepper
  Paprika

1 Preheat oven to 375°F. Cook noodles according to package directions; drain and set aside. In a large skillet cook bacon over medium heat until crisp. Remove bacon with a slotted spoon, reserving drippings in skillet. Drain bacon on paper towels; crumble and set aside. In the same skillet cook onion, carrot, and celery in the reserved drippings over medium heat for 5 minutes. Stir in the 1 teaspoon paprika, the lemon peel, the ¼ teaspoon salt, and the ⅛ teaspoon pepper.

2 Meanwhile, in a medium bowl combine sour cream and flour, stirring until smooth. Gradually whisk in milk. Stir into vegetables in skillet; cook and stir until thickened and bubbly. Stir in cooked noodles and crumbled bacon.

3 Spoon vegetable mixture into an ungreased 9×13-inch baking pan or baking dish. Arrange chicken on top of vegetable mixture. Sprinkle chicken lightly with additional salt, pepper, and paprika. Bake, uncovered, for 35 to 40 minutes or until chicken is no longer pink (170°F).

Makes 6 servings.

Nutrition Facts per serving: 493 cal., 19 g total fat (9 g sat. fat), 141 mg chol., 389 mg sodium, 33 g carbo., 2 g fiber, 45 g pro.

129

LAZY PAELLA

Paella is a Spanish meat and seafood specialty that can take hours to prepare. This easy version uses chicken and shrimp with onion soup mix for added flavor.

Prep: 25 minutes **Bake:** 45 minutes **Stand:** 10 minutes **Oven:** 350°F

Nonstick cooking spray

2½ to 3 pounds chicken thighs, skinned

2 tablespoons cooking oil

1 14-ounce can chicken broth

1 cup long grain rice

1 cup loose-pack frozen peas, thawed

1 cup cooked, peeled, and deveined shrimp

1 4-ounce can (drained weight) sliced mushrooms, drained

2 tablespoons dry onion soup mix

Salt

Black pepper

Paprika

1 Lightly coat a 9×13-inch baking pan or baking dish with nonstick cooking spray; set aside. Preheat oven to 350°F. In a large skillet brown chicken thighs in hot oil, turning to brown evenly. In a large bowl combine broth, uncooked rice, peas, shrimp, mushrooms, and dry soup mix. Spread in prepared pan or dish. Arrange chicken thighs on rice mixture. Sprinkle chicken lightly with salt, pepper, and paprika.

2 Cover dish tightly with foil. Bake about 45 minutes or until chicken is tender and no longer pink (180°F). Let stand, covered, for 10 minutes before serving.

Makes 4 to 6 servings.

Nutrition Facts per serving: 500 cal., 12 g total fat (2 g sat. fat), 212 mg chol., 1,101 mg sodium, 47 g carbo., 3 g fiber, 49 g pro.

CREAMY CHICKEN-BROCCOLI BAKE

This classic for buffet luncheons and dinners stars chicken and vegetables mixed with noodles in a rich sauce. (Pictured on page 109.)

Prep: 30 minutes **Bake:** 55 minutes **Oven:** 350°F

Nonstick cooking spray

- 10 ounces dried medium noodles
- 1½ pounds skinless, boneless chicken breasts, cut into bite-size pieces
- 3 cups sliced fresh mushrooms
- 8 green onions, sliced
- 1 medium red sweet pepper, seeded and coarsely chopped
- 2 10¾-ounce cans condensed cream of broccoli soup
- 2 8-ounce cartons dairy sour cream
- ⅓ cup chicken broth
- 2 teaspoons dry mustard
- ¼ teaspoon black pepper
- 1 16-ounce package frozen chopped broccoli, thawed and drained
- ½ cup fine dry bread crumbs
- 2 tablespoons butter or margarine, melted

1 Coat a 9×13-inch baking pan or baking dish with nonstick cooking spray; set aside. Preheat oven to 350°F.

2 Cook noodles according to package directions; drain. Rinse with cold water; drain again.

3 Meanwhile, coat an unheated large skillet with nonstick cooking spray. Preheat over medium heat. Add chicken to hot skillet. Cook and stir about 3 minutes or until chicken is no longer pink. Transfer chicken to a large bowl.

4 Add mushrooms, green onions, and sweet pepper to skillet. Cook and stir until vegetables are tender. (If necessary, add 1 tablespoon cooking oil during cooking.)

5 Transfer vegetables to bowl with chicken. Stir in cream of broccoli soup, sour cream, broth, mustard, and black pepper. Gently stir in cooked noodles and broccoli.

6 Spoon chicken mixture into prepared pan or dish. In a small bowl combine bread crumbs and melted butter; sprinkle over chicken mixture. Bake, covered, for 30 minutes. Uncover and bake about 25 minutes more or until casserole is heated through.

Makes 12 servings.

Nutrition Facts per serving: 336 cal., 15 g total fat (8 g sat. fat), 79 mg chol., 515 mg sodium, 29 g carbo., 3 g fiber, 21 g pro.

CAJUN CHICKEN PASTA

This one's got a definite kick to it! Cajun seasoning turns chicken and pasta into a mouthwatering and festive dish. If you want less intensity, ease up on the seasoning.

Prep: 50 minutes **Bake:** 25 minutes **Oven:** 350°F

- 1 **pound dried bow tie or rotini pasta**
- 1½ **pounds skinless, boneless chicken breasts, cut into 2-inch pieces**
- 2 **tablespoons all-purpose flour**
- 2 **tablespoons salt-free Cajun seasoning**
- 1 **tablespoon cooking oil**
- 2 **cups whipping cream**
- 2 **cups shredded cheddar and Monterey Jack cheese blend (8 ounces)**
- ½ **teaspoon salt**
- 3 **cups diced seeded tomatoes**
- ¼ **cup sliced green onions**
  Bottled hot pepper sauce (optional)

1 Cook pasta according to package directions; drain. Place in a very large bowl; set aside.

2 In a large resealable plastic bag combine chicken, flour, and 1 tablespoon of the Cajun seasoning. Seal bag; toss to coat. In a large skillet heat oil over medium-high heat. Add chicken; cook and stir until chicken is no longer pink. Transfer chicken to bowl with pasta.

3 Grease a 9×13-inch baking dish; set aside. Preheat oven to 350°F. For cheese sauce, in a medium saucepan bring whipping cream just to boiling over medium heat, stirring occasionally. Remove from heat. Whisk in 1 cup of the cheese, the remaining 1 tablespoon Cajun seasoning, and the salt until cheese is melted and mixture is smooth.

4 Add cheese sauce, tomatoes, and the remaining 1 cup cheese to bowl with chicken and pasta; toss to combine. Transfer to prepared dish.

5 Bake, covered, for 25 to 30 minutes or until heated through. Sprinkle with green onions. If desired, pass hot pepper sauce.

Makes 8 to 10 servings.

Nutrition Facts per serving: 656 cal., 37 g total fat (21 g sat. fat), 207 mg chol., 395 mg sodium, 47 g carbo., 2 g fiber, 34 g pro.

Make-Ahead Directions: *Prepare as directed through step 4. Cover with plastic wrap, then foil, and chill for up to 24 hours. To serve, preheat oven to 350°F. Remove plastic wrap. Bake, covered with foil, for 35 to 40 minutes or until heated through. Sprinkle with green onions, If desired, pass hot pepper sauce.*

COQ AU VIN ROSETTES

All the flavors of the French stew coq au vin get rolled into pasta and baked with a rich cheese sauce. Try this for your next dinner party.

Prep: 45 minutes **Bake:** 35 minutes **Oven:** 325°F

- 2 tablespoons butter or margarine
- 3 cups sliced fresh mushrooms (8 ounces)
- ½ cup chopped onion
- 2 pounds skinless, boneless chicken breasts, cut into 1-inch pieces
- ¾ cup dry white wine
- ½ teaspoon dried tarragon, crushed
- ½ teaspoon white pepper
- ⅛ teaspoon salt
- 8 dried lasagna noodles
- 1 8-ounce package cream cheese, cut up
- ½ cup dairy sour cream
- 2 tablespoons all-purpose flour
- ½ cup half-and-half, light cream, or milk
- 1 cup shredded Gruyère cheese (4 ounces)
- 1 cup shredded Muenster cheese (4 ounces)
  Slivered almonds, toasted (optional)

1 In a large skillet melt butter over medium-high heat. Add mushrooms and onion; cook for 4 to 5 minutes or until tender, stirring occasionally. Add chicken, wine, tarragon, white pepper, and salt. Bring just to boiling; reduce heat. Cover and simmer for 5 minutes, stirring once. Remove from heat.

2 Meanwhile, cook lasagna noodles according to package directions; drain well. Halve each noodle lengthwise. Curl each noodle half into a 2½-inch-diameter ring; place noodle rings, cut sides down, in an ungreased 9×13-inch baking pan or baking dish. Using a slotted spoon, spoon chicken mixture into center of noodle rings, reserving the liquid in skillet. Add the cream cheese to the reserved liquid; heat and stir just until cream cheese is melted.

3 Preheat oven to 325°F. In a small bowl stir together sour cream and flour; stir in half-and-half. Add sour cream mixture, Gruyère cheese, and Muenster cheese to the cream cheese mixture in skillet. Cook and stir over medium heat until thickened and bubbly. Spoon cheese mixture over filled pasta rings in pan or dish. If desired, sprinkle with slivered almonds.

4 Bake, covered, about 35 minutes or until heated through.

Makes 8 servings (16 rosettes).

Nutrition Facts per serving: 731 cal., 32 g total fat (18 g sat. fat), 249 mg chol., 494 mg sodium, 22 g carbo., 1 g fiber, 83 g pro.

CHICKEN TACO PASTA

Mexican meets Italian with a little bit of something to please everyone in the family. Substitute a Mexican cheese blend for the cheddar cheese, if you like.

Prep: 25 minutes **Bake:** 45 minutes **Oven:** 350°F

- 8 ounces dried penne pasta
- 2 pounds uncooked ground chicken
- 1 cup chopped onion
- 1½ cups water
- 1 1¼-ounce envelope taco seasoning mix
- 2 11-ounce cans whole kernel corn with sweet peppers, drained
- 2 cups shredded cheddar cheese (8 ounces)
- 1½ cups sliced pitted ripe olives
- 1 cup purchased salsa
- 2 4-ounce cans diced green chile peppers, drained
- 8 cups shredded lettuce
- 2 medium tomatoes, cut into thin wedges
  Tortilla chips (optional)
  Dairy sour cream (optional)

1 Lightly grease a 9×13-inch baking dish; set aside. Preheat oven to 350°F. Cook pasta according to package directions; drain. Set aside.

2 Meanwhile, in a 12-inch skillet cook ground chicken and onion, half at a time, until chicken is cooked through, using a wooden spoon to break up chicken as it cooks; drain off fat. Return all of the chicken mixture to skillet. Stir in the water and dry taco seasoning mix. Bring to boiling; reduce heat. Simmer, uncovered, for 2 minutes, stirring occasionally. Stir in cooked pasta, corn, half of the cheese, the olives, salsa, and chile peppers. Spoon into prepared dish.

3 Bake, covered, about 45 minutes or until heated through. Remove from oven. Uncover; sprinkle with the remaining cheese.

4 Serve with lettuce, tomato wedges, and, if desired, tortilla chips and sour cream.

Makes 12 servings.

Nutrition Facts per serving: 365 cal., 20 g total fat (4 g sat. fat), 77 mg chol., 926 mg sodium, 27 g carbo., 4 g fiber, 23 g pro.

134

CREAMY CHICKEN ENCHILADAS

If people ask you for the recipe, don't be surprised. This perfect party dish features spinach and chicken dressed up with a luscious sour cream and yogurt sauce.

Prep: 40 minutes **Cook:** 12 minutes **Bake:** 40 minutes **Stand:** 5 minutes **Oven:** 350°F

- 1 **pound skinless, boneless chicken breasts**
- 1 **10-ounce package frozen chopped spinach, thawed and well drained**
- ½ **cup thinly sliced green onions**
- 2 **8-ounce cartons light dairy sour cream**
- ½ **cup plain yogurt**
- ¼ **cup all-purpose flour**
- ½ **teaspoon salt**
- ½ **teaspoon ground cumin**
- 1 **cup milk**
- 2 **4-ounce cans diced green chile peppers, drained**
- 12 **7-inch flour tortillas**
- ⅔ **cup shredded cheddar cheese or Monterey Jack cheese**

  Purchased salsa (optional)

  Sliced green onions (optional)

1 In a large saucepan place chicken in enough water to cover. Bring to boiling; reduce heat. Cover and simmer for 12 to 14 minutes or until chicken is no longer pink (170°F). Drain well. When cool enough to handle, use a fork to shred chicken into bite-size pieces.

2 In a large bowl combine shredded chicken, spinach, and the ½ cup green onions; set aside. For sauce, stir together sour cream, yogurt, flour, salt, and cumin. Stir in milk and chile peppers. Divide sauce in half.

3 Preheat oven to 350°F. For filling, combine one portion of the sauce and the chicken-spinach mixture. Divide filling among tortillas, placing filling near one end of each tortilla. Roll up each tortilla into a spiral. Place filled tortillas, seam sides down, in an ungreased 9×13-inch baking pan or baking dish.

4 Spoon the remaining sauce over tortillas. Bake, uncovered, about 40 minutes or until heated through. Remove from oven; sprinkle with cheese. Let stand for 5 minutes before serving. If desired, serve with salsa and additional green onions.

Makes 12 enchiladas.

Nutrition Facts per enchilada: 247 cal., 9 g total fat (4 g sat. fat), 44 mg chol., 395 mg sodium, 23 g carbo., 1 g fiber, 18 g pro.

POTLUCK CHICKEN TETRAZZINI

Starting with roasted chicken from the grocery store makes this dish super easy. If you have leftover turkey, you can use 3 cups cubed cooked turkey instead.

Prep: 30 minutes **Bake:** 15 minutes **Stand:** 5 minutes **Oven:** 350°F

- 1 purchased deli-roasted chicken
- 8 ounces dried spaghetti or linguine, broken in half
- 12 ounces fresh asparagus, trimmed and cut into 1-inch pieces
- 2 tablespoons butter or margarine
- 8 ounces small whole fresh mushrooms*
- 3 medium red and/or yellow sweet peppers, seeded and cut into 1-inch pieces
- ¼ cup all-purpose flour
- ⅛ teaspoon black pepper
- 1 14-ounce can chicken broth
- ¾ cup milk
- ½ cup shredded Swiss cheese (2 ounces)
- 1 tablespoon finely shredded lemon peel
- 2 slices sourdough bread, cut into cubes (about 1½ cups)
- 1 tablespoon olive oil
- 2 tablespoons snipped fresh parsley

1 Preheat oven to 350°F. Remove meat from bones; discard bones. Cut enough of the chicken pieces into chunks to measure 3 cups. Save remaining chicken for another use.

2 In Dutch oven cook spaghetti according to package directions, adding asparagus for the last minute of cooking. Drain well. Return to Dutch oven.

3 Meanwhile, in a large skillet melt butter over medium heat. Add mushrooms and sweet peppers; cook for 8 to 10 minutes or until mushrooms are tender, stirring occasionally. Stir in flour and black pepper until well mixed. Add broth and milk all at once. Cook and stir until thickened and bubbly.

4 Add mushroom mixture, chicken chunks, Swiss cheese, and half of the lemon peel to the pasta mixture in Dutch oven. Toss gently to coat. Spoon pasta mixture into an ungreased 9×13-inch baking pan or baking dish.

5 In a medium bowl toss together bread cubes, olive oil, and the remaining lemon peel. Spread bread cube mixture over pasta mixture.

6 Bake, uncovered, about 15 minutes or until heated through. Let stand for 5 minutes before serving. Sprinkle with parsley.

Makes 10 servings.

Nutrition Facts per serving: 282 cal., 10 g total fat (4 g sat. fat), 48 mg chol., 258 mg sodium, 28 g carbo., 2 g fiber, 20 g pro.

---

*Test Kitchen Tip: *If mushrooms are large, cut them in half or in quarters so they are all about 1 to 1½ inch pieces.*

CHICKEN AND WILD RICE CASSEROLE

Wild rice, which is really a grain and not rice, adds a nutty flavor to this casserole. Water chestnuts and almonds add a pleasant crunch.

Prep: 30 minutes **Bake:** 35 minutes **Oven:** 350°F

- 1 6-ounce package long grain and wild rice mix
- 3 cups bite-size pieces cooked chicken (about 1 pound)
- 1 14½-ounce can French-cut green beans, drained
- 1 10¾-ounce can condensed cream of celery soup
- 1 8-ounce can sliced water chestnuts, drained
- ½ cup mayonnaise or salad dressing
- ½ cup chopped onion
- 3 tablespoons sliced almonds
- 1 2-ounce jar sliced pimientos, drained
- 1 teaspoon lemon juice
- 1 cup shredded cheddar cheese (4 ounces)

1 Preheat oven to 350°F. Cook rice mix according to package directions. Meanwhile, in a very large bowl combine chicken, green beans, cream of celery soup, water chestnuts, mayonnaise, onion, almonds, pimientos, and lemon juice. Stir in cooked rice mixture. Spoon into an ungreased 9×13-inch baking pan or baking dish.

2 Bake, covered, for 30 minutes. Uncover and sprinkle with cheese. Bake, uncovered, about 5 minutes more or until heated through and cheese is melted.

Makes 8 to 10 servings.

Nutrition Facts per serving: 434 cal., 25 g total fat (6 g sat. fat), 75 mg chol., 971 mg sodium, 30 g carbo., 2 g fiber, 24 g pro.

Make-Ahead Directions: *Prepare as directed in step 1. Cover unbaked casserole; seal cheese in plastic bag. Chill casserole and cheese for up to 24 hours. Preheat oven to 350°F. Bake, covered, for 45 minutes. Uncover and sprinkle with cheese. Bake, uncovered, about 5 minutes more or until heated through and cheese is melted.*

DEEP-DISH CHICKEN POTPIE

Loaded with flavorful vegetables and chicken
baked under a flaky crust, this is what soothing and
satisfying food is all about.

Prep: 50 minutes   **Bake:** 35 minutes   **Stand:** 20 minutes   **Oven:** 400°F

1	recipe Pastry Topper
3	tablespoons butter or margarine
1½	cups chopped leek or onion
1½	cups sliced fresh mushrooms
1¼	cups sliced celery
1	medium red sweet pepper, seeded and chopped
½	cup all-purpose flour
1½	teaspoons poultry seasoning
¼	teaspoon salt
¼	teaspoon black pepper
2¼	cups chicken broth
1½	cups half-and-half, light cream, or milk
3¾	cups chopped cooked chicken (about 1¼ pounds)
1½	cups loose-pack frozen peas or frozen peas and carrots
1	egg, beaten

1 Prepare Pastry Topper; set aside. Preheat oven to 400°F.

2 In a large saucepan melt butter over medium heat. Add leek, mushrooms, celery, and sweet pepper. Cook and stir for 5 to 8 minutes or until vegetables are tender. Stir in flour, poultry seasoning, salt, and black pepper. Add broth and half-and-half all at once. Cook and stir until thickened and bubbly. Stir in cooked chicken and peas. Pour into ungreased 9×13-inch baking pan or baking dish.

3 Place Pastry Topper over chicken mixture in pan or dish. Brush pastry with egg.

4 Bake, uncovered, for 35 to 40 minutes or until topper is golden brown. Let stand for 20 minutes before serving.

Makes 9 servings.

Nutrition Facts per serving: 520 cal., 30 g total fat (11 g sat. fat), 101 mg chol., 644 mg sodium, 38 g carbo., 3 g fiber, 22 g pro.

Pastry Topper: *In a large bowl stir together 2¼ cups all-purpose flour and ¾ teaspoon salt. Using a pastry blender, cut in ⅔ cup shortening until pieces are pea-size. Sprinkle 1 tablespoon cold water over part of the mixture; gently toss with a fork. Push moistened dough to side of bowl. Repeat, using 1 tablespoon cold water at a time, until all of the flour mixture is moistened (7 to 9 tablespoons cold water total). Form dough into a ball. On a lightly floured surface, roll dough into a 9×13-inch rectangle. Using a sharp knife, cut slits in pastry to allow steam to escape, or, if desired, use a small cookie cutter to cut shapes from pastry.*

GREEK CHICKEN AND PITA BAKE

The ingredients are traditionally Greek: feta cheese, kalamata olives, and pita bread. Here they're put together in a deliciously untraditional way.

Prep: 30 minutes **Bake:** 50 minutes **Oven:** 350°F

- 1 10¾-ounce can condensed cream of chicken soup
- 4 cups chopped cooked chicken (about 1¼ pounds)
- 2 medium zucchini, halved lengthwise and cut into ½-inch-thick slices (4 cups)
- ½ cup chicken broth
- ½ cup chopped red onion
- 2 cloves garlic, minced
- ½ teaspoon Greek seasoning
- 3 6-inch pita bread rounds, torn into bite-size pieces
- 1 cup crumbled feta cheese (4 ounces)
- ½ cup pitted kalamata olives, sliced
- 2 tablespoons olive oil
- 2 cups chopped plum tomatoes

1 Preheat oven to 350°F. In a large bowl combine cream of chicken soup, cooked chicken, zucchini, broth, red onion, garlic, and Greek seasoning; mix well. Spoon into an ungreased 9×13-inch baking pan or baking dish.

2 Bake, covered, about 30 minutes or until vegetables are almost tender. Uncover and stir.

3 Meanwhile, in a medium bowl toss together pita bread pieces, feta cheese, olives, and oil. Sprinkle pita mixture and tomatoes over chicken mixture. Bake, uncovered, about 20 minutes more or until top is golden brown.

Makes 4 servings.

Nutrition Facts per serving: 468 cal., 22 g total fat (8 g sat. fat), 109 mg chol., 1,118 mg sodium, 30 g carbo., 3 g fiber, 36 g pro.

TEX-MEX CHICKEN 'N' RICE CASSEROLE

Rice appears twice—as long grain and in a vermicelli mix—in this crowd pleaser. The supportive cast of ingredients, including chile peppers, chili powder, and cumin, contributes to the Tex-Mex flavor.

Prep: 20 minutes **Cook:** 20 minutes **Bake:** 20 minutes **Stand:** 5 minutes **Oven:** 425°F

- 1   cup chopped onion
- 2   tablespoons olive oil
- 1   6.9-ounce package chicken-flavored rice and vermicelli mix
- 1   cup long grain rice
- 2   14-ounce cans chicken broth
- 2½ cups water
- 4   cups chopped cooked chicken (about 1¼ pounds)
- 4   medium tomatoes, chopped
- 1   4-ounce can diced green chile peppers, drained
- 2   teaspoons dried basil, crushed
- 1   tablespoon chili powder
- ¼   teaspoon ground cumin
- ¼   teaspoon black pepper
- 1   cup shredded cheddar cheese (4 ounces)

1 Preheat oven to 425°F. In a 3-quart saucepan cook onion in hot oil until tender. Stir in dry rice and vermicelli mix (including seasoning from package) and uncooked long grain rice. Cook and stir for 2 minutes. Stir in broth and the water. Bring to boiling; reduce heat. Cover and simmer for 20 minutes (liquid will not be fully absorbed).

2 Transfer the rice mixture to a very large bowl. Stir in chicken, tomatoes, chile peppers, basil, chili powder, cumin, and black pepper. Transfer to an ungreased 9×13-inch baking dish.

3 Bake, covered, about 20 minutes or until heated through. Uncover and sprinkle with cheese. Let stand for 5 minutes before serving.

Makes 12 servings.

Nutrition Facts per serving: 287 cal., 10 g total fat (3 g sat. fat), 51 mg chol., 578 mg sodium, 28 g carbo., 2 g fiber, 21 g pro.

SOUTHWEST CHICKEN AND TOMATILLOS

Tomatillos are green tomatolike fruits that come wrapped in husks and add a tart flavor to dishes. Look for them by the tomatoes at your supermarket or at a Hispanic specialty store.

Prep: 30 minutes **Bake:** 35 minutes **Stand:** 10 minutes **Oven:** 350°F

2	tablespoons cooking oil
1	cup chopped onion
1	cup chopped red sweet pepper
2	tomatillos, husks removed, rinsed, and finely chopped (about ½ cup)
1	4-ounce can diced green chile peppers
2	tablespoons finely chopped, seeded fresh jalapeño chile peppers*
¼	cup butter or margarine
¼	cup all-purpose flour
4	teaspoons chili powder
¼	teaspoon salt
2	cups chicken broth
1	8-ounce carton dairy sour cream
10	6-inch tostada shells, coarsely broken
3	cups chopped cooked chicken (about 1 pound)
2	cups crumbled white Mexican cheese (queso fresco) or shredded Monterey Jack cheese (8 ounces)

1 Preheat oven to 350°F. In a large skillet heat oil over medium heat. Add onion, sweet pepper, and tomatillos; cook until tender. Remove from heat; stir in undrained green chile peppers and jalapeño chile peppers. Set aside.

2 For sauce, in a medium saucepan melt butter over medium heat. Stir in flour, chili powder, and salt. Add broth all at once. Cook and stir until thickened and bubbly. Remove from heat. Stir in sour cream.

3 Arrange half of the broken tostada shells in an ungreased 9×13-inch baking pan or baking dish. Layer with half of the chicken, half of the vegetables, half of the sauce, and half of the cheese. Repeat layers once more.

4 Bake, covered, for 35 to 40 minutes or until heated through. Let stand for 10 minutes before serving.

Makes 8 servings.

Nutrition Facts per serving: 408 cal., 26 g total fat (10 g sat. fat), 85 mg chol., 631 mg sodium, 23 g carbo., 3 g fiber, 23 g pro.

*Test Kitchen Tip: *Because chile peppers contain volatile oils that can burn your skin and eyes, avoid direct contact with them as much as possible. When working with chile peppers, wear plastic or rubber gloves. If your bare hands do touch the peppers, wash your hands and nails well with soap and warm water.*

MEXICAN-STYLE CHICKEN

It's a fiesta of flavor in every bite when layers of tortillas, chicken, and a spicy sauce featuring tomatoes combine in this sure-to-please casserole.

Prep: 25 minutes **Bake:** 45 minutes **Stand:** 10 minutes **Oven:** 350°F

- 2   10¾-ounce cans reduced-fat and reduced-sodium condensed cream of chicken soup
- 1   10-ounce can diced tomatoes with green chile peppers, undrained
- ¾   cup chopped green sweet pepper
- ½   cup chopped onion
- 1½ teaspoons chili powder
- ¼   teaspoon black pepper
- 12 6- or 7-inch corn tortillas, cut into thin bite-size strips
- 3   cups cubed cooked chicken (about 1 pound)
- 1   8-ounce package shredded cheddar cheese (2 cups)
    Sliced tomatoes (optional)
    Sliced green onions (optional)

1 Preheat oven to 350°F. In a medium bowl combine cream of chicken soup, undrained tomatoes with chile peppers, sweet pepper, onion, chili powder, and black pepper; set aside.

2 To assemble, sprinkle about one-third of the tortilla strips into an ungreased 9×13-inch baking dish. Layer half of the chicken over tortilla strips; spoon half of soup mixture on top. Sprinkle half of the cheddar cheese and another one-third of the tortilla strips over the soup mixture. Layer with the remaining chicken, the remaining soup mixture, and the remaining tortilla strips.

3 Bake, uncovered, about 45 minutes or until bubbly around edges and heated through. Remove from oven; sprinkle with the remaining cheddar cheese. Let stand for 10 minutes before serving. If desired, top with sliced tomatoes and green onions.

Makes 8 servings.

Nutrition Facts per serving: 380 cal., 16 g total fat (7 g sat. fat), 83 mg chol., 702 mg sodium, 33 g carbo., 2 g fiber, 27 g pro.

HOT CHICKEN SALAD

Try this warm chicken salad for cool-weather lunches. Serve it with homemade biscuits.

Prep: 30 minutes **Bake:** 30 minutes **Stand:** 10 minutes **Oven:** 400°F

- 1 cup coarsely crushed potato chips
- ⅔ cup finely chopped almonds
- 6 cups cubed cooked chicken*
- 3 cups chopped celery
- 1 10¾-ounce can condensed cream of chicken soup
- 2 cups shredded mozzarella cheese (8 ounces)
- 2 8-ounce cartons dairy sour cream or plain yogurt
- ¼ cup chopped onion
- 1 teaspoon dried thyme or basil, crushed
- 4 hard-cooked eggs, chopped

1 Preheat oven to 400°F. In a small bowl combine potato chips and almonds; set aside. In a very large bowl combine cooked chicken, celery, cream of chicken soup, mozzarella cheese, sour cream, onion, and thyme. Gently fold in hard-cooked eggs. Spoon into an ungreased 9×13-inch baking pan or baking dish. Sprinkle with potato chip mixture.

2 Bake, uncovered, for 30 to 35 minutes or until casserole is heated through. Let stand for 10 minutes before serving.

Makes 12 servings.

Nutrition Facts per serving: 398 cal., 25 g total fat (10 g sat. fat), 168 mg chol., 437 mg sodium, 9 g carbo., 2 g fiber, 33 g pro.

*Test Kitchen Tip: *Cook about 2¼ pounds skinless, boneless chicken breasts to yield 6 cups chopped cooked chicken.*

CHICKEN SUPREME CASSEROLE

Remember this chicken dish when
you've got all ages and all kinds of tastes
you want to please.

Prep: 25 minutes **Bake:** 30 minutes **Stand:** 10 minutes **Oven:** 350°F

- 8 ounces dried rotini pasta
- 1 16-ounce package frozen stir-fry vegetables (broccoli, carrots, onions, red peppers, celery, water chestnuts, and mushrooms)
- 2 10¾-ounce cans condensed cream of chicken soup
- 2 cups milk
- ¼ cup mayonnaise or salad dressing
- ¼ teaspoon black pepper
- 2 cups chopped cooked chicken (about 10 ounces)
- 2 cups cubed French bread
- 2 tablespoons butter or margarine, melted
- ¼ teaspoon garlic powder
- 1 tablespoon snipped fresh parsley

1 Preheat oven to 350°F. Cook rotini according to package directions, except add the frozen stir-fry vegetables for the last 5 minutes of cooking; drain well.

2 Meanwhile, in a large bowl stir together cream of chicken soup, milk, mayonnaise, and pepper. Stir in cooked pasta mixture and chicken.

3 Spoon chicken-pasta mixture into an ungreased 9×13-inch baking pan or baking dish. In a medium bowl toss bread cubes with melted butter and garlic powder; sprinkle over pasta mixture.

4 Bake, uncovered, for 30 to 35 minutes or until heated through and bread cubes are golden brown. Let stand for 10 minutes before serving. Sprinkle with parsley.

Makes 6 to 8 servings.

Nutrition Facts per serving: 584 cal., 25 g total fat (8 g sat. fat), 71 mg chol., 1,123 mg sodium, 60 g carbo., 4 g fiber, 28 g pro.

CHICKEN CHOW MEIN CASSEROLE

It's got the crunch of almonds, the crispiness of chow mein noodles, and a colorful mix of vegetables. No wonder this dish is a family favorite.

Prep: 25 minutes **Bake:** 50 minutes **Oven:** 350°F

- 4 cups chopped cooked chicken (about 1¼ pounds)
- 2 cups chopped celery
- 1 cup shredded carrot
- 1 cup chopped green sweet pepper
- 2 4-ounce cans (drained weight) sliced mushrooms, drained
- ⅔ cup sliced or slivered almonds, toasted
- 2 tablespoons diced pimiento, drained
- 2 10¾-ounce cans condensed cream of chicken soup
- 2 cups chow mein noodles

1 Preheat oven to 350°F. In a very large bowl stir together chicken, celery, carrot, sweet pepper, mushrooms, almonds, and pimiento. Add cream of chicken soup to chicken mixture; mix well.

2 Transfer chicken mixture to an ungreased 9×13-inch baking pan or baking dish. Bake, covered, for 45 minutes. Uncover and top with chow mein noodles. Bake, uncovered, for 5 to 10 minutes more or until heated through.

Makes 8 servings.

Nutrition Facts per serving: 366 cal., 19 g total fat (4 g sat. fat), 68 mg chol., 921 mg sodium, 21 g carbo., 4 g fiber, 27 g pro.

CHICKEN BURRITOS

Prep: 25 minutes   **Bake:** 30 minutes   **Oven:** 350°F

- 8   8- to 10-inch flour tortillas
- 1½   cups shredded cooked chicken, beef, or pork (about 8 ounces)
- 1   cup purchased salsa
- 1   3⅛-ounce can jalapeño-flavored bean dip
- 1   teaspoon fajita seasoning
- 8   ounces Monterey Jack cheese or cheddar cheese, cut into eight 5×½-inch sticks
  Shredded lettuce (optional)
  Dairy sour cream (optional)
  Purchased salsa (optional)

1 Preheat oven to 350°F. Wrap tortillas in foil; heat in oven about 10 minutes or until heated through.

2 Meanwhile, in a large bowl stir together shredded chicken, the 1 cup salsa, the bean dip, and fajita seasoning.

3 Grease a 9×13-inch baking dish; set aside. To assemble burritos, place ⅛ cup of the chicken mixture onto each tortilla near one edge. Top chicken mixture on each tortilla with a stick of cheese. Fold in the sides of tortilla and roll up, starting from edge with the filling. Place filled tortillas, seam sides down, in prepared dish.

4 Bake, uncovered, about 30 minutes or until heated through. If desired, serve with lettuce, sour cream, and additional salsa.

Makes 8 burritos.

Nutrition Facts per burrito: 261 cal., 13 g total fat (6 g sat. fat), 48 mg chol., 441 mg sodium, 18 g carbo., 1 g fiber, 17 g pro.

SHORTCUT CHICKEN MANICOTTI

Forget cooking the manicotti shells first. This clever recipe lets the oven do that, delivering a traditional Italian dish that's long on flavor.

Prep: 25 minutes **Bake:** 1 hour **Stand:** 10 minutes **Oven:** 350°F

- 1   egg
- 1   10-ounce package frozen chopped spinach, thawed and well drained
- 1   cup finely chopped cooked chicken or turkey (about 5 ounces)
- ½   cup ricotta cheese or cream-style cottage cheese, drained
- ½   cup grated Parmesan cheese
- 12 dried manicotti shells
- 1   10¾-ounce can condensed cream of chicken soup
- 1   8-ounce carton dairy sour cream
- 1   cup milk
- ½   teaspoon dried Italian seasoning, crushed
- 1   cup boiling water
- 1   cup shredded mozzarella cheese (4 ounces)
- 2   tablespoons snipped fresh parsley (optional)

1 Preheat oven to 350°F. For filling, in a medium bowl beat egg with a fork; stir in spinach, chicken, ricotta cheese, and Parmesan cheese. Spoon about ¼ cup of the filling into each uncooked manicotti shell. Arrange filled shells in an ungreased 9×13-inch baking pan or baking dish, making sure shells do not touch each other.

2 For sauce, in another medium bowl combine cream of chicken soup, sour cream, milk, and Italian seasoning. Pour sauce over filled manicotti shells, spreading to cover shells. Slowly pour the boiling water around the edge of the pan or dish.

3 Cover pan or dish tightly with foil. Bake for 60 to 65 minutes or until manicotti shells are tender. Sprinkle with mozzarella cheese and, if desired, parsley. Let stand for 10 minutes before serving.

Makes 6 servings.

Nutrition Facts per serving: 463 cal., 23 g total fat (13 g sat. fat), 106 mg chol., 758 mg sodium, 35 g carbo., 3 g fiber, 27 g pro.

BUFFET CHICKEN SCALLOP

What makes this perfect for a buffet? With both stuffing and juicy chicken, it looks great and tastes absolutely wonderful.

Prep: 30 minutes **Bake:** 25 minutes **Stand:** 10 minutes **Oven:** 350°F

- 2 tablespoons butter or margarine
- 1 large onion, chopped
- ¾ cup chopped green sweet pepper
- 3 cups herb-seasoned stuffing mix
- 1 cup chicken broth
- 3 eggs, slightly beaten
- 1 10¾-ounce can condensed cream of celery soup
- 4 cups chopped cooked chicken or turkey (about 1¼ pounds)
- 1½ cups cooked rice*
- 1 10¾-ounce can condensed cream of chicken soup
- ½ cup dairy sour cream
- ¼ cup milk

1 Lightly grease a 9×13-inch baking pan or baking dish; set aside. Preheat oven to 350°F. In a large skillet melt butter over medium heat. Add onion and sweet pepper; cook until tender.

2 In large bowl combine stuffing mix and broth; stir in eggs and cream of celery soup. Stir in onion mixture, chicken, and cooked rice. Spread in prepared pan or dish.

3 Bake, uncovered, for 25 to 30 minutes or until an instant-read thermometer inserted in the center registers 160°F. Let stand for 10 minutes before serving.

4 Meanwhile, for sauce, in a small saucepan combine cream of chicken soup, sour cream, and milk; heat and stir until smooth and heated through. Serve sauce with baked chicken mixture.

Makes 12 servings.

Nutrition Facts per serving: 286 cal., 12 g total fat (5 g sat. fat), 106 mg chol., 758 mg sodium, 23 g carbo., 2 g fiber, 19 g pro.

Test Kitchen Tip: *For 1½ cups cooked rice, in a medium saucepan combine 1 cup water and ½ cup uncooked long grain rice. Bring to boiling; reduce heat. Simmer, covered, for 15 to 18 minutes or until rice is tender.*

SMOKY CHICKEN AND CHEESY POTATO CASSEROLE

Smoked chicken and smoked cheddar cheese highlight this comforting casserole. Using frozen hash browns, croutons, and canned soup makes preparation super easy.

Prep: 20 minutes   **Bake:** 40 minutes   **Oven:** 350°F

- 1   10¾-ounce can condensed cream of chicken with herbs soup
- 1   8-ounce carton dairy sour cream
- 1½ cups shredded smoked cheddar cheese (6 ounces)
- 1   28-ounce package loose-pack frozen diced hash brown potatoes with onion and peppers, thawed
- 1   pound smoked or roasted chicken or turkey, cut into bite-size strips (about 3 cups)
- 1   cup crushed croutons
- 1   tablespoon butter or margarine, melted

1 Lightly grease a 9×13-inch baking pan or baking dish; set aside. Preheat oven to 350°F. In a large bowl combine cream of chicken with herbs soup, sour cream, and smoked cheddar cheese. Stir in potatoes and chicken. Spoon into prepared pan or dish.

2 In a small bowl combine crushed croutons and melted butter. Sprinkle crouton mixture over potato mixture in pan or dish.

3 Bake, uncovered, for 40 to 50 minutes or until casserole is heated through.

Makes 6 servings.

Nutrition Facts per serving: 461 cal., 24 g total fat (13 g sat. fat), 89 mg chol., 1,468 mg sodium, 36 g carbo., 3 g fiber, 27 g pro.

149

TURKEY MANICOTTI WITH CHIVE CREAM SAUCE

A simple cream cheese sauce makes these pasta shells filled with turkey and broccoli elegant enough for a special gathering.

Prep: 30 minutes   **Bake:** 30 minutes   **Oven:** 350°F

- 12 dried manicotti shells
- 1   8-ounce tub cream cheese with chive and onion
- ⅔ cup milk
- ¼ cup grated Romano cheese or Parmesan cheese
- 2   cups chopped cooked turkey or chicken (about 10 ounces)
- 1   10-ounce package frozen chopped broccoli, thawed and drained
- 1   4-ounce jar diced pimiento, drained
- ¼ teaspoon black pepper

1 Preheat oven to 350°F. Cook manicotti according to package directions; drain. Rinse with cold water; drain again. Arrange manicotti in a single layer on a piece of greased foil; cool.

2 Meanwhile, for sauce, in a heavy small saucepan heat and stir cream cheese over medium-low heat until melted. Slowly stir in milk until smooth. Stir in Romano cheese.

3 For filling, combine ¾ cup of the sauce, the turkey, broccoli, pimiento, and pepper. Using a small spoon, carefully fill each cooked manicotti shell with ¼ to ⅓ cup filling.

4 Arrange filled shells in an ungreased 9×13-inch baking pan or baking dish. Pour the remaining sauce over shells. Bake, covered, for 30 to 35 minutes or until hot in the center.

Makes 6 servings.

Nutrition Facts per serving: 381 cal., 17 g total fat (10 g sat. fat), 78 mg chol., 256 mg sodium, 32 g carbo., 3 g fiber, 22 g pro.

TURKEY AND STUFFING BAKE

Here's everything you love about turkey dinner in one easy dish, and you don't have to wait for a holiday to enjoy it. Cranberry sauce is the perfect accompaniment.

Prep: 20 minutes **Cook:** 20 minutes **Bake:** 35 minutes **Stand:** 5 minutes **Oven:** 350°F

- 1 cup water
- 1 cup chopped red sweet pepper
- ½ cup long grain rice
- 1 medium onion, chopped
- 1 8-ounce package herb-seasoned stuffing mix
- 2 cups water
- 4 cups diced cooked turkey or chicken (about 1¼ pounds)
- 3 eggs, beaten
- 1 10¾-ounce can condensed cream of chicken soup
- ½ cup dairy sour cream
- ¼ cup milk
- 2 teaspoons dry sherry

1 Grease a 9×13-inch baking pan or baking dish; set aside. Preheat oven to 350°F. In a medium saucepan bring the 1 cup water to boiling. Stir in sweet pepper, uncooked rice, and onion. Reduce heat to low. Cover and cook about 20 minutes or until rice and vegetables are tender and the water is absorbed.

2 In a large bowl combine stuffing mix and the 2 cups water. Stir in turkey, eggs, and half of the cream of chicken soup. Stir in cooked rice mixture. Spread turkey-rice mixture in prepared pan or dish.

3 Bake, uncovered, for 35 to 40 minutes or until casserole is heated through.

4 Meanwhile, for sauce, in a small saucepan combine the remaining cream of chicken soup, the sour cream, and milk. Cook over low heat until heated through. Stir in sherry.

5 Let stand for 5 minutes before serving. Cut into squares. Spoon sauce over individual servings.

Makes 8 servings.

Nutrition Facts per serving: 383 cal., 12 g total fat (4 g sat. fat), 142 mg chol., 765 mg sodium, 38 g carbo., 3 g fiber, 29 g pro.

150

TURKEY-SPINACH CASSEROLE

Not only is this comforting entrée full of flavor, it's extremely adaptable. Another time, substitute broccoli for spinach or chicken for turkey.

Prep: 25 minutes **Bake:** 25 minutes **Oven:** 350°F

- 2 10-ounce packages frozen chopped spinach or chopped broccoli
- 2 10¾-ounce cans reduced-fat and reduced-sodium condensed cream of celery soup
- 2 cups water
- ¼ cup butter or margarine
- 6 cups herb-seasoned stuffing mix
- 4 cups chopped cooked turkey or chicken (about 1¼ pounds)
- ⅔ cup milk
- 2 tablespoons grated Parmesan cheese

1 Preheat oven to 350°F. In a Dutch oven or large saucepan combine spinach, half of the cream of celery soup, the water, and butter. Bring to boiling. (If using spinach, separate it with a fork.) Cover and simmer for 5 minutes.

2 Add the stuffing mix to mixture in saucepan; stir to moisten. Spread in an ungreased 9×13-inch baking pan or baking dish; top with turkey. Stir milk into the remaining cream of celery soup; pour over turkey. Sprinkle with Parmesan cheese.

3 Bake, uncovered, about 25 minutes or until casserole is heated through.

Makes 8 servings.

Nutrition Facts per serving: 375 cal., 12 g total fat (5 g sat. fat), 65 mg chol., 1,065 mg sodium, 44 g carbo., 5 g fiber, 23 g pro.

NACHO TURKEY CASSEROLE

Here is the ideal game-day dish.
It's irresistible—like nachos layered in a
casserole and baked in the oven.

Prep: 20 minutes **Bake:** 30 minutes **Oven:** 350°F

- 5 cups slightly crushed tortilla chips
- 4 cups cubed cooked turkey or chicken (about 1¼ pounds)
- 2 16-ounce jars salsa
- 1 10-ounce package frozen whole kernel corn
- ½ cup dairy sour cream
- 2 tablespoons all-purpose flour
- 1 cup shredded Monterey Jack cheese with jalapeño chile peppers or mozzarella cheese (4 ounces)

1 Lightly grease a 9×13-inch baking dish. Preheat oven to 350°F. Place 3 cups of the tortilla chips in prepared dish. In a large bowl combine turkey, salsa, corn, sour cream, and flour; spoon over tortilla chips.

2 Bake, uncovered, for 25 minutes. Sprinkle with the remaining 2 cups tortilla chips and the cheese. Bake for 5 to 10 minutes more or until heated through.

Makes 8 servings.

Nutrition Facts per serving: 444 cal., 17 g total fat (7 g sat. fat), 74 mg chol., 1,127 mg sodium, 46 g carbo., 4 g fiber, 29 g pro.

152

***Test Kitchen Tip:** Because chile peppers contain volatile oils that can burn your skin and eyes, avoid direct contact with them as much as possible. When working with chile peppers, wear plastic or rubber gloves. If your bare hands do touch the peppers, wash your hands and nails well with soap and warm water.*

TURKEY-WILD RICE BAKE

Two cheeses, a packaged rice mix, and cream of chicken soup transform leftover roasted turkey into a rich oven meal.

Prep: 35 minutes **Bake:** 15 minutes **Oven:** 350°F

- 1 6-ounce package long grain and wild rice mix
- 1 tablespoon butter or margarine
- 1 large onion, chopped
- 3 cloves garlic, minced
- 1 10¾-ounce can condensed cream of chicken soup
- 1 cup milk
- 1½ teaspoons dried basil, crushed
- 2 cups shredded Swiss cheese (8 ounces)
- 3 cups chopped cooked turkey (about 1 pound)
- 1 4-ounce jar (drained weight) sliced mushrooms, drained
- ½ cup shredded Parmesan cheese (2 ounces)
- ⅓ cup sliced almonds, toasted

1 Preheat oven to 350°F. Prepare long grain and wild rice mix according to package directions, except discard the seasoning packet. Set aside.

2 In a 12-inch skillet melt butter over medium heat. Add onion and garlic; cook until onion is tender. Stir in cream of chicken soup, milk, and basil; heat through. Slowly add Swiss cheese, stirring until cheese is melted. Stir in cooked long grain and wild rice, turkey, and mushrooms. Transfer to an ungreased 9×13-inch baking pan or baking dish.

3 Sprinkle with Parmesan cheese. Bake, uncovered, for 15 to 20 minutes or until heated through. Sprinkle with almonds.

Makes 6 servings.

Nutrition Facts per serving: 700 cal., 36 g total fat (19 g sat. fat), 132 mg chol., 1,400 mg sodium, 37 g carbo., 4 g fiber, 56 g pro.

TURKEY-FILLED TORTILLA ROLLS

Olé! Cries of joy and thank yous will erupt when you serve this slimmed-down twist on enchiladas. They're oozing with cheese and stuffed with everything good.

Prep: 40 minutes **Bake:** 45 minutes **Oven:** 350°F

Nonstick cooking spray

½ cup chopped onion

½ of an 8-ounce package reduced-fat cream cheese (Neufchâtel), softened

1 tablespoon water

1 teaspoon ground cumin

¼ teaspoon black pepper

⅛ teaspoon salt

4 cups chopped cooked turkey breast or chicken breast (about 1¼ pounds)

¼ cup chopped pecans, toasted

12 7- to 8-inch flour tortillas

1 10¾-ounce can reduced-fat and reduced-sodium condensed cream of chicken soup

1 8-ounce carton light dairy sour cream

1 cup fat-free milk

2 to 4 tablespoons finely chopped, pickled jalapeño chile peppers*

½ cup shredded reduced-fat sharp cheddar cheese (2 ounces)

Chopped tomatoes (optional)

Chopped green sweet pepper (optional)

Snipped fresh cilantro or parsley (optional)

1 Coat a 9×13-inch baking pan or baking dish with nonstick cooking spray; set aside. Preheat oven to 350°F. For filling, in a covered small saucepan cook onion in a small amount of boiling water until tender; drain. In a medium bowl stir together cream cheese, the 1 tablespoon water, the cumin, black pepper, and salt. Stir in cooked onion, turkey, and pecans. Wrap the tortillas in foil. Heat in the oven about 10 minutes or until softened. (Or wrap tortillas in microwave-safe paper towels. Microwave on 100% [high] power about 30 seconds or until warmed.)

2 Spoon about ¼ cup of the filling onto each tortilla; roll up each tortilla. Place rolls, seam sides down, in the prepared pan or dish.

3 For sauce, in a medium bowl stir together cream of chicken soup, sour cream, milk, and chile peppers. Pour sauce over rolls.

4 Bake, covered, about 40 minutes or until heated through. Uncover; sprinkle with cheddar cheese. Bake, uncovered, about 5 minutes more or until cheese is melted. If desired, top with tomatoes, sweet pepper, and cilantro.

Makes 12 rolls.

Nutrition Facts per roll: 273 cal., 11 g total fat [4 g sat. fat], 55 mg chol., 417 mg sodium, 21 g carbo., 1 g fiber, 21 g pro.

Make-Ahead Directions: *Prepare as directed through step 3. Cover and chill for at least 4 hours or up to 24 hours. Preheat oven to 350°F. Bake, covered, about 1 hour or until heated through. Continue as directed.*

---

*Test Kitchen Tip: *Because chile peppers contain volatile oils that can burn your skin and eyes, avoid direct contact with them as much as possible. When working with chile peppers, wear plastic or rubber gloves. If your bare hands do touch the peppers, wash your hands and nails well with soap and warm water.*

MEATS

Here's a toast to the roast! Whether beef, pork, or lamb—from the simple to the sublime—they're the centerpiece of a dinner, a cause for celebration, and the makings of tomorrow's great sandwiches. They're also easy, which makes them even more lovable. So pull out your roasting rack; the feast is about to begin.

PRIME RIB WITH HORSERADISH CREAM

This king of roasts will make a commanding centerpiece at a special dinner. The horseradish cream also lends a distinctive bite to other meats, such as ham.

Prep: 15 minutes   **Roast:** 1¾ hours   **Stand:** 10 minutes   **Oven:** 350°F

- 1 teaspoon kosher salt or salt
- ½ teaspoon black pepper
- ½ teaspoon dried thyme, crushed
- 1 4- to 6-pound beef rib roast
- 1 8-ounce carton dairy sour cream
- 2 tablespoons grated fresh horseradish or prepared horseradish
- 1 tablespoon finely chopped shallot
- 2 teaspoons white balsamic vinegar or white wine vinegar
- ¼ teaspoon kosher salt or salt

1 Preheat oven to 350°F. In a small bowl combine the 1 teaspoon salt, the pepper, and thyme. Sprinkle evenly over roast; rub in using your fingers. Place roast, fat side up, on a roasting rack in an ungreased 9×13-inch baking pan or baking dish. Insert an oven-going meat thermometer into the center of the roast, making sure tip of the thermometer does not touch bone.

2 Roast, uncovered, until desired doneness. Allow 1¾ to 2¼ hours for medium-rare doneness (135°F) or 2¼ to 2¾ hours for medium doneness (150°F). Cover with foil; let stand for 10 minutes before carving. The temperature of the meat after standing should be 145°F for medium-rare doneness or 160°F for medium doneness.

3 Meanwhile, for the horseradish cream, in a small bowl combine sour cream, horseradish, shallot, vinegar, and the ¼ teaspoon salt. Cover and chill until ready to serve.

4 Serve horseradish cream with sliced meat.

Makes 8 to 10 servings.

Nutrition Facts per serving: 315 cal., 22 g total fat (10 g sat. fat), 86 mg chol., 388 mg sodium, 2 g carbo., 0 g fiber, 26 g pro.

156

RIB ROAST WITH DIJON-SOUR CREAM SAUCE

Infused with aromatic rosemary and marjoram and finished with a mustard-cream sauce, this classic beef roast is ideal for any special occasion.

Prep: 25 minutes **Marinate:** 6 to 24 hours **Roast:** 1¾ hours **Stand:** 15 minutes **Oven:** 350°F

- 1 **4-pound beef rib roast**
- ¾ **cup dry red wine**
- ¼ **cup lemon juice**
- 2 **teaspoons dried rosemary, crushed**
- 2 **teaspoons dried marjoram, crushed**
- ¼ **teaspoon garlic salt**
- 1 **recipe Dijon-Sour Cream Sauce**

1 Place meat in a large resealable plastic bag set in a shallow dish. For marinade, in a small bowl combine wine, lemon juice, rosemary, marjoram, and garlic salt. Pour over meat. Seal bag; turn to coat meat. Marinate in the refrigerator for at least 6 hours or up to 24 hours, turning bag occasionally.

2 Drain meat, discarding marinade. Insert an oven-going meat thermometer into the center of the roast, making sure tip of thermometer does not touch bone.

3 Preheat oven to 350°F. Place roast, fat side up, in an ungreased 9×13-inch baking pan or baking dish. Roast, uncovered, until desired doneness. Allow 1¾ to 2¼ hours for medium-rare doneness (135°F) or 2¼ to 2¾ hours for medium doneness (150°F).

4 Cover with foil; let stand for 15 minutes before carving. The temperature of the meat after standing should be 145°F for medium-rare doneness or 160°F for medium doneness. Carve roast and serve with Dijon-Sour Cream Sauce.

Makes 8 servings.

Nutrition Facts per serving: 274 cal., 15 g total fat (7 g sat. fat), 80 mg chol., 255 mg sodium, 2 g carbo., 0 g fiber, 30 g pro.

Dijon-Sour Cream Sauce: *In a small bowl stir together one 8-ounce carton dairy sour cream, 2 tablespoons Dijon-style mustard, and ½ teaspoon lemon-pepper seasoning. Cover and chill until serving time.*

FENNEL-LIME-CRUSTED BEEF TENDERLOIN

The flavors become even more delightful when this meat is served chilled. Fennel is a bulb vegetable with a licoricelike taste and a celerylike texture.

Prep: 30 minutes **Marinate:** 30 minutes to 1 hour **Roast:** 45 minutes **Stand:** 10 minutes
Chill: 4 to 24 hours **Oven:** 425°F

- ½ cup lime-infused olive oil
- ¼ cup fennel seeds
- ¼ cup snipped fresh tarragon
- ¼ cup finely shredded lime peel (5 or 6 limes)
- 2 teaspoons freshly ground black pepper
- ½ teaspoon salt
- 1 3-pound center-cut beef tenderloin*
- 1 pound peeled onions (such as cipollini onions, pearl onions, and/or cut-up yellow onions)
- 3 cups sliced fennel
- ½ cup dry red wine
- 1 pound fresh green beans, trimmed

1 In a small bowl combine 6 tablespoons of the oil, the fennel seeds, tarragon, lime peel, pepper, and salt. Coat tenderloin with the seed mixture. Place meat on a nonreactive tray; cover loosely with foil. Marinate in the refrigerator for at least 30 minutes or up to 1 hour.

2 Preheat oven to 425°F. Place meat on a roasting rack in an ungreased 9×13-inch baking pan or baking dish. Return any coating left on tray to meat. Insert an oven-going meat thermometer into the thickest portion of meat. In a medium bowl toss together onions and 1 tablespoon of the remaining oil. Place onions on half of the pan or dish alongside meat. Roast, uncovered, for 30 minutes.

3 Meanwhile, toss together fennel and the remaining 1 tablespoon oil. Stir onions and add fennel to other half of pan or dish alongside meat. Roast, uncovered, for 15 to 20 minutes more or until thermometer registers 135°F for medium-rare doneness.

4 Transfer meat to a cutting board; cover with foil. Let stand for 10 to 15 minutes. The temperature of the meat after standing should be 145°F for medium-rare doneness. Wrap roast tightly in plastic wrap; chill for at least 4 hours or up to 24 hours. Transfer onions and fennel to separate bowls. Cover each bowl tightly; chill for at least 4 hours or up to 24 hours.

5 For sauce, pour drippings from the baking pan or dish into a small saucepan, scraping out and including the crusty browned bits. Add red wine to saucepan; cook until bubbly, stirring constantly to dissolve browned bits. Transfer sauce to bowl. Cover; refrigerate until serving.

6 To serve, cook green beans in a small amount of boiling salted water about 5 minutes or until crisp-tender. Drain. Rinse with cold water until chilled; drain again. Toss green beans with the sauce. Arrange on serving platter. Thinly slice tenderloin and arrange on top of beans. Serve with roasted onions and fennel.

Makes 12 servings.

Nutrition Facts per serving: 288 cal., 17 g total fat (4 g sat. fat), 57 mg chol., 165 mg sodium, 7 g carbo., 8 g fiber, 25 g pro.

ROSEMARY BEEF TENDERLOIN

Accordion-sliced beef with goat cheese melting in each cut is a gorgeous presentation and an inspired pairing. Substitute pork loin if you wish.

Prep: 15 minutes   **Roast:** 35 minutes   **Stand:** 15 minutes   **Oven:** 425°F

- 2 tablespoons Dijon-style mustard
- 1 tablespoon olive oil
- 1 tablespoon snipped fresh rosemary
- 3 cloves garlic, minced
- ¾ teaspoon salt
- ¼ teaspoon black pepper
- 1 2½- to 3-pound center-cut beef tenderloin*
- 1 4- to 6-ounce log garlic and herb goat cheese (chèvre), cut crosswise into 8 slices or half of an 8-ounce tub cream cheese spread with chive and onion

Snipped fresh rosemary

1 Preheat oven to 425°F. In a small bowl combine mustard, oil, the 1 tablespoon rosemary, the garlic, salt, and pepper. Spread mixture over the beef tenderloin. Place beef tenderloin on a roasting rack in an ungreased 9×13-inch baking pan or baking dish.

2 Roast, uncovered, until desired doneness. Allow 35 to 40 minutes for medium-rare doneness (135°F) or 45 to 50 minutes for medium doneness (150°F). Cover with foil; let stand for 15 minutes before slicing. The temperature of the meat after standing should be 145°F for medium-rare doneness or 160°F for medium doneness.

3 Make eight slices about 1 to 1½ inches apart, cutting to, but not through, bottom of the meat. Tuck a slice of goat cheese into each cut (or spoon 1 tablespoon cream cheese into each cut). Sprinkle with additional rosemary. To serve, slice through the meat between cheese portions.

Makes 8 servings.

Nutrition Facts per serving: 275 cal., 14 g total fat (6 g sat. fat), 101 mg chol., 440 mg sodium, 1 g carbo., 0 g fiber, 35 g pro.

Rosemary Pork Loin: *Prepare as directed, except substitute one 2½-pound boneless pork top loin roast (single loin) for the beef tenderloin and preheat oven to 325°F. Roast pork for 1¼ to 1¾ hours or until thermometer registers 150°F. Cover with foil; let stand for 15 minutes before slicing. The temperature of the meat after standing should be 160°F.*

Nutrition Facts per serving: 240 cal., 11 g total fat (4 g sat.fat), 96 mg chol., 433 mg sodium, 1 g carbo., 0 g fiber, 33 g pro.

---

*Test Kitchen Tip: *Order a center-cut tenderloin from the butcher or meat counter ahead of time. The center cut holds its shape best during roasting.*

MUSTARD-CRUSTED BEEF TENDERLOIN

The crust not only adds a pungent
accent but also keeps all the juices inside for
melt-in-your mouth beef tenderloin.

Prep: 25 minutes **Roast:** 30 minutes **Stand:** 10 minutes **Oven:** 425°F

¼ cup coarse-grain mustard

2 teaspoons honey

¾ teaspoon dry mustard

¾ teaspoon freshly ground black pepper

½ teaspoon finely shredded orange peel

½ teaspoon finely shredded lemon peel

1 tablespoon olive oil

1 1-pound beef tenderloin roast

1 Preheat oven to 425°F. In a small bowl combine coarse-grain mustard, honey, dry mustard, pepper, orange peel, and lemon peel; set aside.

2 In a heavy large skillet heat oil over medium-high heat. Quickly brown beef tenderloin roast on all sides in hot oil (about 2 minutes total). Transfer meat to a roasting rack set in an ungreased 9×13-inch baking pan or baking dish. Spread mustard mixture over top and sides of roast. Insert an oven-going meat thermometer into center of beef tenderloin roast.

3 Roast, uncovered, for 30 to 40 minutes or until thermometer registers 135°F for medium-rare doneness. Cover meat with foil; let stand for 10 minutes before slicing. The temperature of the meat after standing should be 145°F for medium-rare doneness.

Makes 4 servings.

Nutrition Facts per serving: 234 cal., 12 g total fat (3 g sat. fat), 70 mg chol., 533 mg sodium, 3 g carbo., 0 g fiber, 24 g pro.

OVEN-BARBECUED BEEF BRISKET

Choose your favorite barbecue sauce to serve with this spicy beef. Baking it under foil keeps the meat extra tender and juicy.

Prep: 15 minutes   **Roast:** 3 hours   **Oven:** 325°F

- 1   3- to 3½-pound fresh beef brisket
- ¾   cup water
- ½   cup chopped onion
- 3   tablespoons Worcestershire sauce
- 2   tablespoons cider vinegar or white wine vinegar
- 1   tablespoon chili powder
- 1   teaspoon instant beef bouillon granules
- ⅛   teaspoon cayenne pepper
- 2   cloves garlic, minced
- 1½   cups bottled barbecue sauce

1 Preheat oven to 325°F. Trim fat from brisket. Place brisket in an ungreased 9×13-inch baking pan or baking dish. In a small bowl stir together the water, onion, Worcestershire sauce, vinegar, chili powder, bouillon granules, cayenne pepper, and garlic. Pour over brisket. Cover with foil.

2 Roast about 3 hours or until tender, turning once. Transfer brisket to a cutting board; discard juices. Thinly slice meat across the grain. Place on a serving platter. Serve with barbecue sauce.

Makes 10 to 12 servings.

Nutrition Facts per serving: 244 cal., 7 g total fat (2 g sat. fat), 78 mg chol., 735 mg sodium, 13 g carbo., 0 g fiber, 29 g pro.

SHREDDED BEEF SANDWICHES

Even if grilling season is gone, the barbecue flavor lives on in these crowd-pleasing sandwiches. They're a great choice for weekend lunches.

Prep: 15 minutes   **Roast:** 3½ hours   **Oven:** 350°F

- 1   **5- to 6-pound boneless beef chuck roast**
- 1   **10¾-ounce can condensed cream of onion soup or cream of mushroom soup**
- ¾   **cup bottled barbecue sauce**
- ¼   **cup water**
- 12   **to 16 onion buns or kaiser rolls, split and toasted**

1 Preheat oven to 350°F. Trim fat from roast. Place roast in an ungreased 9×13-inch baking pan or baking dish. In a small bowl combine cream of onion soup, barbecue sauce, and the water; pour over roast.

2 Bake, covered, for 3½ to 4 hours or until very tender.

3 Remove roast from pan or dish. When roast is cool enough to handle, shred it using two forks to pull meat in opposite directions. Skim fat from barbecue sauce mixture in pan or dish. Stir enough of the barbecue sauce mixture into the shredded meat to coat. If necessary, transfer meat mixture to a large saucepan and reheat over medium heat, stirring frequently. Serve meat on buns. Pass the remaining barbecue sauce mixture with sandwiches.

Makes 12 to 16 sandwiches.

Nutrition Facts per sandwich: 401 cal., 12 g total fat (4 g sat. fat), 115 mg chol., 688 mg sodium, 26 g carbo., 1 g fiber, 45 g pro.

NORWEGIAN MEATBALLS

Called *Kjottkaker* in Norwegian, these nutmeg-accented meatballs are terrific served over buttered noodles with the creamy mushroom sauce on top.

Prep: 25 minutes   **Bake:** 30 minutes   **Oven:** 350°F

- 2   eggs
- ½   cup milk
- ⅔   cup crushed saltine crackers (about 18 crackers)
- ⅓   cup finely chopped onion
- ½   teaspoon celery salt
- ½   teaspoon ground nutmeg
- ½   teaspoon black pepper
- 2   pounds lean ground beef
- 1   10¾-ounce can condensed cream of mushroom soup
- ¾   cup milk

1 Grease a 9×13-inch baking pan or baking dish; set aside. Preheat oven to 350°F. In a large bowl beat eggs with a fork; stir in the ½ cup milk. Stir in crushed crackers, onion, celery salt, ¼ teaspoon of the nutmeg, and the pepper. Add ground beef; mix well. Shape mixture into 20 meatballs. Arrange meatballs in prepared pan or dish. Bake about 30 minutes or until done (160°F).*

2 For sauce, in a medium saucepan combine cream of mushroom soup, the ¾ cup milk, and the remaining ¼ teaspoon nutmeg. Cook and stir over medium heat until heated through.

3 To serve, transfer meatballs to a serving bowl. Spoon the sauce over meatballs.

Makes 5 or 6 servings.

Nutrition Facts per serving: 469 cal., 26 g total fat (10 g sat. fat), 204 mg chol., 842 mg sodium, 17 g carbo., 1 g fiber, 39 g pro.

*Test Kitchen Tip: *The internal color of a meatball is not a reliable doneness indicator. A beef meatball cooked to 160°F is safe, regardless of color. To measure the doneness of a meatball, insert an instant-read thermometer into the center of the meatball.*

MEAT AND POTATO LOAVES

When they ask where the potatoes are, say "inside!" It's an all-in-one delicious entrée with cheesy potatoes baked inside traditional meat loaf.

Prep: 25 minutes **Bake:** 35 minutes **Oven:** 350°F

- 1 **egg, beaten**
- ⅓ **cup fine dry bread crumbs**
- ¼ **cup finely chopped onion**
- ¼ **cup beef broth**
- ¼ **teaspoon salt**
- ¼ **teaspoon black pepper**
- 1 **pound ground beef**
- 1¼ **cups loose-pack frozen shredded hash brown potatoes, thawed**
- 1 **cup shredded Mexican cheese blend (4 ounces)**
- ¾ **cup purchased chunky salsa**

1 Preheat oven to 350°F. In a large bowl combine egg, bread crumbs, onion, broth, salt, and pepper. Add ground beef; mix well. Divide beef mixture into four portions.

2 In a medium bowl combine potatoes, ½ cup of the cheese, and ¼ cup of the salsa; set aside.

3 On a sheet of foil, pat each portion of the beef mixture into a 5-inch square. Place one-fourth of the potato mixture down the center of each square, leaving a 1-inch border on each side. Shape beef mixture around potato mixture, pressing to seal. Place loaves, seam sides down, in an ungreased 9×13-inch baking pan or baking dish.

4 Bake, uncovered, about 30 minutes or until done (160°F).* Top with the remaining ½ cup salsa and the remaining ½ cup cheese. Bake for 5 minutes more.

Makes 4 servings.

Nutrition Facts per serving: 612 cal., 45 g total fat (19 g sat. fat), 166 mg chol., 863 mg sodium, 23 g carbo., 2 g fiber, 27 g pro.

***Test Kitchen Tip:** The internal color of a meat loaf is not a reliable doneness indicator. A beef loaf cooked to 160°F is safe, regardless of color. To measure the doneness of a meat loaf, insert an instant-read thermometer into the center of the meat loaf.*

SAGE PORK ROAST WITH APPLE

This recipe pairs the rich flavor of pork with the sweet and tangy tastes of apples and onions. The accompanying chunky compote roasts alongside the meat.

Prep: 30 minutes   **Roast:** 1 hour 25 minutes   **Stand:** 15 minutes   **Oven:** 325°F

- 1   3½- to 4-pound pork loin center rib roast, backbone loosened
- 2   teaspoons snipped fresh sage
- 1½   teaspoons coarsely ground black pepper
- 3   slices bacon
- 6   medium cooking apples, cored and cut into bite-size chunks
- 1   large red onion, cut into thin wedges
- 3   large cloves garlic, peeled and thinly sliced
- 8   whole fresh sage leaves
- ¼   teaspoon salt
- ⅓   cup apple juice

1 Preheat oven to 325°F. Sprinkle roast evenly with snipped sage and 1 teaspoon of the pepper; rub in with your fingers. Place roast, bone side down, in an ungreased 9×13-inch baking pan or baking dish. Place bacon slices across top of roast. Insert an oven-going meat thermometer in center of roast, making sure tip of thermometer does not touch bone. Roast, uncovered, for 1 to 1¼ hours or until thermometer registers 130°F.

2 Remove from oven. Add apples, red onion, garlic, and the whole sage leaves to pan or dish. Sprinkle with salt and the remaining ½ teaspoon pepper. Stir fruit and vegetables to coat with pan juices. Return to oven. Roast for 25 to 35 minutes more or until thermometer registers 150°F; stir apple and onion mixture several times during roasting.

3 Transfer the roast to a serving platter. Cover with foil; let stand for 15 minutes before carving. The temperature of the roast after standing should be 160°F.

4 Using a slotted spoon, transfer the apple and onion mixture to a large bowl; cover and keep warm. Pour drippings from the pan or dish into a small saucepan, scraping out and including the crusty browned bits. Stir in apple juice. Bring mixture just to boiling over medium heat. Pour over the apple mixture, tossing to coat.

5 Serve the apple mixture with the pork roast.

Makes 6 to 8 servings.

Nutrition Facts per serving: 341 cal., 11 g total fat (4 g sat. fat), 82 mg chol., 202 mg sodium, 27 g carbo., 5 g fiber, 34 g pro.

ROAST PORK TANGERINE

Both tangerine peel and juice add a sunny tang to this roast and sauce. If you prefer to use boneless pork, the roasting time will be less.

Prep: 25 minutes   **Roast:** 2 hours   **Stand:** 15 minutes   **Oven:** 325°F

- 1 **4-pound pork loin center rib roast, backbone loosened**
- 1 **teaspoon dry mustard**
- 1 **teaspoon dried marjoram, crushed**
- ½ **teaspoon salt**
- 2 **teaspoons finely shredded tangerine peel or orange peel**
- ½ **cup tangerine juice or orange juice**
- 1 **tablespoon packed brown sugar**
  Chicken broth or beef broth
- ⅔ **cup chicken broth or beef broth**
- 3 **tablespoons all-purpose flour**
- ⅛ **teaspoon dry mustard**
- ⅛ **teaspoon dried marjoram, crushed**
  Salt
  Black pepper
- 3 **tangerines or 2 oranges, peeled, sectioned, and seeded**

1 Preheat oven to 325°F. Place roast, bone side down, in an ungreased 9×13-inch baking pan or baking dish. In a small bowl combine the 1 teaspoon dry mustard, the 1 teaspoon marjoram, and the ½ teaspoon salt. Sprinkle mustard mixture evenly over pork; rub in with your fingers. Insert an oven-going meat thermometer in center of roast, making sure tip of the thermometer does not touch bone. Roast, uncovered, for 1½ hours.

2 In a small bowl stir together peel, juice, and brown sugar; spoon over meat. Roast about 30 minutes more or until thermometer registers 150°F, spooning pan juices over meat once or twice.

3 Transfer meat to serving platter. Cover and let stand for 15 minutes before carving. The temperature of the meat after standing should be 160°F.

4 Meanwhile, strain pan juices. Skim off fat. Measure pan juices; add enough broth to pan juices to equal ¾ cup total liquid. Pour the liquid into a medium saucepan. In a screw-top jar combine the ⅔ cup broth and the flour; shake well. Add to saucepan along with the ⅛ teaspoon dry mustard and the ⅛ teaspoon marjoram. Cook and stir until thickened and bubbly; cook and stir for 1 minute more. Season to taste with additional salt and pepper. Stir in the tangerines or oranges; heat through. Serve with pork.

Makes 10 servings.

Nutrition Facts per serving: 266 cal., 14 g total fat (5 g sat. fat), 87 mg chol., 246 mg sodium, 7 g carbo., 1 g fiber, 26 g pro.

PORK WITH HERBS AND VEGETABLES

This hearty entrée has a hint of fresh tarragon in both the roast and the satisfying side of carrots and fennel.

Prep: 30 minutes   **Roast:** 1½ hours   **Stand:** 15 minutes   **Cook:** 10 minutes   **Oven:** 325°F

- 3 **tablespoons olive oil**
- 1 **teaspoon salt**
- ¼ **teaspoon black pepper**
- 2 **cloves garlic, minced**
- 1 **3½- to 4-pound boneless pork top loin roast (double loin, tied)**
- 2 **tablespoons snipped fresh tarragon**
- 2 **tablespoons finely shredded lemon peel**
- 2 **medium fennel bulbs, cored and cut into wedges**
- 1 **large sweet onion (such as Vidalia, Maui, or Walla Walla), cut into thin wedges**
- 4 **medium carrots, diagonally sliced**
- **Salt**
- **Black pepper**

1 Preheat oven to 325°F. In a small bowl combine oil, the 1 teaspoon salt, the pepper, and garlic; set aside 1 tablespoon of the oil mixture. Untie roast; rub all sides with the remaining oil mixture. In another small bowl combine tarragon and lemon peel; set aside 1 tablespoon of the tarragon mixture. Sprinkle remaining tarragon mixture on top of one of the pork loin pieces. Top with the other pork loin piece and tie with clean 100%-cotton kitchen string.

2 Place roast on a roasting rack in an ungreased 9×13-inch baking pan or baking dish. Insert an oven-going meat thermometer into center of roast. Roast, uncovered, for 1½ to 2¼ hours or until thermometer registers 150°F.

3 Cover meat with foil; let stand for 15 minutes before slicing. The temperature of the meat after standing should be 160°F.

4 While meat stands, in a large saucepan bring 1 inch of water to boiling. Place a steamer basket filled with the fennel, onion, and carrots over boiling water in saucepan. Cook, covered, for 10 minutes. Transfer vegetables to a serving bowl; toss with the reserved 1 tablespoon oil mixture and the reserved 1 tablespoon tarragon mixture. Season to taste with additional salt and pepper. Slice meat and serve with vegetables.

Makes 10 servings.

Nutrition Facts per serving: 301 cal., 13 g total fat (4 g sat. fat), 87 mg chol., 361 mg sodium, 8 g carbo., 3 g fiber, 36 g pro.

APRICOT-GLAZED SPICED PORK ROAST

Cinnamon, ginger, cloves, and cumin give a flavor spike to traditional roasted pork. A glaze of apricot at the end adds the final flourish.

Prep: 20 minutes   **Chill:** 1 to 2 hours   **Roast:** 1¼ hours   **Stand:** 15 minutes   **Oven:** 325°F

- 1½ teaspoons ground cumin
- ½ teaspoon garlic salt
- ½ teaspoon ground cinnamon
- ½ teaspoon ground ginger
- ¼ teaspoon ground cloves
- 1 2½- to 3-pound boneless pork top loin roast (single loin)
- 1 cup apricot preserves
- 2 to 3 tablespoons white wine vinegar

1 For rub, in a small bowl stir together cumin, garlic salt, cinnamon, ginger, and cloves. Sprinkle rub evenly over roast; rub in with your fingers. Wrap roast in plastic wrap. Chill for at least 1 hour or up to 2 hours.

2 Preheat oven to 325°F. Unwrap roast and discard plastic wrap. Place roast on a roasting rack in an ungreased 9×13-inch baking pan or baking dish. Insert an oven-going meat thermometer into center of roast. Roast for 1 to 1½ hours or until meat thermometer registers 135°F.

3 Meanwhile, for apricot glaze, in a small saucepan combine apricot preserves and vinegar; cook and stir over medium heat until preserves are melted. Remove from heat. Brush roast generously with the apricot glaze. Roast about 15 minutes more or until meat thermometer registers 150°F, brushing two or three times with the apricot glaze.

4 Cover with foil; let stand for 15 minutes. The temperature of the roast after standing should be 160°F. Reheat any remaining glaze until boiling; pass with roast.

Makes 8 servings.

Nutrition Facts per serving: 326 cal., 9 g total fat (3 g sat. fat), 77 mg chol., 125 mg sodium, 28 g carbo., 1 g fiber, 31 g pro.

ROAST PORK LOIN WITH DRIED CHERRY AND WILD RICE STUFFING

Cherries, sausage, and wild rice create a moist, flavorful stuffing for this pork loin. A rich pan gravy makes it exceptionally delicious.

Prep: 1 hour **Cook:** 40 minutes **Roast:** 1¾ hours **Stand:** 15 minutes **Oven:** 325°F

- ⅓ cup wild rice
- 1 cup water
- 2 teaspoons snipped fresh rosemary
- ½ teaspoon salt
- ¾ cup coarsely chopped dried tart red cherries or cranberries
- 1 3-pound boneless pork top loin roast (single loin)
- 6 ounces bulk pork sausage
- ½ cup chopped onion
- 1 tablespoon snipped fresh parsley
- 1 teaspoon snipped fresh thyme
- ¼ teaspoon freshly ground black pepper
- 1 cup water
- ⅓ cup cold water
- 2 tablespoons all-purpose flour
- Salt
- Black pepper

1 Rinse wild rice in a strainer under cold running water about 1 minute, lifting the rice with your fingers to thoroughly clean it; drain. In a small saucepan combine the wild rice, 1 cup water, the rosemary, and the ½ teaspoon salt. Bring to boiling; reduce heat. Cover and simmer for 40 to 45 minutes or until wild rice is tender. Remove from heat. Stir in dried cherries. Set aside.

2 Trim fat from pork. Butterfly the meat by making a lengthwise cut down center of meat, cutting to within ½ inch of the other side. Spread open. Place knife in the V of the first cut. Cut horizontally to the cut surface and away from the first cut to within ½ inch of the other side of the meat. Repeat on opposite side of the V. Spread these sections open. Cover the roast with plastic wrap. Working from center to edges, pound with flat side of a meat mallet until meat is ½ to ¾ inch thick. Make sure the meat is a uniform thickness. Remove plastic wrap. Set meat aside.

3 For filling, in a large skillet cook sausage and onion until sausage is browned and onion is tender, using a wooden spoon to break up sausage as it cooks. Drain off fat. Stir in parsley, thyme, and pepper. If necessary, drain the cooked wild rice mixture to remove liquid. Stir cooked wild rice mixture into sausage mixture.

4 Preheat oven to 325°F. Spread the filling over the surface of the butterflied roast. Starting from a long side, roll up into a spiral. Tie in several places with 100%-cotton heavy kitchen string. Place on a roasting rack in an ungreased 9×13-inch baking pan or baking dish. Insert an oven-going meat thermometer in center of roast. Roast, uncovered, about 1¾ hours or until thermometer registers 150°F. Cover loosely with foil; let stand for 15 minutes before slicing. The temperature of the roast after standing should be 160°F.

5 For pan gravy, remove the roast from pan or dish; cover to keep warm. Add 1 cup water to pan or dish, scraping up browned bits. In a small saucepan whisk together the ⅓ cup cold water and the flour. Whisk in pan juices. Cook and stir over medium heat until thickened and bubbly. Cook and stir for 1 minute more. Season to taste with additional salt and pepper.

6 Remove string from pork roast; discard. Slice roast; serve with pan gravy.

Makes 8 to 10 servings.

Nutrition Facts per serving: 377 cal., 15 g total fat (5 g sat. fat), 105 mg chol., 334 mg sodium, 17 g carbo., 1 g fiber, 41 g pro.

CARIBBEAN PORK WITH SWEET POTATOES

This dish is pretty to look at and pretty hot tasting too. Pickapeppa sauce and fruit salsa give the roast and potatoes a Caribbean kick.

Prep: 30 minutes   **Roast:** 1¼ hours   **Stand:** 15 minutes   **Oven:** 325°F

- 4 tablespoons Pickapeppa sauce*
- 2 cloves garlic, minced
- 1 teaspoon snipped fresh thyme or ¼ teaspoon dried thyme, crushed
- 1 2-pound boneless pork loin roast (single loin)
- 2 large sweet potatoes, peeled and cut into ¾-inch pieces (1 to 1¼ pounds total)
- 1 recipe Mango-Jicama Salsa

1 Preheat oven to 325°F. In a small bowl combine 3 tablespoons of the Pickapeppa sauce, the garlic, and thyme; set aside.

2 Trim fat from roast. Brush garlic mixture on all sides of roast. Place roast on a roasting rack in an ungreased 9×13-inch baking pan or baking dish. Insert an oven-going meat thermometer into the center of the roast. Roast, uncovered, for 45 minutes.

3 Meanwhile, in a covered medium saucepan cook sweet potatoes in lightly salted boiling water about 8 minutes or just until tender; drain. Toss sweet potatoes with the remaining 1 tablespoon Pickapeppa sauce. Place sweet potatoes around roast in pan or dish. Continue roasting for 30 to 45 minutes more or until thermometer registers 150°F. Cover meat with foil; let stand for 15 minutes before slicing. The temperature of the meat after standing should be 160°F.

4 Serve meat with sweet potatoes and Mango-Jicama Salsa.

Makes 8 servings.

Nutrition Facts per serving: 265 cal., 7 g total fat (2 g sat. fat), 62 mg chol., 151 mg sodium, 24 g carbo., 3 g fiber, 26 g pro.

Mango-Jicama Salsa: *Drain one 8-ounce can pineapple tidbits (juice pack), reserving 2 tablespoons of the juice. In a medium bowl combine drained pineapple; the reserved 2 tablespoons pineapple juice; 1 cup peeled and chopped jicama; 1 medium mango, peeled, seeded, and chopped; 1 large tomato, seeded and chopped; 1 green onion, sliced; 1 or 2 fresh jalapeño chile peppers, seeded and finely chopped;** 1 tablespoon lime juice; and ⅛ teaspoon salt. Cover and refrigerate until serving time or up to 24 hours.*

---

*Test Kitchen Tip: *If you can't find Pickapeppa sauce, substitute 3 tablespoons Worcestershire sauce mixed with a dash of bottled hot pepper sauce.*

**Test Kitchen Tip: *Because chile peppers contain volatile oils that can burn your skin and eyes, avoid direct contact with them as much as possible. When working with chile peppers, wear plastic or rubber gloves. If your bare hands do touch the peppers, wash your hands and nails well with soap and warm water.*

BARBECUE-STYLE PORK ROAST

Overnight marinating adds a big
dose of flavor. Any leftovers will
make terrific sandwiches.

Prep: 15 minutes   **Marinate:** 6 to 24 hours   **Roast:** 1¼ hours   **Stand:** 15 minutes   **Oven:** 325°F

- 1   3-pound boneless pork top loin roast (single loin)
- ¾   cup dry red wine
- ⅓   cup packed brown sugar
- ¼   cup vinegar
- ¼   cup ketchup
- ¼   cup water
- 1   tablespoon cooking oil
- 1   tablespoon soy sauce
- 1   clove garlic, minced
- 1   teaspoon curry powder
- ½   teaspoon ground ginger
- ¼   teaspoon black pepper
- 2   teaspoons cornstarch

1 Place roast in a large resealable plastic bag set in a large deep bowl. For marinade, in a small bowl combine wine, brown sugar, vinegar, ketchup, the water, oil, soy sauce, garlic, curry powder, ginger, and pepper. Pour marinade over roast. Seal bag; turn to coat roast. Marinate in the refrigerator for at least 6 hours or up to 24 hours, turning the bag several times.

2 Preheat oven to 325°F. Drain meat, reserving 1¼ cups of the marinade; cover reserved marinade and chill. Pat meat dry with paper towels. Place roast on a roasting rack in an ungreased 9×13-inch baking pan or baking dish. Insert an oven-going meat thermometer into center of roast. Roast, uncovered, for 1¼ to 1¾ hours or until meat thermometer registers 150°F.

3 Meanwhile, for sauce, in a small saucepan stir the reserved marinade into the cornstarch. Cook and stir until thickened and bubbly. Cook and stir for 2 minutes more. After 1 hour of roasting, brush the roast frequently with the sauce.

4 Cover meat with foil; let stand for 15 minutes before slicing. The temperature of the meat after standing should be 160°F. Reheat any remaining sauce to boiling; pass sauce with meat.

Makes 8 to 10 servings.

Nutrition Facts per serving: 327 cal., 11 g total fat (4 g sat. fat), 93 mg chol., 265 mg sodium, 12 g carbo., 0 g fiber, 38 g pro.

CHERRY-ALMOND GLAZED PORK

A simple, roasted pork becomes sublime when served with a sweet fruit-nut sauce. Make this combo when you want a special dinner with minimal prep time.

Prep: 25 minutes **Roast:** 1½ hours **Stand:** 15 minutes **Oven:** 325°F

- 1 **3-pound boneless pork loin roast (single loin)**
- **Salt**
- **Black pepper**
- 1 **12-ounce jar cherry preserves**
- ¼ **cup red wine vinegar**
- 2 **tablespoons light-color corn syrup**
- ¼ **teaspoon salt**
- ¼ **teaspoon ground cinnamon**
- ¼ **teaspoon ground nutmeg**
- ¼ **teaspoon ground cloves**
- ¼ **cup slivered almonds, toasted**

1 Preheat oven to 325°F. Sprinkle roast with a little salt and pepper; rub in with your fingers. Place roast on roasting rack in an ungreased 9×13-inch baking pan or baking dish. Insert an oven-going meat thermometer in center of roast. Roast, uncovered, for 1½ to 1¾ hours or until thermometer registers 150°F.

2 Meanwhile, in a small saucepan combine cherry preserves, red wine vinegar, corn syrup, the ¼ teaspoon salt, cinnamon, nutmeg, and cloves. Cook and stir until mixture boils; reduce heat. Simmer, uncovered, for 3 to 5 minutes or until slightly thickened. Stir in almonds. Keep sauce warm.

3 Spoon some of the sauce over the roast for the last 5 minutes of roasting. Cover meat with foil; let stand for 15 minutes before slicing. The temperature of the meat after standing should be 160°F. Reheat any remaining sauce to boiling; pass sauce with meat.

Makes 8 servings.

Nutrition Facts per serving: 391 cal., 10 g total fat (3 g sat. fat), 107 mg chol., 254 mg sodium, 34 g carbo., 1 g fiber, 38 g pro.

MUSTARD-MAPLE PORK ROAST

Maple syrup, orange peel, and mustard add captivating flavor to this succulent roast. Potatoes and carrots roast right alongside the pork. (Pictured on page 103.)

Prep: 20 minutes **Roast:** 1¼ hours **Stand:** 15 minutes **Oven:** 325°F

- 1 2- to 2½-pound boneless pork top loin roast (single loin)
- 2 tablespoons Dijon-style mustard
- 1 tablespoon maple-flavor syrup
- 2 teaspoons dried sage, crushed
- 1 teaspoon finely shredded orange peel
- ¼ teaspoon black pepper
- ⅛ teaspoon salt
- 20 to 24 tiny new potatoes, 1½ to 2 inches in diameter (about 1¾ pounds)*
- 1 1-pound package peeled baby carrots
- 1 tablespoon olive oil
- ¼ teaspoon salt

1 Preheat oven to 325°F. Trim fat from roast. Place roast, fat side up, on a roasting rack in an ungreased 9×13-inch baking pan or baking dish. In a small bowl stir together mustard, syrup, sage, orange peel, pepper, and the ⅛ teaspoon salt. Spoon mixture over roast, spreading evenly over the top. Insert an oven-going meat thermometer into center of roast. Roast, uncovered, for 30 minutes.

2 Meanwhile, peel a strip from the center of each potato. In a covered 4-quart Dutch oven cook potatoes in enough lightly salted boiling water to cover for 5 minutes. Add carrots; cook for 5 minutes more. Drain. Return to saucepan. Add olive oil and the ¼ teaspoon salt; toss gently to coat.

3 Place potato mixture in pan or dish around roast. Roast, uncovered, for 45 minutes to 1 hour more or until meat thermometer registers 150°F. Cover roast tightly with foil; let stand for 15 minutes before slicing. The temperature of the meat after standing should be 160°F.

Makes 8 servings.

Nutrition Facts per serving: 288 cal., 9 g total fat (3 g sat. fat), 62 mg chol., 301 mg sodium, 22 g carbo., 3 g fiber, 27 g pro.

Test Kitchen Tip: *If your potatoes are larger, use fewer potatoes to make 1¾ pounds. Cut any large potatoes in half.*

LEMONY HERBED PORK ROAST

The zing of lemon juice and a little peel brighten this pork roast. For best results, don't marinate it for more than 4 hours.

Prep: 20 minutes **Marinate:** 2 to 4 hours **Roast:** 1¼ hours **Stand:** 15 minutes **Oven:** 325°F

- 1 **2- to 3-pound boneless pork top loin roast (single loin)**
- 2 **teaspoons finely shredded lemon peel**
- 3 **tablespoons lemon juice**
- 2 **tablespoons olive oil**
- 2 **cloves garlic, minced**
- 1 **tablespoon snipped fresh oregano or thyme or 1 teaspoon dried oregano or thyme, crushed**
- ¼ **teaspoon salt**
- ¼ **teaspoon black pepper**

1 Place roast in a large resealable plastic bag set in a shallow dish. For marinade, in a small bowl combine lemon peel, lemon juice, olive oil, garlic, oregano, salt, and pepper. Pour marinade over roast. Seal bag; turn to coat roast. Marinate in the refrigerator for at least 2 hours or up to 4 hours, turning bag occasionally.

2 Preheat oven to 325°F. Drain roast, discarding marinade. Place roast on a roasting rack in an ungreased 9×13-inch baking pan or baking dish. Insert an oven-going meat thermometer into the center of the roast. Roast, uncovered, for 1¼ to 1¾ hours or until thermometer registers 150°F.

3 Cover meat with foil; let stand for 15 minutes before slicing. The temperature of the meat after standing should be 160°F.

Makes 6 to 8 servings.

Nutrition Facts per serving: 264 cal., 14 g total fat (4 g sat. fat), 82 mg chol., 152 mg sodium, 1 g carbo., 0 g fiber, 33 g pro.

174

PORK LOIN ROAST WITH HERBED PEPPER RUB

Rubs are a great way to give meat intense flavor. This peppery mix includes Parmesan cheese in addition to herbs.

Prep: 15 minutes **Roast:** 1¼ hours **Stand:** 15 minutes **Oven:** 350°F

- 2 **tablespoons grated Parmesan cheese**
- 1 **tablespoon cracked black pepper**
- 2 **teaspoons dried basil, crushed**
- 1 **teaspoon dried rosemary, crushed**
- 1 **teaspoon dried thyme, crushed**
- ¼ **teaspoon garlic powder**
- ¼ **teaspoon salt***
- 1 **3-pound boneless pork top loin roast (single loin)***
- 2 **15-ounce cans black-eyed peas, rinsed and drained**
- 1 **16-ounce jar hot, medium, or mild salsa**
- ½ **cup sliced green onions**
- ½ **teaspoon cracked black pepper**
  Lemon wedges (optional)
  Fresh thyme sprigs (optional)

1 Preheat oven to 350°F. For rub, in a small bowl combine Parmesan cheese, the 1 tablespoon black pepper, the basil, rosemary, dried thyme, garlic powder, and salt.

2 Trim fat from roast. Pat dry with paper towels. Sprinkle rub evenly on a sheet of waxed paper. Roll roast in rub to coat on all sides. Place roast on a roasting rack in an ungreased 9×13-inch baking pan or baking dish. Insert an oven-going meat thermometer into the center of the roast. Roast, uncovered, for 1¼ to 1¾ hours or until thermometer registers 150°F.

3 Meanwhile, for black-eyed pea salsa, in a medium bowl stir together black-eyed peas, salsa, green onions, and the ½ teaspoon cracked black pepper. Cover and chill until serving time. (Or if desired, place black-eyed pea salsa in a medium saucepan; bring just to boiling over medium heat.)

4 Cover roast with foil; let stand for 15 minutes. The temperature of the meat after standing should be 160°F. Slice meat and serve with cold or hot black-eyed pea salsa. If desired, garnish with lemon wedges and fresh thyme sprigs.

Makes 12 servings.

Nutrition Facts per serving: 242 cal., 6 g total fat (2 g sat. fat), 63 mg chol., 528 mg sodium, 15 g carbo., 4 g fiber, 30 g pro.

***Test Kitchen Tip:** To keep the sodium in this dish in check, look for natural pork. If using enhanced pork, omit the salt.*

ROASTED PORK TENDERLOIN
WITH CRANBERRY CHUTNEY

Don't save cranberries just for turkey! Here, their lively flavor combines with fresh ginger and curry to pep up roasted pork.

Prep: 30 minutes   **Roast:** 25 minutes   **Cook:** 20 minutes   **Stand:** 10 minutes   **Oven:** 425°F

- 1 tablespoon ground allspice
- 2 to 3 teaspoons cracked black pepper
- 1 teaspoon salt
- 3 1- to 1¼-pound pork tenderloins
- 2 tablespoons cooking oil
- 1 tablespoon butter
- 1 large onion, quartered and thinly sliced
- 1 12-ounce package cranberries
- 1 10-ounce jar currant jelly
- 1 cup cranberry juice
- ¼ cup packed brown sugar
- 3 tablespoons cider vinegar
- 1 tablespoon grated fresh ginger or ½ teaspoon ground ginger
- ½ teaspoon curry powder
- 2 bunches watercress

1 Preheat oven to 425°F. For rub, in a small bowl combine allspice, pepper, and salt. Sprinkle rub evenly on all sides of tenderloins; rub in with your fingers.

2 In a 12-inch skillet heat oil over medium heat. Add tenderloins; cook until browned, turning to brown all sides. Transfer tenderloins to an ungreased 9×13-inch baking pan or baking dish. Roast, uncovered, for 25 to 40 minutes or until done (155°F) and juices run clear. Cover with foil; let stand for 10 minutes before slicing. The temperature of the meat after standing should be 160°F.

3 Meanwhile, for cranberry chutney, add butter and onion to the same 12-inch skillet. Cook about 5 minutes or until nearly tender, stirring occasionally. Add cranberries, jelly, cranberry juice, brown sugar, vinegar, ginger, and curry powder to skillet. Bring mixture to boiling; reduce heat. Boil gently but steadily for 20 to 25 minutes or until mixture is thickened to desired consistency and reduced to about 3 cups.

4 To serve, line a serving platter with watercress. Slice pork and arrange atop watercress; spoon some of the cranberry chutney over pork. Serve remaining chutney with pork.

Makes 12 to 16 servings.

Nutrition Facts per serving: 275 cal., 7 g total fat (2 g sat. fat), 76 mg chol., 259 mg sodium, 29 g carbo., 2 g fiber, 24 g pro.

SESAME PORK TENDERLOIN

Asian chili sauce and
fresh ginger show off
pork's exotic side.

Prep: 25 minutes   **Roast:** 25 minutes   **Stand:** 10 minutes   **Oven:** 425°F

- 2 tablespoons bottled chili sauce or 1 tablespoon Asian chili sauce
- 1 tablespoon reduced-sodium teriyaki sauce
- 2 cloves garlic, minced
- ½ teaspoon grated fresh ginger or ⅛ teaspoon ground ginger
- 1 12- to 16-ounce pork tenderloin
- 1 teaspoon sesame seeds
- 2 teaspoons olive oil
- ⅛ teaspoon salt
- ⅛ teaspoon black pepper
- 4 cups packaged shredded broccoli (broccoli slaw mix)

1 Preheat oven to 425°F. For sauce, in a small bowl stir together chili sauce, teriyaki sauce, half of the garlic, and the ginger.

2 Place tenderloin on a roasting rack in an ungreased 9×13-inch baking pan or baking dish. Spread half of the sauce over tenderloin. Roast, uncovered, for 15 minutes. Spread the remaining sauce over tenderloin; sprinkle tenderloin with sesame seeds. Roast, uncovered, for 10 to 20 minutes more or until done (155°F).

3 Cover tightly with foil; let stand for 10 minutes before slicing. The temperature of the meat after standing should be 160°F.

4 Meanwhile, in a 4-quart Dutch oven heat oil over medium heat. Add the remaining garlic, the salt, and pepper; cook and stir for 15 seconds. Add shredded broccoli. Cook and toss for 1 to 2 minutes or until broccoli is heated through.

5 Slice tenderloin; serve with broccoli mixture.

Makes 4 servings.

Nutrition Facts per serving: 167 cal., 6 g total fat (1 g sat. fat), 55 mg chol., 365 mg sodium, 8 g carbo., 3 g fiber, 21 g pro.

ROAST PORK SALAD
WITH GINGER-PINEAPPLE DRESSING

Here pork and fruit combine with tropical seasonings for a light supper or an impressive lunch. Make the dressing up to 24 hours ahead.

Prep: 25 minutes **Roast:** 25 minutes **Stand:** 10 minutes **Oven:** 425°F

1	12-ounce pork tenderloin
⅛	teaspoon salt
⅛	teaspoon ground black pepper
2	tablespoons honey mustard
6	cups torn romaine and/or fresh spinach
2	cups fresh or canned pineapple chunks and/or sliced fresh nectarines or peaches
	Cracked black pepper (optional)
1	recipe Ginger-Pineapple Dressing

1 Preheat oven to 425°F. Trim fat from pork; sprinkle pork with salt and ground black pepper. Place pork on a roasting rack in an ungreased 9×13-inch baking pan or baking dish. Roast, uncovered, for 20 minutes.

2 Spoon honey mustard onto pork. Roast for 5 to 15 minutes more or until done (155°F) and juices run clear. Cover with foil; let stand for 10 minutes before slicing. The temperature of the meat after standing should be 160°F.

3 Thinly slice pork. Arrange romaine, pork, and fruit on four salad plates. If desired, sprinkle salads with cracked black pepper. Stir Ginger-Pineapple Dressing; drizzle onto salads.

Makes 4 servings.

Nutrition Facts per serving: 289 cal., 14 g total fat (3 g sat. fat), 60 mg chol., 207 mg sodium, 21 g carbo., 3 g fiber, 19 g pro.

Ginger-Pineapple Dressing: *In a small bowl combine ¼ cup mayonnaise or salad dressing, ¼ cup unsweetened pineapple juice or orange juice, 1 tablespoon honey mustard, and 1 teaspoon grated fresh ginger. Cover; chill until serving time or up to 24 hours.*

TWO-POCKET STUFFED CHOPS

Fresh apples, nuts, and spicy Cajun seasoning
make these chops taste doubly good because the
stuffing is in not one but two places.

Prep: 30 minutes   **Bake:** 45 minutes   **Oven:** 375°F

- ¾   cup coarsely chopped roasted and peeled fresh chestnuts* or coarsely chopped canned vacuum-packed whole peeled chestnuts
- ¼   cup chopped hazelnuts (filberts)
- 2   tablespoons butter, melted
- ¼   cup finely chopped apple
- 2   tablespoons finely chopped onion
- ½   teaspoon ground sage
- ¼   cup finely chopped green sweet pepper
- 1   teaspoon Cajun seasoning or Jamaican jerk seasoning
- 4   boneless pork loin chops, cut 1¼ to 1½ inches thick (about 2 pounds total)
- ½   cup apple jelly

1 Preheat oven to 375°F. In a small bowl combine chestnuts and hazelnuts. Drizzle with melted butter; toss to coat. Divide nut mixture evenly between two small bowls.

2 For stuffings, stir apple, 1 tablespoon of the onion, and the sage into nut mixture in one of the bowls. Stir sweet pepper, the remaining 1 tablespoon onion, and the Cajun seasoning into nut mixture in the other bowl.

3 Trim fat from chops. Make two pockets in each chop by cutting horizontally from the fat side, starting just off center for each pocket and working the knife through the chop almost to the other side. Spoon a generous 3 tablespoons of one of the stuffings into one of the pockets in each pork chop. Spoon a generous 3 tablespoons of the other stuffing into the remaining pocket in each pork chop. If necessary, secure openings with wooden toothpicks.

4 Place chops on a roasting rack in an ungreased 9×13-inch baking pan or baking dish. Bake about 45 minutes or until done (160°F) and juices run clear.

5 In a small saucepan melt apple jelly over low heat. Brush chops with melted jelly. Before serving, discard toothpicks.

Makes 4 servings.

Nutrition Facts per serving: 613 cal., 26 g total fat (9 g sat. fat), 160 mg chol., 214 mg sodium, 46 g carbo., 4 g fiber, 49 g pro.

179

*Test Kitchen Tip: *To roast chestnuts, preheat oven to 425°F. Using a sharp knife, cut an X in the flat side of 12 whole fresh chestnuts. (This allows the shells to peel easily and prevents the nuts from exploding during cooking.) Arrange nuts in a single layer in an ungreased 9×13-inch baking pan. Bake about 15 minutes or until shells curl, tossing once or twice. Cool slightly; peel while warm. (You can roast and peel the chestnuts up to 2 days before using. Store, covered, in the refrigerator until needed.)*

PESTO-STUFFED PORK CHOPS

Hidden inside each chop are Mediterranean ingredients—
feta cheese, pesto, and pine nuts. Serve the chops with
hot cooked rice pilaf or couscous.

Prep: 20 minutes   **Bake:** 35 minutes   **Oven:** 375°F

- 3   tablespoons crumbled feta cheese
- 2   tablespoons refrigerated basil pesto
- 1   tablespoon pine nuts, toasted
- 4   boneless pork loin chops, cut 1¼ inches thick
- 1   teaspoon freshly ground black pepper
- 1   teaspoon dried oregano, crushed
- 2   cloves garlic, minced
- ¼   teaspoon crushed red pepper
- ¼   teaspoon dried thyme, crushed
- 1   tablespoon balsamic vinegar

1 Preheat oven to 375°F. For filling, in a small bowl stir together feta cheese, pesto, and pine nuts; set aside.

2 Trim fat from pork chops. Make a pocket in each pork chop by cutting horizontally from the fat side almost to the opposite side. Divide filling among pockets in pork chops. If necessary, secure the openings with wooden toothpicks.

3 For rub, in a small bowl combine black pepper, oregano, garlic, crushed red pepper, and thyme. Sprinkle evenly over all sides of chops; rub in with your fingers. Place chops on a roasting rack in an ungreased 9×13-inch baking pan or baking dish.

4 Bake, uncovered, for 35 to 45 minutes or until done (160°F) and juices run clear. Brush balsamic vinegar onto pork chops for the last 5 minutes of baking. Before serving, discard toothpicks.

Makes 4 servings.

Nutrition Facts per serving: 358 cal., 18 g total fat (5 g sat. fat), 104 mg chol., 201 mg sodium, 4 g carbo., 0 g fiber, 41 g pro.

OVEN-BARBECUED RIBS

These tender, juicy ribs are finger-licking good. If you like lots of sauce, double its ingredients.

Prep: 20 minutes **Bake:** 1¾ hours **Oven:** 350°F

- 3 pounds pork country-style ribs
- Salt
- Black pepper
- ½ cup chopped onion
- 2 cloves garlic, minced
- 1 tablespoon cooking oil
- ¾ cup bottled chili sauce
- ½ cup apple juice, apple cider, or light beer
- ¼ cup honey
- 2 tablespoons Worcestershire sauce
- ½ teaspoon dry mustard

1 Preheat oven to 350°F. Place ribs in an ungreased 9×13-inch baking pan or baking dish. Sprinkle generously with salt and pepper. Bake, uncovered, for 1 hour. Drain off fat.

2 Meanwhile, for sauce, in a medium saucepan cook onion and garlic in hot oil until tender. Stir in chili sauce, apple juice or beer, honey, Worcestershire sauce, and dry mustard. Bring to boiling; reduce heat. Simmer sauce, uncovered, for 20 minutes. (You should have about 1½ cups sauce.)

3 Spoon ⅓ cup of the sauce over the ribs. Bake, covered, for 45 minutes to 1¼ hours more or until tender, turning ribs and spooning another ⅓ cup of the sauce over ribs after 25 minutes. Reheat the remaining sauce until boiling; pass with ribs.

Makes 4 servings.

Nutrition Facts per serving: 473 cal., 19 g total fat (6 g sat. fat), 122 mg chol., 975 mg sodium, 34 g carbo., 3 g fiber, 38 g pro.

Orange-Sesame Ribs: *Prepare as directed, except omit sauce ingredients. For sauce, stir together one 10-ounce jar orange marmalade; one 7¼-ounce jar hoisin sauce; 3 cloves garlic, minced; and 1 teaspoon toasted sesame oil. Spoon ⅔ cup of the sauce over the ribs for the last 15 minutes of baking. Heat remaining sauce until bubbly; pass with ribs.*

Nutrition Facts per serving: 600 cal., 19 g total fat (6 g sat. fat), 123 mg chol., 1,143 mg sodium, 70 g carbo., 2 g fiber, 39 g pro.

OVEN-ROASTED ASIAN-STYLE PORK RIBS

Fruit preserves mixed with soy sauce and ginger create the tantalizing sauce that glazes these ribs. Boiling the ribs first reduces the baking time.

Prep: 20 minutes **Bake:** 15 minutes **Cook:** 20 minutes **Oven:** 350°F

- 3 pounds pork loin back ribs or pork spareribs
- 3 tablespoons pineapple, peach, or apricot preserves
- ⅓ cup ketchup
- 2 tablespoons soy sauce
- 1 teaspoon grated fresh ginger or ¼ teaspoon ground ginger
- 1 clove garlic, minced

1 Cut ribs into serving-size pieces. Place ribs in a 4- to 6-quart Dutch oven. Add enough water to cover. Bring to boiling; reduce heat. Cover and simmer for 20 to 30 minutes or until ribs are tender; drain.

2 Meanwhile, for sauce, cut up any large pieces of fruit in the preserves. In a bowl stir together preserves, ketchup, soy sauce, ginger, and garlic.

3 Preheat oven to 350°F. Brush some of the sauce over both sides of the ribs. Place ribs, bone sides down, in an ungreased 9×13-inch baking pan or baking dish. Bake, uncovered, for 15 to 20 minutes or until glazed and heated through. Brush with the remaining sauce before serving.

Makes 4 servings.

Nutrition Facts per serving: 442 cal., 22 g total fat (7 g sat. fat), 101 mg chol., 797 mg sodium, 16 g carbo., 1 g fiber, 43 g pro.

CHERRY-STUFFED HAM

Plumped dried cherries are placed into slits in the ham and are added to the fruit sauce for a double sweet-tart touch. (Pictured on page 104.)

Prep: 35 minutes **Bake:** 2 hours 10 minutes **Stand:** 15 minutes **Oven:** 325°F

- 1 cup dried tart red cherries, chopped
- ½ cup cherry juice or orange juice
- 1 3- to 4-pound cooked boneless ham
- 1 18-ounce jar peach preserves
- 2 tablespoons lemon juice

1 Preheat oven to 325°F. In a small saucepan combine ½ cup of the dried cherries and the cherry juice; bring to boiling. Remove from heat; let stand for 15 minutes. Drain cherries, discarding juice.

2 Make three or four 1½- to 2-inch-deep slits in ham, cutting at right angles to the direction ham will be sliced and pressing some of the soaked cherries into each slit as it is cut. Place ham on a roasting rack in an ungreased 9×13-inch baking pan or baking dish. Cover with foil. Insert an oven-going meat thermometer in the thickest portion of the ham. Bake about 2 hours or until thermometer registers 140°F.

3 Place peach preserves in a small bowl; snip any large pieces of fruit. Stir in the remaining dried cherries and the lemon juice. Spoon ½ cup of the preserves mixture over ham. Bake, uncovered, for 10 minutes more. In a small saucepan heat the remaining preserves mixture and pass with ham.

Makes 10 to 12 servings.

Nutrition Facts per serving: 413 cal., 12 g total fat (4 g sat. fat), 78 mg chol., 1,795 mg sodium, 52 g carbo., 3 g fiber, 23 g pro.

GLAZED HAM

Studded with cloves, spread with a sweet glaze,
and baked to perfection, this ham is a sure sign of spring
and a long-loved star of the Easter table.

Prep: 15 minutes   **Bake:** 1¼ hours   **Oven:** 325°F

- 1   **3-pound boneless cooked ham (rump half or shank portion)**
- 12   **whole cloves (optional)**
- 1   **recipe Orange Glaze, Chutney Glaze, or Raspberry-Chipotle Glaze**

1 Preheat oven to 325°F. Score ham in a diamond pattern by making shallow diagonal cuts at 1-inch intervals. If desired, stud ham with whole cloves. Place ham on a roasting rack in an ungreased 9×13-inch baking pan or baking dish. Insert an oven-going meat thermometer into center of ham. Bake, uncovered, about 1¼ hours or until thermometer registers 140°F. Brush ham with some of the desired glaze during the last 20 minutes of baking. Serve ham with the remaining desired glaze.

Makes 10 to 12 servings.

Nutrition Facts per 3 ounces meat + about 1 tablespoon Orange Glaze: 156 cal., 7 g total fat (1 g sat. fat), 62 mg chol., 984 mg sodium, 7 g carbo., 0 g fiber, 16 g pro.

Raspberry-Chipotle Glaze: *In a medium saucepan combine ¾ cup seedless raspberry preserves; 1 tablespoon vinegar; 1 or 2 canned chipotle chile peppers in adobo sauce, drained and chopped;* and 2 small cloves garlic, minced. Cook and stir just until boiling. Reduce heat. Cook, uncovered, for 10 minutes more. Makes ¾ cup glaze.*

Nutrition Facts per 3 ounces meat + 1¹⁄₂ tablespoons Raspberry-Chipotle Glaze: 212 cal., 7 g total fat (1 g sat. fat), 62 mg chol., 995 mg sodium, 21 g carbo., 0 g fiber, 16 g pro.

Chutney Glaze: *In a food processor or blender combine ½ cup mango chutney, 2 tablespoons maple syrup, and 1 teaspoon stone-ground mustard. Cover and process or blend until smooth. Makes about ⅔ cup glaze.*

Nutrition Facts per 3 ounces meat + about 1 tablespoon Chutney Glaze: 163 cal., 6 g total fat (1 g sat. fat), 62 mg chol., 1,078 mg sodium, 8 g carbo., 0 g fiber, 16 g pro.

Orange Glaze: *In a medium saucepan combine 1 teaspoon finely shredded orange peel, ½ cup orange juice, ¼ cup packed brown sugar, 2 teaspoons cornstarch, and ¾ teaspoon dry mustard. Cook and stir over medium heat until thickened and bubbly. Cook and stir for 2 minutes more. Makes ⅔ cup glaze.*

*Test Kitchen Tip: *Because chile peppers contain volatile oils that can burn your skin and eyes, avoid direct contact with them as much as possible. When working with chile peppers, wear plastic or rubber gloves. If your bare hands do touch the peppers, wash your hands and nails well with soap and warm water.*

HAM BALLS IN BARBECUE SAUCE

Ham mixes with ground pork and gets a kick from barbecue sauce. For a potluck, plan on one meatball per diner. (Pictured on page 99.)

Prep: 20 minutes **Bake:** 45 minutes **Oven:** 350°F

- 2 eggs, slightly beaten
- 1½ cups soft bread crumbs (2 slices)
- ½ cup finely chopped onion
- 2 tablespoons milk
- 1 teaspoon dry mustard
- ¼ teaspoon black pepper
- 12 ounces ground cooked ham
- 12 ounces ground pork or ground beef
- ¾ cup packed brown sugar
- ½ cup ketchup
- 2 tablespoons vinegar
- 1 teaspoon dry mustard

1 Lightly grease a 9×13-inch baking pan or baking dish; set aside. Preheat oven to 350°F. In a large bowl combine eggs, bread crumbs, onion, milk, 1 teaspoon mustard, and the pepper. Add ground ham and ground pork; mix well. Shape into 12 balls, using about ⅓ cup of the ham mixture for each ball. Place ham balls in prepared pan or dish.

2 In a small bowl combine brown sugar, ketchup, vinegar, and 1 teaspoon mustard. Stir until brown sugar is dissolved. Pour brown sugar mixture over meatballs.

3 Bake, uncovered, about 45 minutes or until done (160°F).*

Makes 6 servings.

Nutrition Facts per serving: 428 cal., 19 g total fat (7 g sat. fat), 144 mg chol., 1,107 mg sodium, 42 g carbo., 1 g fiber, 23 g pro.

*__Test Kitchen Tip:__ The internal color of a meatball is not a reliable doneness indicator. A pork or beef meatball cooked to 160°F is safe, regardless of color. To measure the doneness of a meatball, insert an instant-read thermometer into center of meatball._

INDIVIDUAL SICILIAN MEAT LOAVES

Definitely not your ordinary meat loaf, these little gems boast a melty mozzarella and prosciutto filling. If you can't find prosciutto, use ham instead.

Prep: 20 minutes **Bake:** 20 minutes **Oven:** 400°F

- 1 egg, slightly beaten
- 1 14-ounce jar garlic and onion pasta sauce (1¾ cups)
- ¼ cup seasoned fine dry bread crumbs
- ¼ teaspoon salt
- ¼ teaspoon black pepper
- 12 ounces ground beef
- 2 ounces mozzarella cheese*
- 4 thin slices prosciutto or cooked ham (about 2 ounces)
- 1 9-ounce package refrigerated plain or spinach fettuccine
   Finely shredded Parmesan cheese (optional)

1 Preheat oven to 400°F. In a medium bowl combine egg, ¼ cup of the pasta sauce, the bread crumbs, salt, and pepper. Add ground beef; mix well.

2 Cut mozzarella cheese into four logs (each log should measure approximately 2¼×¾×½ inches). Wrap a slice of prosciutto around each cheese log. Shape one-fourth of the ground beef mixture around each cheese log to form a loaf. Flatten each meat loaf to 1½ inches thick and place in an ungreased 9×13-inch baking pan or baking dish.

3 Bake meat loaves, uncovered, about 20 minutes or until done (160°F).**

4 Meanwhile, prepare fettuccine according to package directions. In a small saucepan heat remaining pasta sauce over medium heat until bubbly.

5 Arrange meat loaves over hot cooked pasta. Spoon sauce over and, if desired, sprinkle with Parmesan cheese.

Makes 4 servings.

Nutrition Facts per serving: 618 cal., 29 g total fat (11 g sat. fat), 171 mg chol., 1,150 mg sodium, 55 g carbo., 3 g fiber, 31 g pro.

*Test Kitchen Tip: *You can substitute two sticks of mozzarella (string) cheese, cut in half crosswise.*

**Test Kitchen Tip: *The internal color of a meat loaf is not a reliable doneness indicator. A beef loaf cooked to 160°F is safe, regardless of color. To measure the doneness of a meat loaf, insert an instant-read thermometer into the center of the meat loaf.*

BALSAMIC-MARINATED LEG OF LAMB

The aroma and flavors of rosemary
and garlic elevate
this lamb to company status.

Prep: 10 minutes **Marinate:** 8 to 24 hours **Roast:** 2 hours **Stand:** 15 minutes **Oven:** 325°F

1   5- to 6-pound leg of lamb, boned, rolled, and tied

4   to 6 cloves garlic, sliced

⅔   cup balsamic vinegar

½   cup olive oil

2   tablespoons Dijon-style mustard

1   tablespoon sugar

2   teaspoons dried basil, crushed

4   cloves garlic, minced

1   teaspoon salt

½   teaspoon black pepper

1 Cut 1-inch-wide pockets into leg of lamb at 3-inch intervals. Place a slice of garlic in each of the pockets. For marinade, in a small bowl combine balsamic vinegar, oil, mustard, sugar, basil, the minced garlic, the salt, and pepper. Place leg of lamb in a large resealable plastic bag set in a shallow dish. Pour marinade over leg of lamb. Seal bag; turn to coat lamb. Marinate in the refrigerator for at least 8 hours or up to 24 hours, turning the bag occasionally.

2 Preheat oven to 325°F. Drain lamb; discard marinade. Place leg of lamb on a roasting rack in an ungreased 9×13-inch baking pan or baking dish. Insert an oven-going meat thermometer into the thickest portion of the leg of lamb. Roast, uncovered, for 2 to 2½ hours or until the thermometer registers 135°F. Cover and let stand for 15 minutes before slicing. The temperature of the meat after standing should be 145°F. Remove and discard strings. Thinly slice leg of lamb.

Makes 12 servings.

Nutrition Facts per serving: 237 cal., 10 g total fat (3 g sat. fat), 101 mg chol., 116 mg sodium, 1 g carbo., 0 g fiber, 32 g pro.

ROAST RACK OF LAMB WITH PEACH-GINGER CHUTNEY

Here is a dish for celebrations. The sauce can be made ahead and the meat roasts in the oven, so you can have time to visit with guests.

Prep: 20 minutes **Roast:** 45 minutes **Stand:** 15 minutes **Oven:** 325°F

- 2 1- to 1½-pound lamb rib roasts (6 to 8 ribs each), with or without backbone
- 3 tablespoons Dijon-style mustard
- 3 tablespoons lemon juice
- 1 tablespoon snipped fresh rosemary or thyme
- ½ teaspoon salt
- ¾ cup soft bread crumbs (1 slice)
- 1 tablespoon butter or margarine, melted
- 1 recipe Peach-Ginger Chutney

1 Preheat oven to 325°F. Trim fat from roasts. In a small bowl stir together mustard, lemon juice, rosemary, and salt; rub evenly onto roasts. In another small bowl toss together bread crumbs and melted butter. Sprinkle evenly over roasts.

2 Place roasts on a roasting rack in an ungreased 9×13-inch baking pan or baking dish. Insert an oven-going meat thermometer in thickest portion of roasts, making sure tip of the thermometer does not touch bone. Roast, uncovered, until desired doneness. Allow 45 minutes to 1 hour for medium-rare doneness (135°F) or 1 to 1½ hours for medium doneness (150°F).

3 Cover with foil and let stand for 15 minutes before carving. The temperature of the meat after standing should be 145°F for medium-rare doneness or 160°F for medium doneness. Serve with warm Peach-Ginger Chutney.

Makes 6 servings.

Nutrition Facts per serving: 299 cal., 9 g total fat (3 g sat. fat), 50 mg chol., 332 mg sodium, 41 g carbo., 3 g fiber, 16 g pro.

188

Peach-Ginger Chutney: *In a medium saucepan stir together ½ cup packed brown sugar, ½ cup dried tart red cherries or raisins, ⅓ cup vinegar, ¼ cup chopped onion, 1 teaspoon grated fresh ginger, and ¼ teaspoon crushed red pepper. Bring to boiling; reduce heat. Simmer, uncovered, for 15 minutes, stirring occasionally. Stir in 3 cups chopped, peeled fresh peaches or chopped thawed unsweetened sliced peaches; heat through. Cover and chill for up to 4 weeks. (Or freeze in an airtight container for up to 12 months.) Reheat before serving. Makes about 2½ cups.*

RACK OF LAMB WITH GARLIC-CHIVE CRUST

To make a bone-in roast look impressive, chefs often french it, by cutting the meat about 1 inch away from the tip of the rib. If you don't want to try frenching yourself, ask your butcher to do it.

Prep: 20 minutes **Roast:** 25 minutes **Stand:** 15 minutes **Oven:** 375°F

- 2 1- to 1½-pound lamb rib roasts (6 to 8 ribs each), with or without backbone, frenched
- ¼ teaspoon salt
- ¼ teaspoon black pepper
- ¾ cup soft bread crumbs (1 slice)
- 2 tablespoons snipped fresh chives
- 2 tablespoons snipped fresh parsley
- 12 cloves garlic, minced
- 1 tablespoon butter or margarine, melted
- 1 tablespoon cooking oil
- 2 tablespoons stone-ground mustard

1 Preheat oven to 375°F. Trim fat from lamb. Cut the roasts in half (3 or 4 ribs each). Sprinkle with salt and pepper. Wrap the exposed bones with foil. In a small bowl combine bread crumbs, chives, parsley, and garlic; add melted butter and toss until evenly moistened. Set crumb mixture aside.

2 In a large skillet heat oil over medium heat. Add half of the lamb; cook about 4 minutes or until browned, turning once. Transfer browned lamb, meat sides up, to an ungreased 9×13-inch baking pan or baking dish. Repeat with remaining lamb. Spread mustard on meat side of each piece of lamb; press crumb mixture into mustard.

3 Roast, uncovered, until desired doneness. Allow about 25 minutes for medium-rare doneness (140°F) or about 35 minutes for medium doneness (155°F). Cover with additional foil; let stand for 15 minutes before serving. The temperature of the meat after standing should be 145°F for medium-rare doneness or 160°F for medium doneness. Uncover and remove foil from exposed bones before serving.

Makes 4 servings.

Nutrition Facts per serving: 357 cal., 20 g total fat (7 g sat. fat), 119 mg chol., 411 mg sodium, 8 g carbo., 1 g fiber, 36 g pro.

BERRY-MUSTARD CRUSTED LAMB

Raspberries add a hint of sweetness to both the mustard crust and mint sauce, and an elegant touch to succulent lamb.

Prep: 20 minutes   **Roast:** 35 minutes   **Stand:** 10 minutes   **Oven:** 375°F

- 2 1-pound or one 1½- to 2-pound lamb rib roast(s), frenched
- Salt
- Black pepper
- 1 tablespoon cooking oil
- ¼ cup seedless raspberry jam or preserves
- 2 tablespoons Dijon-style mustard, stone ground mustard, or Pommery mustard
- 4 cloves garlic, minced
- ¾ cup panko (Japanese-style) bread crumbs
- ½ cup fresh raspberries
- 1 cup beef broth
- 2 tablespoons snipped fresh mint

1 Line a 9×13-inch baking pan or baking dish with foil; set aside. Preheat oven to 375°F. Season lamb generously with salt and pepper. In a very large skillet brown lamb on all sides in hot oil. Set skillet aside. Place lamb, bone side(s) down, in prepared pan or dish.

2 In a small bowl combine jam, mustard, and half of the garlic; spoon over lamb. Sprinkle evenly with bread crumbs. Roast, uncovered, for 35 to 40 minutes for small roasts or 50 to 60 minutes for large roast or until medium-rare doneness (140°F) to medium doneness (155°F).

3 Cover with foil; let stand for 10 minutes before carving. The temperature of the meat after standing should be 145°F for medium-rare doneness to 160°F for medium doneness.

4 Meanwhile, in the large skillet cook raspberries and the remaining garlic for 30 seconds. Add beef broth; heat to boiling. Boil gently, uncovered, for 5 to 8 minutes or until reduced to ⅔ cup. Cool slightly; transfer to a blender. Cover and blend until almost smooth. Stir in mint. Season to taste with additional salt and pepper. Slice lamb between ribs and spoon sauce over lamb.

Makes 8 servings.

Nutrition Facts per serving: 334 cal., 25 g total fat (10 g sat. fat), 58 mg chol., 284 mg sodium, 12 g carbo., 1 g fiber, 13 g pro.

POULTRY DISHES

The favorite alternative to red meat has now moved to front and center on dinner plates across the U.S., and for good reason. Whether you're looking for the main course of a weekly meal or the star of your holiday feast, all you have to do is turn the page and choose a recipe.

ROAST CHICKEN WITH FRUIT AND PESTO

Apricots or peaches lend sweetness to basil pesto. Spreading the pesto under the skin infuses the chicken with an abundance of flavor.

Prep: 20 minutes **Roast:** 1¾ hours **Stand:** 15 minutes **Oven:** 325°F

- 1 cup apricot preserves or peach preserves
- ½ cup snipped dried apricots or peaches
- ¼ teaspoon ground ginger
- ⅔ cup purchased basil pesto
- 1 5- to 6-pound whole roasting chicken

1 Preheat oven to 325°F. In a medium bowl stir together preserves, apricots, and ginger. Remove ⅓ cup of the preserves mixture; place in a small bowl. Stir pesto into preserves mixture in small bowl; set aside. Set aside remaining preserves mixture for sauce.

2 Using your fingers, gently separate the chicken skin from the breast meat of the bird. Spoon some of the preserves-pesto mixture under the skin and spread over the breast meat. Spread some of the mixture into the neck cavity. Pull neck skin to back; fasten with a small skewer. Spread some of the mixture into the body cavity. Rub remaining mixture over outside of chicken. Tuck drumsticks under the band of skin that crosses the tail. If there is no band, use 100%-cotton kitchen string to tie drumsticks to the tail. Twist wing tips under back.

3 Place chicken, breast side up, on a roasting rack in an ungreased 9×13-inch baking pan or baking dish. Insert an oven-going meat thermometer into the center of an inside thigh muscle, making sure tip of the thermometer does not touch bone. Roast, uncovered, for 1¾ to 2½ hours or until thermometer registers 180°F, drumsticks move easily in their sockets, and juices run clear. When the bird is two-thirds done, cut the band of skin or string between the drumsticks so the thighs cook evenly. Transfer chicken to a serving platter. Let stand for 15 to 20 minutes before carving.

4 Meanwhile, for sauce, in a small saucepan heat the reserved preserves mixture over low heat until preserves have melted and mixture is heated through; serve with sliced chicken.

Makes 10 servings.

Nutrition Facts per serving: 565 cal., 36 g total fat (7 g sat. fat), 121 mg chol., 224 mg sodium, 29 g carbo., 1 g fiber, 30 g pro.

ROAST CHICKEN AND POTATOES

Slow down for a Sunday meal that makes the house smell heavenly and everyone happy to come to the table.

Prep: 20 minutes **Bake:** 1 hour 25 minutes **Stand:** 10 minutes **Oven:** 450°F/375°F

- 2 tablespoons olive oil
- 2 tablespoons lemon juice
- 5 to 7 stalks celery
- 1 pound whole carrots
- 1 pound small Yukon gold or red potatoes, halved or quartered
- 1 small lemon, halved (optional)
  Salt
  Black pepper
- 1 3½-pound whole roasting chicken
- ½ of a medium onion, cut into 4 pieces
- 2 or 3 celery leaves (from core)
- ⅓ cup dry white wine

1 Preheat oven to 450°F. In a small bowl stir together oil and lemon juice; set aside. Trim celery to fit a 9×13-inch baking pan or baking dish. Quarter lengthwise any large carrots. Line the bottom of the ungreased pan or dish with celery and carrots. Place potatoes and, if desired, lemon halves on top. Drizzle vegetables with half of the oil mixture. Sprinkle vegetables with salt and pepper. Roast, uncovered, for 15 minutes.

2 Meanwhile, season the body cavity of the chicken with salt and pepper. Stuff chicken cavity with onion pieces and celery leaves. Twist wing tips under back. Reduce oven temperature to 375°F. Push potatoes and lemon halves to the edges of the pan or dish. Place chicken on top of celery and carrots in pan or dish. Baste chicken and potatoes with the remaining oil mixture. Add wine to the pan or dish. Roast for 70 to 75 minutes or until an instant-read thermometer inserted into center of an inside thigh muscle (not touching bone) registers 180°F, the drumsticks move easily in their sockets, juices run clear, and potatoes are tender.

3 Let chicken stand for 10 minutes before carving. To serve, remove onion and celery leaves from chicken and discard. Place chicken on serving platter, draining and discarding any juices from chicken. Add vegetables to platter. If desired, squeeze lemon halves over chicken and vegetables.

Makes 4 to 6 servings.

Nutrition Facts per serving: 523 cal., 31 g total fat (8 g sat. fat), 134 mg chol., 379 mg sodium, 22 g carbo., 4 g fiber, 36 g pro.

ROASTED ITALIAN CHICKEN

The under-the-skin rub in this recipe works like a marinade, adding lots of Italian flavor to the chicken as it roasts.

Prep: 20 minutes   **Roast:** 1¼ hours   **Stand:** 10 minutes   **Oven:** 375°F

- 2   tablespoons balsamic vinegar
- 2   tablespoons olive oil
- 2   tablespoons snipped fresh oregano or 2 teaspoons dried oregano, crushed
- 2   tablespoons snipped fresh basil or 2 teaspoons dried basil, crushed
- 1   tablespoon snipped fresh thyme or 1 teaspoon dried thyme, crushed
- 1   tablespoon lemon juice
- 1   teaspoon salt
- 1   teaspoon coarsely ground black pepper
- 4   cloves garlic, minced
- 1   3- to 3½-pound whole broiler-fryer chicken

1 Preheat oven to 375°F. In a small bowl whisk together balsamic vinegar, oil, oregano, basil, thyme, lemon juice, salt, pepper, and garlic. Divide herb mixture in half; set aside.

2 On one side of the chicken, slip your fingers between the skin and breast meat of the chicken, forming a pocket; repeat on other side of chicken. Divide one portion of the herb mixture between pockets.

3 Using 100%-cotton kitchen string, tie drumsticks to the tail. Twist wing tips under back. Place chicken, breast side up, on a roasting rack in an ungreased 9×13-inch baking pan or baking dish. Insert an oven-going meat thermometer into the center of an inside thigh muscle, making sure tip of the thermometer does not touch bone.

4 Roast, uncovered, for 1 hour. Cut string between drumsticks. Brush chicken with the remaining herb mixture. Roast for 15 to 30 minutes more or until thermometer registers 180°F, drumsticks move easily in their sockets, and juices run clear. Transfer chicken to a serving platter. Cover with foil; let stand for 10 minutes before carving.

Makes 6 servings.

Nutrition Facts per serving: 376 cal., 27 g total fat (7 g sat. fat), 115 mg chol., 476 mg sodium, 3 g carbo., 0 g fiber, 29 g pro.

MEDITERRANEAN HERB-RUBBED ROASTER

Get this bird ready for the oven the night before you plan to serve it. The next day, just add the potatoes, roast in the oven, and enjoy!

Prep: 20 minutes **Chill:** 2 to 24 hours **Roast:** 1¼ hours **Stand:** 10 minutes **Oven:** 375°F

- 1 3½- to 4-pound whole broiler-fryer chicken
- ¼ cup olive oil
- 2 tablespoons herbes de Provence
- 1 teaspoon smoked salt or regular salt
- 1 teaspoon crushed red pepper
- ¾ teaspoon coarsely ground black pepper
- 1½ pounds tiny yellow potatoes, tiny purple potatoes, and/or fingerling potatoes, halved

1 Using 100%-cotton kitchen string, tie chicken drumsticks to tail. Twist wing tips under back. Brush chicken with 2 tablespoons of the oil.

2 In a small bowl stir together herbes de Provence, smoked salt or regular salt, crushed red pepper, and coarsely ground black pepper. Sprinkle 2 tablespoons of the herb mixture evenly over the chicken; rub in with your fingers. Cover the remaining herb mixture; set aside. Place chicken in a large resealable plastic bag. Seal bag. Chill for at least 2 hours or up to 24 hours.

3 Preheat oven to 375°F. Remove chicken from bag. Place chicken, breast side up, on a roasting rack in an ungreased 9×13-inch baking pan or baking dish. Insert an oven-going meat thermometer into center of an inside thigh muscle, making sure the tip of thermometer does not touch bone. In a large bowl combine the remaining 2 tablespoons oil and the remaining herb mixture. Add the potatoes and toss to combine. Arrange potatoes around the chicken. Roast, uncovered, for 1¼ to 1¾ hours or until drumsticks move easily in their sockets and meat thermometer registers 180°F. Remove chicken from oven. Cover with foil; let stand for 10 minutes before carving. Serve chicken with potatoes.

Makes 6 servings.

Nutrition Facts per serving: 543 cal., 35 g total fat (9 g sat. fat), 134 mg chol., 492 mg sodium, 18 g carbo., 3 g fiber, 37 g pro.

LEMONY ROASTED CHICKEN

A consistent winner every time it's served, this
moist bird bursts with the flavors of lemon, fresh herbs, and garlic.

Prep: 20 minutes **Roast:** 1¼ hours **Stand:** 10 minutes **Oven:** 375°F

- 1 3- to 3½-pound broiler-fryer chicken
- 3 cloves garlic, thinly sliced lengthwise
- 2 tablespoons snipped assorted fresh herbs (such as flat-leaf parsley, thyme, and sage)
- 2 tablespoons olive oil
- 1½ teaspoons finely shredded lemon peel
- ¼ teaspoon black pepper
- ½ to 1 teaspoon sea salt or coarse salt
- 1 small onion, quartered

1 Preheat oven to 375°F. With a small knife, cut 8 to 10 small slits in the chicken skin, especially on the breasts and hindquarters. Using your fingers, insert a slice of garlic into each slit, just under the skin. Mince remaining garlic and set aside.

2 In a small bowl combine herbs, oil, lemon peel, pepper, and the minced garlic. Sprinkle chicken evenly with herb mixture; rub in with your fingers. Sprinkle chicken with salt, including cavity. Place onion quarters in cavity. Using 100%-cotton kitchen string, tie drumsticks to tail. Twist wing tips under the back. Place chicken, breast side up, on a roasting rack in an ungreased 9×13-inch baking pan or baking dish.

3 Roast, uncovered, for 1¼ to 1¾ hours or until an instant-read thermometer inserted into the center of an inside thigh muscle (not touching bone) registers 180°F and juices run clear. Remove the onion from the cavity; discard. Cover chicken loosely with foil; let stand for 10 minutes before carving.

Makes 4 servings.

Nutrition Facts per serving: 569 cal., 42 g total fat (11 g sat. fat), 173 mg chol., 364 mg sodium, 3 g carbo., 1 g fiber, 43 g pro.

196

OVEN-BARBECUED CHICKEN

There's no better way to keep a hungry crew happy; remember this
terrific recipe when it's the kids' night to cook.

Prep: 10 minutes **Bake:** 45 minutes **Oven:** 375°F

- 2 to 2½ pounds meaty chicken pieces (breast halves, thighs, and drumsticks), skinned
- ½ cup chopped onion
- 1 clove garlic, minced
- 1 tablespoon cooking oil
- ¾ cup bottled chili sauce
- 2 tablespoons honey
- 2 tablespoons soy sauce
- 1 tablespoon yellow mustard
- ½ teaspoon prepared horseradish
- ¼ teaspoon crushed red pepper

1 Preheat oven to 375°F. Arrange chicken pieces, bone sides up, in an ungreased 9×13-inch baking pan or baking dish. Bake, uncovered, for 25 minutes.

2 Meanwhile, for sauce, in a saucepan cook onion and garlic in hot oil until tender. Stir in chili sauce, honey, soy sauce, mustard, horseradish, and crushed red pepper; heat through.

3 Turn chicken bone sides down. Brush half of the sauce over the chicken. Bake for 20 to 30 minutes more or until chicken is no longer pink (170°F for breasts; 180°F for thighs and drumsticks). In a small saucepan reheat the remaining sauce until boiling; pass with chicken.

Makes 4 servings.

Nutrition Facts per serving: 320 cal., 11 g total fat (3 g sat. fat), 92 mg chol., 1,191 mg sodium, 20 g carbo., 3 g fiber, 32 g pro.

ROAST TARRAGON CHICKEN

Tarragon, known for its aniselike flavor, complements the chicken as well as the sweet roasted tomatoes and shallots in this recipe.

Prep: 20 minutes   **Roast:** 45 minutes   **Oven:** 375°F

- 2½ **to 3 pounds meaty chicken pieces (breast halves, thighs, and drumsticks)**
- 3 **tablespoons olive oil**
- 2½ **teaspoons dried tarragon, crushed**
- 2 **cloves garlic, minced**
- ½ **teaspoon salt**
- ½ **teaspoon coarsely ground black pepper**
- 1 **pound cherry tomatoes**
- 8 **small shallots**
  Fresh tarragon leaves (optional)

1 Preheat oven to 375°F. If desired, skin chicken pieces; set aside.

2 In a medium bowl stir together oil, dried tarragon, garlic, salt, and pepper. Add cherry tomatoes and shallots; toss gently to coat. Using a slotted spoon, remove cherry tomatoes and shallots from bowl, reserving the oil mixture.

3 Place chicken pieces in a single layer in an ungreased 9×13-inch baking pan or baking dish. Add shallots to pan or dish; set cherry tomatoes aside. Brush chicken with the reserved oil mixture. Discard any remaining oil mixture.

4 Roast chicken and shallots, uncovered, for 35 minutes. Add cherry tomatoes; roast for 10 to 12 minutes more or until chicken is tender and no longer pink (170°F for breasts; 180°F for thighs and drumsticks) and vegetables are tender. If desired, garnish with fresh tarragon.

Makes 6 servings.

Nutrition Facts per serving: 309 cal., 17 g total fat (4 g sat. fat), 86 mg chol., 277 mg sodium, 8 g carbo., 1 g fiber, 29 g pro.

CRANBERRY-GLAZED CHICKEN

How could something so easy be so sensational? All you need are four everyday ingredients to turn plain chicken breasts into luscious party fare.

Prep: 15 minutes **Bake:** 1 hour **Oven:** 350°F

- 5 **pounds meaty chicken pieces (breast halves, thighs, and drumsticks)**
- 2 **16-ounce cans whole cranberry sauce**
- 2 **8-ounce bottles reduced-calorie Russian or French salad dressing**
- 1 **2-ounce package (2 envelopes) onion soup mix**

  Hot cooked rice (optional)

1 Preheat oven to 350°F. If desired, skin chicken. Arrange chicken pieces in two ungreased 9×13-inch baking pans or baking dishes. For glaze, in a bowl combine cranberry sauce, salad dressing, and dry soup mix. Pour glaze over chicken in both baking dishes.

2 Bake, uncovered, about 1 hour or until the chicken is no longer pink (170°F for breasts; 180°F for thighs and drumsticks). Stir glaze and spoon over chicken once or twice during baking. If desired, serve chicken and glaze with rice.

Makes 8 servings.

Nutrition Facts per serving: 581 cal., 18 g total fat (5 g sat. fat), 133 mg chol., 880 mg sodium, 62 g carbo., 1 g fiber, 42 g pro.

Make-Ahead Directions: *Prepare as directed in step 1. Cover and chill for at least 6 hours or up to 24 hours. Bake as directed in step 2.*

Test Kitchen Tip: *To make 4 servings, halve the recipe and bake in one 9×13-inch baking pan or baking dish.*

ITALIAN BAKED CHICKEN BREASTS

The secret of this juicy, flavorful chicken is the marinade: a mix of wine, oil, herbs, and lemon. A sprinkling of Parmesan cheese adds the perfect final touch.

Prep: 20 minutes   **Marinate:** 2 to 6 hours   **Bake:** 45 minutes   **Broil:** 4 minutes   **Oven:** 375°F

- 4 bone-in chicken breast halves (about 2¼ pounds total)
- ½ cup dry white wine
- ¼ cup olive oil
- 2 tablespoons white wine vinegar
- 2 tablespoons water
- 1 tablespoon lemon juice
- 1 tablespoon dried Italian seasoning, crushed
- 3 cloves garlic, minced
- ¼ teaspoon salt
- ¼ teaspoon black pepper
- Salt
- Black pepper
- ⅓ cup finely shredded Parmesan cheese

1 If desired, skin chicken. Place chicken in a resealable plastic bag set in a shallow bowl. For marinade, in a small bowl combine dry white wine, oil, white wine vinegar, the water, lemon juice, Italian seasoning, garlic, the ¼ teaspoon salt, and the ¼ teaspoon pepper. Pour over chicken in bag. Seal bag; turn to coat chicken. Marinate in the refrigerator for at least 2 hours or up to 6 hours, turning bag occasionally.

2 Preheat oven to 375°F. Drain chicken, discarding marinade. Sprinkle chicken with additional salt and pepper. Arrange chicken in an ungreased 9×13-inch baking pan. Bake, uncovered, for 45 to 55 minutes or until chicken is tender and no longer pink (170°F). Sprinkle with cheese. Broil 4 to 5 inches from the heat about 4 minutes or until cheese is melted and beginning to brown.

Makes 4 servings.

Nutrition Facts per serving: 689 cal., 45 g total fat (15 g sat. fat), 163 mg chol., 1,103 mg sodium, 4 g carbo., 0 g fiber, 60 g pro.

ROAST CHICKEN WITH OLIVE-RAISIN SAUCE

For quick company fare,
oven-roasted chicken stuffed with fresh
sage leaves does the trick.

Prep: 25 minutes **Roast:** 25 minutes **Oven:** 425°F

- 4 bone-in chicken breast halves (about 2¼ pounds total)
- 8 to 12 fresh sage leaves or 24 sprigs fresh marjoram
- ¼ teaspoon salt
- ¼ teaspoon black pepper
- ½ cup sliced celery (½-inch-wide pieces)
- ½ cup chopped onion
- 2 large cloves garlic, minced
- 2 tablespoons olive oil
- ½ cup chicken broth
- ½ cup dry red wine or ⅓ cup chicken broth plus 2 tablespoons balsamic vinegar
- ½ cup pitted and halved mixed olives or kalamata olives
- ½ cup golden raisins
- ⅛ teaspoon cayenne pepper (optional)
- 1 tablespoon snipped fresh marjoram

1 Preheat oven to 425°F. Using your fingers, gently separate the chicken skin from the meat of the breasts along rib edges. Place two or three of the sage leaves or six sprigs of the marjoram under the skin of each piece of chicken. Sprinkle chicken with salt and black pepper.

2 Place chicken breasts, skin sides up, in an ungreased 9×13-inch baking pan or baking dish. Roast, uncovered, for 25 to 30 minutes or until chicken skin is golden brown and meat no longer pink (170°F).

3 Meanwhile, for sauce, in a large skillet cook celery, onion, and garlic in hot oil until tender. Add broth, wine, olives, raisins, and, if desired, cayenne pepper. Bring mixture to boiling; reduce heat. Simmer, uncovered, about 7 minutes or until slightly thickened. Stir in the snipped marjoram; simmer for 1 minute more.

4 Spoon the sauce over roasted chicken breast halves.

Makes 4 servings.

Nutrition Facts per serving: 542 cal., 28 g total fat (6 g sat. fat), 131 mg chol., 601 mg sodium, 21 g carbo., 2 g fiber, 44 g pro.

PESTO-STUFFED CHICKEN BREASTS

Served cold, these dressed-up chicken breasts become an elegant picnic entrée; served warm, they make a tasty dinner party main dish.

Prep: 20 minutes **Bake:** 45 minutes **Oven:** 375°F

- 4   bone-in chicken breast halves (about 2¼ pounds total)
- ½   cup jarred roasted red sweet peppers, drained and chopped
- ⅓   cup purchased basil pesto
- 2   tablespoons finely shredded Parmesan cheese
     Salt
     Black pepper
- 1   tablespoon butter, melted

1 Preheat oven to 375°F. Lightly grease a 9×13-inch baking pan or baking dish; set aside. Using your fingers, gently separate the chicken skin from the meat of the breasts along rib edges.

2 For stuffing, in a small bowl combine roasted red peppers, pesto, and Parmesan cheese. Spoon a rounded tablespoon of the stuffing between the skin and meat of each breast. Sprinkle stuffed chicken breasts with salt and pepper.

3 Place chicken breasts, bone sides down, in prepared pan or dish. Drizzle chicken with melted butter. Bake, uncovered, for 45 to 55 minutes or until chicken is no longer pink (170°F).

Makes 4 servings.

Nutrition Facts per serving: 421 cal., 27 g total fat (8 g sat. fat), 124 mg chol., 407 mg sodium, 4 g carbo., 1 g fiber, 39 g pro.

SPINACH-SAUCED CHICKEN BREAST HALVES

Skinless chicken breasts get a crunchy cheese coating and a colorful cream sauce with spinach and bits of ham. Serve on fettuccine for a nutritious and delicious family meal.

Prep: 25 minutes   **Bake:** 35 minutes   **Oven:** 350°F

- ⅔ cup Italian-seasoned fine dry bread crumbs
- ¼ cup grated Parmesan cheese
- 8 skinless, boneless chicken breast halves (about 2½ pounds total)
- ½ cup sliced green onions
- 2 tablespoons butter or margarine
- 2 tablespoons all-purpose flour
- 1 cup milk
- 1 10-ounce package frozen chopped spinach, thawed and well drained
- ½ of a 4-ounce package boiled ham slices, diced

1 Preheat oven to 350°F. In a shallow dish combine bread crumbs and Parmesan cheese. Coat chicken breast halves with bread crumb mixture. Arrange chicken in an ungreased 9×13-inch baking pan or baking dish. Set any remaining bread crumb mixture aside.

2 In a saucepan cook green onions in hot butter until tender. Stir in flour. Stir in milk all at once. Cook and stir until thickened and bubbly. Stir in spinach and ham.

3 Spoon spinach mixture over chicken; sprinkle with the remaining bread crumb mixture. Bake, uncovered, for 35 to 40 minutes or until chicken is no longer pink (170°F).

Makes 8 servings.

Nutrition Facts per serving: 273 cal., 7 g total fat (3 g sat. fat), 98 mg chol., 459 mg sodium, 12 g carbo., 2 g fiber, 39 g pro.

ASIAN CHICKEN

Looking for a salad to wow the lunch crowd?
This one does it with layers of fresh spinach, Asian
noodles, and sweet glazed chicken.

Prep: 25 minutes   **Chill:** 1 hour to 2 days   **Bake:** 35 minutes   **Oven:** 375°F

6   skinless, boneless chicken breast halves (about 2 pounds total)

Salt

Black pepper

2   tablespoons bottled hoisin sauce or plum sauce

1   6-ounce package rice sticks

1   recipe Asian Dressing

1   6-ounce package baby spinach

1   tablespoon sesame seeds, toasted

Slivered green onions (optional)

1 Preheat oven to 375°F. Arrange chicken breast halves in an ungreased 9×13-inch baking pan or baking dish. Sprinkle with salt and pepper. Brush tops with hoisin sauce. Bake, uncovered, for 35 to 40 minutes or until chicken is no longer pink (170°F). Cool slightly; cover and chill for at least 1 hour or up to 2 days.

2 Meanwhile, cook rice sticks according to package directions. Drain; rinse with cold water. Drain well. Using kitchen scissors, snip rice sticks in a few places. Place rice sticks in a resealable plastic bag. Seal bag. Chill for at least 1 hour or up to 2 days. Prepare and chill Asian Dressing.

3 To serve, arrange spinach on six serving plates. Place cooked rice sticks on spinach. Place chilled chicken breasts on rice sticks. Drizzle with Asian Dressing. Sprinkle with toasted sesame seeds and, if desired, green onions.

Makes 6 servings.

Nutrition Facts per serving: 434 cal., 16 g total fat (3 g sat. fat), 88 mg chol., 733 mg sodium, 30 g carbo., 1 g fiber, 38 g pro.

203

Asian Dressing: *In a screw-top jar combine ¾ cup rice vinegar, ⅓ cup salad oil, 3 tablespoons bottled hoisin sauce or plum sauce, 2 tablespoons soy sauce, 1½ teaspoons grated fresh ginger or ¼ teaspoon ground ginger, and ¼ teaspoon crushed red pepper. Cover and shake well; chill until ready to serve (up to 1 week).*

WILD RICE-STUFFED CHICKEN WITH RED PEPPER SAUCE

Tender chicken, a ricotta-and-rice stuffing, and a roasted red pepper sauce create an outstanding dish.

Prep: 35 minutes **Bake:** 30 minutes **Oven:** 350°F

- 1 **cup hot cooked wild rice (½ cup uncooked)**
- 1 **cup ricotta cheese**
- ⅓ **cup finely shredded Parmesan cheese**
- 12 **cloves garlic, minced***
- 1 **teaspoon snipped fresh rosemary or ½ teaspoon dried rosemary, crushed**
- ½ **teaspoon snipped fresh parsley (optional)**
-   **Salt**
-   **Black pepper**
- 6 **skinless, boneless chicken breast halves (about 2 pounds total)**
- 2 **tablespoons butter**
- 1 **recipe Red Pepper Sauce**

1 Preheat oven to 350°F. In a medium bowl stir together wild rice, ricotta cheese, Parmesan cheese, garlic, rosemary, and, if desired, parsley. Season to taste with salt and pepper. Set aside.

2 Place each chicken breast half, boned side down, between two pieces of plastic wrap. Using the flat side of a meat mallet and working from the center out, pound each half lightly into a rectangle about ⅛ inch thick. Remove plastic wrap. Spoon about ⅓ cup of the stuffing into the center of each chicken breast piece. Fold in bottom and sides; roll up each piece into a spiral, pressing edges to seal. Secure with wooden toothpicks.

3 In a medium skillet melt butter over medium heat. Add chicken, half at a time; cook until browned, turning to brown evenly. Transfer chicken to an ungreased 9×13-inch baking pan or baking dish. Set the skillet aside for sauce.

4 Bake chicken, uncovered, for 30 to 35 minutes or until chicken is no longer pink. Remove toothpicks.

5 To serve, cut each chicken roll into slices. Spoon Red Pepper Sauce over chicken.

Makes 6 servings.

Nutrition Facts per serving: 483 cal., 27 g total fat (16 g sat. fat), 177 mg chol., 488 mg sodium, 14 g carbo., 2 g fiber, 44 g pro.

Red Pepper Sauce: *In the reserved skillet combine ¼ cup chicken broth and 2 tablespoons dry white wine or chicken broth. Cook over medium heat about 2 minutes or until reduced by half, stirring to loosen browned bits. Stir in 2 tablespoons chopped green onion, 1 tablespoon minced shallot or green onion, 1½ teaspoons snipped fresh parsley, and 1 clove garlic, minced. Cook for 1 minute. Stir in 1 cup whipping cream. Bring to boiling; reduce heat to medium. Cook for 3 to 4 minutes or until slightly thickened, stirring occasionally. Stir in one 12-ounce jar roasted red sweet peppers, drained and cut into strips, and 4 teaspoons snipped fresh chives.*

---

*Test Kitchen Tip: *If you prefer, use 2 tablespoons bottled minced garlic.*

CHICKEN-MOZZARELLA ROLL-UPS

In this baked dish, chicken breasts are rolled up with mozzarella cheese and a lively mix of Italian flavors. Brushing on sherry just before baking intensifies the flavor.

Prep: 30 minutes   **Bake:** 20 minutes   **Oven:** 375°F

- 2 tablespoons olive oil or cooking oil
- ⅓ cup chopped onion
- 6 skinless, boneless chicken breast halves (about 2 pounds total)
- 6 mozzarella cheese slices (about 4½ ounces)
- ¾ teaspoon garlic powder
- ¼ teaspoon black pepper
- 3 tablespoons dry sherry or chicken broth
- ½ cup fine dry bread crumbs
- 3 tablespoons grated Romano cheese
- ¾ teaspoon dried oregano, crushed
- ½ teaspoon onion salt
- 3 tablespoons butter, melted
- 3 cups purchased tomato-base pasta sauce
- Hot cooked fettuccine (optional)

1 Preheat oven to 375°F. Grease a 9×13-inch baking pan or baking dish; set aside. In a small saucepan heat 1 tablespoon of the oil over medium heat. Add onion; cook for 3 to 5 minutes or until tender. Set aside.

2 Place each chicken breast half, boned side down, between two pieces of plastic wrap. Using the flat side of a meat mallet and working from the center out, pound each half lightly into a rectangle about ⅛ inch thick. Remove plastic wrap.

3 Brush tops of chicken breast halves with the remaining 1 tablespoon oil. On boned side of each breast half, place a slice of mozzarella cheese and some of the cooked onion.

4 In a small bowl combine garlic powder and pepper; sprinkle evenly over cheese and onion on chicken breast halves.

5 Fold in sides and bottoms of chicken breast halves; roll up each piece into a spiral, pressing edges to seal. Brush chicken rolls with sherry. In a shallow bowl combine bread crumbs, Romano cheese, oregano, and onion salt. Roll chicken roll-ups in bread crumb mixture to coat. Place in prepared pan or dish. Drizzle with melted butter.

6 Bake, uncovered, for 20 to 25 minutes or until chicken is no longer pink. Meanwhile, in a medium saucepan cook and stir the pasta sauce over medium heat until heated through. Serve chicken roll-ups with warmed pasta sauce and, if desired, hot cooked fettuccine.

Makes 6 servings.

Nutrition Facts per serving: 429 cal., 18 g total fat (8 g sat. fat), 122 mg chol., 1,257 mg sodium, 19 g carbo., 4 g fiber, 44 g pro.

CHILE RELLEÑOS CHICKEN

This signature dish of Mexican restaurants will have your family saying muchas gracias! Seasoned rice and refried beans are the perfect sides.

Prep: 25 minutes **Bake:** 40 minutes **Oven:** 375°F

- 8 skinless, boneless chicken breast halves (about 2½ pounds total)
- 1 cup shredded taco cheese or cheddar cheese (4 ounces)
- ¼ cup finely chopped onion
- ¼ cup snipped fresh cilantro (optional)
- 2 teaspoons chili powder
- 8 canned whole green chile peppers, drained
- 2 eggs, beaten
- 2 tablespoons milk
- ½ cup fine dry bread crumbs
- 1 teaspoon salt

1 Preheat oven to 375°F. Place each chicken breast half, boned side down, between two pieces of plastic wrap. Using the flat side of a meat mallet and working from the center out, pound each half lightly into a rectangle about ¼ inch thick. Remove plastic wrap. Set chicken aside.

2 In a small bowl combine cheese, onion, cilantro (if desired), and half of the chili powder. Stuff some of the cheese mixture into each whole chile pepper.

3 Place a stuffed chile pepper on top of each flattened chicken breast. Roll up chicken around chile pepper, folding in sides. If necessary, secure with wooden toothpicks.

4 In a shallow dish combine eggs and milk. In another shallow dish stir together bread crumbs, the salt, and the remaining chili powder. Dip chicken rolls in egg mixture; coat with bread crumb mixture.

5 Place chicken rolls in an ungreased 9×13-inch baking pan or baking dish. Bake, uncovered, about 40 minutes or until chicken is no longer pink.

Makes 8 servings.

Nutrition Facts per serving: 266 cal., 4 g total fat (4 g sat. fat), 149 mg chol., 720 mg sodium, 6 g carbo., 1 g fiber, 36 g pro.

Make-Ahead Directions: *Prepare as directed through step 4. Cover and chill for up to 2 hours. Bake as directed in step 5.*

BAKED CHICKEN MARSALA

Marsala is an Italian wine fortified with brandy. It adds a rich, smoky flavor to chicken that's baked to perfection with a mozzarella and Parmesan cheese topping.

Prep: 30 minutes **Bake:** 20 minutes **Oven:** 375°F

- 8 skinless, boneless chicken breast halves (about 2 pounds total)
- ⅓ cup all-purpose flour
- 6 tablespoons butter or margarine
- 2 cups sliced fresh mushrooms
- 1 cup dry Marsala
- ⅔ cup chicken broth
- ⅛ teaspoon salt
- ⅛ teaspoon black pepper
- 1 cup shredded mozzarella or fontina cheese (4 ounces)
- ⅔ cup grated Parmesan cheese
- ½ cup thinly sliced green onions

1 Preheat oven to 375°F. Cut each chicken breast half in half lengthwise. Place each chicken breast piece, boned side down, between two pieces of plastic wrap. Using the flat side of a meat mallet and working from the center out, pound each piece into a rectangle about ⅛ inch thick. Remove plastic wrap. Coat chicken lightly with flour.

2 In a 12-inch skillet melt 2 tablespoons of the butter over medium heat. Add half of the chicken pieces. Cook for 4 minutes, turning once. Transfer to an ungreased 9×13-inch baking pan or baking dish. Repeat with another 2 tablespoons of the butter and the remaining chicken pieces.

3 Melt the remaining 2 tablespoons butter in the skillet; add mushrooms. Cook and stir until tender; stir in Marsala, broth, salt, and pepper. Bring to boiling; boil gently about 5 minutes or until mixture is reduced to 1 cup (including the mushrooms). Pour reduced mixture over the chicken.

4 In a medium bowl combine mozzarella cheese, Parmesan cheese, and green onions; sprinkle over the chicken. Bake, uncovered, about 20 minutes or until chicken is no longer pink.

Makes 8 servings.

Nutrition Facts per serving: 364 cal., 17 g total fat (9 g sat. fat), 121 mg chol., 496 mg sodium, 6 g carbo., 0 g fiber, 42 g pro.

CRAB-STUFFED CHICKEN

Tablecloth, candles, and dinner at eight—when the occasion calls for something special, this perfectly elegant and delectable dish is what you want.

Prep: 45 minutes **Bake:** 35 minutes **Oven:** 350°F

- 8 skinless, boneless chicken breast halves (about 2½ pounds total)
- 3 tablespoons butter
- ¼ cup all-purpose flour
- ¾ cup milk
- ¾ cup chicken broth
- ⅓ cup dry white wine
- 1 tablespoon butter or margarine
- 1 cup chopped fresh mushrooms
- ¼ cup chopped onion
- 1 6¼-ounce can crabmeat, drained, flaked, and cartilage removed
- ½ cup coarsely crushed saltine crackers (10 crackers)
- 2 tablespoons snipped fresh parsley
- ½ teaspoon salt
- Dash black pepper
- 2 tablespoons butter
- 1 cup shredded Swiss cheese (4 ounces)
- ½ teaspoon paprika

1 Preheat oven to 350°F. Place each chicken breast half, boned side down, between two pieces of plastic wrap. Using the flat side of a meat mallet and working from the center out, pound each half lightly into a rectangle about ⅛ inch thick. Remove plastic wrap. Set chicken aside.

2 In a medium saucepan melt the 3 tablespoons butter over medium heat; stir in flour. Add milk, chicken broth, and wine all at once; cook and stir until thickened and bubbly. Set aside.

3 In a medium skillet melt the 1 tablespoon butter over medium heat. Add mushrooms and onion; cook until tender. Stir in crabmeat, crushed crackers, parsley, salt, and pepper. Stir in 2 tablespoons of the wine mixture. Top each chicken piece with about ¼ cup of the crab-mushroom mixture. Fold in sides; roll up. If necessary, secure with wooden toothpicks. In a large skillet melt the 2 tablespoons butter over medium heat. Cook the chicken roll-ups in hot butter, half at a time, until browned on all sides.

4 Place chicken roll-ups, seam sides down, in an ungreased 9×13-inch baking pan or baking dish. Pour remaining wine mixture over all. Bake, covered, about 35 minutes or until chicken is no longer pink. Uncover; sprinkle with Swiss cheese and paprika. Bake about 2 minutes more or until cheese is melted.

5 Transfer chicken to a serving platter. Whisk mixture in baking pan or dish; pass with chicken.

Makes 8 servings.

Nutrition Facts per serving: 367 cal., 16 g total fat (9 g sat. fat), 140 mg chol., 542 mg sodium, 9 g carbo., 1 g fiber, 43 g pro.

208

SPINACH-STUFFED CHICKEN ROLLS

These rolls are as good served cold as they are hot. For an impressive presentation, slice the chicken breasts and serve each one on a bed of rice pilaf with sauteed cherry tomatoes on the side.

Prep: 40 minutes   **Bake:** 20 minutes   **Oven:** 350°F

- ⅔ cup chopped onion
- ⅔ cup chopped fresh mushrooms
- 2 cloves garlic, minced
- 2 tablespoons butter or margarine
- 1 10-ounce package frozen chopped spinach, thawed and well drained
- ¾ teaspoon dried oregano, crushed
- ½ teaspoon salt
- ¼ teaspoon black pepper
- 8 skinless, boneless chicken breast halves (about 2½ pounds total)
- ⅔ cup fine dry bread crumbs
- ¼ cup grated Parmesan cheese
- ½ teaspoon paprika
- 2 eggs, beaten
- 1 tablespoon water
- 3 tablespoons butter or margarine, melted

1 Preheat oven to 350°F. Lightly grease a 9×13-inch baking pan or baking dish; set aside. For filling, in a large skillet cook onion, mushrooms, and garlic in the 2 tablespoons hot butter until tender. Stir in spinach, oregano, salt, and pepper; set aside.

2 Place each chicken breast half, boned side down, between two pieces of plastic wrap. Using the flat side of a meat mallet and working from the center out, pound each half lightly into a rectangle about ⅛ inch thick. Remove plastic wrap.

3 Divide the filling evenly among the breast halves. Fold in sides; roll up each piece into a spiral, pressing edges to seal. If necessary, secure with wooden toothpicks.

4 In a shallow dish combine bread crumbs, Parmesan cheese, and paprika. In another shallow dish combine eggs and the water. Dip chicken rolls in the egg mixture; coat with bread crumb mixture. Place rolls, seam sides down, in prepared pan or dish. Drizzle with the melted butter.

5 Bake, uncovered, for 20 to 25 minutes or until chicken is no longer pink.

Makes 8 servings.

Nutrition Facts per serving: 302 cal., 12 g total fat [6 g sat. fat], 156 mg chol., 610 mg sodium, 10 g carbo., 2 g fiber, 38 g pro.

SWEET-AND-SOUR BAKED CHICKEN

Baking makes classic sweet-and-sour chicken easier to make—and more totable. For a family dinner, serve this with hot cooked rice.

Prep: 25 minutes **Bake:** 30 minutes **Oven:** 350°F

- 8 **skinless, boneless chicken breast halves (about 2½ pounds total)**
-    **Salt**
-    **Black pepper**
- 2 **tablespoons cooking oil**
- 1 **20-ounce can pineapple chunks (juice pack)**
- 1 **cup canned jellied cranberry sauce**
- ¼ **cup cornstarch**
- ¼ **cup packed brown sugar**
- ¼ **cup rice vinegar or cider vinegar**
- ¼ **cup frozen orange juice concentrate, thawed**
- ¼ **cup dry sherry, chicken broth, or water**
- ¼ **cup soy sauce**
- ½ **teaspoon ground ginger**
- 2 **medium green sweet peppers, seeded and cut into bite-size strips**

1 Preheat oven to 350°F. Sprinkle chicken lightly with salt and pepper. In a large skillet heat oil over medium-high heat. Add chicken and cook about 4 minutes or until browned, turning once. (If necessary, brown chicken in batches.) Transfer chicken to an ungreased 9×13-inch baking pan or baking dish. Drain pineapple well, reserving ⅔ cup juice. Spoon pineapple chunks evenly over chicken in pan or dish; set aside.

2 For sauce, in a medium saucepan whisk together the reserved pineapple juice, the cranberry sauce, cornstarch, brown sugar, vinegar, orange juice concentrate, sherry, soy sauce, and ginger. Cook and stir over medium heat until thickened and bubbly. Pour over chicken and pineapple in dish.

3 Bake, covered, for 25 minutes. Uncover and add sweet peppers, stirring gently to coat with sauce. Bake about 5 minutes more or until chicken is no longer pink (170°F).

Makes 8 servings.

Nutrition Facts per serving: 354 cal., 5 g total fat (1 g sat. fat), 82 mg chol., 669 mg sodium, 37 g carbo., 2 g fiber, 34 g pro.

CITRUS-MARINATED TURKEY BREAST
WITH CILANTRO DIPPING SAUCE

With a splash of citrus, fresh cilantro, and the kick of jalapeño, this turkey delivers all the sunny flavors of the Southwest.

Prep: 30 minutes **Marinate:** 8 to 24 hours **Roast:** 1 hour 20 minutes **Stand:** 10 minutes **Oven:** 400°F/350°F

- 1 **3- to 3½-pound fresh or frozen bone-in turkey breast half**
- 1 **cup lightly packed fresh cilantro leaves (about ¾ ounce)**
- ⅔ **cup orange juice**
- ¼ **cup lemon juice**
- 6 **cloves garlic, halved**
- 1 **small fresh jalapeño chile pepper, seeded and cut up***
- 1 **teaspoon salt**
- 1 **teaspoon ground cumin**
- ¼ **teaspoon freshly ground black pepper**
- ¾ **cup olive oil**
  Nonstick cooking spray

1 Thaw turkey, if frozen. Using tip of a sharp knife, prick turkey breast in several spots. Place turkey breast half, skin side down, in a very large resealable plastic bag set in a baking dish. Set aside.

2 For cilantro sauce, in a food processor or blender combine cilantro, orange juice, lemon juice, garlic, chile pepper, salt, cumin, and black pepper. Cover and process until almost smooth. With food processor or blender running, slowly add oil in a thin stream. Pour 1 cup of the cilantro sauce into an airtight container. Cover and refrigerate until serving time. Pour the remaining cilantro sauce over turkey breast half. Seal bag; turn to coat turkey. Marinate in the refrigerator for at least 8 hours or up to 24 hours, turning bag occasionally.

3 Preheat oven to 400°F. Coat a 9×13-inch baking pan or baking dish and a roasting rack with nonstick cooking spray. Remove turkey from marinade; discard marinade. Place turkey, bone side down, on the rack in prepared pan or dish. Insert an oven-going meat thermometer into thickest part of the turkey breast half, making sure tip of the thermometer does not touch bone.

4 Roast, uncovered, for 20 minutes. Reduce oven temperature to 350°F. Roast turkey for 1 to 1½ hours more or until thermometer registers 170°F, juices run clear, and turkey is no longer pink. If necessary to prevent overbrowning, cover with foil for the last 15 minutes of roasting. Cover with foil; let stand for 10 minutes before carving. Stir the chilled cilantro sauce; pass with turkey.

Makes 5 or 6 servings.

Nutrition Facts per serving: 612 cal., 39 g total fat (6 g sat. fat), 167 mg chol., 563 mg sodium, 7 g carbo., 1 g fiber, 58 g pro.

*Test Kitchen Tip: *Because chile peppers contain volatile oils that can burn your skin and eyes, avoid direct contact with them as much as possible. When working with chile peppers, wear plastic or rubber gloves. If your bare hands do touch the peppers, wash your hands and nails well with soap and warm water.*

HONEY MUSTARD-GLAZED TURKEY BREAST

Make this for dinner one day
and then layer it with cheese and all the
trimmings for terrific sandwiches the next.

Prep: 20 minutes **Roast:** 1¼ hours **Stand:** 10 minutes **Oven:** 325°F

- 1 **2- to 2½-pound fresh or frozen bone-in turkey breast portion**
- 1 **tablespoon cooking oil**
- ¼ **teaspoon salt**
- ⅛ **teaspoon black pepper**
- 1 **recipe Honey-Mustard Glaze**

1 Thaw turkey, if frozen. Preheat oven to 325°F. Place turkey breast portion, bone side down, on a roasting rack in an ungreased 9×13-inch baking pan or baking dish. Brush with oil; sprinkle with salt and pepper. Insert an oven-going meat thermometer into thickest part of the breast, making sure tip of the thermometer does not touch bone.

2 Roast turkey, uncovered, for 1¼ to 1½ hours or until juices run clear and turkey is no longer pink (170°F), brushing with Honey-Mustard Glaze several times during the last 15 minutes of roasting. Transfer turkey to a cutting board; let stand for 10 to 15 minutes before carving. Heat any remaining glaze until bubbly; serve with turkey.

Makes 6 servings.

Nutrition Facts per serving: 282 cal., 13 g total fat (4 g sat. fat), 88 mg chol., 268 mg sodium, 13 g carbo., 0 g fiber, 28 g pro.

212

Honey-Mustard Glaze: *In a small bowl stir together ¼ cup honey, 1 tablespoon Dijon-style mustard, 1 tablespoon Worcestershire-style marinade for chicken, and 1 tablespoon butter or margarine, melted.*

Maple Barbecue-Glazed Turkey Breast: *Prepare as directed, except omit Honey-Mustard Glaze. In a small saucepan stir together ¼ cup pure maple syrup, 1 tablespoon bottled chili sauce, 1 tablespoon cider vinegar, 2 teaspoons Worcestershire sauce, ¼ teaspoon dry mustard, and ¼ teaspoon black pepper. Heat and stir over medium heat until slightly thickened. Brush on turkey several times during the last 15 minutes of roasting. Heat any remaining glaze until bubbly; serve with turkey.*

Nutrition Facts per serving: 264 cal., 11 g total fat (2 g sat.fat), 88 mg chol., 268 mg sodium, 13 g carbo., 0 g fiber, 28 g pro.

PESTO-RUBBED TURKEY BREAST

Italian favorites, pesto and fresh sage, are placed under the skin, so the turkey breast gets the full intensity of their flavors as it roasts.

Prep: 25 minutes   **Roast:** 1 hour 35 minutes   **Stand:** 10 minutes   **Oven:** 400°F/350°F

1   3- to 3½-pound fresh or frozen bone-in turkey breast half

Nonstick cooking spray

1   7-ounce container refrigerated basil pesto or half of a 10-ounce jar pesto

3   tablespoons finely chopped fresh sage

2   tablespoons finely chopped walnuts

¼   teaspoon salt

¼   teaspoon black pepper

1 Thaw turkey, if frozen. Preheat oven to 400°F. Coat a 9×13-inch baking pan or baking dish and a roasting rack with nonstick cooking spray. Place turkey breast half, bone side down, on the rack in prepared pan or dish; set aside.

2 In a medium bowl combine pesto, sage, walnuts, salt, and pepper; mix well. Reserve half of the pesto mixture to pass with turkey; cover and chill until serving time.

3 Starting at the breast bone of the turkey breast half, slip your fingers between skin and meat to loosen skin, leaving skin attached at top. Rub about two-thirds of the remaining pesto mixture between the skin and meat. Rub remaining pesto mixture over the skin. Insert an oven-going meat thermometer into thickest part of breast, making sure tip of the thermometer does not touch bone.

4 Roast, uncovered, for 20 minutes. Reduce oven temperature to 350°F. Roast for 1¼ to 1½ hours more or until thermometer registers 170°F, juices run clear, and turkey is no longer pink. If necessary to prevent overbrowning, cover with foil for the last 30 to 45 minutes of roasting. Cover with foil; let stand for 10 minutes before carving. Serve with the reserved pesto mixture.

Makes 5 or 6 servings.

Nutrition Facts per serving: 439 cal., 19 g total fat [4 g sat. fat], 145 mg chol., 560 mg sodium, 6 g carbo., 2 g fiber, 58 g pro.

213

Spice-Rubbed Turkey Breast: *Prepare as directed in step 1. Omit pesto, sage, walnuts, salt, and pepper. In a small bowl combine 1 tablespoon packed brown sugar, 1 teaspoon garlic powder, 1 teaspoon salt, 1 teaspoon paprika, 1 teaspoon ground cumin, ¾ teaspoon chili powder, and ½ teaspoon black pepper. Loosen skin of turkey breast half as directed in step 3. Lift skin and spread spice mixture evenly under skin over breast meat. (If desired, you can rub some of the spice mixture onto the outside of the turkey breast for a crusty appearance.) Roast as directed in step 4, except spoon the pan juices over the turkey breast occasionally.*

Nutrition Facts per serving: 256 cal., 2 g total fat [0 g sat. fat], 133 mg chol., 577 mg sodium, 4 g carbo., 1 g fiber, 53 g pro.

HAZELNUT-CRUSTED TURKEY BREAST

If your family prefers white meat over dark, a roasted turkey breast is ideal. This one gets special treatment with a crunchy crust of nuts and spice.

Prep: 20 minutes **Roast:** 1½ hours **Stand:** 15 minutes **Oven:** 375°F

- 1 **3- to 3½-pound fresh or frozen bone-in turkey breast half**
- 1 **tablespoon olive oil or cooking oil**
- 1 **clove garlic, minced**
- ¼ **teaspoon salt**
- ½ **cup hazelnuts (filberts)**
- ½ **teaspoon ground coriander**
- ¼ **teaspoon coarsely ground black pepper**
- ⅛ **teaspoon ground cinnamon**
- ¼ **cup orange marmalade**

1 Thaw turkey, if frozen. Preheat oven to 375°F. Lightly grease a 9×13-inch baking pan or baking dish and a roasting rack. Remove skin from turkey breast. Place turkey breast on the rack in prepared pan or dish. In a small bowl combine oil, garlic, and salt. Brush oil mixture over turkey breast. Insert an oven-going meat thermometer into thickest part of the breast, making sure tip of the thermometer does not touch bone. Roast, uncovered, for 45 minutes.

2 Meanwhile, place hazelnuts in a blender or food processor. Cover and blend or process until finely chopped. Transfer nuts to a small bowl; stir in coriander, pepper, and cinnamon. Set aside.

3 Remove turkey breast from oven. Brush surface with orange marmalade. Sprinkle with nut mixture; press gently so nuts adhere to the turkey breast. Continue roasting for 45 to 60 minutes more or until thermometer registers 170°F. Remove from oven.

4 Cover with foil; let stand for 15 minutes before carving.

Makes 6 to 8 servings.

Nutrition Facts per serving: 374 cal., 14 g total fat (2 g sat. fat), 140 mg chol., 200 mg sodium, 11 g carbo., 1 g fiber, 49 g pro.

BBQ SPICE-RUBBED TURKEY BREAST

A spicy rub goes under the skin of the turkey to infuse the breast with flavor. Cranberries give the barbecue sauce zing.

Prep: 25 minutes   **Roast:** 1 hour 20 minutes   **Stand:** 10 minutes   **Oven:** 400°F/350°F

- 1 3- to 3½-pound fresh or frozen bone-in turkey breast half
- Nonstick cooking spray
- 1 tablespoon packed dark brown sugar
- 1 teaspoon paprika
- 1 teaspoon garlic powder
- ¾ teaspoon salt
- ½ teaspoon ground cumin
- ½ teaspoon chili powder
- ¼ teaspoon freshly ground black pepper
- 1 tablespoon cooking oil
- ½ cup chopped onion
- ½ of a 16-ounce can whole cranberry sauce
- 3 tablespoons bottled chili sauce
- 2 teaspoons cider vinegar
- ½ teaspoon Worcestershire sauce
- ⅛ teaspoon freshly ground black pepper

1 Thaw turkey, if frozen. Preheat oven to 400°F. Coat a 9×13-inch baking pan or baking dish and a roasting rack with nonstick cooking spray. In a small bowl combine brown sugar, paprika, garlic powder, salt, cumin, chili powder, and the ¼ teaspoon pepper. Place turkey breast half, bone side down, on the rack in prepared pan or dish.

2 Starting at breast bone, slip your fingers between the skin and meat to loosen skin, leaving skin attached at top. Lift skin and spread brown sugar mixture evenly under skin over breast meat. Insert an oven-going meat thermometer into thickest part of the breast, making sure tip of the thermometer does not touch bone.

3 Roast, uncovered, on the lowest rack of the oven for 20 minutes. Reduce oven temperature to 350°F. Roast for 1 to 1½ hours more or until thermometer registers 170°F, juices run clear, and turkey is no longer pink, occasionally spooning pan juices over turkey. Cover with foil; let stand for 10 minutes before carving.

4 Meanwhile, for sauce, in a medium saucepan heat oil over medium heat. Add onion; cook and stir about 5 minutes or until tender. Stir in cranberry sauce, chili sauce, vinegar, Worcestershire sauce, and the ⅛ teaspoon pepper. Bring to boiling; reduce heat. Simmer, uncovered, about 5 minutes or until thickened, stirring occasionally. Serve with the turkey.

Makes 6 servings.

Nutrition Facts per serving: 349 cal., 7 g total fat (2 g sat. fat), 139 mg chol., 631 mg sodium, 21 g carbo., 1 g fiber, 48 g pro.

Test Kitchen Tip: *To simplify the preparation, you can rub the brown sugar mixture onto the outside of the turkey breast for a crusty appearance. To prevent burning, cover turkey breast with foil for the last 30 minutes of roasting.*

PROSCIUTTO-STUFFED TURKEY BREAST

This is it—spirals of moist turkey filled with prosciutto and dressing—the perfect recipe for your next dinner party. Not only are the flavors sensational, so is the look.

Prep: 30 minutes   **Roast:** 1¼ hours   **Stand:** 10 minutes   **Oven:** 375°F

- 1 **2- to 2½-pound fresh or frozen bone-in turkey breast half**
- 1 **large leek, thinly sliced (about ½ cup)**
- 4 **teaspoons olive oil or cooking oil**
- ⅓ **cup pine nuts, toasted**
- ¼ **cup grated Parmesan cheese**
- 2 **tablespoons snipped fresh sage or 2 teaspoons dried sage, crushed**
- 2 **tablespoons snipped fresh parsley**
- 2 **ounces thinly sliced prosciutto or cooked ham**
- ¾ **cup chicken broth**
- ¼ **cup dry white wine**

1 Thaw turkey, if frozen. Preheat oven to 375°F. For stuffing, in a small saucepan cook sliced leek in 2 teaspoons of the hot oil until tender. In a small bowl combine cooked leek, nuts, Parmesan cheese, sage, and parsley. Set aside.

2 Remove skin from turkey in one piece; set skin aside. Remove bone. Place breast half, skinned side down, between two pieces of plastic wrap. Using the flat side of a meat mallet, pound to ½-inch thickness.

3 To stuff, arrange prosciutto on top of turkey. Spoon stuffing onto prosciutto. Starting with a short side, roll up turkey and stuffing. Wrap the skin piece around turkey. Tie with 100%-cotton kitchen string. Place on a roasting rack in an ungreased 9×13-inch baking pan or baking dish. Brush with the remaining 2 teaspoons oil. Insert an oven-going meat thermometer into thickest part of turkey breast, making sure tip of the thermometer does not touch bone.

4 Roast, uncovered, for 1¼ to 1½ hours or until thermometer registers 170°F, juices run clear, and turkey is no longer pink. Transfer turkey to a serving platter, reserving 2 tablespoons of the pan drippings. Cover turkey with foil; let stand for 10 minutes before carving.

5 For sauce, spoon reserved pan drippings into a small saucepan. Stir in broth and wine. Bring to boiling; reduce heat. Boil gently about 8 minutes or until reduced to about ½ cup. Serve with turkey.

Makes 6 servings.

Nutrition Facts per serving: 323 cal., 19 g total fat (5 g sat. fat), 93 mg chol., 488 mg sodium, 3 g carbo., 0 g fiber, 34 g pro.

MUSTARD AND GARLIC ROASTED
TURKEY BREAST

Apricot spreadable fruit enhanced with mustard and garlic bastes this turkey breast so it roasts up to a gorgeous color and has just a hint of sweetness.

Prep: 15 minutes   **Roast:** 1¼ hours   **Stand:** 10 minutes   **Oven:** 325°F

- 1 1½- to 2-pound fresh or frozen bone-in turkey breast portion
- 2 tablespoons butter, melted
- ¼ teaspoon salt
- ¼ teaspoon black pepper
- ¼ cup apricot or peach spreadable fruit
- 2 tablespoons coarse-grain brown mustard
- 1½ teaspoons bottled roasted minced garlic

1 Thaw turkey, if frozen. Preheat oven to 325°F. Place turkey breast, bone side down, on a roasting rack in an ungreased 9×13-inch baking pan or baking dish. Brush with 1 tablespoon of the melted butter; sprinkle with salt and pepper. Insert an oven-going meat thermometer into the thickest part of the breast, making sure tip of the thermometer does not touch bone.

2 For glaze, in a small bowl combine the remaining 1 tablespoon butter, the apricot spreadable fruit, mustard, and roasted garlic; set glaze aside.

3 Roast turkey, uncovered, for 1¼ to 1½ hours or until thermometer registers 170°F, juices run clear, and turkey is no longer pink, brushing with glaze several times during the last 15 minutes of roasting. Cover turkey with foil; let stand for 10 minutes before carving.

Makes 4 to 6 servings.

Nutrition Facts per serving: 235 cal., 8 g total fat (3 g sat. fat), 104 mg chol., 254 mg sodium, 9 g carbo., 0 g fiber, 32 g pro.

CORNISH GAME HENS WITH PORT SAUCE

It's always festive to serve guests their own little hen, especially when served with this lively sauce of port, ginger, and blackberry spreadable fruit.

Prep: 20 minutes **Roast:** 55 minutes **Oven:** 375°F

- 2 **1½-pound fresh or frozen Cornish game hens**
- 1 **tablespoon olive oil**
- 1 **recipe Port Sauce**

1 Thaw hens, if frozen. Preheat oven to 375°F. To split hens in half, use kitchen shears to cut out backbone. Lay hens open and use kitchen shears or a large kitchen knife to cut through the breast bone, just off center. Twist wing tips under backs. Place split hens, cut sides down, on a roasting rack in an ungreased 9×13-inch baking pan or baking dish. (Or roast hens whole, breast sides up.) Brush with oil.

2 Roast hens, uncovered, until drumsticks move easily in sockets and juices run clear. Allow 55 to 60 minutes for split hens or 1 to 1¼ hours for whole hens.

3 While hens roast, prepare Port Sauce. Brush hens with Port Sauce during the last 10 to 15 minutes of roasting. Reheat remaining Port Sauce to boiling; serve with hens.

Makes 4 servings.

Nutrition Facts per serving: 473 cal., 26 g total fat (5 g sat. fat), 120 mg chol., 150 mg sodium, 21 g carbo., 0 g fiber, 36 g pro.

218

Port Sauce: *In a small saucepan combine ½ cup orange juice; ⅓ cup water; ¼ cup port wine; ¼ cup blackberry spreadable fruit; 2 tablespoons sherry vinegar; 2 tablespoons minced shallot or chopped onion; 2 teaspoons grated fresh ginger; 2 cloves garlic, minced; ½ teaspoon dried thyme, crushed; ¼ teaspoon instant chicken bouillon granules; ¼ teaspoon cayenne pepper (if desired); and 1 bay leaf. Bring to boiling; reduce heat. Simmer, uncovered, for 5 to 7 minutes or until reduced to 1 cup. Strain port mixture; return to saucepan. In a small bowl stir 2 tablespoons cold water into 1 tablespoon cornstarch. Stir into port mixture. Cook and stir until bubbly. Serve immediately or cover and chill for up to 2 days. If chilled, in a small saucepan reheat sauce over low heat before serving.*

THAI PEANUT CORNISH GAME HENS

This delicious Asian-inspired recipe calls for specialty ingredients, such as red curry paste and unsweetened coconut milk, that may not be available at your local supermarket. Check at a nearby Asian food store.

Prep: 45 minutes **Bake:** 1 hour 50 minutes **Oven:** 300°F

- 2   1- to 1½-pound fresh or frozen Cornish game hens, halved
- 1   13½-ounce can unsweetened coconut milk
- ¼   cup creamy peanut butter
- ⅓   cup chicken broth
- 2   tablespoons soy sauce
- 2   tablespoons rice vinegar
- 1   tablespoon packed brown sugar
- 1   tablespoon toasted sesame oil
- 1   teaspoon red curry paste
- 1   clove garlic, minced
- 1   teaspoon grated fresh ginger
- ⅛   teaspoon cayenne pepper
- ⅔   cup all-purpose flour
- ½   teaspoon salt
- ½   teaspoon black pepper
- 2   tablespoons cooking oil
- 2   tablespoons snipped fresh cilantro
    Hot cooked rice

1 Thaw hens, if frozen; set aside. In a medium saucepan whisk together coconut milk and peanut butter until smooth. Add chicken broth, soy sauce, rice vinegar, brown sugar, sesame oil, curry paste, garlic, ginger, and cayenne pepper. Whisk until smooth. Heat over medium-high heat just until boiling; reduce heat. Simmer, uncovered, for 15 minutes, stirring occasionally.

2 Preheat oven to 300°F. In a heavy large resealable plastic bag combine flour, salt, and black pepper. Add hen halves, one at a time, to flour mixture; close bag and shake to coat. In a large skillet brown hen halves, two to four at a time, in hot oil, turning to brown evenly. Arrange browned halves, meaty sides up, in an ungreased 9×13-inch baking pan or baking dish. Pour peanut butter mixture over hen halves. Cover pan or dish loosely with foil. Bake for 1½ hours, occasionally spooning sauce over hen halves. Remove foil. Bake, uncovered, for 20 to 30 minutes more or until very tender.

3 To serve, arrange hen halves on a serving platter. Skim fat from sauce in pan or dish. Spoon some of the sauce over hen halves. Sprinkle with cilantro. Serve with the remaining sauce and hot cooked rice.

Makes 4 servings.

Nutrition Facts per serving: 718 cal., 45 g total fat (24 g sat. fat), 89 mg chol., 1,091 mg sodium, 50 g carbo., 5 g fiber, 29 g pro.

219

MAPLE-GLAZED STUFFED CORNISH HENS

Make this the star of an autumn or winter dinner. Pair its homey flavors with green beans or broccoli and a tossed salad.

Prep: 30 minutes   **Roast:** 1 hour   **Stand:** 10 minutes   **Oven:** 375°F

- 2 1¼- to 1½-pound fresh or frozen Cornish game hens
- 2 slices bacon
- 1 small leek or 2 green onions, thinly sliced
- 2 tablespoons chopped pecans or walnuts
- ⅛ teaspoon dried thyme or marjoram, crushed
   Dash black pepper
- 1 cup dry bread cubes (1½ slices bread)
- 1 to 2 tablespoons water
   Salt
   Black pepper
- 1 teaspoon butter or margarine, melted
- 2 tablespoons maple-flavored syrup, pure maple syrup, or apricot syrup
- 1 tablespoon butter or margarine, melted
- 2 teaspoons Dijon-style mustard or 1 teaspoon brown mustard

1 Thaw hens, if frozen; set aside. In a medium skillet cook bacon until crisp. Remove bacon and drain on paper towels. Crumble bacon and set aside. Reserve 1 tablespoon of the bacon drippings in skillet.

2 Cook leek and nuts in reserved bacon drippings over medium heat until leek is tender and nuts are toasted; remove from heat. Stir in crumbled bacon, thyme, and the dash pepper. Stir in bread cubes. Drizzle just enough of the water over bread mixture to moisten, tossing lightly until mixed.

3 Preheat oven to 375°F. Lightly season the cavities of the hens with salt and additional pepper. Lightly stuff the hens with the bread mixture. Skewer neck skin, if present, to back of each hen. Twist wing tips under backs. Using 100%-cotton kitchen string, tie legs to tail. Place hens, breast sides up, on a roasting rack in an ungreased 9×13-inch baking pan. Brush with the 1 teaspoon melted butter. Cover loosely with foil. Roast for 1 to 1¼ hours or until tender, no longer pink, and an instant-read thermometer inserted in an inside thigh muscle (not touching bone) registers 180°F.

4 Meanwhile, in a small bowl stir together syrup, the 1 tablespoon melted butter, and the mustard. Uncover hens and brush frequently with the syrup mixture during the last 15 minutes of roasting.

5 Remove hens from oven. Cover hens with foil; let stand for 10 minutes before serving. To serve, use kitchen shears or a long heavy knife to carefully cut each hen in half lengthwise.

Makes 4 servings.

Nutrition Facts per serving: 511 cal., 35 g total fat (11 g sat. fat), 191 mg chol., 385 mg sodium, 16 g carbo., 1 g fiber, 32 g pro.

FISH, SEAFOOD, AND VEGETARIAN DISHES

Today's families like to mix it up. Maybe a meal without meat. Or fish one night, vegetarian the next. Enjoyable meals are all about variety, just like this chapter. You'll find old favorites with new twists, creative and fresh combinations, a range of ethnic to familiar flavors, and one delicious choice after another.

MUSHROOM-DILL BAKED SNAPPER

Dill is a natural pairing for fish. Here it blends with mustard, mushrooms, and spinach for a tasty sauce. If you can't find snapper, any firm white fish will work.

Prep: 20 minutes   **Cook:** 40 minutes   **Bake:** 25 minutes   **Oven:** 375°F

- 2 **pounds fresh or frozen skinless red snapper fillets**
- **Salt**
- **Black pepper**
- 5 **tablespoons butter or margarine**
- 4 **cups sliced fresh mushrooms (about 10 ounces)**
- 1 **cup chopped red onion**
- 2 **cloves garlic, minced**
- 1 **cup whipping cream**
- ½ **cup dry white wine**
- 2 **tablespoons Dijon-style mustard**
- 1 **teaspoon dried dill, crushed**
- 1 **10-ounce package frozen chopped spinach, thawed and well drained**
- ¾ **cup fine dry bread crumbs**
- ¾ **cup grated Parmesan cheese**

1 Thaw fish, if frozen. Rinse fish; pat dry with paper towels. Cut fish fillets into six to eight serving-size portions. Lightly grease a 9×13-inch baking pan or baking dish. Place fish in prepared pan or dish. Sprinkle with salt and pepper. Set aside.

2 In a very large skillet melt 3 tablespoons of the butter over medium heat. Add mushrooms, red onion, and garlic. Cook about 10 minutes or until mushrooms are tender. Add whipping cream and dry white wine. Bring to boiling. Boil gently about 30 minutes or until mixture is reduced to about 1½ cups (mixture will thicken slightly). Stir in mustard and dill. Stir in spinach. Pour mushroom-spinach mixture over fish in pan or dish.

3 Meanwhile, preheat oven to 375°F. In a small saucepan melt the remaining 2 tablespoons butter. Stir in bread crumbs and Parmesan cheese. Sprinkle over mushroom-spinach mixture. Bake, uncovered, for 25 to 30 minutes or until fish flakes easily when tested with a fork.

Makes 6 to 8 servings.

Nutrition Facts per serving: 544 cal., 33 g total fat (17 g sat. fat), 146 mg chol., 968 mg sodium, 19 g carbo., 3 g fiber, 43 g pro.

CURRIED HALIBUT AND COUSCOUS CASSEROLE

An intriguing mix of curry, apples, and tomatoes tops halibut, a firm white, mild fish. Couscous is a North African staple used here as a bed for the fish.

Prep: 25 minutes **Bake:** 20 minutes **Oven:** 450°F

1½ **pounds fresh or frozen halibut steaks or cod fillets**

1 **tablespoon butter or margarine**

1½ **cups thinly sliced onion**

1 **to 2 teaspoons curry powder**

1 **large apple, cored and cut into thin wedges**

1 **cup chopped plum tomatoes**

¼ **teaspoon salt**

⅛ **teaspoon black pepper**

1 **10-ounce package couscous**

2½ **cups chicken broth**

Salt

Black pepper

Chutney (optional)

1 Thaw fish, if frozen. Rinse fish; pat dry with paper towels. If necessary, cut fish into six serving-size portions. Set aside. Preheat oven to 450°F.

2 In a large skillet melt butter over medium heat. Add onion; cook about 5 minutes or until tender. Stir in curry powder. Remove from heat. Stir in apple, tomatoes, the ¼ teaspoon salt, and the ⅛ teaspoon pepper. Set aside.

3 In an ungreased 9×13-inch baking dish combine uncooked couscous and broth. Arrange fish on top in a single layer. Sprinkle with additional salt and pepper. Top with onion-apple mixture.

4 Bake, covered, for 20 to 25 minutes or until fish flakes easily when tested with a fork. If desired, serve with chutney.

Makes 6 servings.

Nutrition Facts per serving: 358 cal., 5 g total fat (1 g sat. fat), 42 mg chol., 612 mg sodium, 45 g carbo., 4 g fiber, 31 g pro.

223

OVEN-ROASTED SALMON

The simplest of preparations lets salmon's rich taste shine. If wild salmon is available, use it. Serve the fish with fresh vegetables and roasted potatoes or rice.

Prep: 10 minutes **Roast:** 4 to 6 minutes per ½-inch thickness of fish **Oven:** 450°F

- 4 5- to 6-ounce fresh or frozen skinless salmon fillets
- 1 tablespoon olive oil or your favorite flavor oil
- 1 teaspoon seasoned salt or your favorite salt blend
- ¼ teaspoon freshly ground black pepper

1 Thaw fish, if frozen. Line a 9×13-inch baking pan or baking dish with parchment paper or foil; set aside. Preheat oven to 450°F. Rinse fish; pat dry with paper towels. Measure the thickest portion of the fillets. Brush fish with oil; sprinkle with seasoned salt and black pepper. Place fish in prepared pan or dish.

2 Bake, uncovered, for 4 to 6 minutes per ½-inch thickness of fish or until fish begins to flake when tested with a fork.

Makes 4 servings.

Nutrition Facts per serving: 195 cal., 8 g total fat (1 g sat. fat), 74 mg chol., 475 mg sodium, 0 g carbo., 0 g fiber, 28 g pro.

TUNA-NOODLE CASSEROLE

This popular dish has been updated with the addition of fresh mushrooms, sweet pepper, and green beans.

Prep: 30 minutes **Bake:** 30 minutes **Oven:** 350°F

- 8 **ounces dried medium noodles**
- 1 **16-ounce package frozen whole or cut green beans**
- ½ **cup fine dry bread crumbs**
- 2 **tablespoons butter or margarine, melted**
- 2 **tablespoons butter or margarine**
- 2 **cups sliced fresh mushrooms**
- 1½ **cups chopped red or green sweet pepper**
- 1 **cup chopped onion**
- 1 **cup sliced celery**
- 2 **cloves garlic, minced**
- 2 **10¾-ounce cans condensed cream of mushroom or cream of celery soup**
- 1 **cup milk**
- 1 **cup shredded process Swiss cheese or American cheese (4 ounces)**
- 2 **9¼-ounce cans tuna (water pack), drained and flaked**

1 Preheat oven to 350°F. Cook noodles according to package directions, adding the green beans for the last 3 minutes of cooking. Drain and set aside. Meanwhile, in a small bowl toss the bread crumbs with the 2 tablespoons melted butter; set aside.

2 In a 12-inch skillet melt 2 tablespoons butter over medium heat. Add mushrooms, sweet pepper, onion, celery, and garlic. Cook and stir until vegetables are tender. Add cream of mushroom soup, milk, and cheese, stirring until cheese is melted. Stir in tuna and the cooked noodles and green beans.

3 Spoon tuna mixture into an ungreased 9×13-inch baking pan or baking dish. Sprinkle bread crumb mixture around outside edge of pan or dish. Bake, uncovered, for 30 to 35 minutes or until heated through and bread crumbs are golden brown.

Makes 12 servings.

Nutrition Facts per serving: 306 cal., 13 g total fat (6 g sat. fat), 57 mg chol., 746 mg sodium, 28 g carbo., 3 g fiber, 19 g pro.

LOBSTER MANICOTTI WITH CHIVE CREAM SAUCE

Succulent lobster, red sweet peppers,
and broccoli make up the flavorful filling of
this elegant seafood dish.

Prep: 45 minutes **Bake:** 30 minutes **Oven:** 350°F

- 12 **dried manicotti shells**
- 1 **tablespoon butter or margarine**
- 1 **tablespoon all-purpose flour**
- 1¼ **cups milk**
- 1 **8-ounce tub cream cheese with chive and onion**
- ¼ **cup grated Romano or Parmesan cheese**
- 12 **ounces chopped cooked lobster or chunk-style imitation lobster (about 2⅔ cups)**
- 1 **10-ounce package frozen chopped broccoli, thawed and well drained**
- ½ **of a 7-ounce jar roasted red sweet peppers, drained and chopped, or one 4-ounce jar diced pimiento, drained**
- ¼ **teaspoon black pepper**
- **Paprika**

1 Preheat oven to 350°F. Cook the manicotti shells according to package directions. Drain; rinse with cold water. Drain again.

2 Meanwhile, for cheese sauce, in a medium saucepan melt butter over medium heat. Add flour and stir until combined. Add 1 cup of the milk. Cook and stir over medium heat until mixture is thickened and bubbly. Turn heat to low. Gradually add cream cheese, stirring until smooth. Stir in Romano cheese.

3 For filling, in a medium bowl combine ¾ cup of the cheese sauce, the lobster, broccoli, roasted sweet peppers, and black pepper. Using a small spoon, carefully fill each cooked manicotti shell with about ⅓ cup of the filling. Arrange the filled shells in an ungreased 9×13-inch baking pan or baking dish. Stir the remaining ¼ cup milk into the remaining cheese sauce. Pour over the shells. Sprinkle with paprika.

4 Bake, covered, for 30 to 40 minutes or until hot in the center.

Makes 6 servings.

Nutrition Facts per serving: 386 cal., 17 g total fat (11 g sat. fat), 90 mg chol., 471 mg sodium, 34 g carbo., 2 g fiber, 21 g pro.

226

CRAWFISH FETTUCCINE

Crawfish, sometimes called crayfish, is a Louisiana specialty that has a sweet rich flavor. Here it stars with fettuccine for a distinctive dinner. Another time substitute shrimp for the crawfish.

Prep: 25 minutes **Bake:** 20 minutes **Oven:** 350°F

- 1 pound fresh or frozen peeled, cooked crawfish tails*
- 1 pound dried fettuccine, broken
- 1 cup coarsely chopped green sweet pepper
- ¾ cup chopped onion
- 4 cloves garlic, minced
- ¼ cup butter or margarine
- 3 tablespoons all-purpose flour
- ¼ to ½ teaspoon cayenne pepper
- ¼ teaspoon salt
- 2 cups half-and-half, light cream, or milk
- 1½ cups shredded American cheese (6 ounces)
- 2 tablespoons snipped fresh parsley
- ⅓ cup grated Parmesan cheese

1 Thaw crawfish, if frozen; set aside. Preheat oven to 350°F. In a Dutch oven cook fettuccine according to package directions. Drain; return to Dutch oven.

2 Meanwhile, for sauce, in a large saucepan cook sweet pepper, onion, and garlic in hot butter about 5 minutes or until tender. Stir in flour, cayenne pepper, and salt. Add half-and-half all at once. Cook and stir over medium heat until thickened and bubbly. Add cheese, stirring until melted. Remove from heat; stir in crawfish and parsley.

3 Pour crawfish mixture over fettuccine, tossing gently to coat. Spoon mixture into an ungreased 9×13-inch baking pan or baking dish. Sprinkle with Parmesan cheese. Bake, covered, for 20 to 25 minutes or until heated through.

Makes 8 servings.

Nutrition Facts per serving: 506 cal., 22 g total fat (13 g sat. fat), 123 mg chol., 574 mg sodium, 51 g carbo., 2 g fiber, 25 g pro.

227

*Test Kitchen Tip: *If you aren't able to find peeled crawfish tails, purchase 4 pounds live whole, head-on crawfish. This will yield 1 pound peeled, cooked crawfish tails. Rinse crawfish under cold running water. In a 12- to 16-quart kettle combine 8 quarts water and ⅓ cup salt. Add crawfish; soak for 15 minutes. Rinse and drain crawfish. Discard liquid in kettle. Fill kettle with another 8 quarts water and 2 teaspoons salt; bring to boiling. Add crawfish. Simmer for 5 to 8 minutes or until shells turn red; drain. To peel crawfish, remove the meat from the shell by gently twisting the tail away from the body. Unwrap the first two or three sections of shell from the tail to expose more meat. Pinch the end of the tail and with the other hand pull out the meat. Allow about 1 hour to peel 4 pounds.*

SHRIMP, CHEESE, AND WILD RICE BAKE

To keep prep time to a minimum,
purchase cooked shrimp from your
supermarket's seafood counter or deli section.

Prep: 25 minutes **Bake:** 40 minutes **Stand:** 10 minutes **Oven:** 375°F

- 1 6-ounce package long grain and wild rice mix
- 1 cup chopped green sweet pepper
- 1 cup chopped celery
- 1 cup chopped onion
- ¼ cup butter or margarine
- 1 10¾-ounce can condensed cream of mushroom soup
- 1 cup shredded cheddar cheese (4 ounces)
- 1 cup shredded Swiss cheese (4 ounces)
- 1 to 1½ pounds cooked, peeled, and deveined shrimp
- ¼ teaspoon black pepper
- 2 lemons, very thinly sliced

1 Preheat oven to 375°F. Prepare rice mix according to package directions. Meanwhile, in a medium saucepan cook and stir sweet pepper, celery, and onion in hot butter about 5 minutes or just until tender.

2 In a very large bowl combine cooked rice, cooked vegetable mixture, cream of mushroom soup, cheddar cheese, and Swiss cheese. Stir in cooked shrimp.

3 Spoon mixture into an ungreased 9×13-inch baking pan or baking dish. Sprinkle with half of the black pepper. Arrange lemon slices over shrimp mixture. Sprinkle with the remaining black pepper.

4 Bake, covered, about 40 minutes or until heated through. Let stand for 10 minutes before serving.

Makes 6 servings.

Nutrition Facts per serving: 488 cal., 26 g total fat (14 g sat. fat), 207 mg chol., 1,313 mg sodium, 33 g carbo., 2 g fiber, 31 g pro.

GREEK ORZO SHRIMP CASSEROLE

This savory combination features shrimp and tangy feta cheese. Be sure to serve with French bread to sop up every bit of the delicious sauce.

Prep: 30 minutes **Bake:** 45 minutes **Stand:** 10 minutes **Oven:** 350°F

- 12 ounces dried orzo pasta
- 1 pound fresh or frozen peeled and deveined medium shrimp
- 1 tablespoon olive oil
- 2 medium green and/or red sweet peppers, seeded and cut into bite-size strips
- 1 8-ounce package sliced fresh mushrooms
- ⅓ cup chopped onion
- 1 clove garlic, minced
- 1 8-ounce package shredded Italian-style cheese blend (2 cups)
- 4 ounces feta cheese or kasseri cheese, crumbled
- ½ cup chopped pitted kalamata olives
- 1 26-ounce jar marinara sauce

1 Cook orzo according to package directions; drain. Set aside. Thaw shrimp, if frozen. Rinse shrimp; pat dry with paper towels. Set aside. Preheat oven to 350°F.

2 In a 12-inch skillet heat oil over medium heat. Add sweet peppers, mushrooms, onion, and garlic; cook until peppers and onion are tender. Add shrimp; cook about 3 minutes or until shrimp are opaque.

3 In a very large bowl combine shrimp mixture, cooked orzo, 1½ cups of the Italian-style cheese, the feta cheese, and olives. Add marinara sauce and stir until well coated. Transfer mixture to an ungreased 9×13-inch baking dish.

4 Bake, covered, about 45 minutes or until heated through. Sprinkle with the remaining ½ cup Italian-style cheese. Let stand for 10 minutes before serving.

Makes 8 servings.

Nutrition Facts per serving: 428 cal., 17 g total fat (7 g sat. fat), 97 mg chol., 878 mg sodium, 44 g carbo., 4 g fiber, 26 g pro.

BAYSIDE ENCHILADAS

Tender shrimp and delicate scallops fill these luscious cheese-sauced enchiladas. Be sure to use small bay scallops, not the larger sea scallops.

Prep: 30 minutes **Bake:** 30 minutes **Stand:** 10 minutes **Oven:** 350°F

- 8 ounces fresh or frozen medium shrimp
- 8 ounces fresh or frozen bay scallops
- 1 8-ounce carton dairy sour cream
- ½ cup purchased salsa
- 2 cups shredded Monterey Jack cheese (8 ounces)
- 6 7- to 8-inch flour tortillas
- ¼ cup cottage cheese
- ¼ cup milk
- 2 tablespoons grated Parmesan cheese
- ¼ cup sliced green onions
- ¼ cup sliced pitted ripe olives

1 Thaw shrimp and scallops, if frozen. Peel and devein shrimp. Rinse shrimp and scallops; pat dry with paper towels. Set aside. Lightly grease a 9×13-inch baking pan or baking dish; set aside. Preheat oven to 350°F.

2 In a large bowl combine sour cream and salsa. Stir in shrimp, scallops, and 1 cup of the Monterey Jack cheese. Spoon about ½ cup of the shrimp mixture onto each tortilla near an edge; roll up. Place filled tortillas, seam sides down, in prepared pan or dish; set aside.

3 In a blender or food processor combine cottage cheese, milk, and Parmesan cheese. Cover and blend or process until nearly smooth (mixture will be thin). Pour mixture over filled tortillas in pan or dish. Sprinkle with green onions and olives.

4 Bake, uncovered, for 25 minutes. Sprinkle with the remaining 1 cup Monterey Jack cheese. Bake about 5 minutes more or until cheese melts. Cover; let stand for 10 minutes before serving.

Makes 6 servings.

Nutrition Facts per serving: 404 cal., 24 g total fat (13 g sat. fat), 109 mg chol., 604 mg sodium, 20 g carbo., 1 g fiber, 27 g pro.

CHEESE 'N' NUT STUFFED SHELLS

These could be habit-forming—triple cheese- and walnut-filled pasta shells baked with a tomato sauce and additional cheese.

Prep: 45 minutes **Bake:** 45 minutes **Oven:** 350°F

- 24 dried jumbo shell macaroni*
- 2 eggs, slightly beaten
- 1 15-ounce carton ricotta cheese
- 1½ cups shredded mozzarella cheese (6 ounces)
- 1 cup shredded Parmesan cheese (4 ounces)
- 1 cup chopped walnuts
- 1 tablespoon snipped fresh parsley
- ½ teaspoon salt
- ¼ teaspoon black pepper
- ⅛ teaspoon ground nutmeg
- 1 26-ounce jar thick and chunky tomato-base pasta sauce (2¾ cups)

1 Preheat oven to 350°F. Cook shell macaroni according to package directions. Drain shells; rinse with cold water and drain well. Set cooked shells aside.

2 Meanwhile, for cheese filling, in a large bowl stir together eggs, ricotta cheese, 1 cup of the mozzarella cheese, ¾ cup of the Parmesan cheese, the walnuts, parsley, salt, pepper, and nutmeg.

3 Spread 1 cup of the pasta sauce in the bottom of an ungreased 9×13-inch baking dish. Using a small spoon, carefully fill each cooked shell with a heaping tablespoon of the cheese filling. Arrange filled shells in the baking dish. Pour the remaining pasta sauce over shells. Sprinkle with the remaining ½ cup mozzarella cheese and the remaining ¼ cup Parmesan cheese. Bake, covered, about 45 minutes or until hot in the center.

Makes 6 servings.

Nutrition Facts per serving: 549 cal., 32 g total fat (12 g sat. fat), 132 mg chol., 1,072 mg sodium, 36 g carbo., 4 g fiber, 30 g pro.

*Test Kitchen Tip: Cook a few extra shells to replace any that tear during cooking.

TOFU MANICOTTI

Used in place of ricotta, tofu adds protein to this vegetarian version of an Italian favorite. It's so delicious, your family will never notice the difference.

Prep: 40 minutes   **Bake:** 32 minutes   **Stand:** 10 minutes   **Oven:** 350°F

8   dried manicotti shells
    Nonstick cooking spray
1   cup chopped fresh mushrooms
½   cup chopped green onions
1   teaspoon dried Italian seasoning, crushed
1   12- to 16-ounce package soft tofu (fresh bean curd), drained
1   egg, slightly beaten
¼   cup finely shredded Parmesan cheese (1 ounce)
1   11-ounce can condensed tomato bisque soup
1   14½-ounce can diced tomatoes with basil, oregano, and garlic, undrained
⅛   teaspoon black pepper
¾   cup shredded Italian-style cheese blend (3 ounces)

1   Cook manicotti shells according to package directions; drain. Rinse in cold water; drain. Set aside.

2   Preheat oven to 350°F. Coat an unheated medium skillet with nonstick cooking spray. Preheat skillet over medium heat. Add mushrooms and green onions; cook until tender. Stir in Italian seasoning; set aside.

3   In a medium bowl mash tofu with a potato masher or fork. Stir in mushroom mixture, egg, and Parmesan cheese. Using a small spoon, carefully fill each cooked manicotti shell with about ¼ cup of the tofu mixture. Arrange filled manicotti shells in a single layer in an ungreased 9×13-inch baking dish.

4   In a medium bowl stir together tomato bisque soup, undrained tomatoes, and pepper. Pour soup mixture over filled manicotti shells.

5   Bake, uncovered, about 30 minutes or until heated through. Sprinkle with Italian-style cheese blend. Bake about 2 minutes more or until cheese melts. Let stand for 10 minutes before serving.

Makes 4 servings.

Nutrition Facts per serving: 411 cal., 13 g total fat (6 g sat. fat), 74 mg chol., 1,383 mg sodium, 53 g carbo., 4 g fiber, 21 g pro.

232

BROCCOLI-CAULIFLOWER TETRAZZINI

Here's a yummy way to get the kids to eat their vegetables—fettuccine mixed with broccoli and cauliflower and baked in a rich, cheesy sauce.

Prep: 35 minutes **Bake:** 15 minutes **Oven:** 400°F

- 8 **ounces dried fettuccine or spaghetti, broken**
- 1 **16-ounce package loose-pack frozen broccoli, carrots, and cauliflower**
- 2 **tablespoons butter or margarine**
- 3 **tablespoons all-purpose flour**
- 2½ **cups milk**
- ½ **cup grated Parmesan cheese**
- ¼ **teaspoon salt**
- ¼ **teaspoon black pepper**
- 1 **4½-ounce jar (drained weight) sliced mushrooms, drained**
- 2 **tablespoons grated Parmesan cheese**

1 Lightly grease a 9×13-inch baking pan or baking dish; set aside. Preheat oven to 400°F. Cook pasta according to package directions; drain. Cook vegetables according to package directions; drain. Set aside.

2 Meanwhile, for cheese sauce, in a medium saucepan melt butter over medium heat. Stir in flour. Add milk all at once. Cook and stir until slightly thickened and bubbly. Cook and stir for 1 minute more. Remove from heat. Stir in the ½ cup Parmesan cheese, the salt, and pepper.

3 In a large bowl toss pasta with ½ cup of the cheese sauce. Spread pasta mixture evenly in prepared pan or dish. Top with cooked vegetables and mushrooms. Pour remaining cheese sauce over all. Sprinkle with the 2 tablespoons Parmesan cheese.

4 Bake, uncovered, about 15 minutes or until mixture is heated through.

Makes 4 servings.

Nutrition Facts per serving: 456 cal., 13 g total fat (8 g sat. fat), 38 mg chol., 602 mg sodium, 61 g carbo., 5 g fiber, 21 g pro.

233

Make-Ahead Directions: *Prepare as directed through step 3. Cover; chill in refrigerator for up to 24 hours. Preheat oven to 400°F. Bake, covered, for 15 minutes. Uncover and bake for 10 to 15 minutes more.*

VEGETABLE PASTITSIO

This delectable meat-free version of the classic Greek casserole is loaded with vegetables and seasoned with mint, oregano, and a hint of cinnamon and nutmeg.

Prep: 35 minutes   **Bake:** 30 minutes   **Stand:** 5 minutes   **Oven:** 350°F

- 8 ounces dried elbow macaroni (about 2 cups)
- 2 eggs, beaten
- ¼ teaspoon salt
- 3 cups fresh spinach leaves, torn
- 3 tablespoons butter or margarine
- ½ cup chopped onion
- 1 clove garlic, minced
- 1 8-ounce can tomato sauce
- 1 cup loose-pack frozen whole kernel corn
- 1 cup cubed cooked potatoes
- ¾ teaspoon dried mint, crushed
- ½ teaspoon dried oregano, crushed
- ¼ teaspoon salt
- ¼ teaspoon ground cinnamon
- ¼ teaspoon black pepper
- ¼ cup all-purpose flour
- ¼ teaspoon ground nutmeg
- 2 cups milk

1 Lightly grease a 9×13-inch baking dish. Preheat oven to 350°F. Cook macaroni according to package directions; drain. Rinse with cold water; drain well. In a large bowl combine cooked macaroni, eggs, and ¼ teaspoon salt. Spread mixture evenly in prepared dish. Arrange spinach over macaroni mixture.

2 In a large skillet melt 1 tablespoon of the butter over medium heat. Add onion and garlic; cook about 3 minutes or until onion is tender. Add tomato sauce, corn, potatoes, mint, oregano, ¼ teaspoon salt, the cinnamon, and pepper; cook and stir until heated through. Spread potato mixture over spinach.

3 In a medium saucepan melt the remaining 2 tablespoons butter over medium heat. Stir in flour and nutmeg. Add milk all at once. Cook and stir until thickened and bubbly. Pour over potato mixture.

4 Bake, uncovered, about 30 minutes or until heated through. Let stand for 5 minutes before serving.

Makes 6 servings.

Nutrition Facts per serving: 343 cal., 10 g total fat (5 g sat. fat), 93 mg chol., 488 mg sodium, 51 g carbo., 3 g fiber, 12 g pro.

BAKED PASTA WITH MUSHROOMS AND SPINACH

On top there's baked cheese. Underneath you'll find pasta, cheese, and vegetables in an herb cream sauce. This is grown-up comfort food even kids will love.

Prep: 45 minutes **Bake:** 30 minutes **Oven:** 350°F

- 12 ounces dried cut ziti or penne pasta (about 4 cups)
- 1 15-ounce carton whole-milk ricotta cheese
- 1 cup half-and-half or light cream
- 1 egg
- 1 teaspoon sugar
- ½ teaspoon salt
- ¼ teaspoon freshly ground black pepper
- ⅛ teaspoon ground nutmeg
- ¼ cup snipped fresh thyme, parsley, basil, and/or rosemary
- ¼ cup cooking oil
- 10 cups sliced fresh mushrooms
- ½ cup chopped onion
- 2 cloves garlic, minced
- 4 cups chopped spinach
- 2 cups shredded Swiss cheese (8 ounces)
- ½ cup shredded Parmesan cheese (2 ounces)

1 Preheat oven to 350°F. Cook pasta according to package directions; drain well.

2 Meanwhile, place the ricotta cheese in a food processor; cover and process until smooth. Add half-and-half, egg, sugar, salt, pepper, and nutmeg; process until well mixed. Stir in thyme. Stir ricotta-thyme mixture into cooked pasta; set aside.

3 In a large skillet heat oil over medium-high heat. Add mushrooms; cook and stir until tender and liquid is reduced. Remove mushrooms from skillet. Add onion and garlic to skillet. Cook and stir until tender and liquid is reduced. Return mushrooms to skillet. Add spinach. Cook and stir for 2 to 3 minutes or until spinach is wilted. Drain mixture well in a colander or sieve. Stir into pasta mixture; stir in half of the Swiss cheese. Transfer to an ungreased 9×13-inch baking pan or baking dish.

4 Cover and bake for 20 minutes. Sprinkle with the remaining Swiss cheese and the Parmesan cheese. Bake, uncovered, for 10 to 15 minutes more or until heated through and the top begins to brown.

Makes 8 servings.

Nutrition Facts per serving: 525 cal., 28 g total fat (14 g sat. fat), 94 mg chol., 371 mg sodium, 43 g carbo., 3 g fiber, 27 g pro.

GREEK PASTA CASSEROLE

Greek olives and feta cheese give a tangy
Mediterranean twist to rotini. Beans make this dish
heartier and add protein and healthful fiber too.

Prep: 25 minutes   **Bake:** 20 minutes   **Stand:** 10 minutes   **Oven:** 375°F

- 12 ounces dried rotini pasta (about 3½ cups)
- 1 15-ounce can tomato sauce
- 1 10¾-ounce can condensed tomato soup
- 1 15-ounce can white kidney beans (cannellini beans) or garbanzo beans (chickpeas), rinsed and drained
- 8 ounces feta cheese, crumbled (2 cups)
- 1 cup coarsely chopped pitted Greek black olives
- ½ cup seasoned fine dry bread crumbs
- 2 tablespoons butter or margarine, melted
- 2 tablespoons finely shredded or grated Parmesan cheese

1 Lightly grease a 9×13-inch baking dish; set aside. Preheat oven to 375°F. Cook pasta according to package directions; drain. In a very large bowl combine cooked pasta, tomato sauce, and tomato soup; toss to coat. Stir in beans, feta cheese, and olives.

2 Spoon pasta mixture into prepared baking dish. In a small bowl stir together bread crumbs, melted butter, and Parmesan cheese; sprinkle over pasta mixture.

3 Bake, uncovered, for 20 to 25 minutes or until heated through and top is lightly browned. Let stand for 10 minutes before serving.

Makes 6 servings.

Nutrition Facts per serving: 553 cal., 19 g total fat (10 g sat. fat), 52 mg chol., 1,890 mg sodium, 74 g carbo., 7 g fiber, 24 g pro.

BAKED ZITI WITH THREE CHEESES

How good is this? Imagine your favorite macaroni and cheese—only richer and creamier—with lots of cheese and a touch of sweet tomato.

Prep: 30 minutes **Bake:** 30 minutes **Oven:** 425°F

- 12 ounces dried cut ziti or penne pasta (about 4 cups)
- 1 14½-ounce can fire-roasted crushed tomatoes or one 14½-ounce can diced tomatoes, undrained
- 2 tablespoons olive oil
- 1 cup chopped onion
- 12 cloves garlic, minced*
- ½ cup dry white wine
- 2 cups whipping cream
- 1 cup shredded Parmesan cheese (4 ounces)
- ¾ cup crumbled Gorgonzola or other blue cheese (3 ounces)
- ½ cup shredded fontina cheese (2 ounces)
- ¾ teaspoon salt
- ¼ teaspoon black pepper
- Snipped fresh flat-leaf parsley (optional)

1 Preheat oven to 425°F. Cook pasta according to package directions; drain. Place in an ungreased 9×13-inch baking dish; stir in the undrained tomatoes. Set aside.

2 Meanwhile, in a large saucepan heat oil over medium heat. Add onion and garlic; cook just until tender. Carefully stir in dry white wine and cook about 3 minutes or until liquid is reduced by half. Add whipping cream; heat to boiling. Boil gently, uncovered, about 5 minutes or until mixture thickens slightly, stirring frequently. Remove from heat. Stir in Parmesan cheese, Gorgonzola cheese, fontina cheese, salt, and pepper.

3 Pour cheese mixture over pasta. Bake, covered, for 30 to 35 minutes or until sauce is bubbly. Stir pasta to coat. If desired, sprinkle with snipped parsley.

Makes 6 servings.

Nutrition Facts per serving: 748 cal., 47 g total fat (27 g sat. fat), 145 mg chol., 1,088 mg sodium, 55 g carbo., 3 g fiber, 23 g pro.

Test Kitchen Tip: If you prefer, use 2 tablespoons bottled minced garlic.

ROASTED VEGETABLES AND SPINACH WITH PASTA

It's fun to go meatless now and then—especially with flavor-packed recipes like this one. Six ounces of spinach may look like a lot at first, but as you stir, it wilts to the right amount.

Prep: 30 minutes **Roast:** 30 minutes **Bake:** 15 minutes **Oven:** 400°F

- 1 pound eggplant, peeled and cut into 1-inch chunks
- 1 large red onion, cut into thin wedges
- 2 yellow and/or green sweet peppers, seeded and coarsely chopped
- 1 tablespoon olive oil
- ½ teaspoon salt
- 1 teaspoon olive oil
- ½ teaspoon dried thyme, crushed
- ¼ teaspoon fennel seeds, crushed
- ¼ teaspoon black pepper
- ⅛ teaspoon crushed red pepper
- 2 cloves garlic, minced
- 1 11-ounce can condensed tomato bisque soup
- 1 cup water
- 12 ounces dried cut ziti or rotini pasta (about 4 cups)
- 1 6-ounce bag prewashed baby spinach (about 8 cups)
- 1 cup shredded mozzarella cheese (4 ounces)

1 Preheat oven to 400°F. In an ungreased 9×13-inch baking dish combine eggplant, red onion, sweet peppers, and the 1 tablespoon olive oil. Sprinkle with salt. Roast, uncovered, for 30 to 35 minutes or until vegetables begin to brown, stirring twice.

2 Meanwhile, in a small saucepan heat the 1 teaspoon olive oil over medium heat. Add thyme, fennel seeds, black pepper, crushed red pepper, and garlic. Cook and stir for 2 minutes. Stir in tomato bisque soup and the water. Bring to boiling; reduce heat. Simmer, uncovered, for 5 minutes, stirring occasionally.

3 Meanwhile, cook pasta according to package directions; drain well and return to pan. Add tomato bisque soup mixture and roasted vegetables; toss to coat. Stir in spinach.

4 Spoon pasta mixture into the same baking dish. Sprinkle with cheese. Bake, uncovered, for 15 to 20 minutes or until heated through and cheese is melted.

Makes 6 to 8 servings.

Nutrition Facts per serving: 382 cal., 8 g total fat (3 g sat. fat), 14 mg chol., 775 mg sodium, 63 g carbo., 8 g fiber, 15 g pro.

TORTELLINI VEGETABLE BAKE

A colorful mix of fresh vegetables and creamy herb sauce turns tortellini into a deliciously satisfying entrée. Serve with a fresh green salad and breadsticks.

Prep: 30 minutes Bake: 30 minutes Oven: 350°F

- 2 9-ounce packages refrigerated cheese tortellini
- 1½ cups fresh sugar snap peas, trimmed and halved crosswise
- ½ cup thinly sliced carrot
- 1 tablespoon butter or margarine
- 1 cup sliced fresh mushrooms
- ⅓ cup vegetable broth or chicken broth
- 2 teaspoons all-purpose flour
- 1½ teaspoons dried oregano, crushed
- ½ teaspoon garlic salt
- ½ teaspoon black pepper
- 1 cup milk
- 1 8-ounce package cream cheese, cubed and softened
- 1 tablespoon lemon juice
- 1 cup quartered cherry tomatoes
- ½ cup coarsely chopped red or green sweet pepper
- 2 tablespoons grated Parmesan cheese

1 Preheat oven to 350°F. Cook tortellini according to package directions, adding the sugar snap peas and the carrot for the last 1 minute of cooking; drain well.

2 Meanwhile, in a 12-inch skillet melt butter over medium heat; add mushrooms. Cook and stir about 5 minutes or until mushrooms are tender. Remove from skillet.

3 In a screw-top jar combine broth, flour, oregano, garlic salt, and pepper. Cover and shake until smooth. Add to skillet along with milk. Cook and stir until thickened and bubbly; add cream cheese. Cook and stir until cream cheese is smooth. Remove from heat; stir in lemon juice. Stir in tortellini mixture, mushroom mixture, cherry tomatoes, and sweet pepper. Transfer to an ungreased 9×13-inch baking dish.

4 Bake, covered, about 30 minutes or until heated through. Sprinkle with Parmesan cheese.

Makes 8 servings.

Nutrition Facts per serving: 353 cal., 17 g total fat (9 g sat. fat), 69 mg chol., 468 mg sodium, 37 g carbo., 1 g fiber, 15 g pro.

VEGETABLE PRIMAVERA CASSEROLE

A medley of vegetables adds
vibrant color and fresh flavor to
good ol' mac and cheese.

Prep: 30 minutes **Bake:** 30 minutes **Stand:** 5 minutes **Oven:** 375°F

- 1½ **cups dried elbow macaroni (6 ounces)**
- 1 **16-ounce package loose-pack frozen vegetable blend (any combination)**
- 2 **medium zucchini, halved lengthwise and sliced**
- ½ **cup chopped red sweet pepper**
- 2 **12-ounce cans evaporated milk**
- 1 **cup vegetable broth or chicken broth**
- ⅓ **cup all-purpose flour**
- 1 **teaspoon dried oregano, crushed**
- ½ **teaspoon garlic powder**
- ½ **teaspoon salt**
- ½ **teaspoon black pepper**
- ¾ **cup grated Parmesan cheese or Romano cheese**
- 1 **medium tomato, halved and sliced**

1 Lightly grease a 9×13-inch baking pan or baking dish; set aside. Preheat oven to 375°F. In a 4- to 5-quart Dutch oven cook macaroni in lightly salted boiling water for 8 minutes, adding the frozen vegetables, zucchini, and sweet pepper for the last 3 minutes of cooking; drain. Return macaroni mixture to the hot Dutch oven.

2 Meanwhile, in a medium saucepan whisk together evaporated milk, broth, flour, oregano, garlic powder, salt, and black pepper. Cook and stir over medium heat until thickened and bubbly. Add to macaroni mixture; toss to coat. Stir in ½ cup of the Parmesan cheese. Transfer macaroni mixture to prepared pan or dish.

3 Bake, uncovered, for 25 minutes. Top with tomato slices and the remaining ¼ cup Parmesan cheese. Bake about 5 minutes more or until heated through. Let stand for 5 minutes before serving.

Makes 8 servings.

Nutrition Facts per serving: 280 cal., 9 g total fat (5 g sat. fat), 31 mg chol., 499 mg sodium, 35 g carbo., 3 g fiber, 13 g pro.

ROTINI-BEAN BAKE

A vegetarian pasta with a little Greek influence describes this hearty one-dish entrée. Plain yogurt gives the sauce creaminess.

Prep: 35 minutes **Bake:** 35 minutes **Stand:** 10 minutes **Oven:** 375°F

- 12 ounces dried rotini pasta (about 4 cups)
- ½ cup bottled balsamic vinaigrette
- 1 pound plum tomatoes, coarsely chopped
- 1 15-ounce can white kidney beans (cannellini beans) or garbanzo beans (chickpeas), rinsed and drained
- 8 ounces feta cheese, crumbled
- 1 cup coarsely chopped pitted Greek black olives
- ½ cup seasoned fine dry bread crumbs
- 1 8-ounce carton plain low-fat yogurt
- ¾ cup milk
- ⅓ cup grated Parmesan cheese
- 1 tablespoon all-purpose flour

1 Lightly grease a 9×13-inch baking dish; set aside. Preheat oven to 375°F. Cook pasta according to package directions. Drain. In a very large bowl combine balsamic vinaigrette and cooked pasta; toss to coat. Stir in tomatoes, beans, feta cheese, and olives.

2 Sprinkle ¼ cup of the bread crumbs into prepared dish. Spoon pasta mixture into dish. In a medium bowl stir together yogurt, milk, Parmesan cheese, and flour until smooth. Pour evenly over pasta mixture. Sprinkle with the remaining ¼ cup bread crumbs.

3 Bake, covered, for 25 minutes. Uncover; bake for 10 to 15 minutes more or until heated through and top is lightly browned. Let stand for 10 minutes before serving.

Makes 8 servings.

Nutrition Facts per serving: 425 cal., 15 g total fat (6 g sat. fat), 31 mg chol., 1,045 mg sodium, 57 g carbo., 6 g fiber, 19 g pro.

THREE-BEAN TAMALE PIE

The ingredients are so simple,
but the results are just what makes a
sure-to-please potluck dish.

Prep: 30 minutes **Bake:** 20 minutes **Oven:** 400°F

- 1 tablespoon cooking oil
- 1 cup chopped green sweet pepper
- 1 cup chopped onion
- 3 cloves garlic, minced
- 1 15- to 16-ounce can kidney beans, rinsed, drained, and slightly mashed
- 1 15- to 16-ounce can pinto beans, rinsed, drained, and slightly mashed
- 1 15-ounce can black beans, rinsed, drained, and slightly mashed
- 1 11½-ounce can vegetable juice
- 1 4-ounce can diced green chile peppers
- 1¼ teaspoons chili powder
- ¾ teaspoon ground cumin
- 1 8½-ounce package corn muffin mix
- ½ cup shredded cheddar cheese (2 ounces)
- ¼ cup snipped fresh cilantro or parsley
  Purchased salsa (optional)
  Dairy sour cream (optional)

1 Grease a 9x13-inch baking dish; set aside. Preheat oven to 400°F.

2 In a large skillet heat oil over medium heat. Add sweet pepper, onion, and garlic; cook and stir until tender. Stir in kidney beans, pinto beans, black beans, vegetable juice, undrained chile peppers, chili powder, and cumin; heat through. Spoon bean mixture into prepared dish.

3 Prepare corn muffin mix according to package directions. Add cheese and cilantro to muffin mix, stirring just until combined. Dollop corn muffin mixture evenly over top of bean mixture. Bake, uncovered, for 20 to 25 minutes or until topping is golden brown. If desired, serve with salsa and sour cream.

Makes 8 servings.

Nutrition Facts per serving: 313 cal., 8 g total fat (3 g sat. fat), 8 mg chol., 994 mg sodium, 51 g carbo., 11 g fiber, 14 g pro.

ROASTED VEGETABLES PARMIGIANA

Garbanzo beans add a meaty
texture to an aromatic mix of vegetables,
finished with cheese sprinkled on top.

Prep: 20 minutes   **Roast:** 17 minutes   **Oven:** 450°F

- 2 medium zucchini, cut into 1-inch chunks
- 1 medium yellow summer squash, cut into 1-inch chunks
- 1 medium red or green sweet pepper, seeded and cut into 1-inch pieces
- 8 ounces fresh mushrooms (stems removed, if desired)
- 2 tablespoons olive oil
- ½ teaspoon dried rosemary, crushed
- ¼ teaspoon salt
- ¼ teaspoon cracked black pepper
- 1 15-ounce can garbanzo beans (chickpeas), rinsed and drained
- 1 14½-ounce can Italian-style stewed tomatoes, undrained
- ⅓ cup shredded mozzarella cheese
- ⅓ cup finely shredded Parmesan cheese

1 Preheat oven to 450°F. In an ungreased 9×13-inch baking dish combine zucchini, yellow summer squash, sweet pepper, and mushrooms. Drizzle vegetable mixture with oil; sprinkle with rosemary, salt, and pepper. Toss lightly to coat.

2 Roast, uncovered, for 12 minutes. Remove from oven. Gently stir in garbanzo beans and undrained tomatoes. Roast about 5 minutes more or just until vegetables are tender. Transfer vegetable mixture to a serving dish; sprinkle with the shredded mozzarella cheese and Parmesan cheese.

Makes 6 servings.

Nutrition Facts per serving: 223 cal., 10 g total fat (3 g sat. fat), 9 mg chol., 558 mg sodium, 26 g carbo., 6 g fiber, 10 g pro.

BEAN AND CHEESE BURRITOS

This is a go-to standard of Mexican-food lovers. Have the children help fill and roll these, then it's just 10 minutes in the oven until dinner is ready.

Prep: 20 minutes   **Bake:** 10 minutes   **Oven:** 350°F

- 8   7- or 8-inch flour tortillas
- 1   cup chopped onion
- 1   tablespoon cooking oil
- 1   16-ounce can refried beans
- 1   cup shredded cheddar cheese (4 ounces)
- 1   cup shredded lettuce
- ⅓   cup purchased salsa
      Dairy sour cream (optional)
      Guacamole (optional)

1 Preheat oven to 350°F. Stack tortillas and wrap tightly in foil. Heat in oven for 10 minutes to soften.

2 Meanwhile, for filling, in a large skillet cook onion in hot oil until tender. Add refried beans; cook and stir until heated through. Spoon about ¼ cup of the filling onto each tortilla just below center and to within 1 inch of the edge. Divide cheese among tortillas. Fold bottom edge of each tortilla up and over filling. Fold opposite sides in over filling. Roll up from the bottom. Place in an ungreased 9×13-inch baking pan or baking dish.

3 Bake about 10 minutes or until heated through. Serve with lettuce and salsa. If desired, top with sour cream and/or guacamole.

Makes 4 servings.

Nutrition Facts per serving: 453 cal., 19 g total fat (8 g sat. fat), 39 mg chol., 886 mg sodium, 53 g carbo., 8 g fiber, 18 g pro.

POTATO ENCHILADAS

Calling all mashed-potato lovers: This one's for you. Creamy spuds with a dash of cumin fill tortillas that are rolled, then baked with a creamy sauce.

Prep: 30 minutes   **Cook:** 20 minutes   **Bake:** 35 minutes   **Oven:** 350°F

- 2   pounds baking potatoes, peeled and quartered
- 3   tablespoons butter or margarine
- ½   teaspoon ground cumin
- ⅛   teaspoon cayenne pepper
- 4   to 6 tablespoons milk
- 1   4-ounce can diced green chile peppers
- 8   7- to 8-inch flour tortillas
- 1   10¾-ounce can condensed cream of celery soup
- 1   8-ounce carton dairy sour cream
- ¾   cup milk
- 1   cup shredded Colby and Monterey Jack cheese or taco cheese (4 ounces)
    Sliced pitted ripe olives (optional)
    Sliced green onions (optional)

1 Grease a 9×13-inch baking pan or baking dish; set aside. Preheat oven to 350°F. In a covered medium saucepan cook potatoes in enough boiling lightly salted water to cover for 20 to 25 minutes or until tender; drain. Mash with a potato masher or beat with an electric mixer on low speed. Add butter, cumin, and cayenne pepper. Beat in enough of the 4 to 6 tablespoons milk to make mixture light and fluffy. Stir in undrained green chile peppers.

2 Meanwhile, wrap tortillas tightly in foil. Bake for 10 minutes to soften.

3 Divide potato mixture evenly among warmed tortillas; roll up tortillas. Arrange filled tortillas, seam sides down, in prepared pan or dish. In a medium bowl stir together cream of celery soup, sour cream, and the ¾ cup milk. Pour soup mixture over enchiladas in pan or dish.

4 Bake, covered, for 30 minutes. Sprinkle with cheese. Bake, uncovered, for 5 to 10 minutes more or until heated through and cheese is melted. If desired, top with ripe olives and green onions.

Makes 8 enchiladas.

Nutrition Facts per enchilada: 359 cal., 20 g total fat (11 g sat. fat), 44 mg chol., 643 mg sodium, 36 g carbo., 2 g fiber, 9 g pro.

CHILLY VEGGIE PIZZA

This unbeatable pizza features a prebaked crust spread with a dill-flavored cream cheese sauce and topped with olives, veggies, and cheese. Make this ahead for lunch.

Prep: 30 minutes   **Bake:** 8 minutes   **Chill:** 2 to 4 hours   **Oven:** 375°F

- 1 8-ounce package (8) refrigerated crescent rolls
- 1 8-ounce package cream cheese, softened
- ⅓ cup mayonnaise or salad dressing
- 2 tablespoons thinly sliced green onion
- ½ teaspoon dried dill
- ½ cup shredded lettuce
- ⅓ cup sliced pitted ripe olives or pimiento-stuffed green olives
- ¼ cup chopped green and/or yellow sweet pepper
- ¼ cup chopped seeded cucumber
- 1 medium tomato, seeded and chopped
- 1 cup crumbled garlic-and-herb feta cheese

1 Preheat oven to 375°F. Lightly grease a 9×13-inch baking pan or baking dish. Unroll crescent rolls. Press the dough over the bottom and about ½ inch up the sides of prepared pan or dish; press dough perforations to seal. Bake for 8 to 10 minutes or until light brown. Cool.

2 Meanwhile, in a medium bowl combine cream cheese, mayonnaise, green onion, and dill. Spread cream cheese mixture over cooled crust. Top with lettuce, olives, sweet pepper, and cucumber. Sprinkle with tomato and feta cheese. Cover and chill for at least 2 hours or up to 4 hours before serving.

Makes 6 servings.

Nutrition Facts per serving: 408 cal., 31 g total fat (14 g sat. fat), 68 mg chol., 706 mg sodium, 23 g carbo., 2 g fiber, 11 g pro.

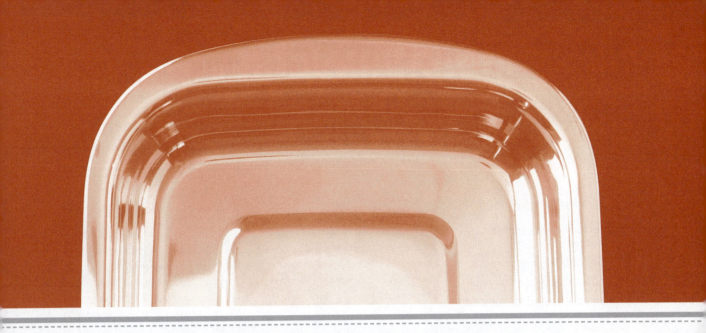

SIDES AND SALADS

The sides. The go-withs. The rest of the meal. Never the stars. It's a wonder vegetable dishes and salads don't have an inferiority complex! But, hey, they know how good they are. They're nutritious. They can liven up a plate or change deliciously with the seasons. Most important, no meal would be complete without them.

ROASTED ASPARAGUS WITH FRESH TARRAGON BUTTER

This herb butter is magic on roasted asparagus but would also be wonderful with grilled chicken and broiled fish or scrambled with eggs.

Prep: 15 minutes   **Chill:** 1 hour (butter)   **Roast:** 20 minutes   **Stand:** 30 minutes   **Oven:** 400°F

- 1 recipe Fresh Tarragon Butter
- 1½ pounds fresh asparagus
- 1 to 2 tablespoons olive oil
- 1 to 2 cloves garlic, minced

1 Preheat oven to 400°F. Prepare the Fresh Tarragon Butter. Wash asparagus; break off woody bases where spears snap easily. If desired, scrape off scales.

2 Line a 9×13-inch baking pan or baking dish with foil. Place asparagus in a large resealable plastic bag. Add oil and garlic to bag. Seal bag. Roll bag to massage the seasonings onto the asparagus spears.

3 Place asparagus in prepared pan or dish. Drizzle oil in the bag over asparagus. Roast, uncovered, about 20 minutes or until crisp-tender.

4 Arrange asparagus on a serving platter. Cut Fresh Tarragon Butter into ½-inch-thick slices. Place desired number of slices of butter on top of asparagus. (Store remaining Fresh Tarragon Butter in refrigerator for up to 2 weeks.)

Makes 6 to 8 servings.

Nutrition Facts per serving asparagus and 2 teaspoons butter: 105 cal., 10 g total fat (4 g sat. fat), 22 mg chol., 83 mg sodium, 3 g carbo., 1 g fiber, 1 g pro.

Fresh Tarragon Butter: *Allow ½ cup butter to stand at room temperature for 30 minutes. In a small bowl stir together the softened butter; 2 tablespoons finely snipped fresh tarragon; 1 teaspoon finely shredded lemon peel; 1 clove garlic, minced; and ⅛ teaspoon salt until well mixed. Transfer to a sheet of waxed paper. Shape into a 4-inch-long log. Wrap in waxed paper; twist ends to seal. Chill for at least 1 hour or until firm. Makes about ½ cup.*

QUICK-ROASTED ASPARAGUS WITH
PARMESAN CHEESE

Asparagus, one of nature's most elegant vegetables, has a distinctive, delectable flavor when it's quickly roasted. It's perfect with a simple steak or grilled fish.

Prep: 10 minutes **Roast:** 15 minutes **Oven:** 450°F

1½ pounds fresh asparagus
⅛ teaspoon black pepper
4 teaspoons olive oil
¼ cup grated Parmesan cheese

1 Preheat oven to 450°F. Wash asparagus; break off woody bases where spears snap easily. If desired, scrape off scales. Place asparagus in an ungreased 9×13-inch baking pan or baking dish. Sprinkle with pepper. Drizzle with oil. Roast, uncovered, about 15 minutes or until crisp-tender, using tongs to lightly toss twice during roasting. Transfer asparagus to a warm serving platter. Sprinkle with Parmesan cheese.

Makes 6 servings.

Nutrition Facts per serving: 56 cal., 4 g total fat (1 g sat. fat), 3 mg chol., 52 mg sodium, 2 g carbo., 1 g fiber, 3 g pro.

ROASTED HERBED GREEN BEANS

Want a fresh way to do green beans?
Try roasting them! Just a few minutes in the oven
produces beans bursting with flavor.

Prep: 15 minutes **Roast:** 8 minutes **Oven:** 450°F

- 1 pound fresh green beans, trimmed
- 2 tablespoons desired snipped fresh herbs or 2 teaspoons desired dried herbs, crushed (optional)
- 2 tablespoons olive oil
- ¼ teaspoon salt
  Several dashes freshly ground black pepper
- 1 ounce Parmesan cheese, shaved

1 Preheat oven to 450°F. Heat an ungreased 9×13-inch baking pan in the oven for 5 minutes. In a covered large saucepan cook green beans in a large amount of boiling water for 2 minutes; drain.

2 In a large bowl toss green beans with herbs (if desired), oil, salt, and pepper.

3 Spread green beans in a single layer in the hot baking pan. Return to oven. Roast, uncovered, for 8 to 10 minutes or until tender when pierced with the tip of a knife, stirring occasionally. Transfer green beans to a serving platter. Sprinkle with shaved Parmesan cheese.

Makes 4 to 6 servings.

Nutrition Facts per serving: 123 cal., 9 g total fat (2 g sat. fat), 5 mg chol., 266 mg sodium, 8 g carbo., 4 g fiber, 5 g pro.

ROSEMARY ROASTED VEGETABLES

Green beans and Brussels sprouts are a delectable pair when roasted with aromatic rosemary and smoky bacon. (Pictured on page 105.)

Prep: 30 minutes **Roast:** 20 minutes **Oven:** 425°F

- 1 **pound fresh Brussels sprouts**
- 12 **ounces fresh whole green beans**
- 1 **bunch green onions, trimmed and cut up**
- 12 **fresh rosemary sprigs**
- 8 **slices pancetta or bacon, partially cooked, drained, and cut up**
- 2 **tablespoons olive oil**
  Salt
  Freshly ground black pepper
- 1 **lemon, halved**

1 Preheat oven to 425°F. Wash Brussels sprouts and green beans; drain. Halve any large Brussels sprouts. In a covered large saucepan cook Brussels sprouts in a small amount of lightly salted boiling water for 3 minutes; add green beans and cook for 5 minutes more. Drain.

2 Transfer Brussels sprouts and green beans to an ungreased 9×13-inch baking pan or baking dish. Add green onions and rosemary sprigs; toss to combine. Top with partially cooked pancetta or bacon. Drizzle vegetable mixture with oil. Sprinkle with salt and pepper.

3 Roast, uncovered, about 20 minutes or until vegetables are crisp-tender and pancetta is crisp. Transfer to a serving platter. Squeeze juice from lemon over vegetables.

Makes 12 servings.

Nutrition Facts per serving: 143 cal., 10 g total fat (4 g sat. fat), 10 mg chol., 275 mg sodium, 6 g carbo., 3 g fiber, 4 g pro.

GREEN BEAN AND SWEET ONION GRATIN

Traditional green bean casserole gets a delicious makeover with layers of sweet onions and green beans baked with a cream sauce and a cheesy crumb layer on top.

Prep: 30 minutes **Bake:** 35 minutes **Stand:** 10 minutes **Oven:** 325°F

252

POTLUCK ● FAVORITE

2	16-ounce packages frozen cut green beans
1½	pounds sweet onions (such as Vidalia or Maui), halved and thinly sliced
⅓	cup butter or margarine
⅓	cup all-purpose flour
1	teaspoon salt
¼	teaspoon black pepper
⅛	teaspoon ground nutmeg
1	14-ounce can chicken broth
1½	cups half-and-half, light cream, or milk
2¼	cups soft bread crumbs (4 to 5 slices)
⅓	cup grated Parmesan cheese
3	tablespoons olive oil

1 Preheat oven to 325°F. Cook green beans according to package directions; drain well and set aside.

2 Meanwhile, in a large saucepan or Dutch oven cook sliced onion in a small amount of boiling water for 4 to 5 minutes or until tender. Drain; set aside.

3 For sauce, in the same saucepan or Dutch oven melt butter over medium heat. Stir in flour, salt, pepper, and nutmeg. Add broth and half-and-half; cook and stir until mixture is thickened and bubbly.

4 In an ungreased 9×13-inch baking pan or baking dish layer half of the the beans, the sliced onion, and the remaining beans. Spoon sauce over all.

5 In a small bowl toss together bread crumbs, Parmesan cheese, and oil; sprinkle over vegetables. Bake, uncovered, for 35 to 40 minutes or until hot and bubbly. Let stand for 10 minutes before serving.

Makes 8 to 10 servings.

Nutrition Facts per serving: 278 cal., 19 g total fat (9 g sat. fat), 39 mg chol., 575 mg sodium, 23 g carbo., 4 g fiber, 6 g pro.

Make-Ahead Directions: *Prepare as directed, except do not top with bread crumb mixture. Cover pan or dish; chill for up to 24 hours. Wrap bread crumb mixture separately; chill. To serve, preheat oven to 325°F. Sprinkle bread crumb mixture over vegetables. Bake, uncovered, for 50 to 55 minutes or until hot and bubbly. Let stand for 10 minutes before serving.*

SQUASH CASSEROLE

If you like, team this tantalizing mix of squash, eggs, and corn with a tossed salad for a light lunch or supper.

Prep: 40 minutes **Bake:** 40 minutes **Stand:** 10 minutes **Oven:** 350°F

- 2 pounds butternut or acorn squash, peeled, seeded, and cubed
- 6 slices white bread, toasted
- ½ cup butter or margarine, melted
- 6 eggs, slightly beaten
- 1⅓ cups milk
- 1 teaspoon salt
- ½ teaspoon black pepper
- 2 15¼-ounce cans whole kernel corn, drained
- 2 medium onions, finely chopped

1 In a covered large saucepan cook squash in lightly salted boiling water about 20 minutes or until tender. Drain. Set aside.

2 Meanwhile, preheat oven to 350°F. Place toasted bread, half at a time, in a food processor, tearing to fit as necessary. Cover and process until crumbs are fine (should have 1⅔ cups crumbs total). Set aside. Pour melted butter into a 9×13-inch baking pan or baking dish; set aside.

3 In a large bowl combine eggs, milk, salt, and pepper. Stir in corn, onions, drained squash, and bread crumbs. Pour mixture into pan or dish with butter.

4 Bake, uncovered, about 40 minutes or until center is set and edges are slightly puffed. Let stand for 10 minutes before serving.

Makes 10 to 12 servings.

Nutrition Facts per serving: 294 cal., 14 g total fat (7 g sat. fat), 154 mg chol., 717 mg sodium, 37 g carbo., 4 g fiber, 10 g pro.

TUSCAN STUFFED PEPPERS

What could be more tempting than this robust medley of Italian ingredients: eggplant, fennel, and olives? Try it in early fall when sweet peppers are in abundance.

Prep: 40 minutes **Broil:** 12 minutes **Cool:** 15 minutes **Bake:** 20 minutes **Oven:** 375°F

- 6 red and/or yellow sweet peppers (about 8 ounces each)
- 1 large eggplant (about 1½ pounds)
- 1 to 2 teaspoons salt
- 3 tablespoons olive oil
- 1 medium fennel bulb, chopped (about 1 cup)
- 8 cloves garlic, minced
- ⅓ cup drained capers, rinsed
- 8 to 10 canned anchovies, drained and finely chopped (optional)
- ¾ cup ripe or green olives, pitted and quartered
- ½ cup snipped fresh flat-leaf parsley
- ¼ cup snipped fresh sage
- 2 tablespoons freshly grated Parmesan cheese

1 Preheat broiler. Slice the stem end off each sweet pepper and carefully remove the core and seeds; discard stem end, core, and seeds. Place sweet peppers on a foil-lined baking sheet. Broil about 4 inches from the heat for 12 to 15 minutes or until charred, turning to char all sides. Place in a closed container or wrap in foil and cool for 15 minutes; carefully peel off skins. Set aside.

2 Meanwhile, for filling, cut eggplant into ½-inch-thick slices. Lightly sprinkle both sides of each eggplant slice with salt. Let stand for 30 minutes to drain. Wipe excess salt off eggplant slices; cut eggplant into ½-inch cubes.

3 Preheat oven to 375°F. In a large skillet heat oil over medium heat. Add fennel; cook for 4 minutes. Add eggplant and garlic to skillet; cook for 8 minutes more. Stir in capers and, if desired, anchovies. Remove skillet from heat.

4 Stir olives, parsley, and sage into the eggplant mixture. Divide filling among sweet peppers. Arrange filled peppers in a single layer in an ungreased 9×13-inch baking pan or baking dish. Sprinkle filled peppers with grated Parmesan cheese. Bake, uncovered, for 20 to 25 minutes or until filling is heated through and slightly browned.

Makes 6 servings.

Nutrition Facts per serving: 170 cal., 10 g total fat (2 g sat. fat), 6 mg chol., 1,001 mg sodium, 18 g carbo., 10 g fiber, 5 g pro.

SWISS VEGETABLE MEDLEY

Nothing could be easier: Swiss cheese
and sour cream meld into
a rich sauce for frozen veggies.

Prep: 15 minutes **Bake:** 35 minutes **Oven:** 350°F

- 2 16-ounce packages loose-pack frozen broccoli, cauliflower, and carrots, thawed
- 2 10¾-ounce cans condensed cream of mushroom soup
- 2 cups shredded Swiss cheese (8 ounces)
- ⅔ cup dairy sour cream
- ½ teaspoon black pepper
- 2 2.8-ounce cans French-fried onions

1 Preheat oven to 350°F. In a large bowl combine thawed vegetables, cream of mushroom soup, half of the Swiss cheese, the sour cream, and pepper. Stir in half of the French-fried onions. Spoon vegetable mixture into an ungreased 9×13-inch baking pan or baking dish.

2 Bake, covered, for 30 minutes. Uncover and sprinkle with the remaining Swiss cheese and the remaining French-fried onions. Bake about 5 minutes more or until mixture is heated through.

Makes 12 servings.

Nutrition Facts per serving: 249 cal., 17 g total fat (6 g sat. fat), 22 mg chol., 589 mg sodium, 14 g carbo., 3 g fiber, 9 g pro.

ROASTED VEGETABLES WITH FETA CHEESE

Roasting intensifies the flavors
of these make-ahead veggies, while feta
cheese adds a tasty accent.

Prep: 20 minutes **Roast:** 30 minutes **Chill:** 2 to 24 hours **Oven:** 350°F

- 1 medium eggplant, cut into 1-inch cubes
- 1 medium zucchini, cut into 1-inch cubes
- 1 medium onion, cut into wedges
- 1 medium red sweet pepper, seeded and cut into 1-inch pieces
- 1 medium orange or yellow sweet pepper, seeded and cut into 1-inch pieces
- ½ teaspoon salt
- ¼ cup olive oil
- 4 ounces feta cheese, crumbled (1 cup)
- ¼ cup slivered fresh basil
- Cracked black pepper

1 Preheat oven to 350°F. In an ungreased 9×13-inch baking pan or baking dish combine eggplant cubes, zucchini cubes, onion wedges, and sweet pepper pieces. Sprinkle vegetables with the salt. Drizzle with oil; toss to coat vegetables. Roast, uncovered, for 30 minutes, stirring once or twice. Transfer to a large serving bowl. Set aside to cool completely. Stir in feta cheese and basil. Cover and chill for at least 2 hours or up to 24 hours.

2 Serve vegetable mixture cold or let stand at room temperature for 30 minutes before serving. Sprinkle with cracked black pepper.

Makes 6 servings.

Nutrition Facts per serving: 166 cal., 13 g total fat (4 g sat. fat), 17 mg chol., 391 mg sodium, 9 g carbo., 2 g fiber, 4 g pro.

VEGETABLE CASSEROLE

Reminiscent of ratatouille, a dish from the Provençal region of France, this casserole is loaded with vegetables and herbs. Serve it with a simple roast or grilled chicken.

Prep: 35 minutes **Roast:** 35 minutes **Oven:** 425°F

- 2 14½-ounce cans Italian-style stewed tomatoes
- 1 medium eggplant (about 1 pound), peeled if desired and cut into 1-inch pieces (about 5½ cups)
- 4½ cups fresh mushrooms, halved (12 ounces)
- 2 medium zucchini, cut into 1-inch pieces (3½ cups)
- 1 cup chopped onion
- 2 tablespoons olive oil
- 2 teaspoons dried basil, crushed
- 1 teaspoon salt
- ¾ teaspoon dried oregano, crushed
- ½ teaspoon black pepper
- ½ cup shredded mozzarella cheese (2 ounces)
- ½ cup shredded Parmesan cheese (2 ounces)

1 Preheat oven to 425°F. Drain tomatoes in a colander while preparing recipe (do not chill). In an ungreased 9×13-inch baking pan or baking dish combine eggplant, mushrooms, zucchini, and onion. Sprinkle with oil, basil, salt, oregano, and pepper; toss to coat.

2 Roast, uncovered, about 30 minutes or until vegetables are tender, stirring twice. Stir in drained tomatoes. Sprinkle with mozzarella cheese and Parmesan cheese. Roast about 5 minutes more or until cheeses are melted.

Makes 10 servings.

Nutrition Facts per serving: 108 cal., 5 g total fat (2 g sat. fat), 6 mg chol., 630 mg sodium, 13 g carbo., 4 g fiber, 6 g pro.

SLOW AND SAVORY ROOT VEGETABLES

Wow! Roasting and a little honey give these vegetables an incredibly delicious caramelized flavor.

Prep: 25 minutes   **Roast:** 35 minutes   **Oven:** 425°F

- 2 medium parsnips, peeled, halved lengthwise, and cut into 1-inch pieces
- 2 medium turnips, peeled and cut into 1-inch pieces, or 1 medium rutabaga, peeled and cut into 1-inch pieces
- 2 small Yukon gold potatoes, peeled and cut into quarters, or 1 medium sweet potato, peeled and cut into 1-inch pieces
- 2 medium carrots, halved lengthwise and cut into 1-inch pieces
- 1 medium yellow onion, cut into 1-inch-wide wedges
- 4 fresh sage leaves, slivered
- 2 tablespoons olive oil
- ¾ teaspoon salt
- ¼ teaspoon freshly ground black pepper
- 2 tablespoons honey
- 1 fresh sage leaf, snipped

1 Grease a 9×13-inch baking pan or baking dish. Preheat oven to 425°F. In prepared pan or dish combine parsnips, turnips or rutabaga, potatoes, carrots, onion, and the slivered sage. In a small bowl combine oil, salt, and pepper; drizzle over vegetables in pan or dish. Toss lightly to coat.

2 Roast, uncovered, for 30 to 35 minutes or until vegetables are lightly browned and tender, stirring occasionally. Drizzle honey over vegetables. Stir gently to coat. Roast for 5 minutes more. To serve, sprinkle with the snipped sage.

Makes 4 servings.

Nutrition Facts per serving: 209 cal., 7 g total fat (1 g sat. fat), 0 mg chol., 506 mg sodium, 36 g carbo., 5 g fiber, 3 g pro.

ROASTED VEGETABLES WITH POLENTA AND BABY GREENS

Top Parmesan-seasoned polenta with roasted vegetables and fresh baby greens for a beautiful presentation and a terrific blend of flavors.

Prep: 25 minutes **Roast:** 30 minutes **Oven:** 350°F

- 6 cups cut-up fresh vegetables (such as cut-up asparagus, red or green sweet pepper wedges, zucchini slices, quartered mushrooms, and/or red onion slices)
- ¼ cup olive oil
- ¼ teaspoon kosher salt or regular salt
- 1 tablespoon olive oil
- 1 clove garlic, minced
- ¼ to ½ teaspoon crushed red pepper
- 2 cups milk
- 2 cups water
- 1 cup cornmeal
- ½ cup finely shredded Parmesan cheese (2 ounces)
- 1 tablespoon snipped fresh basil
- ½ teaspoon kosher salt or regular salt

Finely shredded Parmesan cheese

Mixed baby greens

1 Preheat oven to 350°F. In an ungreased 9×13-inch baking pan or baking dish combine vegetables, the ¼ cup oil, and the ¼ teaspoon salt; toss to coat vegetables. Roast, uncovered, about 30 minutes or until crisp-tender, stirring once.

2 Meanwhile, for polenta, in a large saucepan heat the 1 tablespoon oil over medium heat. Add garlic; cook for 1 minute. Stir in crushed red pepper. Stir in milk and 1 cup of the water. Bring just to boiling. In a small bowl stir together cornmeal and the remaining 1 cup water. Slowly add the cornmeal mixture to the hot milk mixture, stirring constantly. Return to boiling; reduce heat to low. Cook, uncovered, for 5 to 10 minutes more or until mixture is very thick, stirring frequently. Stir in the ½ cup Parmesan cheese, the basil, and the ½ teaspoon salt.

3 To serve, spoon polenta mixture into a shallow bowl. Spoon roasted vegetables on top of polenta. Sprinkle with additional Parmesan cheese and top with mixed baby greens. Serve immediately.

Makes 6 servings.

Nutrition Facts per serving: 272 cal., 16 g total fat (4 g sat. fat), 11 mg chol., 404 mg sodium, 26 g carbo., 4 g fiber, 9 g pro.

ROASTED SUMMER VEGETABLES

When you come home with a basketful of produce from the farmer's market, remember this recipe. A simple dressing and quick roasting are all it takes to punch up the flavors of fresh summer vegetables.

Prep: 20 minutes **Roast:** 25 minutes **Oven:** 425°F

- 3 red, yellow, and/or green sweet peppers, seeded and cut into ½-inch-wide strips
- 2 medium red onions, each cut into 8 wedges
- 2 small yellow summer squash, cut into ½-inch-thick slices
- 2 small zucchini, cut into ½-inch-wide strips
- 4 cloves garlic, thinly sliced
- 2 tablespoons snipped fresh parsley
- 2 tablespoons balsamic vinegar
- 1 tablespoon olive oil
- 1 teaspoon dried oregano, crushed
- ½ teaspoon salt
- ¼ teaspoon black pepper

1 Preheat oven to 425°F. In an ungreased 9×13-inch baking pan or baking dish combine sweet peppers, red onions, yellow squash, zucchini, and garlic.

2 In a screw-top jar combine parsley, balsamic vinegar, oil, oregano, salt, and black pepper. Cover and shake well. Pour over the vegetables; toss to coat.

3 Roast, uncovered, about 25 minutes or until crisp-tender, stirring twice.

Makes 8 servings.

Nutrition Facts per serving: 45 cal., 2 g total fat (0 g sat. fat), 0 mg chol., 137 mg sodium, 7 g carbo., 1 g fiber, 1 g pro.

VEGETABLE PASTA BAKE

Pasta is the perfect foil for this golden rich mix of roasted tomatoes and zucchini seasoned with fresh basil.

Prep: 20 minutes **Roast:** 20 minutes **Bake:** 10 minutes **Oven:** 400°F

- 9 medium plum tomatoes, cored and cut into ¼-inch-thick slices
- 2 medium zucchini, halved lengthwise and cut into ½-inch-thick slices
- 4 teaspoons olive oil
- 4 cloves garlic, minced
- ½ teaspoon salt
- ¼ teaspoon black pepper
- 6 ounces dried penne or rotini pasta
- 3 tablespoons Italian-style tomato paste
- ½ cup finely shredded Parmesan cheese (2 ounces)
- ¼ cup slivered fresh basil

1 Preheat oven to 400°F. In an ungreased 9×13-inch baking dish combine plum tomatoes and zucchini. In a small bowl combine oil, garlic, salt, and pepper; drizzle over vegetables. Roast, uncovered, for 20 minutes, stirring once.

2 Meanwhile, cook pasta according to package directions; drain. Stir pasta and tomato paste into the roasted vegetable mixture. Bake, uncovered, for 10 minutes more.

3 To serve, stir pasta and vegetable mixture. Divide mixture among eight serving plates. Sprinkle individual servings with Parmesan cheese and basil.

Makes 8 servings.

Nutrition Facts per serving: 148 cal., 4 g total fat (1 g sat. fat), 4 mg chol., 289 mg sodium, 22 g carbo., 2 g fiber, 8 g pro.

OVEN-ROASTED VEGETABLE COMBO

Sweet potato wedges and new potatoes drizzled with olive oil and balsamic vinegar roast to a delicious finish in the oven, and the last-minute addition of spinach adds extra color and nutrients.

Prep: 20 minutes   **Roast:** 25 minutes   **Stand:** 5 minutes   **Oven:** 425°F

- 2 medium sweet potatoes (about 1 pound), peeled and each cut lengthwise into about 10 wedges
- 8 ounces new potatoes, scrubbed and halved
- 1 large red or green sweet pepper, seeded and cut into 1-inch-wide slices
- 2 tablespoons olive oil
- 1 to 2 tablespoons balsamic vinegar
- 1 teaspoon coarse salt
- 1 cup packed fresh spinach leaves

1 Preheat oven to 425°F. In an ungreased 9×13-inch baking pan or baking dish toss together sweet potato wedges, new potatoes, sweet pepper, oil, 1 tablespoon of the balsamic vinegar, and the salt. Roast, uncovered, for 25 to 30 minutes or until vegetables are lightly browned and tender, stirring or tossing once or twice.

2 Remove from oven. Add spinach; cover with foil. Let stand for 5 minutes. Toss to combine.

3 Transfer vegetable mixture to a large serving bowl. If desired, drizzle with the remaining 1 tablespoon balsamic vinegar.

Makes 6 servings.

Nutrition Facts per serving: 117 cal., 5 g total fat (1 g sat. fat), 0 mg chol., 298 mg sodium, 18 g carbo., 3 g fiber, 2 g pro.

SCALLOPED POTATOES

Every mom and grandmother has her favorite recipe for these creamy taters. Here's one more. Feel free to add cheese if you like. Either way, they're hard to beat.

Prep: 30 minutes **Bake:** 1 hour 25 minutes **Stand:** 10 minutes **Oven:** 350°F

1	cup chopped onion
2	cloves garlic, minced
¼	cup butter or margarine
¼	cup all-purpose flour
½	teaspoon salt
¼	teaspoon black pepper
2½	cups milk
8	cups thinly sliced red, white, long white, or yellow potatoes (about 2½ pounds)

1 Grease a 9×13-inch baking pan or baking dish; set aside. Preheat oven to 350°F. For sauce, in a medium saucepan cook onion and garlic in hot butter until tender. Stir in flour, salt, and pepper. Add milk all at once. Cook and stir over medium heat until thickened and bubbly.

2 Place half of the sliced potatoes in prepared pan or dish. Top with half of the sauce. Repeat layers.

3 Bake, covered, for 45 minutes. Uncover and bake for 40 to 50 minutes more or until potatoes are tender. Let stand for 10 minutes before serving.

Makes 10 servings.

Nutrition Facts per serving: 178 cal., 6 g total fat (4 g sat. fat), 17 mg chol., 183 mg sodium, 27 g carbo., 2 g fiber, 5 g pro.

Cheesy Scalloped Potatoes: *Prepare as directed, except gradually add 1½ cups shredded cheddar or Swiss cheese (6 ounces) to the thickened sauce, stirring until cheese melts. Nutrition Facts per serving: 247 cal., 12 g total fat (7 g sat. fat), 35 mg chol., 289 mg sodium, 27 g carbo., 2 g fiber, 9 g pro.*

ROASTED CHEDDAR POTATOES

How do you make potato wedges even better? Add a crunchy cheese topping. Serve this easy-does-it dish to snack on while watching the ball game on television or as a side at dinner.

Prep: 10 minutes **Bake:** according to package directions

- 1 **24-ounce package frozen oven-fried potato wedges (skins on)**
- 2 **tablespoons cooking oil**
- 4 **cloves garlic, minced**
- 1 **teaspoon smoked paprika or paprika**
- ¼ **teaspoon salt**

  Nonstick cooking spray
- 1 **cup shredded white cheddar cheese or other cheddar cheese (4 ounces)**
- ⅔ **cup crushed croutons (about 1 cup croutons)**

  Dairy sour cream (optional)

1 Preheat oven according to package directions for potatoes. Place frozen potatoes in a large resealable plastic bag. In a small bowl combine oil, garlic, paprika, and salt; drizzle over potato wedges. Seal bag; shake to coat potatoes.

2 Lightly coat a 9×13-inch baking pan or baking dish with nonstick cooking spray. Spread potatoes in a single layer in prepared pan or dish. Bake potato wedges according to package directions, turning once.

3 In another small bowl combine cheddar cheese and crushed croutons. Sprinkle over potatoes for the last 3 minutes of baking. Using a large spatula, transfer potato wedges to a platter or large plate (keep potatoes in a single layer). If desired, serve with sour cream.

Makes 6 to 8 servings.

Nutrition Facts per serving: 226 cal., 11 g total fat (5 g sat. fat), 20 mg chol., 291 mg sodium, 25 g carbo., 2 g fiber, 7 g pro.

POTATOES WITH CARAMELIZED ONIONS AND HAM

In this better-than-ever version of scalloped potatoes, sweet caramelized onions and ham are layered with potatoes for comfort food with fantastic flavor.

Prep: 30 minutes   **Cook:** 25 minutes   **Bake:** 1 hour   **Stand:** 15 minutes   **Oven:** 350°F

- 1 tablespoon olive oil
- 1 tablespoon butter
- 2 large yellow onions, peeled and cut into thin wedges
- 1½ cups whipping cream
- ½ cup milk
- 2 tablespoons snipped fresh sage or 1 teaspoon dried sage, crushed
- 3 cloves garlic, minced
- 1 teaspoon salt
- ¼ teaspoon black pepper
- 3 pounds Yukon gold or other yellow-fleshed potatoes, thinly sliced (about 8 cups)
- 8 ounces thinly sliced cooked ham, cut into bite-size strips (about 1½ cups)
- 8 ounces aged white cheddar cheese, shredded (2 cups)

1 For caramelized onions, in a large skillet combine oil and butter; heat over medium heat until butter is melted. Stir in onion wedges; cook, uncovered, about 20 minutes or until onions are tender, stirring frequently. (If necessary, reduce heat to medium-low to prevent overbrowning before onions are tender.) Increase heat to medium-high and cook about 5 minutes more or until onions are golden brown, stirring frequently. Remove from heat. Set aside.

2 In a medium bowl stir together whipping cream, milk, sage, garlic, salt, and pepper. Lightly grease a 9×13-inch baking pan or baking dish; set aside.

3 Preheat oven to 350°F. Arrange half of the potatoes in the prepared pan or dish, overlapping as necessary. Sprinkle with ham and caramelized onions. Sprinkle with half of the white cheddar cheese. Layer the remaining potatoes over the cheese. Pour cream mixture over; top with the remaining cheese.

4 Bake, uncovered, for 60 to 65 minutes or until top is golden brown and potatoes are tender. Cover; let stand for 15 minutes before serving.

Makes 12 servings.

Nutrition Facts per serving: 333 cal., 21 g total fat (12 g sat. fat), 75 mg chol., 588 mg sodium, 25 g carbo., 3 g fiber, 11 g pro.

MASHED BAKED POTATOES WITH
GARDEN CONFETTI

A colorful saute of carrots and celery tops these creamy mashed spuds. They're a great choice for buffets or family gatherings.

Prep: 35 minutes **Bake:** 1 hour 55 minutes **Oven:** 425°F/325°F

- 1 5-pound bag red potatoes (about 15 medium potatoes)
  Nonstick cooking spray
- 1 8-ounce package cream cheese or reduced-fat cream cheese (Neufchâtel), cut up and softened
- 1½ cups half-and-half, light cream, or fat-free evaporated milk
- 1 teaspoon salt
- 1 teaspoon cracked black pepper
- 1 recipe Garden Confetti
- 2 tablespoons butter, melted

1 Preheat oven to 425°F. Scrub potatoes thoroughly with a brush; pat dry with paper towels. Prick potatoes with a fork. Bake for 40 to 60 minutes or until tender.

2 Reduce oven temperature to 325°F. Coat a 9×13-inch baking pan or baking dish with nonstick cooking spray; set aside. While the potatoes are still hot, transfer half of the potatoes to a very large bowl. (Cut any large potatoes in half or quarters for easier mashing.) Using a potato masher or an electric mixer, mash the potatoes (with their skins still on) until slightly lumpy; transfer to another bowl. Use the same bowl to mash the remaining potatoes. Return all potatoes to the very large bowl; add cream cheese, half-and-half, salt, and pepper. Beat or stir until combined. Spoon the potato mixture into the prepared pan or dish; set aside.

3 Spoon Garden Confetti over the potato mixture. Drizzle with melted butter.

4 Bake, uncovered, about 1¼ hours or until hot in the center.

Makes 10 to 12 servings.

Nutrition Facts per serving: 304 cal., 17 g total fat (11 g sat. fat), 51 mg chol., 386 mg sodium, 33 g carbo., 3 g fiber, 7 g pro.

Garden Confetti: *In a large skillet melt 3 tablespoons butter or margarine over medium-high heat. Add 3 medium carrots, shredded; 2 stalks celery, finely chopped; and 1 medium onion, halved and thinly sliced. Cook and stir for 4 to 5 minutes or until vegetables are tender.*

Make-Ahead Directions: *Prepare as directed through step 3. Cover with foil. Chill for up to 24 hours. Preheat oven to 325°F. Bake, covered, for 1 hour. Uncover; bake for 1 to 1¼ hours more or until heated through.*

LEMON-DILL POTATOES

Fresh dill, lemon juice, and a hint of garlic salt give a refreshing twist to twice-baked potatoes. Serve them with a meat loaf, a roast, or the perfect grilled steak.

Prep: 25 minutes **Bake:** 1 hour **Oven:** 425°F

- 4 large baking potatoes
- ⅓ cup dairy sour cream
- ¼ cup butter or margarine, melted
- 2 tablespoons finely snipped fresh dill or 1½ teaspoons dried dill
- 1 tablespoon lemon juice
- ½ teaspoon garlic salt
- ⅛ teaspoon black pepper
   Paprika (optional)

1 Preheat oven to 425°F. Scrub potatoes thoroughly with a brush; pat dry with paper towels. Prick potatoes with a fork. Bake for 40 to 60 minutes or until tender.

2 Cut potatoes in half lengthwise. Gently scoop pulp out of each potato half, leaving a thin shell. Place potato pulp in a large bowl. Add sour cream, 3 tablespoons of the melted butter, the dill, lemon juice, garlic salt, and pepper; beat with an electric mixer on low speed until mixture is smooth. Mound the mixture into the potato shells.

3 Arrange filled potato shells in an ungreased 9×13-inch baking pan or baking dish. Brush potatoes with the remaining 1 tablespoon melted butter. If desired, sprinkle with paprika. Bake, uncovered, about 20 minutes or until lightly browned.

Makes 8 servings.

Nutrition Facts per serving: 156 cal., 8 g total fat (5 g sat. fat), 19 mg chol., 112 mg sodium, 20 g carbo., 2 g fiber, 3 g pro.

HASH BROWN CASSEROLE

Eggs—any way you like them—are ideal partners for these crispy baked potatoes. Make the casserole the night before, then bake and serve it hot with eggs for breakfast.

Prep: 20 minutes   **Bake:** 1 hour   **Oven:** 350°F

- 1 **16-ounce carton dairy sour cream**
- 1 **10¾-ounce can condensed cream of chicken soup**
- 1 **32-ounce package loose-pack frozen diced hash brown potatoes**
- 2 **cups diced cooked ham**
- 2 **cups cubed American cheese (8 ounces)**
- ½ **cup chopped onion**
- ¼ **teaspoon black pepper**
- 2 **cups crushed cornflakes**
- ⅓ **cup butter or margarine, melted**

1 In a very large bowl combine sour cream and cream of chicken soup. Stir in frozen potatoes, ham, American cheese, onion, and pepper. Spread mixture evenly in an ungreased 9×13-inch baking pan or baking dish.

2 Preheat oven to 350°F. In a medium bowl combine cornflakes and melted butter; sprinkle over the potato mixture. Bake, uncovered, about 1 hour or until hot and bubbly.

Makes 12 servings.

Nutrition Facts per serving: 382 cal., 24 g total fat (13 g sat. fat), 64 mg chol., 998 mg sodium, 30 g carbo., 1 g fiber, 13 g pro.

Make-Ahead Directions: *Prepare as directed in step 1. Cover and chill for at least 8 hours or up to 24 hours. To serve, continue with step 2, except bake for 50 to 55 minutes or until hot and bubbly.*

BALSAMIC ROASTED POTATOES
AND CARROTS

The slightly sweet taste of
balsamic vinegar infuses these vegetables
with a rich, caramelized flavor.

Prep: 15 minutes   **Roast:** 30 minutes   **Oven:** 425°F

1½	pounds tiny new potatoes, halved
½	of a 16-ounce package peeled baby carrots
1	medium red onion, cut into wedges
3	tablespoons olive oil or cooking oil
1	teaspoon dried rosemary, crushed
¾	teaspoon salt
¼	teaspoon black pepper
3	tablespoons balsamic vinegar

1 Lightly grease a 9×13-inch baking pan or baking dish. Preheat oven to 425°F. In prepared pan or dish combine potatoes, carrots, and onion. In a small bowl stir together oil, rosemary, salt, and pepper. Drizzle over vegetables; toss to coat.

2 Roast, uncovered, for 30 to 35 minutes or until potatoes and onion are tender, stirring twice. Drizzle with balsamic vinegar; toss to coat. Serve immediately.

Makes 6 servings.

Nutrition Facts per serving: 179 cal., 7 g total fat (1 g sat. fat), 0 mg chol., 327 mg sodium, 27 g carbo., 3 g fiber, 3 g pro.

AU GRATIN POTATOES AND PEAS

Dill, cheddar cheese, and pimiento flavor
this great-tasting potato dish. A cracker-crumb
topper adds crunch.

Prep: 35 minutes **Bake:** 30 minutes **Oven:** 350°F

1½ **pounds potatoes, peeled and cut into ½-inch cubes**

1 **cup coarsely crushed rich round crackers or shredded wheat wafers**

2 **tablespoons butter or margarine, melted**

⅓ **cup butter or margarine**

⅓ **cup all-purpose flour**

1 **teaspoon dried dill**

¾ **teaspoon salt**

¼ **teaspoon black pepper**

2½ **cups milk**

1½ **cups shredded sharp cheddar cheese (6 ounces)**

1 **16-ounce package frozen peas, thawed**

1 **4-ounce jar diced pimiento, drained**

1 Preheat oven to 350°F. In a large saucepan combine potatoes and enough water to cover. Bring to boiling. Cover and cook for 3 minutes. Drain; set aside.

2 Meanwhile, grease a 9×13-inch baking pan or baking dish; set aside. In a small bowl combine crushed crackers and the melted butter; set aside.

3 For sauce, in a large saucepan melt the ⅓ cup butter. Stir in flour, dill, salt, and pepper. Add milk all at once. Cook and stir over medium heat until thickened and bubbly. Remove from heat. Add sharp cheddar cheese, stirring until melted.

4 In the prepared pan or dish combine potatoes, peas, and pimiento; pour sauce over all. Sprinkle with crushed cracker mixture. Bake, uncovered, about 30 minutes or until potatoes are tender.

Makes 10 servings.

Nutrition Facts per serving: 322 cal., 18 g total fat (10 g sat. fat), 46 mg chol., 523 mg sodium, 30 g carbo., 4 g fiber, 11 g pro.

BAKED SWEET POTATO AND CHILI WEDGES

These spuds are sensational! Honey tempers a good dose of chili powder to season potatoes that are served with a cooling sour cream sauce.

Prep: 20 minutes   **Bake:** 25 minutes   **Oven:** 450°F

- 2 pounds round sweet potatoes (5 or 6 large)
- 1 tablespoon olive oil
- ½ teaspoon salt
- ⅛ teaspoon black pepper
- ¼ cup orange juice
- 1 tablespoon honey
- 1¾ teaspoons chili powder
- ½ cup dairy sour cream
- ¼ cup snipped fresh cilantro

1 Preheat oven to 450°F. Cut each unpeeled sweet potato into 1-inch-thick wedges. Place sweet potato wedges in a large resealable plastic bag. Add oil, salt, and pepper to sweet potatoes in plastic bag; toss to coat. Arrange sweet potatoes in an ungreased 9×13-inch baking pan or baking dish.

2 Meanwhile, in a small bowl combine orange juice, honey, and 1½ teaspoons of the chili powder; set aside.

3 Bake sweet potatoes, uncovered, for 25 to 30 minutes or until tender, shaking occasionally to rearrange and brushing three times with the orange juice mixture.

4 Meanwhile, in a small bowl combine sour cream, cilantro, and the remaining ¼ teaspoon chili powder. Transfer sweet potatoes to a serving dish. Pass sour cream mixture with potatoes.

Makes 6 servings.

Nutrition Facts per serving: 166 cal., 6 g total fat (2 g sat. fat), 7 mg chol., 272 mg sodium, 27 g carbo., 4 g fiber, 2 g pro.

CORN BREAD FOR A CROWD

This moist sweet corn bread goes great with soups, especially chili. Enjoy it while it's warm.

Prep: 10 minutes **Bake:** 35 minutes **Oven:** 350°F

Nonstick cooking spray
2½ cups all-purpose flour
2 cups yellow cornmeal
½ cup sugar
4 teaspoons baking powder
1 teaspoon salt
3 eggs
2¼ cups milk
½ cup butter, melted

1 Coat a 9×13-inch baking pan or baking dish with nonstick cooking spray; set aside. Preheat oven to 350°F.

2 In an extra-large bowl stir together flour, cornmeal, sugar, baking powder, and salt. In a medium bowl stir together eggs, milk, and melted butter. Add egg mixture to the flour mixture, stirring just until combined. Do not overmix.

3 Pour into prepared pan or dish. Bake, uncovered, for 35 to 40 minutes or until a toothpick inserted in center comes out clean. Serve warm.

Makes 24 servings.

Nutrition Facts per serving: 163 cal., 5 g total fat (3 g sat. fat), 38 mg chol., 203 mg sodium, 28 g carbo., 1 g fiber, 3 g pro.

- -

Fiesta Corn Bread: *Prepare as directed, except fold ¾ cup shredded cheddar cheese and one 4-ounce can diced green chile peppers, undrained, into the batter.*

Nutrition Facts per serving: 178 cal., 6 g total fat (4 g sat. fat), 42 mg chol., 239 mg sodium, 28 g carbo., 1 g fiber, 4 g pro.

24-HOUR DILLED VEGETABLE SALAD

Creamy dressing and cheese
top layers of greens and vegetables in
this make-ahead salad.

Prep: 30 minutes **Chill:** 2 to 24 hours

- 5 cups torn iceberg lettuce, romaine, leaf lettuce, butterhead (Boston or Bibb) lettuce, and/or fresh spinach
- Salt (optional)
- Black pepper (optional)
- 1½ cups sliced fresh mushrooms, broccoli florets, or loose-pack frozen peas
- 1½ cups shredded carrots
- 2 hard-cooked eggs, sliced
- 6 slices bacon, crisp-cooked, drained, and crumbled
- 1 cup shredded American cheese, cheddar cheese, or Swiss cheese (4 ounces)
- ⅓ cup thinly sliced green onions
- 1 cup mayonnaise or salad dressing
- 1 tablespoon lemon juice
- 2 teaspoons snipped fresh dill or ½ teaspoon dried dill
- Thinly sliced green onions (optional)

1 Spread lettuce evenly in a 9×13-inch baking dish. If desired, sprinkle with salt and pepper. Layer on top of lettuce in the following order: mushrooms, carrots, hard-cooked eggs, crumbled bacon, ⅔ cup of the shredded cheese, and the ⅓ cup green onions.

2 For dressing, in small bowl combine mayonnaise, lemon juice, and dill. Spread dressing over salad. Sprinkle with the remaining ⅓ cup cheese. If desired, garnish with additional green onions. Cover tightly with plastic wrap. Chill for at least 2 hours or up to 24 hours. To serve, toss to coat vegetables.

Makes 8 servings.

Nutrition Facts per serving: 326 cal., 31 g total fat (8 g sat. fat), 83 mg chol., 536 mg sodium, 5 g carbo., 1 g fiber, 8 g pro.

LAYERED VEGETABLE SALAD

Not your everyday salad, this tasty medley has crunchy fennel layered with sweet pepper, cherry tomatoes, and garbanzo beans.

Prep: 25 minutes   **Chill:** 4 to 24 hours

- 6   cups torn mixed salad greens
- 1   15-ounce can garbanzo beans (chickpeas), rinsed and drained, or one 10-ounce package frozen peas, thawed
- 1   cup cherry tomatoes, quartered or halved
- 1   cup thinly sliced fennel bulb or broccoli florets
- 1   cup chopped yellow and/or red sweet pepper
- 1   cup diced cooked ham (about 5 ounces)
- ¼   cup thinly sliced green onions
- 1   cup mayonnaise or salad dressing
- 2   tablespoons milk
- 1   tablespoon snipped fennel tops (optional)
- ⅛   teaspoon white pepper or black pepper
- ¾   cup shredded cheddar cheese (3 ounces)

1 Spread salad greens evenly in a 9×13-inch baking dish. Layer ingredients in the following order: garbanzo beans, cherry tomatoes, sliced fennel or broccoli florets, sweet pepper, ham, and green onions.

2 For dressing, in a small bowl stir together mayonnaise, milk, snipped fennel tops (if desired), and white pepper. Spread dressing over salad. Cover tightly with plastic wrap. Chill for at least 4 hours or up to 24 hours.

3 Before serving, top salad with cheddar cheese; toss lightly to coat evenly.

Makes 8 to 10 servings.

Nutrition Facts per serving: 352 cal., 29 g total fat (6 g sat. fat), 34 mg chol., 676 mg sodium, 13 g carbo., 6 g fiber, 10 g pro.

24-HOUR VEGETABLE SALAD
WITH ORANGE MAYONNAISE DRESSING

This super-easy, always colorful 24-hour salad has a fresh taste with feta cheese, olives, and a lively orange-accented dressing.

Prep: 25 minutes   **Chill:** 2 to 24 hours

- 1 medium carrot
- 6 cups torn mixed salad greens
- 1 cup sliced fresh mushrooms
- 1 medium cucumber, halved, seeded, and cut into ¼-inch-thick slices (1¾ cups)
- ½ cup sliced radishes
- ⅔ cup mayonnaise or salad dressing
- ⅓ cup plain low-fat yogurt
- 1 teaspoon finely shredded orange peel
- ½ to ¾ teaspoon crushed red pepper
- ⅛ to ¼ teaspoon black pepper
- ¼ cup sliced green onions
- ¼ cup coarsely chopped pitted kalamata olives
- ¼ cup crumbled feta cheese (1 ounce)

1 Peel carrot. Using a vegetable peeler, carefully cut carrot lengthwise into long, paper-thin ribbons; set aside.

2 Spread salad greens evenly in a 9×13-inch baking dish. Layer ingredients in the following order: carrot ribbons, mushrooms, cucumber, and radishes.

3 For dressing, in a small bowl stir together mayonnaise, yogurt, orange peel, crushed red pepper, and black pepper. Spread dressing over salad. Cover tightly with plastic wrap. Chill for at least 2 hours or up to 24 hours.

4 To serve, sprinkle with green onions, olives, and feta cheese.

Makes 8 servings.

Nutrition Facts per serving: 175 cal., 16 g total fat (3 g sat. fat), 11 mg chol., 213 mg sodium, 6 g carbo., 2 g fiber, 3 g pro.

LAYERED BLACK BEAN SALAD

This easy, kind of spicy salad is all about layering one good thing on top of another, adding the dressing, and then chilling.

Prep: 25 minutes   **Chill:** 4 to 24 hours

- 4 cups shredded iceberg lettuce
- 2 15-ounce cans black beans, rinsed and drained
- 2 tablespoons snipped fresh cilantro
- 1 cup chopped red onion
- 2 cups chopped red and/or green sweet pepper
- 1 4-ounce can chopped green chile peppers, drained
- 1½ cups dairy sour cream
- 2 tablespoons lime juice
- 1 teaspoon chili powder
- ½ teaspoon salt
- ¼ teaspoon garlic powder
- ¾ cup chopped seeded tomato

1 Spread lettuce evenly in a 9×13-inch baking dish. Layer ingredients in the following order: black beans, cilantro, red onion, sweet pepper, and chile peppers.

2 For dressing, in a small bowl stir together sour cream, lime juice, chili powder, salt, and garlic powder. Spread dressing over salad. Cover tightly with plastic wrap. Chill for at least 4 hours or up to 24 hours.

3 Sprinkle with chopped tomato before serving.

Makes 8 to 12 servings.

Nutrition Facts per serving: 173 cal., 8 g total fat (5 g sat. fat), 16 mg chol., 492 mg sodium, 22 g carbo., 7 g fiber, 9 g pro.

24-HOUR TEX-MEX SALAD

This Mexicali masterpiece is chock-full of goodness. Layers upon layers of ingredients soak up flavor while this favorite party salad chills.

Prep: 45 minutes   **Chill:** 6 to 24 hours

- 6 cups torn lettuce
- 1 15-ounce can black beans, black-eyed peas, or pinto beans, rinsed and drained
- 3 medium tomatoes, seeded and chopped
- 1 10-ounce package frozen whole kernel corn
- 1 cup chopped red, green, and/or yellow sweet pepper
- 1 cup peeled and cubed jicama or shredded carrot
- 1 cup diced cooked ham or chicken
- ¼ cup thinly sliced green onions
- 4 ounces Monterey Jack cheese with jalapeño chile peppers, shredded (1 cup)
- 1 cup mayonnaise or salad dressing
- 1 8-ounce carton dairy sour cream
- 1½ teaspoons chili powder
- ½ cup sliced radishes
- 2 tablespoons snipped fresh cilantro or parsley

1 Spread 3 cups of the lettuce evenly in a 9×13-inch baking dish. Layer ingredients in the following order: black beans, tomatoes, corn, sweet pepper, jicama, the remaining 3 cups lettuce, the ham, green onions, and Monterey Jack cheese.

2 For dressing, in a small bowl stir together mayonnaise, sour cream, and chili powder. Spread dressing over salad. Cover tightly with plastic wrap. Chill for at least 6 hours or up to 24 hours.

3 To serve, top with radish slices and sprinkle with cilantro.

Makes 8 to 10 servings.

Nutrition Facts per serving: 443 cal., 35 g total fat (10 g sat. fat), 45 mg chol., 625 mg sodium, 23 g carbo., 5 g fiber, 13 g pro.

ROASTED BEET AND POTATO SALAD

Colorful and flavorful, this terrific
combination highlights the sweetness of fresh
beets and baby new potatoes.

Prep: 25 minutes   **Roast:** 40 minutes   **Oven:** 375°F

- 12   ounces fresh baby beets or 3 medium fresh beets
- 12   ounces tiny new potatoes, halved
- 4   ounces pearl onions, peeled
- ¼   cup olive oil
- 6   cloves garlic, minced
- 1   tablespoon snipped fresh rosemary or basil
- ½   teaspoon salt
- ½   teaspoon coarsely ground black pepper
- 2   tablespoons balsamic vinegar
- 1   tablespoon snipped fresh chives
- 1   tablespoon water
- 6   cups torn butterhead (Boston or Bibb) lettuce

1 Preheat oven to 375°F. Scrub beets; trim off stems and root ends. (If using medium beets, peel them and cut into 1-inch pieces.) In an ungreased 9×13-inch baking pan or baking dish combine beets, potatoes, and pearl onions.

2 In a small bowl combine 2 tablespoons of the oil, the garlic, rosemary, salt, and pepper. Drizzle over vegetables in pan or dish. Toss lightly to coat. Cover pan or dish with foil. Roast for 30 minutes. Uncover; continue roasting for 10 to 20 minutes more or until vegetables are tender. Cool vegetables to room temperature; drain, reserving pan drippings.

3 For dressing, in a screw-top jar combine the reserved pan drippings, the remaining 2 tablespoons oil, the balsamic vinegar, snipped chives, and the water. Cover and shake well.

4 Divide lettuce among six salad plates. Top with roasted vegetable mixture; drizzle with dressing. Serve immediately.

Makes 6 servings.

Nutrition Facts per serving: 172 cal., 9 g total fat (1 g sat. fat), 0 mg chol., 245 mg sodium, 20 g carbo., 3 g fiber, 3 g pro.

MISSISSIPPI CORN BREAD SALAD

This hearty make-ahead salad features crumbled corn bread layered with corn, beans, tomatoes, bacon, and always good ranch salad dressing.

Prep: 35 minutes   **Bake:** according to package directions   **Chill:** 3 to 24 hours

- 1   8½-ounce package corn muffin mix
- 1   cup mayonnaise or salad dressing
- 1   8-ounce carton dairy sour cream
- 1   1-ounce envelope ranch salad dressing mix
- 2   15¼-ounce cans whole kernel corn, drained
- 2   15-ounce cans pinto beans, rinsed and drained
- 3   large tomatoes, chopped (about 3 cups)
- ½   cup chopped red sweet pepper
- ½   cup chopped green sweet pepper
- ½   cup chopped green onions
- 2   cups shredded cheddar cheese (8 ounces)
- 10 slices bacon, crisp-cooked, drained, and crumbled

1 Prepare corn muffin mix according to package directions for corn bread. Cool and crumble (should have about 5 cups). Set aside.

2 For dressing, in a medium bowl combine mayonnaise, sour cream, and dry salad dressing mix. In a large bowl combine corn, pinto beans, tomatoes, sweet peppers, and green onions.

3 In a 9×13-inch baking dish layer half of the crumbled corn bread, half of the bean mixture, half of the cheddar cheese, and half of the bacon. Spread dressing over. Repeat with remaining corn bread, bean mixture, cheese, and bacon. Cover and chill for at least 3 hours or up to 24 hours. To serve, toss to coat evenly.

Makes 18 to 20 servings.

Nutrition Facts per serving: 339 cal., 21 g total fat (6 g sat. fat), 35 mg chol., 735 mg sodium, 30 g carbo., 4 g fiber, 10 g pro.

FRESH TOMATO AND MOZZARELLA SALAD

The unbeatable flavor of garden fresh tomatoes shines through when layered with fresh mozzarella cheese, drizzled with vinaigrette, and sprinkled with basil.

Start to Finish: 20 minutes

- 1½ pounds tomatoes, thinly sliced
- 8 ounces fresh mozzarella cheese, thinly sliced
- 3 tablespoons olive oil
- 3 tablespoons balsamic vinegar
- 2 tablespoons Dijon-style mustard
- 2 cloves garlic, minced
- ⅛ teaspoon salt
- ¼ cup shredded fresh basil leaves

1 Arrange tomato slices and fresh mozzarella cheese slices alternately in a 9×13-inch baking dish.

2 In a small bowl whisk together oil, balsamic vinegar, mustard, garlic, and salt. Drizzle over tomato mixture. Sprinkle with fresh basil.

Makes 8 servings.

Nutrition Facts per serving: 153 cal., 12 g total fat (4 g sat. fat), 22 mg chol., 309 mg sodium, 6 g carbo., 1 g fiber, 8 g pro.

FANCY STRAWBERRY-NUT SALAD

Strawberries, pineapple, and bananas fill berry gelatin with refreshing fruit flavors, while a layer of sour cream adds richness.

Prep: 25 minutes   **Chill:** 5½ hours   **Freeze:** 10 minutes

- 1   6-ounce package strawberry-flavor gelatin
- 1   cup boiling water
- 2   10-ounce packages frozen sliced strawberries in syrup, thawed
- 1   20-ounce can crushed pineapple, drained
- 3   medium bananas, sliced
- 1   cup coarsely chopped walnuts, toasted
- 2   8-ounce cartons dairy sour cream

1 In a large bowl stir gelatin into boiling water until gelatin is dissolved. Stir in undrained strawberries. Chill in the refrigerator about 1½ hours or until partially set (the consistency of unbeaten egg whites).

2 Stir in pineapple, bananas, and walnuts. Spoon half of the mixture into a 9×13-inch baking dish. Cover and chill in the freezer for 10 to 12 minutes or just until firm. (Let remaining mixture stand at room temperature so it does not set up.)

3 Spread sour cream evenly over strawberry mixture in dish. Spoon remaining strawberry mixture over sour cream. Cover and chill in the refrigerator for at least 4 hours or until firm.

Makes 24 servings.

Nutrition Facts per serving: 152 cal., 8 g total fat (3 g sat. fat), 8 mg chol., 22 mg sodium, 21 g carbo., 1 g fiber, 2 g pro.

ORANGE-GINGER SALAD

Crystallized ginger and ginger ale give this orange-and-apple gelatin salad a double dose of lively flavor.

Prep: 15 minutes **Chill:** 4 hours

- 2 6-ounce packages orange-flavor gelatin
- 2 cups water
- 3 tablespoons finely chopped crystallized ginger
- 4 cups ginger ale, chilled
- 2 medium apples, cored and chopped
- 1 11-ounce can mandarin oranges, drained
- ¾ cup chopped pecans, toasted
- ½ cup shredded carrot
- 1 8-ounce carton dairy sour cream
- ⅓ cup sugar
- 1 teaspoon vanilla

1 In a large saucepan combine gelatin, the water, and crystallized ginger; heat and stir until gelatin dissolves. Remove from heat. Carefully stir in ginger ale, stopping occasionally to let foam subside if necessary. Transfer to a very large bowl. Cover and chill for 1 to 1½ hours or until partially set (the consistency of unbeaten egg whites). Fold in apples, mandarin oranges, pecans, and carrot.

2 Pour into a 9×13-inch baking dish. Cover; chill for at least 3 hours or until firm. In a small bowl combine sour cream, sugar, and vanilla. Cover and chill until serving time.

3 To serve, cut gelatin mixture into squares. Top individual servings with dollops of the sour cream mixture.

Makes 15 servings.

Nutrition Facts per serving: 233 cal., 8 g total fat (3 g sat. fat), 7 mg chol., 51 mg sodium, 38 g carbo., 1 g fiber, 3 g pro.

YUM-YUM RIBBON SALAD

The name says it all. Raspberry, lemon, and lime gelatin are filled with delectable ingredients such as marshmallows, pineapple, and whipped cream. (Pictured on page 107.)

Prep: 25 minutes   **Chill:** 6¾ hours

- 1   6-ounce package raspberry- or strawberry-flavor gelatin
- 1   3-ounce package lemon-flavor gelatin
- 1   cup boiling water
- 1   cup tiny marshmallows
- 1   3-ounce package cream cheese, softened
- ¾   cup mayonnaise or salad dressing
- 1   8-ounce can crushed pineapple
- ½   cup whipping cream
- 1   3-ounce package lime-flavor gelatin
-      Whipped cream (optional)

1 Prepare raspberry- or strawberry-flavor gelatin according to package directions. Pour gelatin into a 9×13-inch baking dish. Chill gelatin about 1 hour or until almost firm (sticky to touch).

2 In a large bowl dissolve lemon-flavor gelatin in the 1 cup boiling water. Add marshmallows; whisk until marshmallows are melted. Whisk in cream cheese and mayonnaise until combined. Stir in undrained crushed pineapple. In a small bowl beat whipping cream until soft peaks form. Gently fold whipped cream into pineapple mixture. Carefully stir mixture to distribute the crushed pineapple evenly; spoon over chilled gelatin. Chill about 1 hour or until almost firm (sticky to touch).

3 Prepare lime-flavor gelatin according to package directions. Chill about 45 minutes or until partially set (consistency of unbeaten egg whites). Pour over the chilled lemon mixture. Cover and chill at least 4 hours or until firm.

4 If desired, top individual servings with whipped cream.

Makes 15 servings.

Nutrition Facts per serving: 238 cal., 14 g total fat (4 g sat. fat), 23 mg chol., 145 mg sodium, 27 g carbo., 0 g fiber, 3 g pro.

STRAWBERRY PRETZEL SALAD

Crunchy pretzels are the surprise ingredient in this company-pleasing gelatin salad. Take it to your next potluck.

Prep: 20 minutes **Bake:** 10 minutes **Chill:** 4 hours **Oven:** 350°F

- 3 cups finely crushed pretzels
- ½ cup sugar
- ¾ cup butter or margarine, melted
- 1 8-ounce package cream cheese, softened
- 1 cup sugar
- 1 8-ounce container frozen whipped dessert topping, thawed
- 2 10-ounce packages frozen strawberries in syrup, thawed
- 2 3-ounce packages strawberry-flavor gelatin
- 2 cups boiling water

1 Preheat oven to 350°F. For crust, in a medium bowl combine crushed pretzels and the ½ cup sugar. Add melted butter; stir well to combine. Press pretzel mixture into an ungreased 9×13-inch baking pan or baking dish. Bake for 10 minutes. Cool in pan or dish on a wire rack.

2 In a large bowl combine cream cheese and the 1 cup sugar; beat with an electric mixer on medium speed until well mixed. Slowly beat in the dessert topping. Spread over cooled crust.

3 In another large bowl combine strawberries and gelatin. Stir in the boiling water. Stir about 2 minutes or until gelatin is dissolved. Carefully pour gelatin mixture over the cream cheese layer. Cover and chill for at least 4 hours or until set.

Makes 24 servings.

Nutrition Facts per serving: 252 cal., 11 g total fat (8 g sat. fat), 26 mg chol., 240 mg sodium, 35 g carbo., 1 g fiber, 3 g pro.

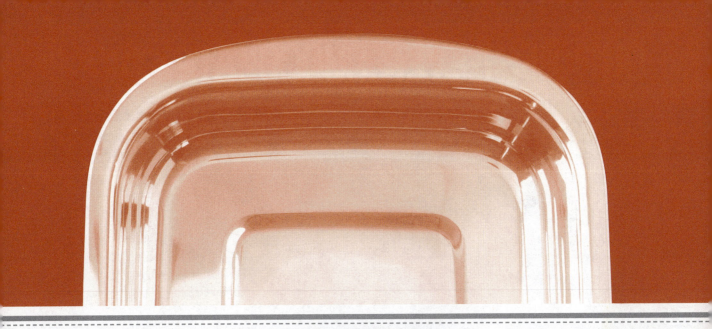

CAKES FOR
ALL OCCASIONS

When you're celebrating a special occasion, such as a birthday, or you need to tote something sweet to a potluck or office party, serve up pieces worth remembering. You'll find a wide range of cakes, from oven-warm upside down cakes to rich and decadent chocolate specialties. Busy cooks can have their cake, too, when they try our easy

OUR BEST-EVER CHOCOLATE CAKE

A classic 1950s recipe, this is still one of the richest, chocolatiest cakes ever. A sour cream-chocolate frosting makes it nearly irresistible.

Prep: 50 minutes **Stand:** 30 minutes **Bake:** 35 minutes **Oven:** 350°F (baking pan) or 325°F (baking dish)

- ¾ **cup butter**
- 3 **eggs**
- 2 **cups all-purpose flour**
- ¾ **cup unsweetened cocoa powder**
- 1 **teaspoon baking soda**
- ¾ **teaspoon baking powder**
- ½ **teaspoon salt**
- 2 **cups sugar**
- 2 **teaspoons vanilla**
- 1½ **cups milk**
- 1 **recipe Chocolate-Sour Cream Frosting**

1 Allow butter and eggs to stand at room temperature for 30 minutes. Meanwhile, lightly grease a 9×13-inch baking pan or baking dish; set pan or dish aside. Preheat oven to 350°F if using a baking pan or 325°F if using a baking dish.

2 In a medium bowl stir together flour, cocoa powder, baking soda, baking powder, and salt; set aside.

3 In a large bowl beat butter with an electric mixer on medium to high speed for 30 seconds. Gradually add sugar, about ¼ cup at a time, beating on medium speed until well mixed (3 to 4 minutes). Scrape side of bowl; continue beating on medium speed for 2 minutes. Add eggs, one at a time, beating after each addition (about 1 minute total). Beat in vanilla.

4 Alternately add flour mixture and milk to beaten mixture, beating on low speed after each addition just until combined. Beat on medium to high speed for 20 seconds more. Spread batter evenly in prepared pan or dish.

5 Bake for 35 to 40 minutes or until a toothpick inserted in the center comes out clean. Cool in pan or dish on a wire rack.

6 Spread Chocolate-Sour Cream Frosting over the cake. Cover and store in the refrigerator within 2 hours.

Makes 15 servings.

Nutrition Facts per serving: 458 cal., 19 g total fat (11 g sat. fat), 80 mg chol., 290 mg sodium, 68 g carbo., 1 g fiber, 4 g pro.

Chocolate-Sour Cream Frosting: *In a large saucepan combine 1 cup semisweet chocolate pieces and ¼ cup butter; cook and stir over low heat until melted. Cool for 5 minutes. Stir in ½ cup dairy sour cream. Gradually add 2¼ to 2½ cups powdered sugar, beating with an electric mixer until smooth. (Mixture may be slightly warm when powdered sugar is added.)*

DEVIL'S FOOD CAKE WITH GANACHE

So beautiful and chocolaty, it's almost sinful. A rich bittersweet chocolate glaze makes this classic hard to resist.

Prep: 40 minutes **Bake:** 30 minutes **Oven:** 350°F (baking pan) or 325°F (baking dish)

- 2¼ cups all-purpose flour
- ½ cup unsweetened cocoa powder
- 1½ teaspoons baking powder
- 1 teaspoon baking soda
- ¼ teaspoon salt
- ½ cup shortening
- 1¾ cups sugar
- 1 teaspoon vanilla
- 3 eggs
- 1⅓ cups cold water
- 9 ounces bittersweet chocolate, chopped
- 1 cup whipping cream

1 Grease a 9×13-inch baking pan or baking dish; set aside. Preheat oven to 350°F if using a baking pan or 325°F if using a baking dish. In a large bowl combine flour, cocoa powder, baking powder, baking soda, and salt; set aside.

2 In a large bowl beat shortening with an electric mixer on medium to high speed for 30 seconds. Add sugar and vanilla; beat until well mixed. Add eggs, one at a time, beating well after each addition. Alternately add flour mixture and the water to beaten mixture, beating on low speed after each addition just until combined. Spread batter evenly in prepared pan or dish.

3 Bake for 30 to 40 minutes or until a toothpick inserted near the center comes out clean. Cool in pan or dish on a wire rack.

4 For ganache, place the chocolate in a medium bowl. In a small saucepan heat whipping cream over medium heat just until boiling, watching very carefully. Pour hot cream over chopped chocolate; whisk until smooth. Allow the ganache to cool slightly. Starting at the center of the cake and working outward, pour ganache over cake.

Makes 15 servings.

Nutrition Facts per serving: 382 cal., 21 g total fat (10 g sat. fat), 65 mg chol., 181 mg sodium, 49 g carbo., 3 g fiber, 3 g pro.

RED WALDORF CAKE

Yes, it really is red! Kids will love this velvety chocolate cake that is big on flavor and has a creamy white frosting. Red food coloring is the key.

Prep: 30 minutes   **Stand:** 30 minutes   **Bake:** 30 minutes   **Oven:** 350°F (baking pan) or 325°F (baking dish)

  2   eggs
  ½   cup unsweetened cocoa powder
  2   ounces red food coloring (¼ cup)
2¼   cups sifted cake flour or 2 cups sifted all-purpose flour
  ½   teaspoon salt
  ½   cup shortening
1½   cups sugar
  1   teaspoon vanilla
  1   cup buttermilk or sour milk*
  1   teaspoon baking soda
  1   teaspoon vinegar
  1   recipe Creamy Frosting

1 Allow eggs to stand at room temperature for 30 minutes. Meanwhile, grease a 9×13-inch baking pan or baking dish; set aside. Preheat oven to 350°F if using a baking pan or 325°F if using a baking dish. In a small bowl stir together cocoa powder and food coloring; set aside. In another small bowl stir together flour and salt; set aside.

2 In a large bowl beat shortening with an electric mixer on medium to high speed for 30 seconds. Add sugar and vanilla; beat until well mixed. Add eggs, one at a time, beating on medium speed after each addition until combined. Beat in cocoa mixture. Alternately add flour mixture and buttermilk to beaten mixture, beating on low to medium speed after each addition just until combined. In small bowl stir together baking soda and vinegar. Add to batter, stirring until combined. Spread batter evenly in prepared pan or dish.

3 Bake about 30 minutes or until a toothpick inserted near center comes out clean. Cool in pan or dish on a wire rack.

4 Spread Creamy Frosting over cake. Cover and store in the refrigerator within 2 hours.

Makes 15 servings.

Nutrition Facts per serving: 426 cal., 20 g total fat (10 g sat. fat), 63 mg chol., 283 mg sodium, 54 g carbo., 0 g fiber, 4 g pro.

Creamy Frosting: *In a medium saucepan whisk together 1 cup milk and 3 tablespoons all-purpose flour. Cook and stir over medium heat until thickened and bubbly. Reduce heat; cook and stir for 2 minutes more. Cover surface with plastic wrap. Cool to room temperature (do not stir). In a medium bowl combine 1 cup butter, softened; 1 cup sugar; and 1 teaspoon vanilla; beat with an electric mixer on medium speed until light and fluffy. Add the cooled milk mixture to the butter mixture, ¼ cup at a time, beating on low speed after each addition until smooth.*

*Test Kitchen Tip: *To make 1 cup sour milk, place 1 tablespoon lemon juice or vinegar in a glass measuring cup. Add enough milk to make 1 cup total liquid; stir. Let stand for 5 minutes before using.*

Make-Ahead Directions: *Prepare as directed, except cover and store in the refrigerator for up to 3 days.*

CHOCOLATE-BUTTERMILK CAKE

With a texture like a cake brownie, tons of chocolaty flavor, and a light chocolate icing, this cake will keep you coming back for more. And more.

Prep: 30 minutes **Bake:** 35 minutes **Oven:** 350°F (baking pan) or 325°F (baking dish)

- 2 **cups all-purpose flour**
- 2 **cups sugar**
- 1 **teaspoon baking soda**
- ¼ **teaspoon salt**
- 1 **cup butter**
- 1 **cup water**
- ⅓ **cup unsweetened cocoa powder**
- 2 **eggs**
- ½ **cup buttermilk or sour milk***
- 1½ **teaspoons vanilla**
- 1 **recipe Chocolate-Buttermilk Frosting**

1 Grease a 9×13-inch baking pan or baking dish; set aside. Preheat oven to 350°F if using a baking pan or 325°F if using a baking dish. In a large bowl combine flour, sugar, baking soda, and salt; set aside.

2 In a medium saucepan combine butter, the water, and cocoa powder. Bring just to boiling, stirring constantly. Remove from heat. Add the chocolate mixture to the flour mixture; beat with an electric mixer on medium speed until combined. Add the eggs, buttermilk, and vanilla. Beat for 1 minute (batter will be thin). Spread batter evenly in prepared pan or dish.

3 Bake about 35 minutes or until a toothpick inserted in center comes out clean.

4 Pour warm Chocolate-Buttermilk Frosting over warm cake, spreading evenly. Cool in pan or dish on a wire rack.

Makes 15 servings.

Nutrition Facts per serving: 279 cal., 5 g total fat (3 g sat. fat), 39 mg chol., 172 mg sodium, 57 g carbo., 1 g fiber, 2 g pro.

Chocolate-Buttermilk Frosting: *In a medium saucepan combine ¼ cup butter, 3 tablespoons unsweetened cocoa powder, and 3 tablespoons buttermilk or sour milk.* Bring mixture to boiling. Remove from heat. Add 2¼ cups powdered sugar and ½ teaspoon vanilla. Beat until smooth. If desired, stir in ¾ cup coarsely chopped pecans.*

***Test Kitchen Tip:** To make ¾ cup sour milk, place 2 teaspoons lemon juice or vinegar in a glass measuring cup. Add enough milk to make ¾ cup total liquid; stir. Let mixture stand for 5 minutes before using. Use ½ cup in the cake and 3 tablespoons in the frosting; discard remaining.*

Make-Ahead Directions: *Cover and store in refrigerator for up to 3 days. (Or place pieces in a single layer in an airtight container. Cover and seal. Freeze for up to 3 months.)*

DARK COCOA BUTTERMILK CAKE
WITH COCOA MASCARPONE FROSTING

A richer, moister, more chocolaty cake is hard to find. Look for mascarpone, an Italian cream cheese with a buttery flavor, in your store's specialty cheese section.

Prep: 30 minutes **Stand:** 30 minutes **Bake:** 45 minutes **Oven:** 350°F (baking pan) or 325°F (baking dish)

- ¾ cup butter
- 3 eggs
- 2⅓ cups all-purpose flour
- ¾ cup Dutch-process unsweetened cocoa powder or regular unsweetened cocoa powder
- 1 teaspoon baking soda
- ¾ teaspoon baking powder
- ½ teaspoon salt
- 1 cup granulated sugar
- 1 cup packed brown sugar
- 2 teaspoons vanilla
- 1½ cups buttermilk or sour milk*
- 1 recipe Cocoa Mascarpone Frosting
  White and dark chocolate shavings (optional)

1 Allow butter and eggs to stand at room temperature for 30 minutes. Meanwhile, lightly grease a 9×13-inch baking pan or baking dish; set pan or dish aside. Preheat oven to 350°F if using a baking pan or 325°F if using a baking dish.

2 In a medium bowl stir together flour, cocoa powder, baking soda, baking powder, and salt; set aside.

3 In a large bowl beat butter with an electric mixer on medium to high speed for 30 seconds. In a small bowl combine granulated sugar and brown sugar. Gradually add sugar mixture to butter, about ¼ cup at a time, beating on medium speed until well mixed (3 to 4 minutes). Scrape side of bowl; continue beating on medium speed for 2 minutes. Add eggs, one at a time, beating well after each addition. Beat in vanilla.

4 Alternately add flour mixture and buttermilk to beaten mixture, beating on low speed after each addition just until combined. Beat on medium to high speed for 20 seconds more. Spread batter evenly in prepared pan or dish.

5 Bake for 45 to 50 minutes or until a toothpick inserted in the center comes out clean. Cool in pan or dish on wire rack.

6 Spread Cocoa Mascarpone Frosting over cake. If desired, top with chocolate shavings. Cover and store in the refrigerator.

Makes 15 servings.

Nutrition Facts per serving: 414 cal., 16 g total fat (10 g sat. fat), 81 mg chol., 310 mg sodium, 65 g carbo., 2 g fiber, 4 g pro.

Cocoa Mascarpone Frosting: *In a medium bowl combine ¼ cup mascarpone cheese or 2 ounces cream cheese, softened; ¼ cup butter, softened; 3 tablespoons unsweetened cocoa powder; 1 tablespoon milk; and 1 teaspoon vanilla. Beat with an electric mixer on medium to high speed until creamy. Gradually add 2⅓ cups powdered sugar, beating until smooth. Beat in enough additional milk, 1 teaspoon at a time, to reach spreading consistency. Makes about 1½ cups.*

---

*Test Kitchen Tip: *To make 1½ cups sour milk, place 4½ teaspoons lemon juice or vinegar in a glass measuring cup. Add enough milk to make 1½ cups total liquid; stir. Let mixture stand for 5 minutes before using.*

GERMAN CHOCOLATE CAKE

For many, this is the best of all chocolate cakes because it not only has chocolate but a chewy and gooey coconut-pecan frosting.

Prep: 30 minutes   **Stand:** 30 minutes   **Bake:** 40 minutes   **Oven:** 350°F (baking pan) or 325°F (baking dish)

- 1 4-ounce package sweet baking chocolate, chopped
- 1½ cups milk
- ¾ cup butter
- 3 eggs
- 2 cups all-purpose flour
- 1 teaspoon baking soda
- ¾ teaspoon baking powder
- ½ teaspoon salt
- 1¾ cups sugar
- 2 teaspoons vanilla
- 1 recipe Coconut-Pecan Frosting

1 In a small saucepan combine chocolate and milk. Cook and stir over low heat until melted; set aside to cool.

2 Allow butter and eggs to stand at room temperature for 30 minutes. Meanwhile, lightly grease a 9×13-inch baking pan or baking dish; set aside. Preheat oven to 350°F if using a baking pan or 325°F if using a baking dish. In a medium bowl stir together flour, baking soda, baking powder, and salt; set aside.

3 In a large bowl beat butter with an electric mixer on medium to high speed for 30 seconds. Gradually add sugar, about ¼ cup at a time, beating on medium speed until well mixed (about 3 minutes). Scrape sides of bowl; continue beating on medium speed for 2 minutes more. Add eggs, one at a time, beating after each addition (about 1 minute total). Beat in vanilla.

4 Alternately add flour mixture and chocolate mixture to beaten mixture, beating on low speed after each addition just until combined. Beat on medium to high speed for 20 seconds more. Spread batter evenly in prepared pan or dish.

5 Bake for 40 to 45 minutes or until a toothpick inserted near the center comes out clean. Cool in pan or dish on a wire rack.

6 Spread Coconut-Pecan Frosting over cake. Cover and store in the refrigerator.

Makes 15 servings.

Nutrition Facts per serving: 450 cal., 23 g total fat (14 g sat. fat), 94 mg chol., 328 mg sodium, 57 g carbo., 2 g fiber, 5 g pro.

291

Coconut-Pecan Frosting: *In a medium saucepan slightly beat 1 egg. Stir in one 5-ounce can (⅔ cup) evaporated milk, ⅔ cup sugar, and ¼ cup butter. Cook and stir over medium heat for 6 to 8 minutes or until thickened and bubbly. Remove from heat; stir in 1⅓ cups flaked coconut and ½ cup chopped pecans. Cover and cool completely.*

ORANGE-CHOCOLATE CAKE

Yogurt, orange juice, and egg whites make this devil's food cake light and refreshing. Two icings, one chocolate and one orange, are drizzled on top.

Prep: 15 minutes   **Bake:** 35 minutes   **Oven:** 350°F (baking pan) or 325°F (baking dish)

Nonstick cooking spray

Unsweetened cocoa powder

1   package 2-layer-size devil's food cake mix

1   8-ounce carton low-fat or fat-free plain yogurt

2   tablespoons finely shredded orange peel

½   cup orange juice

½   cup water

1   egg

2   egg whites

2   tablespoons cooking oil

1   teaspoon ground cinnamon

1   recipe Chocolate Icing

1   recipe Orange Icing

1 Coat a 9×13-inch baking pan or baking dish with nonstick cooking spray; dust with unsweetened cocoa powder. Set aside. Preheat oven to 350°F if using a baking pan or 325°F if using a baking dish.

2 In a large bowl combine dry cake mix, yogurt, orange peel, orange juice, the water, egg, egg whites, oil, and cinnamon. Beat with an electric mixer on low speed for 4 minutes. Spread batter evenly in prepared pan or dish.

3 Bake for 35 to 40 minutes or until a toothpick inserted near center comes out clean. Cool in pan or dish on a wire rack. Drizzle Chocolate Icing and Orange Icing over cake.

Makes 15 servings.

Nutrition Facts per serving: 221 cal., 8 g total fat (2 g sat. fat), 15 mg chol., 311 mg sodium, 36 g carbo., 1 g fiber, 4 g pro.

Chocolate Icing: *In a small bowl combine ½ cup powdered sugar, 1 tablespoon unsweetened cocoa powder, 2 teaspoons orange juice, and ¼ teaspoon vanilla. Stir in enough additional orange juice, 1 teaspoon at a time, to make icing of drizzling consistency. Makes about 2 tablespoons.*

Orange Icing: *In another small bowl combine ½ cup powdered sugar, 1 teaspoon orange juice, and ¼ teaspoon vanilla. Stir in enough additional orange juice, 1 teaspoon at a time, to make icing of drizzling consistency. Makes about 2 tablespoons.*

CHOCOLATE CHIP-OATMEAL CAKE

This down-homey cake has the nuttiness of oats and the sweetness of chocolate. More chocolate pieces and walnuts create the tasty topping.

Prep: 25 minutes **Bake:** 40 minutes **Oven:** 350°F (baking pan) or 325°F (baking dish)

1	cup quick-cooking rolled oats
1¾	cups boiling water
1	cup granulated sugar
1	cup packed brown sugar
½	cup butter, cut up
2	eggs
1¾	cups all-purpose flour
1	tablespoon unsweetened cocoa powder
1	teaspoon baking soda
½	teaspoon salt
1	12-ounce package semisweet chocolate pieces
¾	cup chopped walnuts

1 Place rolled oats in a large bowl. Pour the boiling water over the oats; let stand for 10 minutes. Meanwhile, grease and flour a 9×13-inch baking pan or baking dish; set aside. Preheat oven to 350°F if using a baking pan or 325°F if using a baking dish.

2 Add granulated sugar, brown sugar, and butter to oat mixture, stirring until butter is melted. Stir in eggs until combined. Stir in flour, cocoa powder, baking soda, and salt until combined. Stir in 1 cup of the chocolate pieces. Spread batter evenly in prepared pan or dish. Sprinkle with chopped walnuts and the remaining chocolate pieces.

3 Bake about 40 minutes or until a toothpick inserted near the center comes out clean. Cool in pan or dish on a wire rack.

Makes 15 servings.

Nutrition Facts per serving: 403 cal., 18 g total fat (8 g sat. fat), 46 mg chol., 243 mg sodium, 51 g carbo., 5 g fiber, 4 g pro.

CHOCOLATE CANDY-GRAHAM CAKE

It's a dream come true. Chocolate cake has chocolate peanut butter candy baked inside, then gets more candy and chocolate melted on top.

Prep: 25 minutes **Bake:** 55 minutes **Chill:** 10 minutes **Oven:** 350°F (baking pan) or 325°F (baking dish)

Nonstick cooking spray

1¼ cups finely crushed graham crackers

¼ cup sugar

⅓ cup butter

4 2.1-ounce bars chocolate-covered crisp peanut butter candy bars, chilled and crushed

1 package 2-layer-size Swiss chocolate or devil's food cake mix

1¼ cups water

½ cup cooking oil

3 eggs

1 cup milk chocolate pieces

1 Line a 9×13-inch baking pan or baking dish with foil, extending foil over the edges of the pan or dish. Lightly coat foil with nonstick cooking spray. Set aside. Preheat oven to 350°F if using a baking pan or 325°F if using a baking dish.

2 In a medium bowl combine crushed graham crackers and sugar. Using a pastry blender, cut in butter until mixture resembles coarse crumbs. Press crumb mixture evenly into prepared pan or dish. Bake for 10 minutes. Remove from oven and sprinkle with half of the crushed candy bars.

3 In a large bowl combine dry cake mix, the water, cooking oil, and eggs. Beat with an electric mixer on low speed for 30 seconds, scraping side of bowl constantly. Beat on high speed for 2 minutes. Spread batter evenly over the candy in pan or dish. Bake about 45 minutes or until a toothpick inserted near the center comes out clean.

4 Remove from oven and immediately sprinkle with the remaining crushed candy bars and the milk chocolate pieces. Cool in pan or dish on a wire rack. Chill about 10 minutes or until chocolate is firm.

5 Using the edges of the foil, lift the uncut cake out of the pan or dish. Cut into pieces.

Makes 15 servings.

Nutrition Facts per serving: 472 cal., 24 g total fat (10 g sat. fat), 58 mg chol., 403 mg sodium, 58 g carbo., 2 g fiber, 6 g pro.

COCOA-COLA CAKE

Soft melting marshmallows blend with toasty pecans and chocolate to create a Southern-style cake and a sure crowd-pleaser.

Prep: 40 minutes **Bake:** 30 minutes **Oven:** 350°F (baking pan) or 325°F (baking dish)

- 2 cups all-purpose flour
- 2 cups granulated sugar
- 1 cup butter
- 1 cup cola
- 2 tablespoons unsweetened cocoa powder
- 2 eggs, slightly beaten
- ½ cup buttermilk or sour milk*
- 1 teaspoon baking soda
- 1 teaspoon vanilla
- 2 cups tiny marshmallows
- 1 recipe Cocoa-Cola Frosting
- ½ cup chopped pecans, toasted

1 Grease a 9×13-inch baking pan or baking dish; set aside. Preheat oven to 350°F if using a baking pan or 325°F if using a baking dish. In a large bowl stir together flour and the granulated sugar. Set aside.

2 In medium saucepan combine butter, cola, and cocoa powder. Cook and stir over medium heat until butter melts. Pour over flour mixture. Add eggs, buttermilk, baking soda, and vanilla; mix well. Stir in tiny marshmallows. Spread batter evenly in prepared pan or dish.

3 Bake for 30 to 35 minutes or until a toothpick inserted near center comes out clean. Cool in pan or dish on a wire rack.

4 Spread Cocoa-Cola Frosting over cake. Sprinkle with pecans.

Makes 15 servings.

Nutrition Facts per serving: 500 cal., 20 g total fat (11 g sat. fat), 72 mg chol., 227 mg sodium, 79 g carbo., 1 g fiber, 2 g pro.

295

Cocoa-Cola Frosting: *In a medium bowl beat ⅓ cup butter with an electric mixer on medium to high speed for 30 seconds. Slowly add 2 cups powdered sugar and 2 tablespoons unsweetened cocoa powder, beating until combined. Add ¼ cup cola, beating until combined. Gradually beat in 1¾ cups additional powdered sugar until combined. If necessary, beat in enough additional cola, 1 teaspoon at a time, to make frosting of spreadable consistency.*

*Test Kitchen Tip: *To make ½ cup sour milk, place 1½ teaspoons lemon juice or vinegar in a glass measuring cup. Add enough milk to make ½ cup total liquid; stir. Let stand for 5 minutes before using.*

GOOEY CHOCO-CARAMEL CAKE

A rich caramel sauce is poured over and oozes throughout the cake. If it sounds incredibly gooey and good, just wait until you taste it.

Prep: 15 minutes   **Bake:** according to package directions

- 1 **package 2-layer-size German chocolate cake mix**
- 1 **14-ounce can sweetened condensed milk**
- 1 **12- to 12.5-ounce jar caramel ice cream topping**
- 1 **8-ounce carton frozen whipped dessert topping, thawed**
- 3 **1.4-ounce bars chocolate-covered English toffee, chopped**

1 Preheat oven according to package directions for cake mix. Prepare cake mix according to package directions using a 9×13-inch baking pan or baking dish. Spread batter evenly in prepared pan or dish. Bake according to package directions. Cool in pan or dish on a wire rack.

2 Using the handle of a wooden spoon, poke holes about 1 inch apart over surface of cake. Pour the sweetened condensed milk over the cake. Pour caramel topping over cake. Spread dessert topping evenly over top. Cover and store in the refrigerator within 2 hours.* Sprinkle with the chopped toffee bars before serving.

Makes 24 servings.

Nutrition Facts per serving: 268 cal., 9 g total fat (5 g sat. fat), 6 mg chol., 233 mg sodium, 40 g carbo., 0 g fiber. 3 g pro.

*Test Kitchen Tip: *For best results, do not store this cake longer than 24 hours.*

MISSISSIPPI MUD CAKE

It's got a funny name, but this old-time Southern favorite is a deep, dark chocolate and peanutty cake that tastes like a slice of heaven.

Prep: 15 minutes **Stand:** 15 minutes **Bake:** 30 minutes **Oven:** 350°F (baking pan) or 325°F (baking dish)

- 1 package 2-layer-size chocolate cake mix
- 1¼ cups water
- ⅓ cup cooking oil
- ⅓ cup creamy peanut butter
- 3 eggs
- 1 cup semisweet chocolate pieces
- 1 cup tiny marshmallows
- 1 6-ounce can chocolate fudge frosting
- 1 cup chopped peanuts

1 Grease a 9×13-inch baking pan or baking dish; set aside. Preheat oven to 350°F if using a baking pan or 325°F if using a baking dish.

2 In a large bowl combine dry cake mix, the water, oil, peanut butter, and eggs; beat with an electric mixer on low speed until moistened. Beat on medium speed for 2 minutes. Stir in chocolate pieces. Spread batter evenly in prepared pan or dish. Bake for 30 to 35 minutes or until a toothpick inserted in center comes out clean.

3 Sprinkle the hot cake with tiny marshmallows; let stand for 15 minutes. Drop spoonfuls of the frosting over the cake; spread evenly. Sprinkle with peanuts. Cool in pan or dish on a wire rack.

Makes 15 servings.

Nutrition Facts per serving: 484 cal., 27 g total fat (8 g sat. fat), 42 mg chol., 366 mg sodium, 57 g carbo., 2 g fiber, 7 g pro.

SHORTCUT MALTED CHOCOLATE CAKE

Mom made a chocolate layer cake and frosting from scratch. You can doctor up a cake mix and canned frosting and have a homemade cake in no time.

Prep: 15 minutes   **Bake:** 30 minutes   **Oven:** 350°F (baking pan) or 325°F (baking dish)

1 package 2-layer-size dark chocolate fudge or devil's food cake mix

⅓ cup vanilla malted milk powder

1 12-ounce can whipped chocolate frosting

¼ cup vanilla malted milk powder

1½ cups coarsely crushed malted milk balls

1 │ Grease a 9×13-inch baking pan or baking dish; set aside. Preheat oven to 350°F if using a baking pan or 325°F if using a baking dish. Prepare cake mix according to package directions, except add the ⅓ cup malted milk powder to the batter. Spread batter evenly in prepared pan or dish.

2 │ Bake for 30 to 35 minutes or until a toothpick inserted near center comes out clean. Cool in pan or dish on a wire rack.

3 │ In a medium bowl stir together chocolate frosting and the ¼ cup malted milk powder. Spread mixture evenly over cake. Sprinkle with crushed malted milk balls.

Makes 20 servings.

Nutrition Facts per serving: 231 cal., 7 g total fat (2 g sat. fat), 2 mg chol., 281 mg sodium, 41 g carbo., 1 g fiber, 3 g pro.

MARBLE CAKE

A traditional marble cake nestles underneath a butter-rich chocolate frosting, decorated with sprinkles of crushed English toffee.

Prep: 30 minutes **Bake:** 30 minutes **Oven:** 350°F (baking pan) or 325°F (baking dish)

3	cups all-purpose flour
2½	teaspoons baking powder
¾	teaspoon baking soda
¼	teaspoon salt
¾	cup butter, softened
2	cups sugar
1	tablespoon vanilla
3	eggs
1½	cups milk
½	cup chocolate-flavor syrup
1	recipe Chocolate Butter Frosting
2	1.4-ounce bars chocolate-covered English toffee, chopped (optional)

1 Grease a 9×13-inch baking pan or baking dish; set aside. Preheat oven to 350°F if using a baking pan or 325°F if using a baking dish. In a medium bowl combine flour, baking powder, baking soda, and salt; set aside.

2 In a large bowl beat butter with an electric mixer on medium to high speed for 30 seconds. Add sugar and vanilla; beat until fluffy. Add eggs, one at a time, beating well after each addition. Alternately add flour mixture and milk to beaten mixture, beating on low speed after each addition just until combined.

3 Transfer 1½ cups of the batter to a medium bowl; stir in chocolate-flavor syrup. Spread light batter evenly in prepared pan or dish. Spoon chocolate batter over light batter. Using a table knife, gently cut through batters to marble.

4 Bake for 30 to 35 minutes or until a toothpick inserted in center comes out clean. Cool in pan or dish on a wire rack. Spread Chocolate Butter Frosting over cake. If desired, sprinkle with chopped toffee.

Makes 16 servings.

Nutrition Facts per serving: 453 cal., 16 g total fat (9 g sat. fat), 79 mg chol., 332 mg sodium, 74 g carbo., 1 g fiber, 5 g pro.

299

Chocolate Butter Frosting: *In a large bowl combine 6 tablespoons butter and ½ cup unsweetened cocoa powder; beat with an electric mixer on medium speed until fluffy. Gradually add 2 cups powdered sugar, beating until well mixed. Slowly beat in ¼ cup milk and 1½ teaspoons vanilla. Slowly beat in 2 cups additional powdered sugar. If necessary, beat in enough additional milk, 1 teaspoon at a time, to make spreading consistency. Makes 2 cups.*

MERINGUE-TOPPED SPICE CAKE

In 1937, *Better Homes and Gardens*® magazine included this
light spice cake covered with a fluffy meringue in its revised cookbook.
It was sensational then and it still is today.

Prep: 30 minutes **Bake:** 55 minutes **Oven:** 350°F (baking pan) or 325°F (baking dish)

- 2   eggs
- 2⅓   cups all-purpose flour
- 1½   teaspoons baking powder
- 1   teaspoon ground cinnamon
- ¾   teaspoon salt
- ½ to 1 teaspoon ground cloves
- ½   teaspoon baking soda
- ¾   cup shortening
- 2   cups packed brown sugar
- 1   teaspoon vanilla
- 1¼   cups buttermilk or sour milk*
- 1   cup packed brown sugar
- ½   cup coarsely chopped walnuts

1 Grease a 9×13-inch baking pan or baking dish; set aside. Preheat oven to 350°F if using a baking pan or 325°F if using a baking dish. Separate eggs; set aside. In a medium bowl combine flour, baking powder, cinnamon, salt, cloves, and baking soda; set aside.

2 In a large bowl beat shortening with electric mixer on medium to high speed for 30 seconds. Beat in the 2 cups brown sugar until well mixed. Beat in the egg yolks and vanilla until well mixed. Alternately add flour mixture and buttermilk to beaten mixture, beating on low speed after each addition just until combined. Spread batter evenly in prepared pan or dish.

3 Bake about 45 minutes or until toothpick inserted near center comes out clean.

4 Meanwhile, thoroughly wash beaters in warm soapy water. For meringue, in a medium bowl beat egg whites with electric mixer on high speed until soft peaks form (tips curl over). Gradually add the 1 cup brown sugar, beating until stiff peaks form (tips stand straight). Dollop spoonfuls of the egg white mixture over the hot cake. Gently spread to an even layer. Sprinkle with walnuts. Bake about 10 minutes more or until meringue is lightly browned. Cool in pan or dish on a wire rack. Cover and store in the refrigerator within 2 hours.

Makes 15 servings.

Nutrition Facts per serving: 370 cal., 13 g total fat (3 g sat. fat), 29 mg chol., 231 mg sodium, 60 g carbo., 1 g fiber, 3 g pro.

***Test Kitchen Tip:** To make 1¼ cups sour milk, place 4 teaspoons lemon juice or vinegar in a 2-cup glass measure. Add enough milk to make 1¼ cups total liquid; stir. Let mixture stand for 5 minutes before using.*

NUTMEG CAKE WITH LEMON SAUCE

Nutmeg has a pungent and spicy flavor that lights up this tender cake. A warm and slightly tart lemon sauce perfectly complements it.

Prep: 35 minutes   **Bake:** 30 minutes   **Oven:** 350°F (baking pan) or 325°F (baking dish)

- 2 cups all-purpose flour
- 1 teaspoon baking powder
- 1 teaspoon ground nutmeg
- ½ teaspoon baking soda
- ¼ teaspoon salt
- ¼ cup butter, softened
- ¼ cup shortening
- 1½ cups sugar
- ½ teaspoon vanilla
- 3 eggs
- 1 cup buttermilk or sour milk*
- 1 recipe Lemon Sauce

1 Grease a 9×13-inch baking pan or baking dish; set aside. Preheat oven to 350°F if using a baking pan or 325°F if using a baking dish. In a medium bowl combine flour, baking powder, nutmeg, baking soda, and salt; set aside.

2 In a large bowl combine butter and shortening; beat with an electric mixer on medium to high speed for 30 seconds. Add sugar and vanilla; beat until combined. Add eggs, one at a time, beating well after each addition. Alternately add flour mixture and buttermilk to beaten mixture, beating on low speed after each addition just until combined. Spread batter evenly in prepared pan or dish.

3 Bake for 30 to 35 minutes or until a toothpick inserted near center comes out clean. Cool slightly in pan or dish on a wire rack. Serve warm cake with Lemon Sauce.

Makes 15 servings.

Nutrition Facts per serving: 275 cal., 9 g total fat (4 g sat. fat), 55 mg chol., 172 mg sodium, 45 g carbo., 1 g fiber, 2 g pro.

301

Lemon Sauce: *In a small saucepan stir together ¾ cup sugar, 5 teaspoons cornstarch, and dash salt. Stir in 1 cup water. Cook and stir over medium heat until thickened and bubbly. Cook and stir for 2 minutes more. Remove from heat. Stir in 1 teaspoon finely shredded lemon peel, 3 tablespoons lemon juice, 2 tablespoons butter, and, if desired, 1 drop yellow food coloring.*

---

*Test Kitchen Tip: *To make 1 cup sour milk, place 1 tablespoon lemon juice or vinegar in a glass measuring cup. Add enough milk to make 1 cup total liquid; stir. Let mixture stand for 5 minutes before using.*

GINGERBREAD CAKE

With its old-fashioned and comforting flavors, this cake is ideal when there's a chill in the air. Serve it warm with whipped cream.

Prep: 20 minutes   **Stand:** 30 minutes   **Bake:** 40 minutes   **Cool:** 30 minutes
Oven: 350°F (baking pan) or 325°F (baking dish)

½   cup butter
2   eggs
2⅓   cups all-purpose flour
1½   teaspoons baking powder
1   teaspoon ground ginger
½   teaspoon baking soda
½   teaspoon ground cinnamon
¼   teaspoon salt
¼   teaspoon ground cloves
½   cup granulated sugar
1   cup mild-flavor molasses
1¼   cups cold water
Powdered sugar

1 Allow butter and eggs to stand at room temperature for 30 minutes. Meanwhile, grease a 9×13-inch baking pan or baking dish; set aside. Preheat oven to 350°F if using a baking pan or 325°F if using a baking dish. In a medium bowl stir together flour, baking powder, ginger, baking soda, cinnamon, salt, and cloves; set aside.

2 In a large bowl beat butter with an electric mixer on medium to high speed for 30 seconds. Add granulated sugar; beat until well mixed. Add eggs, one at a time, beating well after each addition. Add molasses; beat until well mixed. Alternately add flour mixture and the cold water to beaten mixture, beating on low speed after each addition just until combined. Spread batter evenly in prepared pan or dish.

3 Bake for 40 to 50 minutes or until a toothpick inserted near center comes out clean. Cool in pan or dish on a wire rack for 30 minutes. Sprinkle cake with powdered sugar and serve warm.

Makes 16 servings.

Nutrition Facts per serving: 213 cal., 7 g total fat (4 g sat. fat), 42 mg chol., 156 mg sodium, 36 g carbo., 1 g fiber, 1 g pro.

OATMEAL CAKE

The addition of rolled oats ensures this cake will be nice and moist, but it's the chewy coconut and walnut topping that will win you over.

Prep: 30 minutes **Stand:** 20 minutes **Bake:** 30 minutes **Oven:** 350°F (baking pan) or 325°F (baking dish)

- 1 cup quick-cooking rolled oats
- 1½ cups boiling water
- 1½ cups all-purpose flour
- 1½ teaspoons ground cinnamon
- 1 teaspoon baking soda
- ½ teaspoon salt
- ½ cup shortening
- 1 cup granulated sugar
- 1 cup packed brown sugar
- 2 eggs
- 1 cup flaked or shredded coconut
- ⅔ cup packed brown sugar
- 6 tablespoons butter
- 2 tablespoons milk
- ⅔ cup chopped walnuts

1 Grease a 9×13-inch baking pan or baking dish; set aside. Preheat oven to 350°F if using a baking pan or 325°F if using a baking dish. In a small bowl combine oats and the boiling water; let stand for 20 minutes. Meanwhile, in a medium bowl combine flour, cinnamon, baking soda, and salt.

2 In a large bowl combine shortening, granulated sugar, and the 1 cup brown sugar; beat with an electric mixer on medium speed until combined. Beat in eggs. Beat in oatmeal mixture. Add flour mixture; beat until combined. Spread batter evenly in prepared pan or dish.

3 Bake for 30 to 35 minutes or until a toothpick inserted near center comes out clean. Place pan or dish on a wire rack.

4 For topping, in a small saucepan combine coconut, the ⅔ cup brown sugar, the butter, and milk; cook and stir until boiling. Stir in nuts. Spoon topping over hot cake; cool completely.

Makes 16 servings.

Nutrition Facts per serving: 358 cal., 17 g total fat (6 g sat. fat), 39 mg chol., 218 mg sodium, 80 g carbo., 2 g fiber, 4 g pro.

CARROT CAKE

Eating your veggies is a piece of cake—a rich and spicy, nut-filled one to be exact. With a cream cheese icing, this is an all-time family favorite.

Prep: 55 minutes **Bake:** 40 minutes **Oven:** 350°F (baking pan) or 325°F (baking dish)

- 2 cups all-purpose flour
- 2 cups sugar
- 2 teaspoons baking powder
- 1 teaspoon ground cinnamon
- ½ teaspoon baking soda
- 3 cups finely shredded carrots
- 1 cup cooking oil
- 4 eggs
- 1 cup chopped pecans
- 1 recipe Cream Cheese Frosting

1 Grease a 9×13-inch baking pan or baking dish; set aside. Preheat oven to 350°F if using a baking pan or 325°F if using a baking dish. In a large bowl stir together flour, sugar, baking powder, cinnamon, and baking soda. Add finely shredded carrots, cooking oil, and eggs. Beat with an electric mixer just until combined. Stir in chopped pecans. Spread batter evenly in prepared pan or dish.

2 Bake for 40 to 45 minutes or until a toothpick comes out clean. Cool in pan or dish on a wire rack. Spread Cream Cheese Frosting over the cake. Cover and store in the refrigerator.

Makes 16 to 24 servings.

Nutrition Facts per serving: 481 cal., 24 g total fat (5 g sat. fat), 65 mg chol., 145 mg sodium, 65 g carbo., 2 g fiber, 5 g pro.

Cream Cheese Frosting: *In a medium bowl combine 6 ounces cream cheese, softened, and 2 teaspoons vanilla; beat with an electric mixer on medium speed until light and fluffy. Gradually add 2 cups powdered sugar, beating well. Gradually beat in enough of 2 to 2½ cups additional powdered sugar to reach spreading consistency. Makes about 1½ cups.*

PUMPKIN CAKE

A moist cake with a cream cheese frosting, this is a delicious treat anytime, but especially at Halloween when decorated with candy corn.

Prep: 25 minutes **Bake:** 25 minutes **Oven:** 350°F (baking pan) or 325°F (baking dish)

1⅔   cups all-purpose flour
1¼   cups sugar
1½   teaspoons baking powder
1½   teaspoons ground cinnamon
¾   teaspoon baking soda
¼   teaspoon salt
⅛   teaspoon ground cloves
3   eggs, slightly beaten
1   cup canned pumpkin
⅔   cup cooking oil
1   16-ounce can cream cheese frosting
2   cups candy corn or candy pumpkins (optional)

1 Preheat oven to 350°F if using a baking pan or 325°F if using a baking dish. In a large bowl stir together flour, sugar, baking powder, cinnamon, baking soda, salt, and cloves. Stir in eggs, pumpkin, and oil until combined. Spread batter evenly in an ungreased 9×13-inch baking pan or baking dish.

2 Bake for 25 to 30 minutes or until a toothpick inserted near center comes out clean. Cool in pan or dish on a wire rack. Spread frosting over cake. If desired, sprinkle frosted cake with candy.

Makes 24 servings.

Nutrition Facts per serving: 217 cal., 10 g total fat (2 g sat. fat), 26 mg chol., 132 mg sodium, 31 g carbo., 1 g fiber, 1 g pro.

APPLE UPSIDE-DOWN SPICE CAKE

Flip this over while it's still warm and serve with vanilla ice cream. Buttery Brazil nuts are a flavorful addition. Cake mix makes it easy.

Prep: 25 minutes **Bake:** 40 minutes **Cool:** 10 minutes **Oven:** 350°F (baking pan) or 325°F (baking dish)

- 3 tablespoons butter
- 2 large cooking apples, peeled, cored, and thinly sliced (about 2¾ cups)
- ½ cup chopped Brazil nuts
- 3 tablespoons packed brown sugar
- 1 package 2-layer-size spice cake mix
- 3 tablespoons molasses
- ½ cup whipping cream (optional)

1 Grease a 9×13-inch baking pan or baking dish; set aside. Preheat oven to 350°F if using a baking pan or 325°F if using a baking dish.

2 In a large skillet melt butter over medium heat. Add apples and nuts; cook about 5 minutes or until apples are tender. Remove from heat; stir in brown sugar. Spread mixture evenly in the prepared pan or dish.

3 Prepare cake mix according to package directions, except reduce the water called for to 1 cup. Stir molasses into batter. Pour batter evenly over apple mixture.

4 Bake for 40 to 45 minutes or until a toothpick inserted near center comes out clean. Cool in pan or dish on wire rack for 10 minutes. Using a knife, loosen sides of cake from pan or dish; invert cake onto serving plate.

5 If desired, in a chilled small bowl beat whipping cream until soft peaks form. Serve cake warm with whipped cream.

Makes 15 servings.

Nutrition Facts per serving: 283 cal., 14 g total fat (4 g sat. fat), 49 mg chol., 278 mg sodium, 38 g carbo., 1 g fiber, 2 g pro.

PECAN-PRALINE CAKE

This nutty treat is so simple you can enjoy
it any time. Serve it with a generous scoop
of ice cream on the side.

Prep: 20 minutes **Bake:** according to package directions

- 1 **package 2-layer-size butter pecan cake mix**
- 1 **cup caramel ice cream topping**
- 1 **cup chopped pecans, toasted**

1 Preheat oven according to package directions for cake mix. Prepare cake mix according to package directions using a 9×13-inch baking pan or baking dish. Spread batter evenly in prepared pan or dish. Bake according to package directions. Cool in pan or dish on a wire rack.

2 Drizzle caramel topping over cake. Sprinkle with pecans.

Makes 15 servings.

Nutrition Facts per serving: 361 cal., 18 g total fat (6 g sat. fat), 64 mg chol., 228 mg sodium, 49 g carbo., 2 g fiber, 3 g pro.

CANDY LANE CAKE

Feature this festive cake at your next
holiday gathering. You can opt for
either red or green peppermint candies.

Prep: 15 minutes **Bake:** according to package directions

- 1 **package 2-layer-size white cake mix**
- ½ **teaspoon mint extract or peppermint extract**
- 1 **16-ounce can vanilla frosting**
- **Round peppermint candies, crushed***

1 Preheat oven according to package directions for cake mix. Prepare cake mix according to package directions using a 9×13-inch baking pan or baking dish, except add the extract with the egg whites. Spread batter evenly in prepared pan or dish. Bake according to package directions. Cool in pan or dish on a wire rack.

2 Spread cake with vanilla frosting. Sprinkle with candies.

Makes 15 servings.

Nutrition Facts per serving: 286 cal., 10 g total fat (2 g sat. fat), 0 mg chol., 296 mg sodium, 50 g carbo., 0 g fiber, 2 g pro.

***Test Kitchen Tip:** Use green-and-white striped candies for a mint-flavored cake or red-and-white candies for a peppermint-flavored cake.*

APPLE DAPPLE CAKE

A warm, brown sugar cream sauce is poured over this apple cake while it's warm to make it even moister, richer, and more scrumptious.

Prep: 30 minutes   **Bake:** 45 minutes   **Oven:** 350°F (baking pan) or 325°F (baking dish)

- 3   cups all-purpose flour
- 2   cups granulated sugar
- 1   teaspoon baking soda
- ½   teaspoon salt
- 3   eggs, beaten
- 1   cup cooking oil
- ½   cup apple juice
- 2   teaspoons vanilla
- 3   cups finely chopped cooking apples
- 1   cup chopped walnuts or pecans
- 1   cup packed brown sugar
- ⅓   cup whipping cream
- ¼   cup butter

1 Grease and flour a 9×13-inch baking pan or baking dish; set aside. Preheat oven to 350°F if using a baking pan or 325°F if using a baking dish. In a very large bowl combine flour, granulated sugar, baking soda, and salt; make a well in center and set aside. In a medium bowl combine eggs, oil, apple juice, and vanilla; stir in apples and nuts. Add egg mixture to flour mixture, stirring just until moistened. Spread batter evenly in prepared pan or dish.

2 Bake for 45 to 50 minutes or until a toothpick inserted in center comes out clean. Cool in pan or dish on a wire rack.

3 For sauce, in a small saucepan combine brown sugar, whipping cream, and butter. Cook and stir over medium heat just until bubbly and all of the sugar is dissolved. Cool slightly. Drizzle warm sauce over cake.

Makes 20 servings.

Nutrition Facts per serving: 376 cal., 20 g total fat (5 g sat. fat), 44 mg chol., 162 mg sodium, 48 g carbo., 1 g fiber, 4 g pro.

APPLESAUCE CAKE

This moist cake, filled with raisins and nuts and tasting of spice, is a perennial favorite. Penuche frosting, a brown sugar confection, is the ideal finishing touch.

Prep: 20 minutes **Bake:** 40 minutes **Oven:** 350°F (baking pan) or 325°F (baking dish)

- 2½ cups all-purpose flour
- 1½ teaspoons baking powder
- 1 teaspoon ground cinnamon
- ¾ teaspoon ground nutmeg
- ½ teaspoon salt
- ½ teaspoon ground cloves
- ¼ teaspoon baking soda
- ½ cup butter, softened
- 2 cups sugar
- 2 eggs
- 1½ cups applesauce
- ½ cup raisins
- ½ cup chopped walnuts
- 1 recipe Penuche Frosting

1 Grease a 9×13-inch baking pan or baking dish; set aside. Preheat oven to 350°F if using a baking pan or 325°F if using a baking dish. In a medium bowl combine flour, baking powder, cinnamon, nutmeg, salt, cloves, and baking soda. Set aside.

2 In a large bowl beat butter with an electric mixer on medium to high speed about 30 seconds or until softened. Add sugar; beat until combined. Add eggs, one at a time, beating well after each addition. Alternately add flour mixture and applesauce to beaten mixture, beating on low to medium speed after each addition just until combined. Stir in raisins and walnuts. Spread batter evenly in prepared pan or dish.

3 Bake for 40 to 45 minutes or until a toothpick inserted in center comes out clean. Cool in pan or dish on a wire rack. Quickly spread Penuche Frosting over cake.

Makes 15 servings.

Nutrition Facts per serving: 517 cal., 16 g total fat (8 g sat. fat), 61 mg chol., 229 mg sodium, 93 g carbo., 1 g fiber, 2 g pro.

Penuche Frosting: *In a 2-quart saucepan melt ½ cup butter over medium heat; stir in 1 cup packed brown sugar. Cook and stir over medium heat until bubbly. Remove from heat. Add ¼ cup milk and 1 teaspoon vanilla. Stir with a wooden spoon until combined and smooth. Stir in 3½ cups powdered sugar. Continue beating with the wooden spoon about 3 minutes or until smooth and thickened. Immediately spread over cake. (If frosting becomes too thick to spread, add hot water, a few drops at a time, until spreadable.)*

Make-Ahead Directions: *Prepare and bake as directed, except do not frost cake. Tightly cover cooled, unfrosted cake with heavy foil. Freeze for up to 1 month. Thaw and frost cake before serving.*

BANANA-NUT CAKE

It's all the richness and goodness of banana bread baked in a cake. And it's easier than ever to make because you start with a mix.

Prep: 20 minutes **Bake:** according to package directions

1 package 2-layer-size yellow cake mix

⅔ cup mashed ripe banana (2 medium)

⅔ cup buttermilk or sour milk*

¼ teaspoon ground nutmeg

½ cup chopped walnuts or pecans, toasted

1 16-ounce can cream cheese frosting

½ cup miniature semisweet chocolate pieces

1 Preheat oven according to package directions for cake mix. Prepare cake mix according to package directions using a 9×13-inch baking pan or baking dish, except use 1 more egg than the package directs, omit the water called for, and add the banana, buttermilk, and nutmeg. Fold walnuts into batter. Spread batter evenly in prepared pan or dish. Bake according to package directions. Cool in pan or dish on a wire rack.

2 Spread frosting over cake. Sprinkle with miniature chocolate pieces. Cover and store in the refrigerator.

Makes 15 servings.

Nutrition Facts per serving: 405 cal., 19 g total fat (5 g sat. fat), 59 mg chol., 306 mg sodium, 57 g carbo., 1 g fiber, 4 g pro.

----

*Test Kitchen Tip: *To make ⅔ cup sour milk, place 2 teaspoons lemon juice or vinegar in a glass measuring cup. Add enough milk to make ⅔ cup total liquid; stir. Let mixture stand for 5 minutes before using.*

BANANA CAKE WITH STRAWBERRIES AND PEPPERED PECANS

A ripe banana is the star of this moist cake. A sprinkling of cayenne perks up the pecans and contrasts with the sweet berry topping.

Prep: 40 minutes **Bake:** 30 minutes **Oven:** 350°F (baking pan) or 325°F (baking dish)

1½ cups sugar

1 cup butter, softened

4 eggs

1 large banana, mashed (½ cup)

½ cup dairy sour cream

½ cup milk

1 teaspoon vanilla

3 cups all-purpose flour

2 teaspoons baking powder

½ teaspoon salt

¼ teaspoon baking soda

2 cups sliced fresh strawberries

1 tablespoon sugar (optional)

1 recipe Peppery-Spiced Pecans

Sweetened whipped cream

1 Grease a 9×13-inch baking pan or baking dish; set aside. Preheat oven to 350°F if using a baking pan or 325°F if using a baking dish.

2 In a large bowl beat the 1½ cups sugar and the butter until well mixed. Add eggs, one at a time, beating well after each addition. In a medium bowl combine mashed banana, sour cream, milk, and vanilla. In another bowl combine flour, baking powder, salt, and baking soda. Alternately add flour mixture and banana mixture to beaten mixture, beating on low speed after each addition just until combined.

3 Spread batter evenly in prepared pan or dish. Bake for 30 to 35 minutes or until a toothpick inserted near center comes out clean. Cool in pan or dish on a wire rack.

4 If desired, in a medium bowl combine strawberries and the 1 tablespoon sugar. Top cake with strawberries, Peppery-Spiced Pecans, and whipped cream.

Makes 15 servings.

Nutrition Facts per serving: 455 cal., 27 g total fat (12 g sat. fat), 116 mg chol., 259 mg sodium, 49 g carbo., 2 g fiber, 6 g pro.

311

Peppery-Spiced Pecans: *Line a 9×9-inch baking pan with foil; lightly coat foil with nonstick cooking spray. Preheat oven to 325°F. In a medium bowl combine 1 cup broken pecans, 3 tablespoons sugar, 2 tablespoons light-color corn syrup, ½ teaspoon apple pie spice or pumpkin pie spice, and ¼ teaspoon cayenne pepper. Spread nut mixture in prepared pan. Bake for 15 minutes, stirring twice. Turn out onto a buttered piece of foil; cool. Break into clusters.*

PINEAPPLE CAKE

A coconut-pecan topping gets toasty as it
bakes to make this super-moist pineapple cake
a standout. (Pictured on page 112.)

Prep: 25 minutes   **Bake:** 30 minutes   **Oven:** 350°F (baking pan) or 325°F (baking dish)

- 1 20-ounce can crushed pineapple
- 2½ cups all-purpose flour
- 1½ teaspoons baking powder
- ½ teaspoon baking soda
- ¼ teaspoon salt
- ½ cup butter, softened
- 1 cup granulated sugar
- 2 eggs
- ¾ cup packed brown sugar
- ¾ cup chopped pecans
- ¾ cup flaked or shredded coconut

1 Grease a 9×13-inch baking pan or baking dish; set aside. Preheat oven to 350°F if using a baking pan or 325°F if using a baking dish. Drain crushed pineapple, reserving juice. In a medium bowl combine flour, baking powder, baking soda, and salt; set aside.

2 In a large bowl beat butter with an electric mixer on medium to high speed for 30 seconds. Add granulated sugar; beat until fluffy. Add eggs; beat until smooth. Alternately add flour mixture and reserved pineapple juice to beaten mixture, beating on low speed after each addition just until combined. Fold in drained pineapple. Spread batter evenly in prepared pan or dish.

3 In a small bowl combine brown sugar, chopped pecans, and coconut; sprinkle over batter. Bake for 30 to 35 minutes or until a toothpick inserted in center comes out clean. Cool slightly in pan or dish on wire rack. Serve warm.

Makes 16 servings.

Nutrition Facts per serving: 285 cal., 12 g total fat (5 g sat. fat), 43 mg chol., 189 mg sodium, 43 g carbo., 1 g fiber, 3 g pro.

CITRUS YELLOW CAKE

Add an extra special touch by sprinkling
the top of the frosted cake with toasted coconut or
toasted chopped pecans.

Prep: 20 minutes   **Stand:** 30 minutes   **Bake:** 25 minutes   **Oven:** 375°F (baking pan) or 350°F (baking dish)

¾	cup butter
3	eggs
2½	cups all-purpose flour
2½	teaspoons baking powder
½	teaspoon salt
1¾	cups sugar
1½	teaspoons vanilla
1¼	cups milk
2	teaspoons shredded lemon peel or orange peel
1	recipe Citrus Butter Frosting

1 Allow butter and eggs to stand at room temperature for 30 minutes. Meanwhile, grease and lightly flour a 9×13-inch baking pan or baking dish; set aside. Preheat oven to 375°F if using a baking pan or 350°F if using a baking dish.

2 In a medium bowl stir together flour, baking powder, and salt; set aside.

3 In a large bowl beat butter with an electric mixer on medium to high speed for 30 seconds. Gradually add sugar, about ¼ cup at time, beating on medium speed until well mixed and scraping side of bowl occasionally. Beat on medium speed for 2 minutes more. Add eggs, one at a time, beating well after each addition. Beat in vanilla. Alternately add flour mixture and milk to butter mixture, beating on low speed after each addition just until combined. Stir in lemon peel. Spread batter evenly in prepared pan or dish.

4 Bake for 25 to 30 minutes or until a toothpick inserted near the center comes out clean. Cool cake in pan or dish on wire rack. Spread with Citrus Butter Frosting.

Makes 12 to 16 servings.

Nutrition Facts per serving: 545 cal., 19 g total fat (11 g sat. fat), 99 mg chol., 294 mg sodium, 91 g carbo., 1 g fiber, 3 g pro.

Citrus Butter Frosting: *In a large bowl beat ⅓ cup butter, softened, with an electric mixer on medium to high speed until smooth. Gradually add 1 cup powdered sugar, beating well. Beat in ¼ teaspoon finely shredded lemon peel or ½ teaspoon finely shredded orange peel, 3 tablespoons lemon juice or orange juice, and 1 teaspoon vanilla. Gradually beat in 3 cups additional powdered sugar. Beat in additional lemon juice or orange juice or additional powdered sugar to reach spreading consistency. Makes about 2¼ cups.*

CHEERY CHERRY-LEMON CAKE

How delightful! Pretty specks of cherry dot this yummy lemony cake. Top with the cream cheese frosting or serve with whipped cream and a cherry.

Prep: 40 minutes **Bake:** 30 minutes **Oven:** 375°F (baking pan) or 350°F (baking dish)

- 1½ cups coarsely chopped pitted fresh dark sweet cherries
- 2½ cups all-purpose flour
- 2½ teaspoons baking powder
- ½ teaspoon salt
- ¾ cup butter, softened
- 1¾ cups sugar
- 1½ teaspoons vanilla
- 3 eggs
- 1¼ cups milk
- 2 teaspoons finely shredded lemon peel
- 1 recipe Lemony Cream Cheese Frosting
- Fresh dark sweet cherries with stems, pitted
- Fresh mint leaves

1 Grease a 9×13-inch baking pan or baking dish; set aside. Preheat oven to 375°F if using a baking pan or 350°F if using a baking dish. To prevent bleeding, pat the coarsely chopped dark sweet cherries as dry as possible with paper towels; set aside. In a medium bowl combine flour, baking powder, and salt; set aside.

2 In a large bowl beat butter with an electric mixer on medium to high speed for 30 seconds. Add sugar and vanilla; beat until well mixed. Add eggs, one at a time, beating for 1 minute after each addition. Alternately add flour mixture and milk to beaten mixture, beating on low speed after each addition just until combined. Stir lemon peel into batter. Spread batter evenly in prepared pan or dish. Sprinkle the coarsely chopped cherries evenly on top of batter. (The cherries will sink during baking.)

3 Bake for 30 to 35 minutes or until a toothpick inserted near center comes out clean. Cool in pan or dish on a wire rack.

4 To serve, cut cake into 15 pieces. Top each piece with a generous dollop of Lemony Cream Cheese Frosting. Add a pitted cherry and a mint leaf to each piece.

Makes 15 servings.

Nutrition Facts per serving: 554 cal., 24 g total fat (15 g sat. fat), 107 mg chol., 309 mg sodium, 81 g carbo., 1 g fiber, 4 g pro.

Lemony Cream Cheese Frosting: *In a large bowl combine one 8-ounce package cream cheese, softened; ⅔ cup butter, softened; 2 teaspoons finely shredded lemon peel; and 2 tablespoons lemon juice. Beat with an electric mixer on medium speed until light and fluffy. Gradually add 3 cups powdered sugar, beating well. Gradually beat in about 1½ cups additional powdered sugar to reach a consistency that will dollop.*

CHERRY-COLA CAKE

This is a cause for celebration: German chocolate cake that's spread with a luscious cherry-flavored frosting.

Prep: 30 minutes   **Bake:** according to package directions   **Chill:** 5 to 25 hours

1   package 2-layer-size German chocolate cake mix

Cherry cola

1½   teaspoons ground ginger

1   teaspoon finely shredded lime peel

1   recipe Celebration Icing

12   fresh dark sweet cherries with stems, pitted (optional)

1 Well-grease and flour a 9×13-inch baking pan or baking dish; set aside. Preheat oven according to package directions for cake mix. Prepare cake mix according to package directions, except substitute cherry cola for the liquid called for and add the ginger and lime peel. Spread batter evenly in prepared pan or dish. Bake according to package directions. Cool in pan or dish on a wire rack.

2 Spread cake with Celebration Icing. Refrigerate cake about 1 hour or until icing is set. Cover cake with plastic wrap. Refrigerate for 4 to 24 hours before serving. If desired, top individual servings with sweet cherries.

Makes 15 servings.

Nutrition Facts per serving: 381 cal., 11 g total fat (5 g sat. fat), 11 mg chol., 267 mg sodium, 64 g carbo., 0 g fiber, 3 g pro.

Celebration Icing: *You'll need a 1-pound box powdered sugar (about 4½ cups) for this recipe. In a medium bowl beat ⅓ cup butter with an electric mixer on medium to high speed until smooth. Gradually add 1 cup of the powdered sugar, beating well. Slowly beat in 3 tablespoons milk and 1 teaspoon vanilla. Gradually beat in another 2 cups of the powdered sugar. Add ¼ cup cherry spreadable fruit and enough red food coloring to make a pink icing. Beat until well mixed. Gradually beat in enough of the remaining powdered sugar to make spreading consistency. Makes about 2½ cups total icing.*

HAZELNUT PICNIC CAKE

Here's a dense, moist cake that is studded with toasted nuts, miniature chocolate pieces, and chunks of toffee. Starting with a pound cake mix makes it a quick-fix.

Prep: 15 minutes **Bake:** 30 minutes **Oven:** 350°F (baking pan) or 325°F (baking dish)

- 1 **16-ounce package pound cake mix**
- 2 **tablespoons chocolate-hazelnut spread (such as Nutella®)**
- ⅓ **cup hazelnuts (filberts), toasted, skinned,* and chopped**
- ⅓ **cup toffee pieces**
- ⅓ **cup chocolate-hazelnut spread (such as Nutella®)**
- ¾ **cup miniature semisweet chocolate pieces**

1 Grease a 9×13-inch baking pan or baking dish; set aside. Preheat oven to 350°F if using a baking pan or 325°F if using a baking dish.

2 In a large bowl prepare cake mix according to package directions, except add the 2 tablespoons chocolate-hazelnut spread to bowl before beating the batter. Spread batter evenly in prepared pan or dish. In a small bowl combine hazelnuts, toffee pieces, and the ⅓ cup chocolate-hazelnut spread (mixture will be thick). Spoon mixture on top of cake in 25 to 30 small mounds (each about 1 rounded teaspoon).

3 Bake for 30 to 35 minutes or until a toothpick inserted near the center comes out clean. Sprinkle chocolate pieces on top of hot cake. Cool in pan or dish on a wire rack. If chocolate pieces are too soft after cooling cake, chill the cake for 15 minutes before serving.

Makes 16 to 18 servings.

Nutrition Facts per serving: 222 cal., 10 g total fat (3 g sat. fat), 31 mg chol., 132 mg sodium, 32 g carbo., 1 g fiber, 3 g pro.

*Test Kitchen Tip: *To toast hazelnuts, preheat oven to 350°F. Spread hazelnuts in a single layer in a shallow baking pan. Bake about 10 minutes or until toasted, stirring once. Place warm nuts on a clean cloth kitchen towel. Rub nuts with towel to remove loose skins.*

ROOT BEER FLOAT CAKE

Ingenious! Using root beer instead of the liquid called for in a packaged mix creates a refreshingly light cake. (Pictured on page 97.)

Prep: 20 minutes **Bake:** according to package directions **Oven:** 350°F (baking pan) or 325°F (baking dish)

1   package 2-layer-size caramel or yellow cake mix

     Root beer

1½   teaspoons vanilla

1   teaspoon finely shredded lemon peel

1   recipe Root Beer Icing

1 Grease a 9×13-inch baking pan or baking dish; set aside. Preheat oven to 350°F if using a baking pan or 325°F if using a baking dish. Prepare cake mix according to package directions, except substitute root beer for the liquid called for and add the vanilla and lemon peel. Spread batter evenly in prepared pan or dish. Bake according to package directions. Cool in pan or dish on a wire rack for 10 minutes. Carefully invert cake onto a wire rack; remove pan or dish. Cool completely. Invert again onto another wire rack.

2 Using a serrated knife, cut top of cake to make it level. Trim edges of cake. Discard trimmed pieces. Cut cake in half lengthwise into two 4½×13-inch rectangles. Place one cake rectangle on a serving platter. Spread with half of the Root Beer Icing. Top with second cake rectangle. Spread top with the remaining icing.

Makes 15 servings.

Nutrition Facts per serving: 342 cal., 13 g total fat (4 g sat. fat), 55 mg chol., 265 mg sodium, 55 g carbo., 0 g fiber, 2 g pro.

317

Root Beer Icing: *In a medium bowl beat ⅓ cup butter with an electric mixer on medium to high speed until smooth. Gradually add 1 cup powdered sugar, beating well. Slowly beat in 3 tablespoons root beer and 1 teaspoon vanilla. Gradually beat in 2 cups additional powdered sugar. If necessary, beat in a little more root beer or powdered sugar to make icing of spreading consistency.*

PRALINE CRUNCH CAKE

Coffee crystals flavor both the cake and the frosting of this festive cake that has a delicious, home-baked, crunchy pecan mixture sprinkled on top.

Prep: 30 minutes **Bake:** 30 minutes **Oven:** 350°F (baking pan) or 325°F (baking dish)

POTLUCK ● FAVORITE

318

- 2 **tablespoons molasses**
- **Water**
- 1 **tablespoon instant coffee crystals**
- 1 **package 2-layer-size yellow cake mix**
- 3 **eggs**
- ⅓ **cup cooking oil**
- ⅓ **cup all-purpose flour**
- 1 **tablespoon packed brown sugar**
- ½ **teaspoon ground cinnamon**
- 3 **tablespoons butter**
- ⅓ **cup chopped pecans**
- ¼ **cup butter, softened**
- 3½ **cups powdered sugar**
- ¼ **cup half-and-half, light cream, or milk**
- 1 **teaspoon instant coffee crystals**
- 1 **teaspoon vanilla**
- **Half-and-half, light cream, or milk**

1 Grease a 9×13-inch baking pan or baking dish; set aside. Preheat oven to 350°F if using a baking pan or 325°F if using a baking dish. Place molasses in a 2-cup glass measure; add enough water to measure 1⅓ cups total liquid and stir to combine. Transfer to a large bowl. Add 1 tablespoon coffee crystals; stir to dissolve. Add dry cake mix, eggs, and oil. Beat with an electric mixer on low speed until combined. Beat on medium speed for 2 minutes. Spread batter evenly in prepared pan or dish. Bake about 30 minutes or until a toothpick inserted in center comes out clean. Cool cake in pan or dish on a wire rack.

2 While cake is cooling, if necessary, raise oven temperature to 350°F. In a small bowl stir together flour, brown sugar, and cinnamon. Using a pastry blender, cut in the 3 tablespoons butter until crumbly. Stir in pecans. Knead with fingers until mixture starts to cling together (mixture should form small moist clumps). Spread clumps evenly in a 10×15-inch baking pan. Bake in the 350°F oven about 10 minutes or until lightly golden brown. Transfer to a piece of foil to cool.

3 For frosting, in a large bowl beat the ¼ cup butter with an electric mixer on medium speed for 30 seconds. Add 1 cup of the powdered sugar; beat until combined. In a small bowl stir together the ¼ cup half-and-half and the 1 teaspoon instant coffee crystals until coffee crystals are dissolved. Add to powdered sugar mixture along with vanilla. Beat until combined. (Mixture may appear curdled.) Gradually add the remaining 2½ cups powdered sugar, beating until smooth. If necessary, beat in enough additional half-and-half to make frosting of spreading consistency. Spread frosting over cooled cake; sprinkle with toasted pecan mixture.

Makes 16 servings.

Nutrition Facts per serving: 369 cal., 15 g total fat (6 g sat. fat), 54 mg chol., 263 mg sodium, 58 g carbo., 0 g fiber, 2 g pro.

BARS

Someone, many years ago, must have decided it was easier to make cookies in a pan. Voilà! Bars. Chewy, gooey, caramely, chocolaty, fruity, nutty—they are the quick-to-bake answer to the sweet tooth. One after another—the usual way they disappear—they are always a delicious reward.

APPLE-RAISIN COOKIE BARS

Make your own granola bars for the family. This easy recipe combines cereal with dried apples and raisins for a chewy, nutritious snack.

Prep: 20 minutes **Bake:** 30 minutes **Oven:** 350°F

- 4 cups granola cereal
- ¼ cup all-purpose flour
- ¼ teaspoon salt
- ⅓ cup butter, melted
- 1 cup chopped dried apples
- ½ cup golden raisins
- 1 14-ounce can sweetened condensed milk

1 Line a 9×13-inch baking pan or baking dish with foil, extending foil over the edges of the pan. Well-grease foil; set aside. Preheat oven to 350°F. For crust, in a food processor combine granola, flour, and salt; cover and process just until mixture is combined. Add butter; process with several on-off turns just until mixture is combined. Press cereal mixture evenly into prepared pan or dish. Bake for 10 minutes.

2 Sprinkle dried apples and golden raisins over crust. Pour or spoon the sweetened condensed milk evenly over top.

3 Bake about 20 minutes or until top is golden brown, being careful not to overbake. Cool in pan or dish on a wire rack. Using the edges of the foil, lift the uncut bars out of the pan or dish. Cut into bars.

Makes 36 bars.

Nutrition Facts per bar: 113 cal., 3 g total fat (2 g sat. fat), 8 mg chol., 75 mg sodium, 20 g carbo., 1 g fiber, 2 g pro.

To store: *Layer bars between waxed paper in an airtight storage container. Cover; seal. Store in the refrigerator for up to 2 days.*

SUPER-EASY CHOCOLATE BARS

As quick as these are to make, that's how fast these will disappear off the plate. They're a great choice for packing and mailing.

Prep: 20 minutes **Bake:** 35 minutes **Oven:** 350°F

- 1 cup butter, softened
- ½ cup sugar
- ⅛ teaspoon salt
- 2 cups all-purpose flour
- 1 14-ounce can sweetened condensed milk
- 1 cup semisweet chocolate pieces
- ½ cup chopped walnuts or pecans
- ½ teaspoon vanilla

1 Preheat oven to 350°F. For crust, in a large bowl beat butter with an electric mixer on medium to high speed for 30 seconds. Add sugar and salt; beat until combined, scraping side of bowl occasionally. Beat in the flour on low speed until combined. Press two-thirds of the crust mixture evenly into an ungreased 9×13-inch baking pan or baking dish.

2 For filling, in a medium saucepan combine sweetened condensed milk and chocolate pieces. Cook and stir over low heat until chocolate melts and mixture is smooth. Remove from heat. Stir in nuts and vanilla. Spread hot mixture over the crust. Sprinkle remaining crust mixture over chocolate mixture.

3 Bake about 35 minutes or until golden brown. Cool in pan or dish on a wire rack. Cut into bars.

Makes about 25 bars.

Nutrition Facts per bar: 217 cal., 12 g total fat (7 g sat. fat), 25 mg chol., 85 mg sodium, 25 g carbo., 1 g fiber, 2 g pro.

To store: *Layer bars between waxed paper in an airtight container. Cover; seal. Store in the refrigerator for up to 3 days or freeze for up to 3 months. Thaw, if frozen, before serving.*

FIVE-LAYER BARS

Only five words describe these all-time favorites of young and old: easy, gooey, chewy, deliciously good.

Prep: 10 minutes **Bake:** 37 minutes **Oven:** 350°F

- 2 **13-ounce packages (32 cookies) soft coconut macaroon cookies**
- ¾ **cup sweetened condensed milk**
- ¾ **cup semisweet chocolate pieces**
- ¾ **cup raisins, dried cranberries, golden raisins, and/or dried tart red cherries**
- 1 **cup coarsely chopped peanuts**

1 Grease a 9×13-inch baking pan or baking dish. Preheat oven to 350°F. Arrange cookies in prepared pan or dish. Press cookies together to form a crust. Bake for 12 minutes.

2 Remove from oven. Drizzle crust evenly with sweetened condensed milk. Sprinkle with chocolate pieces and raisins; sprinkle with peanuts. Bake about 25 minutes more or until edges are lightly browned. Cool in pan or dish on a wire rack. Cut into bars.

Makes 30 bars.

Nutrition Facts per bar: 181 cal., 7 g total fat (4 g sat. fat), 3 mg chol., 86 mg sodium, 28 g carbo., 1 g fiber, 3 g pro.

To store: *Place bars in a single layer in an airtight container. Cover; seal. Store at room temperature for up to 3 days.*

CHOCOLATE-MINT BARS

This recipe is proof that it doesn't take a lot of work—or ingredients—to turn out incredibly good mint bars.

Prep: 10 minutes **Bake:** 20 minutes **Oven:** 350°F

- 1 tablespoon butter
- 1½ cups finely crushed chocolate wafers (about 25)
- 1½ cups chopped nuts
- 1¼ cups mint-flavor semisweet chocolate pieces
- 1½ cups flaked coconut
- 1 14-ounce can sweetened condensed milk

1 Line a 9×13-inch baking pan or baking dish with nonstick foil; generously grease the foil with the butter. Preheat oven to 350°F. Sprinkle crushed wafers evenly into pan or dish; sprinkle evenly with nuts and chocolate pieces. Sprinkle evenly with coconut. Drizzle sweetened condensed milk evenly over all.

2 Bake for 20 to 25 minutes or until coconut is golden brown around edges. Cool in pan or dish on a wire rack. Using the edges of the foil, lift the uncut bars out of the pan. Cut into bars.

Makes 48 bars.

Nutrition Facts per bar: 112 cal., 7 g total fat (4 g sat. fat), 4 mg chol., 42 mg sodium, 12 g carbo., 1 g fiber, 1 g pro.

To store: *Tightly cover pan or dish and store in the refrigerator for up to 3 days.*

LEMON BARS DELUXE

The sweet-tart taste of lemon bars is a favorite for dessert tables everywhere. These are extra lemony with real pucker appeal and a light dusting of powdered sugar.

Prep: 20 minutes **Bake:** 45 minutes **Oven:** 350°F

2 cups all-purpose flour
½ cup powdered sugar
1 cup butter, softened
4 eggs
1½ cups granulated sugar
1 tablespoon finely shredded lemon peel (set aside)
⅓ cup lemon juice
¼ cup all-purpose flour
Powdered sugar

1 Line a 9×13-inch baking pan with foil, extending foil over the edges of the pan; set aside. Preheat oven to 350°F. In a large bowl stir together the 2 cups flour and the ½ cup powdered sugar. Add butter and beat with an electric mixer on low to medium speed just until mixture begins to cling together. Press evenly into prepared pan or dish. Bake about 25 minutes or until lightly browned.

2 In a medium bowl beat eggs with a whisk; whisk in granulated sugar and lemon juice until well mixed. Whisk in the ¼ cup flour and the lemon peel. Pour evenly over baked crust.

3 Bake about 20 minutes more or until edges begin to brown and center is set. Cool in pan on a wire rack. Using the edges of the foil, lift the uncut bars out of the pan. Sift additional powdered sugar over top. Cover and store in the refrigerator within 2 hours. Cut into bars.

Makes 30 bars.

Nutrition Facts per bar: 147 cal., 7 g total fat (4 g sat. fat), 44 mg chol., 53 mg sodium, 20 g carbo., 0 g fiber, 2 g pro.

ALMOND SQUARES

These dressy little numbers have toasted almonds on top, a crunchy almond middle, and a buttery crust. Cut them into diamonds for a pretty look.

Prep: 25 minutes   Bake: 20 minutes   Broil: 1 minute   Oven: 350°F

- 2   eggs
- 1   cup sugar
- 1   cup butter, melted
- 1   cup all-purpose flour
- ½   cup butter
- ½   cup sugar
- ½   cup sliced almonds
- 1   tablespoon all-purpose flour
- 1   tablespoon milk

1 Grease and lightly flour a 9×13-inch baking pan; set pan aside. Preheat oven to 350°F.

2 For crust, in a medium bowl combine eggs and the 1 cup sugar; beat with an electric mixer on medium speed about 8 minutes or until thick and lemon-colored. Stir in the 1 cup melted butter and the 1 cup flour. Pour into prepared pan.

3 Bake for 20 to 25 minutes or until a toothpick inserted near center comes out clean and edges begin to pull away from pan.

4 Meanwhile, for topping, in a small saucepan combine the ½ cup butter, the ½ cup sugar, the almonds, the 1 tablespoon flour, and the milk. Cook and stir over medium heat until mixture comes to a boil.

5 Adjust oven rack so top of pan is 3 to 4 inches from heat. Turn oven to broil. Spoon almond mixture over hot crust. Broil about 1 minute or until golden brown, watching carefully to avoid burning. Cool in pan on a wire rack. Cut into bars.

Makes 32 bars.

Nutrition Facts per bar: 147 cal., 11 g total fat (6 g sat. fat), 38 mg chol., 97 mg sodium, 12 g carbo., 0 g fiber, 1 g pro.

BUTTERSCOTCH BARS

All kinds of goodies come together for these treats, from peanut butter in the crust to butterscotch in the filling and chopped peanuts on top.

Prep: 20 minutes   **Chill:** 2 hours

1   9-ounce package chocolate wafers

1½   cups powdered sugar

1   cup creamy peanut butter

6   tablespoons butter, melted

1   11-ounce package (2 cups) butterscotch-flavor pieces

¼   cup whipping cream

¾   cup chopped peanuts

1 | Crush chocolate wafers for a total of 2 cups. In a large bowl stir together powdered sugar, peanut butter, and butter. Stir in crushed chocolate wafers. Press mixture evenly into an ungreased 9×13-inch baking pan or baking dish.

2 | In a heavy medium saucepan combine butterscotch-flavor pieces and whipping cream. Cook and stir over low heat just until pieces are melted. Carefully spoon butterscotch mixture over crumb mixture, spreading evenly. Sprinkle peanuts over butterscotch mixture. Cover and chill for at least 2 hours. Cut into bars.

Makes 48 bars.

Nutrition Facts per bar: 130 cal., 8 g total fat (4 g sat. fat), 6 mg chol., 96 mg sodium, 13 g carbo., 0 g fiber, 2 g pro.

To store: *Layer bars between waxed paper in an airtight container. Cover; seal. Store in the refrigerator for up to 1 week or freeze for up to 3 months. Thaw, if frozen, before serving.*

MOCHA-CHOCOLATE CHIP CHEESECAKE BARS

If mocha lattes are your drink of choice,
these bars are for you. Refrigerated cookie dough is
used as the crust to make preparation a snap.

Prep: 15 minutes   **Bake:** 20 minutes   **Oven:** 350°F

- 1   18-ounce package refrigerated chocolate chip cookie dough
- 1   8-ounce package cream cheese or reduced-fat cream cheese (Neufchâtel), softened
- ⅓   cup sugar
- 1   egg
- 1   tablespoon instant coffee crystals
- 1   teaspoon vanilla
- 1   teaspoon water
- ½   cup miniature semisweet chocolate pieces

1 Preheat oven to 350°F. For crust, crumble cookie dough into an ungreased 9×13-inch baking pan or baking dish. Press evenly into the pan or dish; set aside.

2 In a medium bowl combine cream cheese, sugar, and egg; beat with a wooden spoon until smooth. In a small bowl or custard cup combine coffee crystals, vanilla, and the water, stirring until coffee crystals are dissolved. Stir coffee mixture into cream cheese mixture. Spread evenly over crust; sprinkle with the chocolate pieces.

3 Bake about 20 minutes or until completely set. Cool in pan or dish on a wire rack. Cover and store in the refrigerator within 2 hours. Cut into bars.

Makes 36 bars.

Nutrition Facts per bar: 109 cal., 6 g total fat (3 g sat. fat), 15 mg chol., 71 mg sodium, 12 g carbo., 0 g fiber, 1 g pro.

To store: *Place bars in a single layer in an airtight container. Cover; seal. Store in the refrigerator for up to 3 days or freeze for up to 1 month. Thaw, if frozen, before serving.*

CANDY BAR COOKIE BARS

Is it a candy or cookie? You decide. Either way, these treats are always a hit at potlucks and family gatherings. (Pictured on page 101.)

Prep: 30 minutes **Bake:** 10 minutes **Oven:** 375°F

- 1 cup packed brown sugar
- ⅔ cup butter
- ¼ cup dark- or light-color corn syrup
- ¼ cup peanut butter
- 1 teaspoon vanilla
- 3½ cups quick-cooking rolled oats
- 2 cups semisweet chocolate pieces
- 1 cup butterscotch-flavor pieces
- ⅔ cup peanut butter
- ½ cup chopped peanuts

1 Line a 9×13-inch baking pan or baking dish with foil, extending foil over the edges of the pan or dish; set aside. Preheat oven to 375°F. In a medium saucepan combine brown sugar, butter, and corn syrup; cook and stir over medium-low heat until combined. Remove saucepan from heat; stir in the ¼ cup peanut butter and the vanilla until smooth.

2 For crust, place rolled oats in a very large bowl. Pour brown sugar mixture over oats, stirring gently until combined. Press oat mixture evenly into prepared pan or dish. Bake for 10 to 12 minutes or until edges are lightly browned.

3 Meanwhile, in the same saucepan combine chocolate pieces and butterscotch pieces; cook and stir over low heat until melted. Stir in the ⅔ cup peanut butter until mixture is smooth. Slowly pour mixture over the hot crust, spreading evenly; sprinkle with peanuts.

4 Cool in pan or dish on a wire rack for several hours or until chocolate layer is firm. (If necessary, chill until chocolate is set.) Using the edges of the foil, lift the uncut bars out of the pan or dish. Cut into bars.

Makes 48 bars.

Nutrition Facts per bar: 166 cal., 9 g total fat (4 g sat. fat), 7 mg chol., 64 mg sodium, 16 g carbo., 2 g fiber, 3 g pro.

SALTED PEANUT BARS

The taste is somewhere between a cookie and a candy and altogether scrumptious with peanuts three ways and marshmallows in the filling.

Prep: 25 minutes **Chill:** 1 hour

Nonstick cooking spray

4 cups dry-roasted or honey-roasted peanuts

1 10½-ounce package tiny marshmallows

½ cup butter

1 14-ounce can sweetened condensed milk

1 10-ounce package peanut butter-flavor pieces

½ cup creamy peanut butter

1 Line a 9×13-inch baking pan or baking dish with heavy foil, extending foil over the edges of the pan or dish. Coat foil with nonstick cooking spray. Spread half of the peanuts evenly in the prepared pan or dish.

2 In a 3-quart saucepan combine marshmallows and butter; cook and stir over medium-low heat until melted. Stir in sweetened condensed milk, peanut butter pieces, and peanut butter until smooth. Quickly pour peanut butter mixture over peanuts in pan or dish. Sprinkle the remaining peanuts on top. Gently press peanuts into peanut butter mixture.

3 Chill about 1 hour or until firm. Using the edges of the foil, lift the uncut bars out of the pan or dish. Cut into bars.

Makes 60 bars.

Nutrition Facts per bar: 144 cal., 10 g total fat [3 g sat. fat], 7 mg chol., 128 mg sodium, 12 g carbo., 1 g fiber, 4 g pro.

To store: *Layer bars between waxed paper in an airtight container. Cover; seal. Store in the refrigerator for up to 3 days.*

CARAMEL APPLE BARS

Chewy apple bars are drizzled with caramel, then coated with peanuts, treating you to one of the best tastes of autumn.

Prep: 20 minutes   **Chill:** 15 minutes

Nonstick cooking spray

1   10½-ounce package (about 6 cups) tiny marshmallows

3   tablespoons butter, cut up

6   cups apple-and-cinnamon-flavor round toasted cereal

1   cup snipped dried apples

½   of a 14-ounce package (about 24 caramels) vanilla caramels, unwrapped

1   tablespoon milk

1   tablespoon butter

1   cup coarsely chopped peanuts or cashews

1 Line a 9×13-inch baking pan or baking dish with foil, extending foil over the edges of the pan or dish. Lightly coat foil with nonstick cooking spray; set aside.

2 In a large microwave-safe bowl combine marshmallows and the 3 tablespoons butter. Microwave on 100% power (high) for 1 to 2 minutes or until melted, stirring twice. Stir mixture until smooth. Stir in cereal and dried apples.

3 Spoon cereal mixture into prepared pan or dish. Using the back of a buttered spoon, press cereal mixture evenly into pan or dish. Cool. Using the edges of the foil, lift the uncut bars out of the pan or dish. Cut into 1½×2-inch bars.

4 In a medium microwave-safe bowl combine caramels, milk, and the 1 tablespoon butter. Microwave on 100% power (high) for 45 to 60 seconds or until melted and smooth, stirring twice.

5 Line a baking sheet with foil; set aside. Place peanuts in a small bowl. Drizzle one-third of each bar with caramel mixture; dip the caramel-coated portion of each bar into the peanuts. Place bars on prepared baking sheet. Chill about 15 minutes or until caramel is set.

Makes 32 bars.

Nutrition Facts per bar: 121 cal., 5 g total fat (1 g sat. fat), 4 mg chol., 63 mg sodium, 19 g carbo., 1 g fiber, 2 g pro.

To store: *Layer bars between waxed paper in an airtight container. Cover; seal. Store at room temperature for up to 3 days or freeze for up to 3 months. Thaw bars, if frozen, before serving.*

STREUSEL STRAWBERRY BARS

These are like pretty little strawberry sandwiches and as sweet to eat as they sound. Try them another time with raspberry jam as the filling.

Prep: 20 minutes **Bake:** 45 minutes **Oven:** 350°F

- 2 cups butter, softened
- 2 cups granulated sugar
- 2 eggs
- 4 cups all-purpose flour
- 1½ cups pecans, coarsely chopped
- 2 10-ounce jars (2 cups) strawberry preserves or seedless red raspberry preserves
- 1 recipe Powdered Sugar Icing

1 Preheat oven to 350°F. In a large bowl combine butter and granulated sugar; beat with an electric mixer on medium speed until combined, scraping side of bowl occasionally. Beat in eggs. Beat in as much of the flour as you can with the mixer. Using a wooden spoon, stir in any remaining flour and the pecans (mixture will be crumbly). Set aside 2 cups of the pecan mixture.

2 Press the remaining pecan mixture evenly into an ungreased 9×13-inch baking pan or baking dish. Spread preserves to within ½ inch of the edges. Sprinkle the reserved 2 cups pecan mixture on top of the preserves.

3 Bake about 45 minutes or until top is golden brown. Cool in pan or dish on a wire rack. Drizzle with Powdered Sugar Icing. Cut into bars.

Makes 48 bars.

Nutrition Facts per bar: 205 cal., 11 g total fat (5 g sat. fat), 31 mg chol., 89 mg sodium, 26 g carbo., 1 g fiber, 2 g pro.

Powdered Sugar Icing: *In a small bowl combine 1 cup powdered sugar, 1 tablespoon milk, and ¼ teaspoon vanilla. Stir in additional milk, 1 teaspoon at a time, until icing is of drizzling consistency.*

CARAMEL-NUT REVEL BARS

This easy-to-make recipe features peanuts, marshmallows, chocolate pieces, and caramels.

Prep: 30 minutes **Bake:** 30 minutes **Oven:** 350°F

- ½ cup butter, softened
- 1 cup packed brown sugar
- ½ teaspoon baking soda
- 1 egg
- 1 teaspoon vanilla
- 1¼ cups all-purpose flour
- 1½ cups quick-cooking rolled oats
- 20 vanilla caramels, unwrapped
- 2 tablespoons milk
- 2 cups tiny marshmallows
- 1 cup dry-roasted peanuts
- 1½ cups semisweet chocolate pieces
- 1 14-ounce can sweetened condensed milk
- 2 tablespoons butter
- 2 teaspoons vanilla

1 Line a 9×13-inch baking pan or baking dish with foil, extending foil over the edges of the pan or dish; set aside. Preheat oven to 350°F. In a large bowl beat the ½ cup butter with an electric mixer on medium to high speed for 30 seconds. Add brown sugar and baking soda. Beat until combined, scraping side of bowl occasionally. Beat in egg and the 1 teaspoon vanilla. Beat in as much of the flour as you can with the mixer. Using a wooden spoon, stir in any remaining flour. Stir in oats. Set aside ⅔ cup of the oat mixture. With floured hands, press the remaining oat mixture evenly into prepared pan or dish. Set aside.

2 In a small saucepan combine caramels and milk. Cook and stir over low heat just until caramels are melted. Drizzle caramel mixture over oat mixture. Sprinkle with 1⅓ cups of the tiny marshmallows and ⅔ cup of the peanuts; set aside.

3 In a medium saucepan combine chocolate pieces, sweetened condensed milk, and the 2 tablespoons butter. Cook over low heat until chocolate melts, stirring occasionally. Remove from heat. Stir in the 2 teaspoons vanilla. Pour chocolate mixture evenly over the tiny marshmallows and peanuts in pan or dish. Spoon small mounds of the reserved ⅔ cup oat mixture evenly over chocolate mixture. Sprinkle evenly with the remaining ⅔ cup marshmallows and the remaining ⅓ cup peanuts. Bake about 30 minutes or until golden brown. Cool in pan or dish on a wire rack.

4 Using the edges of the foil, lift the uncut bars out of the pan or dish. Cut into bars.

Makes about 36 bars.

Nutrition Facts per bar: 222 cal., 9 g total fat (4 g sat. fat), 19 mg chol., 78 mg sodium, 32 g carbo., 2 g fiber, 4 g pro.

To store: *Place bars in a single layer in an airtight container. Cover; seal. Store at room temperature for up to 3 days or freeze for up to 3 months. Thaw, if frozen, before serving.*

PEANUT BUTTER BLONDIE BARS

They're peanutty through and through, from the peanut butter cookie dough to peanut butter frosting and peanut butter candies on top.

Prep: 25 minutes **Bake:** 20 minutes **Oven:** 350°F

- 1 32-ounce tube or two 16½-ounce tubes refrigerated peanut butter cookie dough
- 1⅓ cups finely crushed graham crackers
- 1 recipe Peanut Butter Frosting
- ⅔ cup candy-coated peanut butter-flavor pieces
- ½ cup chopped peanuts
- ½ cup miniature semisweet chocolate pieces

1 Line a 9×13-inch baking pan or baking dish with foil, extending foil over the edges of the pan or dish; set aside. Preheat oven to 350°F.

2 For crust, in a large bowl combine cookie dough and crushed graham crackers; knead with your hands until combined (dough will be stiff). Press dough evenly into prepared pan or dish. Bake about 20 minutes or until crust is evenly puffed and lightly brown across the top. Cool in pan or dish on a wire rack (crust will fall slightly during cooling).

3 Spread Peanut Butter Frosting evenly over crust. Immediately sprinkle with peanut butter pieces, peanuts, and chocolate pieces.

4 Using the edges of the foil, lift the uncut bars out of the pan or dish. Cut into bars.

Makes 36 bars.

Nutrition Facts per bar: 225 cal., 12 g total fat (4 g sat. fat), 10 mg chol., 154 mg sodium, 27 g carbo., 1 g fiber, 4 g pro.

Peanut Butter Frosting: *In a medium saucepan combine ¼ cup peanut butter and ¼ cup butter; cook and stir just until melted. Stir in 2 cups powdered sugar and 1 teaspoon vanilla. Stir in enough milk (about 2 tablespoons) to make a frosting of spreading consistency. Makes about 1 cup.*

To store: *Layer bars between waxed paper in an airtight container. Cover; seal. Store at room temperature for up to 3 days or freeze for up to 3 months. Thaw bars, if frozen, before serving.*

CARROT AND ZUCCHINI BARS

You love carrots and zucchini in cakes. Now they're bringing their moist and delicious flavors to bars. (Pictured on page 106.)

Prep: 20 minutes   **Bake:** 25 minutes   **Oven:** 350°F (baking pan) or 325°F (baking dish)

1½   cups all-purpose flour
  1   teaspoon baking powder
  ½   teaspoon ground ginger
  ¼   teaspoon baking soda
  2   eggs, slightly beaten
1½   cups shredded carrots
  1   medium zucchini, shredded (1 cup)
  ¾   cup packed brown sugar
  ½   cup raisins
  ½   cup chopped walnuts
  ½   cup cooking oil
  ¼   cup honey
  1   teaspoon vanilla
  1   recipe Citrus-Cream Cheese Frosting

1 Preheat oven to 350°F if using a baking pan or 325°F if using a baking dish. In a large bowl combine flour, baking powder, ginger, and baking soda. In another large bowl stir together eggs, carrots, zucchini, brown sugar, raisins, walnuts, oil, honey, and vanilla. Add carrot mixture to flour mixture, stirring just until combined. Spread batter evenly into an ungreased 9×13-inch baking pan or baking dish.

2 Bake about 25 minutes or until a toothpick inserted in center comes out clean. Cool in pan or dish on a wire rack. Frost with Citrus-Cream Cheese Frosting. Cut into bars.

Makes 36 bars.

Nutrition Facts per bar: 125 cal., 7 g total fat (2 g sat. fat), 19 mg chol., 44 mg sodium, 16 g carbo., 1 g fiber, 2 g pro.

Citrus-Cream Cheese Frosting: *In a medium bowl combine one 8-ounce package cream cheese, softened, and 1 cup powdered sugar; beat with an electric mixer on medium speed until fluffy. Stir in 1 teaspoon finely shredded lemon peel or orange peel.*

RAIN FOREST BARS

Grown in tropical rain forests, Brazil nuts have a distinctive creamy flavor. Here they combine with coconut to create wonderfully rich and buttery bars.

Prep: 25 minutes **Bake:** 30 minutes **Oven:** 350°F

- ¾ cup butter, softened
- ½ cup packed brown sugar
- 1 egg yolk
- 1 teaspoon vanilla
- 2 cups all-purpose flour
- 1 cup packed brown sugar
- 3 eggs
- 1 teaspoon vanilla
- 3 tablespoons all-purpose flour
- ¼ teaspoon salt
- 2 cups chopped Brazil nuts
- 1 cup flaked or shredded coconut

1 Preheat oven to 350°F. In a medium bowl beat butter with an electric mixer on medium to high speed for 30 seconds. Add the ½ cup brown sugar; beat until combined, scraping side of bowl occasionally. Beat in egg yolk and 1 teaspoon vanilla until combined. Beat in the 2 cups flour until combined. Pat dough evenly into an ungreased 9×13-inch baking pan. Bake for 10 minutes. Cool in pan on a wire rack for 5 minutes.

2 Meanwhile, in a large bowl stir together the 1 cup brown sugar, the eggs, and 1 teaspoon vanilla. Beat with an electric mixer on medium speed until combined. Beat in the 3 tablespoons flour and the salt until combined. Stir in Brazil nuts and coconut. Spread evenly over baked crust. Bake about 20 minutes more or until set. Cool in pan on wire rack. Cover and store in the refrigerator within 2 hours. Cut into bars.

Makes 40 bars.

Nutrition Facts per bar: 154 cal., 10 g total fat (4 g sat. fat), 30 mg chol., 56 mg sodium, 15 g carbo., 1 g fiber, 2 g pro.

To store: *Layer bars between waxed paper in an airtight container. Cover; seal. Store in the refrigerator for up to 3 days.*

CHERRY-WALNUT BARS

Bits of sweet cherries and chopped nuts top the squares that have pretty drizzles of cherry icing.

Prep: 25 minutes   Bake: 45 minutes   Oven: 350°F

- 2¼   cups all-purpose flour
- ½   cup granulated sugar
- 1   cup butter, softened
- 3   eggs
- 1½   cups packed brown sugar
- ¾   teaspoon baking powder
- ¾   teaspoon salt
- ¾   teaspoon vanilla
- 1   6-ounce jar maraschino cherries, drained and chopped (reserve ¼ cup liquid)
- ½   cup chopped walnuts
- 2   cups powdered sugar
- 2   tablespoons butter, softened

1 Lightly grease a 9×13-inch baking pan; set aside. Preheat oven to 350°F. In a large bowl combine flour and granulated sugar. Using a pastry blender, cut in the 1 cup butter until mixture is crumbly. Press evenly into prepared pan. Bake for 20 minutes.

2 Meanwhile, in a medium bowl stir together eggs, brown sugar, baking powder, salt, and vanilla. Stir in chopped cherries and walnuts. Spoon evenly on top of baked crust. Bake for 25 minutes more. Cool in pan on a wire rack.

3 For icing, in a small bowl combine powdered sugar, the 2 tablespoons butter, and enough of the reserved cherry liquid (3 to 4 tablespoons) to make icing of spreading consistency. Spread or pipe icing over bars. Cut into bars.

Makes 48 bars.

Nutrition Facts per bar: 119 cal., 5 g total fat (3 g sat. fat), 25 mg chol., 88 mg sodium, 17 g carbo., 0 g fiber, 1 g pro.

CHOCOLATE CARAMEL-NUT BARS

Milk chocolate pieces and peanuts make these creamy bars a sweet and salty, hard-to-resist snack. Cake mix and ice cream topping keep prep to a minimum.

Prep: 20 minutes **Bake:** 30 minutes **Oven:** 350°F

Nonstick cooking spray
1 package 2-layer-size white cake mix
1 cup quick-cooking rolled oats
½ cup peanut butter
1 egg
2 tablespoons milk
1 8-ounce package reduced-fat cream cheese (Neufchâtel), softened
1 12¼-ounce jar caramel ice cream topping
1 11½-ounce package milk chocolate pieces
1 cup cocktail peanuts

1 Coat a 9×13-inch baking pan or baking dish with nonstick cooking spray; set aside. Preheat oven to 350°F. For crumb mixture, in a large bowl combine dry cake mix and oats. Using a pastry blender, cut in peanut butter until mixture resembles fine crumbs. In a small bowl beat egg with milk; add to crumb mixture, stirring until well mixed. Set aside ¾ cup of the crumb mixture. Press the remaining crumb mixture evenly into bottom of the prepared pan or dish.

2 For filling, in a large bowl beat cream cheese with an electric mixer on medium speed until smooth. Add caramel topping and beat until mixed. Spread evenly on top of crumb mixture. Sprinkle chocolate pieces on top; sprinkle the cocktail peanuts over to cover. Sprinkle evenly with the reserved ¾ cup crumb mixture. Bake for 30 minutes. Cool in pan or dish on a wire rack. Cover and store in the refrigerator within 2 hours. Cut into bars.

Makes 24 bars.

Nutrition Facts per bar: 311 cal., 14 g total fat (5 g sat. fat), 16 mg chol., 273 mg sodium, 41 g carbo., 1 g fiber, 7 g pro.

RHUBARB BARS

One of early summer's treasured fruits, rhubarb is cooked into a sauce that makes the filling for these slightly tart treats. Use frozen rhubarb when fresh is not available.

Prep: 30 minutes **Bake:** 30 minutes **Oven:** 375°F

- 3 **cups fresh or frozen unsweetened sliced rhubarb**
- 1 **cup granulated sugar**
- ¼ **cup water**
- ½ **cup granulated sugar**
- 2 **tablespoons all-purpose flour**
- 1 **teaspoon vanilla**
- 1½ **cups all-purpose flour**
- 1½ **cups quick-cooking rolled oats**
- 1 **cup packed brown sugar**
- ¼ **teaspoon baking soda**
- 1 **cup shortening**
- ½ **cup chopped pecans or walnuts**
- **Chopped pecans or walnuts (optional)**

1 Grease a 9×13-inch baking pan or baking dish; set aside. For filling, in a medium saucepan combine rhubarb, the 1 cup granulated sugar, and the water. Bring to boiling; reduce heat. Cover and simmer for 5 minutes. Meanwhile, in a small bowl combine the ½ cup granulated sugar and the 2 tablespoons flour. Stir into rhubarb mixture. Cook and stir about 1 minute more or until thick. Remove from heat; stir in vanilla. Set aside.

2 Preheat oven to 375°F. In a medium bowl combine the 1½ cups flour, the oats, brown sugar, and baking soda. Using a pastry blender, cut in shortening until the mixture resembles coarse crumbs. Stir in the ½ cup pecans. Set aside 1 cup of the crumb mixture.

3 Press the remaining crumb mixture evenly into prepared pan or dish. Spread the rhubarb mixture evenly over the top. Sprinkle with the reserved 1 cup crumb mixture. If desired, sprinkle with additional chopped pecans. Bake for 30 to 35 minutes or until the top is golden brown. Cool in pan or dish on a wire rack. Cut into bars.

Makes 45 bars.

Nutrition Facts per bar: 122 cal., 5 g total fat (1 g sat. fat), 0 mg chol., 10 mg sodium, 17 g carbo., 1 g fiber, 1 g pro.

CHOCOLATE-HAZELNUT MARSHMALLOW BARS

These luscious bars, studded with chips, chunks, and ethereal bits of sticky goodness, are just about as decadent as it gets. Mmmm.

Prep: 25 minutes   **Chill:** 30 minutes

- 1   10½-ounce package tiny marshmallows
- 1   cup hazelnuts (filberts), toasted, skinned,* and coarsely chopped, or coarsely chopped peanuts
- 2½   cups semisweet chocolate pieces
- ½   cup chocolate-hazelnut spread (such as Nutella®)
- ½   cup whipping cream
- ¼   cup butter, softened

      Powdered sugar (optional)

1 Line a 9×13-inch baking pan or baking dish with foil, extending foil over the edges of the pan or dish; set aside. In an extra-large bowl combine marshmallows and nuts; set aside. In a medium saucepan combine chocolate pieces, chocolate-hazelnut spread, whipping cream, and butter; cook and stir over medium-low heat until mixture is smooth.

2 Add chocolate mixture to marshmallow mixture; stir to coat well. Spoon mixture evenly into prepared pan or dish, pressing down lightly. Cover and chill for 30 minutes.

3 Using the edges of the foil, lift the uncut bars out of the pan or dish. Cut into 18 bars while cold. Cut each bar diagonally in half to make triangles. Store in the refrigerator (bars soften at room temperature). If desired, sprinkle with powdered sugar.

Makes 36 triangles.

Nutrition Facts per triangle: 151 cal., 9 g total fat (4 g sat. fat), 8 mg chol., 25 mg sodium, 17 g carbo., 1 g fiber, 1 g pro.

339

***Test Kitchen Tip:** To toast hazelnuts, preheat oven to 350°F. Place the nuts in a single layer in a shallow baking pan. Bake about 10 minutes or until nuts are toasted, stirring once. Place the warm nuts on a clean kitchen towel. Rub nuts with the towel to remove loose skins.*

To store: *Layer bars between waxed paper in an airtight container. Cover; seal. Store in the refrigerator for up to 3 days or freeze for up to 3 months. Keep chilled until ready to serve (bars soften at room temperature).*

RASPBERRY-OATMEAL BARS

The easiest of treats is also super adaptable. If you prefer apricot preserves, try that. Blackberry or peach jam also works. Any way you make them, they're delicious.

Prep: 15 minutes **Bake:** 20 minutes **Oven:** 375°F

- 1 package 2-layer-size yellow or white cake mix
- 2½ cups quick-cooking rolled oats
- ¾ cup butter, melted
- 1 12-ounce jar seedless raspberry jam, seedless blackberry jam, or apricot or peach preserves (about 1 cup)
- 1 tablespoon water

1 | Line a 9×13-inch baking pan or baking dish with foil, extending foil over the edges of the pan or dish. Grease the foil; set aside. Preheat oven to 375°F.

2 | In a very large bowl stir together dry cake mix and rolled oats; stir in melted butter until crumbly. Press half (about 3 cups) of the crumb mixture evenly into prepared pan or dish.

3 | In a small bowl combine jam or preserves and the water; spread over crust to within ½ inch of the edges. Sprinkle evenly with the remaining crumb mixture.

4 | Bake for 20 to 25 minutes or until golden brown. Cool in pan or dish on a wire rack. Using the edges of the foil, lift the uncut bars out of the pan or dish. Cut into bars.

Makes 40 bars.

Nutrition Facts per bar: 135 cal., 5 g total fat (3 g sat. fat), 10 mg chol., 122 mg sodium, 20 g carbo., 1 g fiber, 2 g pro.

PINEAPPLE-COCONUT BARS

Thoughts of ocean breezes and island flavors inspired these refreshing bars. They're quick to make and bake, and are filled with pineapple, coconut, and nuts.

Prep: 20 minutes   **Bake:** 35 minutes   **Oven:** 350°F (baking pan) or 325°F (baking dish)

- 1½   cups all-purpose flour
- 1½   cups sugar
- ½   teaspoon baking soda
- 4   eggs, beaten
- 1   20-ounce can crushed pineapple, drained
- ½   cup butter, melted
- ½   cup chopped nuts
- ½   cup shredded coconut

1 Grease a 9×13-inch baking pan or baking dish; set aside. Preheat oven to 350°F if using a baking pan or 325°F if using a baking dish. In a large bowl stir together flour, sugar, and baking soda. Stir in eggs, drained pineapple, and melted butter until combined. Fold in nuts and coconut. Spread batter evenly in prepared pan or dish.

2 Bake about 35 minutes or until a toothpick inserted near the center comes out clean. Cool in pan or dish on a wire rack. Cut into bars.

Makes 24 bars.

Nutrition Facts per bar: 160 cal., 7 g total fat (3.g sat. fat), 45 mg chol., 66 mg sodium, 23 g carbo., 1 g fiber, 2 g pro.

CHOCOLATE-PEANUT BUTTER BARS

If ever there was a flavor match made in heaven, it's peanut butter and chocolate. Enjoy the blend in these candylike bars.

Prep: 30 minutes **Bake:** 10 minutes **Chill:** 2½ hours **Oven:** 300°F

- 1¾ cups finely crushed graham crackers or vanilla wafers
- ½ cup butter, melted
- ¼ cup unsweetened cocoa powder
- 1⅓ cups semisweet chocolate pieces
- ⅔ cup butter
- 2½ cups peanut butter
- ¾ cup butter, softened
- 1 tablespoon vanilla
- 3 cups powdered sugar

342

1 Preheat oven to 300°F. For crust, in a medium bowl stir together crushed graham crackers, the ½ cup melted butter, and the cocoa powder. Press evenly into an ungreased 9×13-inch baking pan or baking dish. Bake for 10 minutes. Cool in pan or dish on a wire rack.

2 In a medium saucepan combine chocolate pieces and the ⅔ cup butter; cook and stir over low heat until melted. Carefully spread half of the chocolate mixture evenly over crust. Chill about 30 minutes or until chocolate mixture is set. Cover the remaining chocolate mixture; set aside at room temperature.

3 In a large bowl combine peanut butter, the ¾ cup softened butter, and the vanilla. Beat with an electric mixer on medium speed until smooth. Gradually beat in as much of the powdered sugar as you can with the mixer. Using a wooden spoon, stir in any remaining powdered sugar. Pat evenly over chocolate layer in pan.

4 Spread the remaining chocolate mixture evenly over peanut butter layer. Cover and chill for 2 hours. Cut into bars.

Makes about 60 bars.

Nutrition Facts per bar: 170 cal., 13 g total fat (6 g sat. fat), 16 mg chol., 115 mg sodium, 13 g carbo., 1 g fiber, 3 g pro.

COCONUT-ALMOND DELIGHT BARS

They're delicious, delightful, and a great dessert for a special lunch. Almond paste doubles up with toasted almonds and coconut in this chewy treat.

Prep: 30 minutes **Bake:** 28 minutes **Cool:** 20 minutes **Oven:** 350°F

- 1 cup butter, softened
- ½ cup sugar
- 1 8-ounce can almond paste made without syrup or glucose
- 1 cup all-purpose flour
- 1½ cups quick-cooking rolled oats
- 1 cup flaked coconut
- ½ cup finely ground, toasted almonds

1 Line a 9×13-inch baking pan or baking dish with foil, extending foil over the edges of the pan or dish. Grease foil; set aside. Preheat oven to 350°F.

2 In a very large bowl beat butter with an electric mixer on medium to high speed for 30 seconds. Add sugar, beating until combined. Break up almond paste and add to butter mixture; beat until well mixed. Beat in flour. Stir in oats, ¾ cup of the coconut, and the almonds until well mixed. Press mixture evenly into prepared pan or dish. Sprinkle with the remaining ¼ cup coconut.

3 Bake for 28 to 30 minutes or until top is golden brown. Cool for 20 minutes. Using the edges of the foil, lift the uncut bars out of the pan or dish. Place on cutting board; cool completely. Using a long-bladed knife, cut straight down into bars.

Makes 24 bars.

Nutrition Facts per bar: 201 cal., 13 g total fat (7 g sat. fat), 20 mg chol., 69 mg sodium, 19 g carbo., 2 g fiber, 2 g pro.

343

MAPLE-HAZELNUT BARS

A buttery crust with cream cheese forms the base for a nutty, pielike filling that will delight maple fans. A chocolate drizzle adds the perfect finish.

Prep: 25 minutes **Bake:** 40 minutes **Oven:** 350°F

- 2 3-ounce packages cream cheese, softened
- ½ cup butter, softened
- ½ cup packed brown sugar
- 1 teaspoon vanilla
- 2 cups all-purpose flour
- 3 eggs
- 1 cup packed brown sugar
- ⅔ cup light-color corn syrup
- ¼ cup pure maple syrup or maple-flavor syrup
- ¼ cup whipping cream
- ¼ cup butter, melted
- ⅛ teaspoon salt
- 2 cups hazelnuts (filberts), toasted, skinned,* and chopped
- 2 ounces semisweet chocolate, chopped
- ½ teaspoon shortening

1 Lightly grease a 9×13-inch baking pan; set aside. Preheat oven to 350°F. For crust, in a large bowl combine cream cheese, the ½ cup butter, the ½ cup brown sugar, and the vanilla. Beat with an electric mixer on medium to high speed until well mixed. Beat in as much of the flour as you can with the mixer. Using a wooden spoon, stir in any remaining flour. Pat mixture evenly into prepared pan. Bake for 15 to 18 minutes or until edge is lightly brown.

2 For filling, in a medium bowl beat eggs with a fork. Stir in the 1 cup brown sugar, the corn syrup, maple syrup, whipping cream, the ¼ cup melted butter, and the salt. Mix well. Stir in hazelnuts. Pour filling evenly over crust in pan. Bake for 25 to 30 minutes or until mixture is golden brown and bubbly. Cool in pan on a wire rack.

3 In a small saucepan combine semisweet chocolate and shortening; heat and stir over low heat until melted. Drizzle chocolate mixture over bars in a decorative pattern. Let stand until set. Cover and store in the refrigerator within 2 hours. Cut into bars.

Makes 36 bars.

Nutrition Facts per bar: 193 cal., 12 g total fat (5 g sat. fat), 35 mg chol., 62 mg sodium, 21 g carbo., 1 g fiber, 2 g pro.

---

*Test Kitchen Tip: *To toast hazelnuts, preheat oven to 350°F. Place the nuts in a shallow baking pan. Bake about 10 minutes or until nuts are toasted, stirring once. Place the warm nuts on a clean kitchen towel. Rub nuts with the towel to remove the loose skins.*

To store: *Layer chocolate-drizzled bars between waxed paper in an airtight container. Cover; seal. Store in the refrigerator for up to 3 days. (Or layer undrizzled bars between waxed paper in an airtight container. Cover; seal. Freeze for up to 3 months. Thaw bars; drizzle with chocolate as directed in step 3.)*

COFFEE CHEESECAKE BARS

Have a little kick with your after-dinner coffee. If you're not a fan of coffee liqueur, substitute milk.

Prep: 25 minutes   **Bake:** 25 minutes   **Oven:** 350°F

- 2 cups finely crushed chocolate wafers (about 44 wafers or one 9-ounce package)
- ⅓ cup butter, melted
- 1 8-ounce package cream cheese, softened
- 1 3-ounce package cream cheese, softened
- ⅔ cup sugar
- ½ teaspoon vanilla
- 4 eggs
- 2 tablespoons coffee liqueur or milk
- ½ cup sliced almonds

1 Grease a 9×13-inch baking pan or baking dish; set aside. Preheat oven to 350°F. For crust, in a medium bowl combine crushed chocolate wafers and melted butter. Press crumb mixture evenly into prepared pan or dish; set aside.

2 For filling, in a large bowl combine cream cheese, sugar, and vanilla; beat with an electric mixer on medium to high speed until combined. Add eggs all at once. Beat on low speed just until combined. Stir in liqueur or milk. Pour filling evenly over the crust. Sprinkle with almonds.

3 Bake for 25 to 30 minutes or until center appears set. Cool in pan or dish on a wire rack. Cover and store in the refrigerator within 2 hours. Cut into bars.

Makes 32 bars.

Nutrition Facts per bar: 124 cal., 8 g total fat (4 g sat. fat), 42 mg chol., 99 mg sodium, 11 g carbo., 0 g fiber, 2 g pro.

MIXED NUT BARS

Nuts about nuts? Look no more. These bars are loaded with nuts in a lightly sweet filling on top of a butter crust. Chill first for easy cutting.

Prep: 20 minutes   **Bake:** 35 minutes   **Chill:** 1 to 2 hours   **Oven:** 350°F

- 1¾ cups all-purpose flour
- ¾ cup butter, softened
- ⅓ cup packed brown sugar
- 1⅔ cups granulated sugar
- 1 cup buttermilk or sour milk*
- 3 eggs
- ¼ cup all-purpose flour
- ¼ cup butter, melted
- 1½ teaspoons vanilla
- 2 cups coarsely chopped mixed nuts (no peanuts)
  Powdered sugar (optional)

1 Preheat oven to 350°F. In a large bowl combine the 1¾ cups flour, the ¾ cup butter, and the brown sugar. Beat with an electric mixer on medium to high speed until combined (mixture will be crumbly). Pat mixture evenly into the bottom and ½ inch up the sides of an ungreased 9×13-inch baking pan. Bake for 10 minutes.

2 Meanwhile, in a clean bowl combine granulated sugar, buttermilk, eggs, the ¼ cup flour, the ¼ cup melted butter, and the vanilla; beat with an electric mixer on low speed until combined. Stir in nuts. Pour evenly into crust.

3 Bake about 25 minutes or until golden brown and center is set. Cool in pan on a wire rack. Cover and chill for at least 1 hour or up to 2 hours. Cut into bars. If desired, sprinkle with powdered sugar.

Makes 32 bars.

Nutrition Facts per bar: 194 cal., 11 g total fat (5 g sat. fat), 35 mg chol., 58 mg sodium, 21 g carbo., 1 g fiber, 2 g pro.

*Test Kitchen Tip: *To make 1 cup sour milk, place 1 tablespoon lemon juice or vinegar in a glass measuring cup. Add enough milk to make 1 cup total liquid; stir. Let mixture stand for 5 minutes before using.*

To store: *Layer bars between waxed paper in an airtight container. Cover; seal. Store in the refrigerator for up to 3 days or freeze for up to 3 months. Thaw, if frozen, before serving.*

CRANBERRY-MACADAMIA BARS

There are no nuts like macadamias to enrich a recipe. Here they add a tropical taste to cranberry and coconut bars that have a hint of orange.

Prep: 20 minutes   **Bake:** 40 minutes   **Oven:** 350°F

1¼   cups all-purpose flour
¾   cup sugar
½   cup butter
1   cup finely chopped macadamia nuts, hazelnuts (filberts), or pecans
1¼   cups sugar
2   eggs, slightly beaten
2   tablespoons milk
1   teaspoon finely shredded orange peel
1   teaspoon vanilla
1   cup finely chopped fresh cranberries
½   cup flaked or shredded coconut

1 Preheat oven to 350°F. For crust, in a medium bowl stir together flour and the ¾ cup sugar. Using a pastry blender, cut in butter until mixture resembles coarse crumbs. Stir in ½ cup of the nuts. Press the flour mixture evenly into an ungreased 9×13-inch baking pan.

2 Bake for 10 to 15 minutes or until the crust is light brown around the edges.

3 Meanwhile, for topping, in a medium bowl combine the 1¼ cups sugar, the eggs, milk, orange peel, and vanilla; beat with an electric mixer on low to medium speed until combined. Pour over the hot crust. Sprinkle with the remaining ½ cup nuts, the cranberries, and coconut.

4 Bake about 30 minutes more or until golden brown. Cool slightly in pan on a wire rack. Cut into bars while warm. Cool completely.

Makes 24 bars.

Nutrition Facts per bar: 176 cal., 8 g total fat (4 g sat. fat), 28 mg chol., 46 mg sodium, 24 g carbo., 0 g fiber, 2 g pro.

To store: *Layer bars between waxed paper in an airtight container. Cover; seal. Store in the refrigerator for up to 3 days.*

MYSTICAL LAYERED BARS

Like magic, the ingredients layer one on top of another and bake into the most chewy, chocolaty, raisin-y, yummy bars. Who can resist?

Prep: 15 minutes **Bake:** 25 minutes **Oven:** 350°F

- ⅓ cup butter, melted
- 1 cup finely crushed graham crackers
- ½ cup rolled oats
- 1 14-ounce can sweetened condensed milk
- 1 cup flaked coconut
- ¾ cup semisweet chocolate pieces
- ¾ cup golden raisins
- 1 cup coarsely chopped peanuts or pecans

1 Preheat oven to 350°F. Pour melted butter into a 9×13-inch baking pan or baking dish; tilt pan or dish to coat bottom evenly. Sprinkle crushed graham crackers evenly over melted butter; sprinkle with rolled oats. Drizzle with sweetened condensed milk. Sprinkle with coconut, chocolate pieces, and raisins; top with peanuts.

2 Bake for 25 to 30 minutes or until edges are lightly browned. Cool in pan or dish on a wire rack for 5 minutes. Cut into bars and cool completely.

Makes 36 bars.

Nutrition Facts per bar: 127 cal., 7 g total fat (3 g sat. fat), 9 mg chol., 46 mg sodium, 15 g carbo., 1 g fiber, 3 g pro.

To store: *Tightly cover pan or dish and store at room temperature for up to 2 days.*

EASY GINGERBREAD BARS

Here's an old-fashioned, sure-to-please specialty for today's busy cooks. Start with a mix, add nutritious dried fruits, and serve with cold milk.

Prep: 10 minutes **Bake:** 20 minutes **Oven:** 350°F (baking pan) or 325°F (baking dish)

1   14½-ounce package gingerbread mix
1   7-ounce package mixed dried fruit bits
1   cup chopped pecans
¾   cup water
1   egg
1   cup powdered sugar
⅛   teaspoon ground ginger
3   to 4 teaspoons milk

1 Grease a 9×13-inch baking pan or baking dish; set aside. Preheat oven to 350°F if using a baking pan or 325°F if using a baking dish. In a medium bowl stir together dry gingerbread mix, fruit bits, pecans, the water, and egg just until combined. Spread batter evenly in prepared pan or dish.

2 Bake for 20 to 25 minutes or until a toothpick inserted near the center comes out clean. Cool in pan or dish on a wire rack.

3 For glaze, in a small bowl stir together powdered sugar, ginger, and enough of the milk to make a glaze of spreading consistency. Spread glaze over top. Cut into bars.

Makes 24 bars.

Nutrition Facts per bar: 145 cal., 6 g total fat (1 g sat. fat), 9 mg chol., 130 mg sodium, 24 g carbo., 0 g fiber, 2 g pro.

To store: *Layer unglazed bars between waxed paper in an airtight container. Cover; seal. Store at room temperature for up to 3 days or freeze for up to 3 months. Thaw, if frozen. Prepare glaze and spread over bars.*

GOOEY PECAN PIE BARS

Here's everything that makes pecan pie an irresistible item on the holiday table—a rich, buttery crust with a sweet filling, chock-full of pecans.

Prep: 25 minutes   **Bake:** 45 minutes   **Oven:** 350°F

- 2 cups all-purpose flour
- ½ cup granulated sugar
- ⅛ teaspoon salt
- ¾ cup butter
- 1 cup packed brown sugar
- 1 cup light-color corn syrup
- ½ cup butter
- 4 eggs, slightly beaten
- 2½ cups finely chopped pecans
- 1 teaspoon vanilla

1 Grease a 9×13-inch baking pan; set aside. Preheat oven to 350°F. In a large bowl stir together flour, granulated sugar, and salt. Using a pastry blender, cut in the ¾ cup butter until the mixture resembles fine crumbs. Press the crumb mixture evenly into the prepared pan. Bake for 15 to 18 minutes or until lightly browned; set aside.

2 For filling, in a medium saucepan combine brown sugar, corn syrup, and the ½ cup butter. Bring to boiling over medium heat, stirring constantly. Remove from heat.

3 Place eggs in a medium bowl. Gradually stir about ½ cup of the hot mixture into the eggs. Return all mixture to saucepan. Stir in pecans and vanilla. Pour nut mixture evenly over baked crust.

4 Bake for 30 to 32 minutes more or until the filling is set. Cool in the pan on a wire rack. Cut into bars.

Makes 20 to 32 bars.

Nutrition Facts per bar: 363 cal., 23 g total fat (9 g sat. fat), 75 mg chol., 175 mg sodium, 39 g carbo., 2 g fiber, 4 g pro.

OATMEAL-CHEESECAKE-CRANBERRY BARS

These are just too good to save for holiday eating. Creamy cheesecake gets a topping of cranberry sauce and a dusting of crumbs.

Prep: 20 minutes **Bake:** 55 minutes **Chill:** 3 hours **Oven:** 350°F

- 2 **cups all-purpose flour**
- 1¼ **cups quick-cooking rolled oats**
- ¾ **cup packed brown sugar**
- 1 **cup butter**
- 12 **ounces cream cheese, softened**
- ½ **cup granulated sugar**
- 2 **eggs**
- 2 **teaspoons lemon juice**
- 1 **teaspoon vanilla**
- 1 **16-ounce can whole cranberry sauce**
- 2 **teaspoons cornstarch**

1 Grease a 9×13-inch baking pan; set aside. Preheat the oven to 350°F. For crust, in a large bowl stir together flour, rolled oats, and brown sugar. Using a pastry blender, cut in butter until mixture resembles coarse crumbs. Set aside 1½ cups of the crumbs. Press the remaining crumbs evenly into prepared pan. Bake for 15 minutes.

2 Meanwhile, in a medium bowl combine cream cheese and granulated sugar; beat with an electric mixer on medium speed until light and fluffy. Beat in eggs, lemon juice, and vanilla. Spread cream cheese mixture evenly over baked crust.

3 In a small bowl stir together cranberry sauce and cornstarch; carefully spoon over cream cheese layer. Sprinkle with the reserved 1½ cups crumbs. Bake about 40 minutes or until set. Cool in pan on a wire rack. Cover and chill for at least 3 hours. Cut into bars.

Makes 36 bars.

Nutrition Facts per bar: 166 cal., 9 g total fat (5 g sat. fat), 36 mg chol., 74 mg sodium, 20 g carbo., 1 g fiber, 2 g pro.

To store: *Place bars in a single layer in an airtight container. Cover; seal. Store in the refrigerator for up to 3 days or freeze for up to 3 months. Thaw, if frozen, before serving.*

HOLIDAY LAYER BARS

Layered with tasty jewels—gingersnaps, white chocolate, cranberries, orange peel, and coconut—these make beautiful treats.

Prep: 25 minutes **Bake:** 25 minutes **Oven:** 350°F

½   cup butter, melted

1½   cups finely crushed gingersnaps (about 25 cookies)

6   ounces white chocolate baking squares (with cocoa butter), chopped, or white baking pieces

⅔   cup dried cranberries or dried tart red cherries, snipped

⅓   cup diced candied orange peel

1   cup pistachio nuts, chopped

1   14-ounce can sweetened condensed milk

1⅓   cups flaked or shredded coconut

1 Preheat oven to 350°F. Pour melted butter into a 9×13-inch baking pan or baking dish. Tilt pan or dish to coat the bottom with butter. Sprinkle crushed gingersnaps evenly over butter in pan or dish.

2 Layer white chocolate, cranberries, candied orange peel, and pistachio nuts on top of crushed gingersnaps. Pour sweetened condensed milk evenly over fruit and nut layers. Sprinkle with coconut.

3 Bake about 25 minutes or until coconut is lightly golden brown. Cool in pan or dish on a wire rack. Cut into bars.

Makes 42 bars.

Nutrition Facts per bar: 134 cal., 7 g total fat (4 g sat. fat), 10 mg chol., 68 mg sodium, 16 g carbo., 1 g fiber, 2 g pro.

To store: *Place bars in a single layer in an airtight container. Cover; seal. Store in the refrigerator for up to 3 days or freeze for up to 3 months. Thaw, if frozen, before serving.*

HONEY-NUT BARS

Baked golden and chewy with coconut and walnuts, these bars are so rich you only need one, but they're just too good to stop there.

Prep: 25 minutes **Bake:** 25 minutes **Oven:** 350°F

½ cup butter, softened
¼ cup shortening
1 cup honey
1 teaspoon baking powder
¼ teaspoon salt
3 eggs
1 teaspoon vanilla
1½ cups all-purpose flour
1 cup flaked or shredded coconut
1 cup chopped walnuts
1 cup powdered sugar
Milk
¼ teaspoon vanilla
Chopped walnuts

1 Grease a 9×13-inch baking pan or baking dish; set aside. Preheat oven to 350°F. In a large bowl combine butter and shortening; beat with an electric mixer on medium to high speed for 30 seconds. Add honey, baking powder, and salt. Beat until combined. Beat in eggs and vanilla until combined. Beat in as much of the flour as you can with the mixer. Using a wooden spoon, stir in any remaining flour. Stir in coconut and the 1 cup nuts.

2 Spread batter evenly in prepared pan or dish. Bake for 25 to 30 minutes or until a toothpick inserted near the center comes out clean. Cool in pan or dish on a wire rack.

3 Meanwhile, for the powdered sugar icing, in a small bowl stir together powdered sugar, 1 tablespoon milk, and the vanilla. Stir in enough additional milk, 1 teaspoon at a time, to make icing of drizzling consistency.

4 Drizzle powdered sugar icing over cooled cookies in pan or dish; sprinkle with additional nuts. Cut into bars.

Makes 24 bars.

Nutrition Facts per bar: 197 cal., 11 g total fat (4 g sat. fat), 38 mg chol., 92 mg sodium, 23 g carbo., 1 g fiber, 3 g pro.

353

To store: *Place iced bars in a single layer in an airtight container. Cover; seal. Store in the refrigerator for up to 3 days. (Or place uncut, uniced bars in a freezer container; freeze for up to 1 month. Before serving, cut into bars and thaw for 15 minutes. Drizzle with the powdered sugar icing; sprinkle with nuts.)*

ORANGE-CHOCOLATE CHEESECAKE BARS

These decadent bars—creamy, fresh, and chocolaty all at once—will produce oohs and aahs whenever they're served.

Prep: 35 minutes **Bake:** 55 minutes **Cool:** 1½ hours **Chill:** 4 to 24 hours **Oven:** 350°F

1 recipe Graham Cracker Crust

3 8-ounce packages cream cheese, softened

1¼ cups packed brown sugar

3 eggs

3 tablespoons frozen orange juice concentrate, thawed

1½ teaspoons finely shredded orange peel

½ teaspoon vanilla

¼ teaspoon salt

6 ounces semisweet chocolate, cut up

2 tablespoons butter

1½ cups dairy sour cream

⅓ cup granulated sugar

Ground cinnamon (optional)

1 Preheat oven to 350°F. Prepare Graham Cracker Crust; set aside. For cream cheese filling, in a large bowl combine cream cheese and brown sugar; beat with an electric mixer on medium speed until mixed. Add eggs, one at a time, beating on low speed after each addition just until combined. Stir in thawed orange juice concentrate, orange peel, vanilla, and salt. Pour 1 cup of the cream cheese filling into a medium bowl. Set both bowls aside.

2 In a small saucepan combine chocolate and butter; cook and stir over very low heat just until melted and smooth. Stir chocolate mixture into the reserved 1 cup cream cheese filling. Carefully spread the chocolate filling evenly over the Graham Cracker Crust. Bake for 15 minutes. Remove from oven. Carefully pour the remaining cream cheese filling over the baked chocolate layer, spreading evenly.

3 Bake for 40 to 45 minutes or just until mixture is set in the center. Remove from oven; cool for 30 minutes in pan on a wire rack. Meanwhile, in a small bowl combine sour cream and granulated sugar. Cover; let stand at room temperature while bars cool.

4 Gently spread the sour cream mixture onto bars. Cool for 1 hour more. Cover and chill for at least 4 hours or up to 24 hours before cutting. Using the edges of the foil, lift the uncut bars out of the pan. If desired, sprinkle with cinnamon just before serving. Cut into bars.

Makes 32 bars.

Nutrition Facts per bar: 215 cal., 14 g total fat (9 g sat. fat), 54 mg chol., 146 mg sodium, 20 g carbo., 0 g fiber, 3 g pro.

Graham Cracker Crust: *Line a 9×13-inch baking pan with heavy foil, extending foil over the edges of the pan. Lightly grease foil; set aside. In a large bowl stir together 1¼ cups finely crushed graham crackers and ¼ cup granulated sugar. Add ⅓ cup butter, melted; mix well. Press evenly onto the bottom of the prepared pan.*

To store: *Place bars in a single layer in an airtight container. Cover; seal. Store in the refrigerator for up to 3 days.*

HONEY-ROASTED PEANUT BUTTER BARS

Kids (and adults!) who like honey on their PB sandwiches will devour these. A layer of chocolate makes the bars extra scrumptious.

Prep: 30 minutes   **Chill:** 1 hour

- 1 **cup honey-roasted peanut butter**
- ⅓ **cup honey**
- 2 **tablespoons butter, melted**
- 2 **cups finely crushed graham crackers**
- 2 **cups semisweet chocolate pieces, melted***
- ⅔ **cup honey-roasted peanuts, chopped if desired**

1 In a large bowl combine peanut butter, honey, and melted butter. Stir in crushed graham crackers to form a thick mixture.

2 Press graham cracker mixture evenly into an ungreased 9×13-inch baking pan or baking dish. Spread melted chocolate evenly over graham cracker layer. Sprinkle with peanuts. Chill about 1 hour or until set. Cut into bars.

Makes 36 bars.

Nutrition Facts per bar: 138 cal., 9 g total fat (3 g sat. fat), 2 mg chol., 85 mg sodium, 15 g carbo., 1 g fiber, 3 g pro.

Test Kitchen Tip: To melt the chocolate pieces, place in a medium microwave-safe bowl; microwave on 50% power (medium) for 1 to 2 minutes or until chocolate is melted and smooth, stirring two or three times.

To store: Place bars in a single layer in an airtight container. Cover; seal. Store in the refrigerator for up to 3 days.

LEMONY GLAZED SHORTBREAD BARS

Butter makes these bars rich
and flaky while fresh lemon peel adds zest to the
sweet lemon mixture.

Prep: 40 minutes **Bake:** 40 minutes **Oven:** 300°F

- 3 **cups all-purpose flour**
- ⅓ **cup cornstarch**
- 1¼ **cups powdered sugar**
- ¼ **cup finely shredded lemon peel (6 to 7 lemons)**
- 1½ **cups butter, softened**
- 1 **tablespoon lemon juice**
- ½ **teaspoon salt**
- ½ **teaspoon vanilla**
- 1 **recipe Lemony Glaze**

1 Line a 9×13-inch baking pan or baking dish with heavy foil, extending foil over the edges of the pan or dish. Lightly grease foil; set aside. Preheat oven to 300°F.

2 In a medium bowl stir together flour and cornstarch. In a small bowl combine powdered sugar and lemon peel. Using your fingers or pressing against side of bowl with a wooden spoon, work lemon peel into powdered sugar until sugar is yellow and very fragrant.* Set aside.

3 In a large bowl combine butter, lemon juice, salt, and vanilla; beat with an electric mixer on medium speed until combined. Gradually beat in sugar mixture. Stir in flour mixture.

4 With lightly floured fingers, press dough evenly into the prepared pan or dish. Bake on the center rack of the oven about 40 minutes or until pale golden brown in center and edges begin to brown.

5 Remove from oven. Immediately dollop Lemony Glaze over top and gently spread to evenly distribute the glaze. Cool in pan or dish on a wire rack. Using the edges of the foil, lift the uncut bars out of the pan or dish. Cut into bars.

Makes 32 bars.

Nutrition Facts per bar: 181 cal., 9 g total fat (5 g sat. fat), 23 mg chol., 98 mg sodium, 25 g carbo., 0 g fiber, 0 g pro.

Lemony Glaze: *In a medium bowl combine 2½ cups powdered sugar, 2 teaspoons finely shredded lemon peel, 3 tablespoons lemon juice, 1 tablespoon light-color corn syrup, and ½ teaspoon vanilla. Whisk until smooth.*

----

*Test Kitchen Tip: *Rubbing the lemon peel with the powdered sugar releases the lemon oil.*

LINZER BARS

The classic Austrian linzertorte is deliciously transformed into bars that have a rich crust and a filling of raspberry jam. Sprinkle with powdered sugar, if desired.

Prep: 30 minutes **Chill:** 1¼ hours **Bake:** 30 minutes **Oven:** 350°F

⅔ cup butter

⅔ cup granulated sugar

½ teaspoon ground cinnamon

¼ teaspoon ground cloves

1 egg

1 tablespoon cherry liqueur, cherry brandy, or milk

1½ cups all-purpose flour

1 cup ground hazelnuts (filberts) or almonds

1 teaspoon finely shredded lemon peel

2 tablespoons all-purpose flour

1 cup seedless red raspberry jam

Powdered sugar (optional)

1 In a medium bowl beat butter with an electric mixer on medium to high speed for 30 seconds. Add granulated sugar, cinnamon, and cloves; beat until combined. Beat in egg and liqueur until combined. Using a wooden spoon, stir in the 1½ cups flour, the hazelnuts, and lemon peel. Divide dough in half; stir the 2 tablespoons flour into one portion of the dough. Wrap doughs in plastic wrap (label the one with additional flour); chill for 1 hour.

2 Roll the dough with the additional flour between two pieces of waxed paper into a 10×15-inch rectangle. Remove top piece of waxed paper. Cut rectangle into 10×½-inch strips. Slide dough, with waxed paper, onto a large baking sheet. Chill dough strips about 15 minutes or until firm and easy to handle.

3 Meanwhile, preheat oven to 350°F. Line a 9×13-inch baking pan or baking dish with foil, extending foil over the edges of the pan or dish. Grease foil. Pat the dough without the additional flour evenly into prepared pan or dish. Spread jam evenly over dough in pan or dish. Using a long narrow-bladed metal spatula, peel dough strips from waxed paper. Carefully place half of the dough strips across jam about ½ inch apart. Trim ends and piece strips of dough together as necessary by overlapping slightly. Place remaining dough strips diagonally across jam, making a diamond pattern.

4 Bake about 30 minutes or until crust is golden brown. Cool in pan or dish on a wire rack. Using the edges of the foil, lift the uncut bars out of the pan or dish. Cut into bars. Just before serving, if desired, sift powdered sugar over bars.

Makes 32 bars.

Nutrition Facts per bar: 131 cal., 7 g total fat (3 g sat. fat), 17 mg chol., 33 mg sodium, 17 g carbo., 1 g fiber, 1 g pro.

To store: *Layer bars between waxed paper in an airtight storage container. Cover; seal. Store in the refrigerator for up to 3 days or freeze for up to 3 months. Thaw, if frozen, before serving.*

APPLE-CHEESE BARS

If you'd like sweeter bars, make this recipe with mildly tart Golden Delicious, Jonathan, Rome Beauty, or Newtown Pippin apples. For treats with tang, use Granny Smiths.

Prep: 25 minutes **Bake:** 40 minutes **Oven:** 350°F

- 2 cups all-purpose flour
- 1 cup butter, softened
- ½ cup granulated sugar
- 2 egg yolks
- 1 teaspoon baking powder
- 4 medium cooking apples (such as Golden Delicious, Rome Beauty, Granny Smith, Jonathan, or Newtown Pippin), peeled and shredded
- 1 cup shredded cheddar cheese (4 ounces)
- ¾ cup granulated sugar
- ¼ cup all-purpose flour
- 1 teaspoon ground cinnamon
- 2 egg whites
- 1½ cups powdered sugar
- ¼ cup cream cheese, softened (about 2 ounces)

1 Preheat oven to 350°F. For crust, in a medium bowl combine the 2 cups flour, the butter, the ½ cup granulated sugar, the egg yolks, and baking powder; beat with an electric mixer on low to medium speed until mixture is crumbly. Press half of the crumb mixture into an ungreased 9×13-inch baking pan or baking dish. Bake for 10 to 12 minutes or until lightly browned. Set aside.

2 In a large bowl combine shredded apples, cheddar cheese, the ¾ cup granulated sugar, the ¼ cup flour, and the cinnamon. Spread over crust. Sprinkle with the remaining crumb mixture. Set aside.

3 In a small bowl beat egg whites with an electric mixer on medium speed until soft peaks form. Gradually beat in powdered sugar and cream cheese. Spoon over crumb mixture. Bake for 30 to 35 minutes more or until browned. Cool in pan or dish on a wire rack. Cover and store in the refrigerator within 2 hours. Cut into bars.

Makes 36 bars.

Nutrition Facts per bar: 147 cal., 7 g total fat (4 g sat. fat), 31 mg chol., 94 mg sodium, 19 g carbo., 0 g fiber, 2 g pro.

BROWNIES

Warning: The following chapter may make you swoon, grow weak in the knees, and beg for just one more bite. Brownies just seem to do that. Their deep, rich, and luscious nature is irresistible. So perhaps the best thing to do is bake a batch and indulge.

FUDGY ALMOND BROWNIES

What makes these chewy morsels so irresistible is a mild coffee flavor and a hint of cinnamon. Skip the coffee crystals if you prefer.

Prep: 20 minutes **Bake:** 35 minutes **Oven:** 350°F

- 9 ounces unsweetened chocolate, coarsely chopped
- 1 cup butter
- ⅓ cup water
- 4 teaspoons instant coffee crystals
- 1½ cups granulated sugar
- 1½ cups packed brown sugar
- 5 eggs
- 1½ teaspoons vanilla
- 2 cups all-purpose flour
- ¾ cup ground almonds
- ½ teaspoon ground cinnamon
- ¼ teaspoon salt
- 3 tablespoons powdered sugar (optional)
- ¼ teaspoon unsweetened cocoa powder (optional)

1 Line a 9×13-inch baking pan or baking dish with foil, extending foil over the edges of the pan or dish. Grease foil; set aside. Preheat oven to 350°F.

2 In a large microwave-safe bowl combine chocolate, butter, the water, and coffee crystals. Microwave, uncovered, on 100% power (high) for 2 to 4 minutes or until butter is melted, stirring once or twice. Remove bowl from microwave oven. Stir until chocolate is completely melted.

3 Add granulated sugar and brown sugar to chocolate mixture; beat with an electric mixer on low to medium speed until combined. Add eggs and vanilla; beat on medium speed for 2 minutes. Add flour, almonds, cinnamon, and salt. Beat on low speed until combined. Spread batter evenly in prepared pan or dish.

4 Bake about 35 minutes or until top appears set and dry. Cool in pan or dish on a wire rack. Using the edges of the foil, lift the uncut brownies out of the pan or dish. Cut into bars. If desired, stir together the powdered sugar and cocoa powder; sift over brownies.

Makes 24 brownies.

Nutrition Facts per brownie: 302 cal., 17 g total fat (9 g sat. fat), 66 mg chol., 127 mg sodium, 37 g carbo., 2 g fiber, 4 g pro.

CREAM CHEESE BROWNIES

These are every bit as rich and decadent as you could hope for, with swirls of cream cheese through chocolate and toasty bits of macadamia nuts.

Prep: 30 minutes **Bake:** 45 minutes **Chill:** 1 hour **Oven:** 350°F

- 8 ounces semisweet chocolate, chopped
- 3 tablespoons butter
- 4 eggs
- 1¼ cups sugar
- ⅓ cup water
- 2 teaspoons vanilla
- 1 cup all-purpose flour
- 1 teaspoon baking powder
- ¼ teaspoon salt
- ¾ cup chopped macadamia nuts, toasted
- 1 8-ounce package cream cheese, softened
- ⅔ cup sugar
- 2 tablespoons all-purpose flour
- 1 tablespoon lemon juice
- 1 recipe Chocolate Glaze
- 32 whole macadamia nuts (optional)

1 Line a 9×13-inch baking pan or baking dish with foil, extending foil over the edges of the pan or dish. Grease foil; set aside. Preheat oven to 350°F. In a heavy large saucepan combine chocolate and butter; cook and stir over low heat until chocolate is melted. Set aside to cool.

2 In a large bowl beat two of the eggs with an electric mixer on medium speed until foamy. Add the 1¼ cups sugar, the water, and 1 teaspoon of the vanilla; beat about 5 minutes or until thick and lemon-colored. Beat in cooled chocolate mixture. Stir in the 1 cup flour, the baking powder, and salt. Stir in the ¾ cup nuts. Spread half of the chocolate batter evenly in prepared pan or dish; set pan or dish and the remaining chocolate batter aside.

3 In a medium bowl combine the remaining 2 eggs, the cream cheese, the ⅔ cup sugar, the 2 tablespoons flour, the lemon juice, and the remaining 1 teaspoon vanilla; beat with an electric mixer on medium speed until smooth. Spread evenly over chocolate batter in pan or dish. Spoon the remaining chocolate batter evenly over cream cheese mixture. Using a table knife, swirl batter to marble.

4 Bake for 45 minutes. Cool in pan or dish on a wire rack. Spread Chocolate Glaze over cooled brownies or, if desired, top each brownie with a small amount of the Chocolate Glaze and a whole macadamia nut. Chill about 1 hour or until glaze is set. Cut into bars.

Makes 32 brownies.

Nutrition Facts per brownie: 199 cal., 12 g total fat (6 g sat. fat), 41 mg chol., 72 mg sodium, 23 g carbo., 1 g fiber, 3 g pro.

Chocolate Glaze: *In a small saucepan combine 6 ounces semisweet chocolate, finely chopped, and ⅓ cup whipping cream; cook and stir over low heat until chocolate is melted.*

DEEP CHOCOLATE BROWNIES

Bittersweet and semisweet chocolates flavor this luscious dark brownie that gets even better with a gooey butterscotch and pecan topping.

Prep: 25 minutes   **Bake:** 35 minutes   **Oven:** 350°F

- 1   egg
- 1   cup butterscotch-flavor ice cream topping
- 2   cups coarsely chopped pecans
- 2   cups flaked coconut
- ¾   cup butter, softened
- 1½ cups packed dark brown sugar
- 8   ounces bittersweet chocolate, melted and cooled
- 2   eggs
- 2   teaspoons vanilla
- 2   cups all-purpose flour
- 1   teaspoon baking powder
- ½   teaspoon baking soda
- ½   teaspoon salt
- 1   12-ounce package semisweet chocolate pieces

1 Lightly grease a 9×13-inch baking pan or baking dish; set aside. Preheat oven to 350°F.

2 In a medium bowl beat the 1 egg with an electric mixer on medium speed until fluffy and light colored. Stir in butterscotch topping. Fold in pecans and coconut; set aside.

3 In a large bowl beat butter with an electric mixer on medium to high speed for 30 seconds. Beat in brown sugar until fluffy. Beat in cooled chocolate, the 2 eggs, and the vanilla. In a small bowl stir together flour, baking powder, baking soda, and salt; beat or stir into chocolate mixture (batter will be thick). Stir in chocolate pieces. Spread batter evenly in prepared pan or dish; spread pecan mixture over batter.

4 Bake about 35 minutes or until golden and set. Cool in pan or dish on a wire rack. Cut into bars.

Makes 24 brownies.

Nutrition Facts per brownie: 404 cal., 23 g total fat (11 g sat. fat), 43 mg chol., 221 mg sodium, 50 g carbo., 4 g fiber, 5 g pro.

MALTED FUDGE BROWNIES

Are chocolate malts your favorite? Then take a bite of these. They not only have malted milk powder but malted milk balls mixed into every tasty bite.

Prep: 30 minutes **Bake:** 35 minutes **Oven:** 325°F

- 1½ cups all-purpose flour
- ⅓ cup malted milk powder
- ½ teaspoon salt
- 1 cup butter
- 4 ounces unsweetened chocolate, cut up
- 2 cups sugar
- 4 eggs
- 1 teaspoon vanilla
- 1 cup chopped walnuts, toasted
- 4 ounces malted milk balls, coarsely crushed (about 1 cup)
- ½ of a 15- to 16-ounce can chocolate fudge frosting

1 Lightly grease a 9×13-inch baking pan or baking dish; set aside. Preheat oven to 325°F. In a medium bowl combine flour, malted milk powder, and salt; set aside.

2 In a medium saucepan combine butter and chocolate; cook and stir over low heat until melted. Remove from heat; stir in sugar. Add eggs, one at a time, beating with a wooden spoon after each addition just until combined. Add vanilla. Stir in flour mixture, walnuts, and half of the crushed malted milk balls. Spread in prepared pan or dish.

3 Bake for 35 minutes. Cool in pan or dish on a wire rack. Spread cooled brownies with frosting; sprinkle with the remaining crushed malted milk balls. Cut into bars.

Makes 30 brownies.

Nutrition Facts per brownie: 245 cal., 14 g total fat (5 g sat. fat), 47 mg chol., 140 mg sodium, 29 g carbo., 1 g fiber, 3 g pro.

ROCKY ROAD BROWNIES

Rocky road is a kid favorite for lots of yummy reasons. Chocolate, roasted peanuts, and tiny marshmallows load these brownies with rich and chewy flavor.

Prep: 30 minutes **Bake:** 40 minutes **Oven:** 350°F

- 2   cups all-purpose flour
- 2   cups sugar
- 1   teaspoon baking soda
- ¼   teaspoon salt
- 1   cup butter
- 1   cup water
- ⅓   cup unsweetened cocoa powder
- 2   eggs
- ½   cup buttermilk or sour milk*
- 1½   teaspoons vanilla
- 1½   cups chopped dry-roasted peanuts
- 3   cups tiny marshmallows
- 1   recipe Chocolate Drizzle

1 Line a 9×13-inch baking pan or baking dish with foil, extending foil over the edges of the pan or dish. Grease foil; set aside. Preheat oven to 350°F. In a large bowl combine flour, sugar, baking soda, and salt; set aside.

2 In a medium saucepan combine butter, the water, and cocoa powder. Bring just to boiling, stirring constantly. Remove saucepan from heat. Add the chocolate mixture to the flour mixture; beat with an electric mixer on medium speed until combined. Add eggs, buttermilk, and vanilla. Beat for 1 minute more (batter will be thin). Stir in 1 cup of the peanuts. Spread batter evenly in prepared pan or dish.

3 Bake about 40 minutes or until a toothpick inserted in the center comes out clean.

4 Sprinkle the remaining ½ cup chopped peanuts and the tiny marshmallows over hot brownies. Top with Chocolate Drizzle. Cool in pan or dish on a wire rack.

5 Using the edges of the foil, lift the uncut brownies out of the pan or dish. Cut into bars.

Makes 32 brownies.

Nutrition Facts per brownie: 237 cal., 13 g total fat (6 g sat. fat), 33 mg chol., 119 mg sodium, 27 g carbo., 2 g fiber, 3 g pro.

Chocolate Drizzle: *In a medium saucepan combine 6 ounces semisweet chocolate pieces, ¼ cup whipping cream, and 2 tablespoons butter. Cook and stir over medium-low heat until melted. Drizzle over brownies.*

*Test Kitchen Tip: *To make ½ cup sour milk, place 1½ teaspoons lemon juice or vinegar in a glass measuring cup. Add enough milk to make ½ cup liquid; stir. Let the mixture stand for 5 minutes before using.*

CHOCOLATE BROWNIES WITH PEANUT BUTTER SWIRL

Ribbons of peanut butter throughout chewy chocolate result in the ultimate of rich delights. A drizzle of chocolate on top just adds to the joy.

Prep: 25 minutes **Bake:** 45 minutes **Oven:** 350°F

- 8 ounces semisweet chocolate, chopped
- 3 tablespoons butter
- 4 eggs
- 1¼ cups sugar
- ⅓ cup water
- 1 teaspoon vanilla
- 1 cup all-purpose flour
- 1 teaspoon baking powder
- ¼ teaspoon salt
- ⅔ cup sugar
- 1 3-ounce package cream cheese, softened
- ½ cup peanut butter
- 2 tablespoons all-purpose flour
- ½ cup semisweet chocolate pieces
- 1 teaspoon shortening

1 Line a 9×13-inch baking pan or baking dish with foil, extending foil over the edges of the pan or dish. Grease foil; set aside. Preheat oven to 350°F.

2 In a large heavy saucepan combine chocolate and butter; cook and stir over low heat until chocolate melts. Remove from heat; cool for 15 minutes.

3 Meanwhile, in a large bowl beat two of the eggs with an electric mixer on medium speed until foamy. Add the 1¼ cups sugar, the water, and vanilla; beat on medium speed about 5 minutes or until mixture thickens. Beat in cooled chocolate mixture. Stir in the 1 cup flour, the baking powder, and salt. Spread half of the chocolate batter evenly in prepared pan or dish; set pan or dish and the remaining chocolate batter aside.

4 In a medium bowl combine the remaining 2 eggs, the ⅔ cup sugar, the cream cheese, peanut butter, and the 2 tablespoons flour; beat with an electric mixer on medium speed until smooth. Spread evenly over chocolate batter in pan or dish. Spoon the remaining chocolate batter evenly over cream cheese mixture. Using a table knife, swirl batter to marble. Bake for 45 minutes. Cool in pan or dish on a wire rack.

5 In a small saucepan combine semisweet chocolate pieces and shortening; cook and stir over low heat until chocolate is melted and smooth. Drizzle over cooled brownies. Let stand until chocolate is firm. Using the edges of the foil, lift the uncut brownies out of the pan or dish. Cut into bars.

Makes 32 brownies.

Nutrition Facts per brownie: 160 cal., 8 g total fat (3 g sat. fat), 32 mg chol., 71 mg sodium, 21 g carbo., 1 g fiber, 3 g pro.

BLACK FOREST BROWNIES

The traditional combination of cherries and chocolate creates a brownie sure to please any chocolate lover.

Prep: 30 minutes **Bake:** 35 minutes **Oven:** 350°F

- 2 10-ounce jars maraschino cherries, drained
- 1 cup semisweet chocolate pieces
- ½ cup butter
- 3 eggs, slightly beaten
- 1¼ cups granulated sugar
- 1¼ cups all-purpose flour
- 1 teaspoon vanilla
- ¾ teaspoon salt
- ½ teaspoon baking powder
- 1 cup white baking pieces
- ½ cup slivered almonds, toasted
- 1 3-ounce package cream cheese, softened
- ⅔ cup powdered sugar

1 Grease a 9×13-inch baking pan or baking dish; set aside. Preheat oven to 350°F. Remove stems from 1 cup of the maraschino cherries, if necessary; coarsely chop these cherries. Drain on paper towels. Set aside the chopped cherries and the remaining whole cherries.

2 In a large microwave-safe bowl combine chocolate pieces and butter. Microwave on 100% power (high) for 1 minute; stir. Microwave for 10 to 20 seconds more or until mixture is melted and smooth. Add eggs, granulated sugar, flour, vanilla, salt, and baking powder. Stir until combined. Fold in chopped cherries, white baking pieces, and toasted almonds. Spread batter evenly in prepared pan or dish.

3 Bake for 35 minutes. Cool in pan or dish on a wire rack. Cut into bars.

4 Just before serving, in a medium bowl beat cream cheese and powdered sugar with an electric mixer on medium speed until smooth. Pipe on cooled brownies. If necessary, remove stems from the remaining whole maraschino cherries; coarsely chop cherries and sprinkle on brownies. Cut into bars.

Makes 24 brownies.

Nutrition Facts per brownie: 240 cal., 11 g total fat (5 g sat. fat), 40 mg chol., 128 mg sodium, 33 g carbo., 1 g fiber, 3 g pro.

To store: *Place bars in a single layer in an airtight container. Cover; seal. Store in the refrigerator for up to 3 days.*

BLACK-AND-WHITE BROWNIES

White baking pieces and semisweet chocolate pieces dress up a packaged mix in this so-easy recipe. (Pictured on page 110.)

Prep: 25 minutes **Bake:** 31 minutes **Cool:** 1½ hours **Oven:** 350°F

- 1 **19- to 21-ounce package fudge brownie mix**
- 1 **10- to 12-ounce package white baking pieces**
- 1 **cup semisweet chocolate pieces**
- ½ **cup pecan pieces**
- ¼ **cup butter, melted**
- 3 **tablespoons hot water**
- 2 **cups powdered sugar**
- ¼ **cup unsweetened cocoa powder**
- 1 **teaspoon vanilla**
- ¾ **cup pecan pieces**

1 Grease bottom of a 9×13-inch baking pan or baking dish; set aside. Preheat oven to 350°F. Prepare brownie mix according to package directions. Stir in half of the white baking pieces, all of the semisweet chocolate pieces, and the ½ cup pecans. Spread batter evenly in prepared pan or dish.

2 Bake about 30 minutes or until center is set. Sprinkle with the remaining white baking pieces; return to oven for 1 minute. Cool in pan or dish on a wire rack

3 For frosting, in a medium bowl combine melted butter and hot water; stir in powdered sugar, cocoa powder, and vanilla. Using a wooden spoon, beat by hand until smooth; spoon on brownies. Sprinkle with the ¾ cup pecans. Cool about 1½ hours or until frosting is set. Cut into bars.

Makes 36 brownies.

Nutrition Facts per brownie: 221 cal., 12 g total fat [4 g sat. fat], 18 mg chol., 67 mg sodium, 25 g carbo., 1 g fiber, 2 g pro.

BANANA SPLIT BROWNIES

Oh my, what a treat! Strawberry and cream cheese frosting adds the crowning touch to ultramoist chocolate and banana brownies.

Prep: 20 minutes **Bake:** 20 minutes **Oven:** 350°F

- ½ cup butter, softened
- 1 cup sugar
- 1 teaspoon baking powder
- ½ teaspoon baking soda
- ⅛ teaspoon salt
- 1 cup mashed ripe banana (3 medium)
- 2 eggs
- 1 cup all-purpose flour
- ⅓ cup unsweetened cocoa powder
- 1 recipe Strawberry and Cream Cheese Frosting

1 Grease a 9×13-inch baking pan or baking dish; set aside. Preheat oven to 350°F. In a large bowl beat butter with an electric mixer on medium to high speed for 30 seconds. Add sugar, baking powder, baking soda, and salt. Beat until combined, scraping side of bowl occasionally. Beat in mashed banana and eggs. Beat or stir in flour and cocoa powder. Spread batter evenly in prepared pan or dish.

2 Bake about 20 minutes or until a toothpick inserted into the center comes out clean.

3 Cool in pan or dish on a wire rack. Spread with Strawberry and Cream Cheese Frosting. Cover and store in refrigerator within 2 hours. Cut into bars.

Makes 24 brownies.

Nutrition Facts per brownie: 182 cal., 6 g total fat (3 g sat. fat), 32 mg chol., 102 mg sodium, 33 g carbo., 1 g fiber, 1 g pro.

Strawberry and Cream Cheese Frosting: *In a small bowl combine half of an 8-ounce tub cream cheese with strawberries and 1 cup powdered sugar; beat with an electric mixer on medium speed until combined. Beat in ½ cup frozen strawberries, thawed, cut up, and well drained (about ¼ cup). Beat in 2½ to 3 cups powdered sugar or enough to make a spreading consistency (frosting will stiffen with chilling). Makes about 1⅔ cups.*

To store: *Place bars in a single layer in an airtight container. Cover; seal. Store in the refrigerator for up to 3 days.*

BUTTERSCOTCH BROWNIES

Here are the brownies for those who want rich and chewy without chocolate. Coconut, pecans, and tiny marshmallows make these too good to pass up.

Prep: 30 minutes **Bake:** 20 minutes **Oven:** 350°F

- ⅓ cup butter
- ⅔ cup packed brown sugar
- 1⅓ cups flaked or shredded coconut
- ¾ cup chopped pecans
- ½ cup butter, softened
- 1 cup packed brown sugar
- ½ teaspoon baking soda
- ¼ teaspoon salt
- 3 eggs
- ½ teaspoon vanilla
- 1½ cups all-purpose flour
- ½ cup chopped pecans
- ½ cup tiny marshmallows
- Caramel-flavor ice cream topping (optional)

1 Grease a 9×13-inch baking pan or baking dish; set aside. Preheat oven to 350°F. In a small saucepan melt the ⅓ cup butter; stir in the ⅔ cup brown sugar. Stir in the coconut and the ¾ cup pecans. Pat evenly into prepared pan or dish; set aside.

2 In a large bowl beat the ½ cup butter with an electric mixer on medium to high speed for 30 seconds. Add the 1 cup brown sugar, the baking soda, and salt; beat until combined. Beat in eggs and vanilla until combined. Add flour and beat until combined. Stir in the ½ cup pecans and the marshmallows. Spoon small mounds of the marshmallow mixture over the coconut mixture in pan or dish. Carefully spread to cover.

3 Bake about 20 minutes or until evenly browned (center may jiggle slightly when shaken). Cool in pan or dish on a wire rack. Cut into bars. If desired, drizzle with caramel topping.

Makes 24 brownies.

Nutrition Facts per brownie: 211 cal., 13 g total fat (6 g sat. fat), 43 mg chol., 113 mg sodium, 23 g carbo., 1 g fiber, 2 g pro.

RASPBERRY CHEESECAKE BROWNIES

An elegant and decadent brownie with a dark chocolate crust, a creamy rich cheesecake filling, and a jeweled top of fresh raspberries.

Prep: 30 minutes   **Bake:** 35 minutes   **Chill:** 6 to 24 hours   **Oven:** 350°F

- 4 ounces bittersweet or semisweet chocolate, chopped
- 2 ounces unsweetened chocolate, chopped
- ½ cup unsalted butter
- 1¼ cups sugar
- 3 eggs
- 1½ teaspoons vanilla
- ½ teaspoon salt
- ¾ cup all-purpose flour
- 1 8-ounce package cream cheese, softened
- ⅔ cup sugar
- 2 teaspoons lemon juice
- 1 egg
- ½ teaspoon vanilla
- 2 tablespoons all-purpose flour
- 1½ cups fresh raspberries
- 1 tablespoon sugar

1 Grease and flour a 9×13-inch baking pan or baking dish; set aside. Preheat oven to 350°F.

2 For brownie layer, set a metal bowl over a saucepan of barely simmering water. Add bittersweet chocolate, unsweetened chocolate, and butter to bowl; heat and stir until melted. Remove bowl from saucepan and cool. Whisk in the 1¼ cups sugar and the 3 eggs, one at a time. Whisk in the 1½ teaspoons vanilla and the salt. Add the ¾ cup flour; stir just until combined. Spread batter evenly in prepared pan or dish.

3 For cheesecake layer, in a medium bowl combine cream cheese and the ⅔ cup sugar; beat with an electric mixer on medium speed until combined. Add lemon juice, the 1 egg, and the ½ teaspoon vanilla; beat just until combined. Beat in the 2 tablespoons flour until combined. Spread mixture evenly over brownie layer in pan or dish. Scatter raspberries over top; sprinkle with the 1 tablespoon sugar.

4 Bake for 35 to 40 minutes or until top is puffed and golden brown and the edges start to brown. Cool in pan or dish on a wire rack. Cover and chill for at least 6 hours or up to 24 hours. Cut into bars. Serve cold or at room temperature.

Makes 32 brownies.

Nutrition Facts per brownie: 150 cal., 8 g total fat (5 g sat. fat), 42 mg chol., 67 mg sodium, 18 g carbo., 1 g fiber, 2 g pro.

To store: *Layer brownies between waxed paper in an airtight container. Cover; seal. Store in the refrigerator for up to 1 week.*

CHERRY AND CHOCOLATE CHUNK BROWNIES

Bits of tart cherry and dark chunks of chocolate make already fudgy brownies even more scrumptious and a perfect choice for the holidays.

Prep: 20 minutes **Bake:** 30 minutes **Oven:** 350°F

- 1 **cup butter**
- 6 **ounces unsweetened chocolate, coarsely chopped**
- 2 **cups sugar**
- 4 **eggs**
- 2 **teaspoons vanilla**
- 1⅓ **cups all-purpose flour**
- ½ **teaspoon baking soda**
- ¼ **teaspoon salt**
- ¼ **teaspoon ground cardamom**
- 1 **cup dried tart red cherries**
- 2 **ounces bittersweet or semisweet chocolate, chopped**

1 Grease a 9×13-inch baking pan or baking dish; set aside. Preheat oven to 350°F. In a large saucepan combine butter and unsweetened chocolate; cook and stir over low heat until melted. Remove from heat; cool.

2 Stir sugar into cooled chocolate mixture in saucepan. Add eggs, one at a time, beating with a wooden spoon after each addition just until combined. Stir in vanilla.

3 In a medium bowl combine flour, baking soda, salt, and cardamom. Add flour mixture to chocolate mixture; stir just until combined. Stir in cherries and bittersweet or semisweet chocolate. Spread batter evenly in prepared pan or dish.

4 Bake for 30 minutes. Cool in pan or dish on a wire rack. Cut into bars.

Makes 24 brownies.

Nutrition Facts per brownie: 242 cal., 13 g total fat (8 g sat. fat), 56 mg chol., 121 mg sodium, 32 g carbo., 2 g fiber, 2 g pro.

POTLUCK ● FAVORITE

To store: *Layer bars between waxed paper in an airtight container. Cover; seal. Store at room temperature for up to 3 days or freeze for up to 3 months. Thaw brownies, if frozen, before serving.*

ESPRESSO BROWNIES

It's the mocha lover's dream bar. This fudge brownie for grown-ups is not too sweet, yet ultrarich with coffee accents and a chocolate glaze.

Prep: 25 minutes **Bake:** 25 minutes **Stand:** 20 minutes **Chill:** 2 hours **Oven:** 350°F

- 1 **cup butter, cut into pieces**
- 6 **ounces unsweetened chocolate, coarsely chopped**
- 1½ **cups all-purpose flour**
- 1 **teaspoon baking powder**
- ½ **teaspoon salt**
- 4 **eggs**
- 2½ **cups sugar**
- ¼ **cup instant espresso powder or instant coffee powder**
- ¼ **cup coffee liqueur**
- 2 **teaspoons vanilla**
- 1 **recipe Chocolate Glaze**
  Chocolate-covered coffee beans (optional)

1 Line a 9×13-inch baking pan or baking dish with foil, extending foil over the edges of the pan or dish. Grease foil; set aside. Preheat oven to 350°F. In a small saucepan combine butter and unsweetened chocolate; cook and stir over low heat until melted. Cool to room temperature.

2 Meanwhile, in a medium bowl stir together flour, baking powder, and salt; set aside. In a large bowl combine eggs, sugar, espresso powder, coffee liqueur, and vanilla; beat with an electric mixer on medium speed until combined. Beat in cooled chocolate mixture. Add flour mixture, stirring just until combined. Spread batter evenly in prepared pan or dish.

3 Bake for 25 to 30 minutes or until top appears set and dry. Cool in pan or dish on a wire rack. Pour Chocolate Glaze evenly over brownies. Cover and chill about 2 hours or until glaze is set.

4 Before serving, let stand at room temperature for 20 to 30 minutes. Using the edges of the foil, lift the uncut brownies out of the pan or dish. Cut into bars. If desired, garnish with chocolate-covered coffee beans.

Makes 48 brownies.

Nutrition Facts per brownie: 144 cal., 9 g total fat (5 g sat. fat), 31 mg chol., 91 mg sodium, 16 g carbo., 1 g fiber, 2 g pro.

Chocolate Glaze: *In a medium saucepan combine 6 ounces semisweet chocolate, coarsely chopped; ¼ cup butter; and 2 tablespoons milk. Cook and stir over low heat until melted and smooth.*

GINGER-PEAR BROWNIES

These beautiful brownies are rich with flavors that are fresh and spicy, deep and chocolaty. All they need is a dusting of ginger-accented powdered sugar.

Prep: 30 minutes **Bake:** 40 minutes **Oven:** 350°F

8	ounces bittersweet chocolate, chopped
3	tablespoons butter
4	eggs
1¾	cups granulated sugar
⅓	cup water
¾	teaspoon almond extract
1	cup all-purpose flour
1	teaspoon baking powder
¼	teaspoon salt
1	8-ounce package cream cheese, softened
2	tablespoons all-purpose flour
1	cup chopped, peeled, cored pears
1	cup chopped walnuts (optional)
1¼	teaspoons ground ginger
2	tablespoons powdered sugar

1 Line a 9×13-inch baking pan or baking dish with foil, extending foil over the edges of the pan or dish. Grease foil; set aside. Preheat oven to 350°F. In a heavy small saucepan combine chocolate and butter; cook and stir over low heat until melted. Remove from heat; cool.

2 In a large bowl beat two of the eggs with an electric mixer on medium speed until foamy. Add 1¼ cups of the granulated sugar, the water, and ½ teaspoon of the almond extract. Beat about 5 minutes or until mixture is lemon-colored. Beat in cooled chocolate mixture. Stir in the 1 cup flour, the baking powder, and salt. Spread 2 cups of the chocolate batter evenly in the prepared pan or dish. Set the pan or dish and the remaining chocolate batter aside. Wash beaters thoroughly with warm, soapy water.

3 For pear filling, in a medium bowl beat cream cheese with an electric mixer until smooth. Add the remaining ½ cup granulated sugar, the remaining 2 eggs, the remaining ¼ teaspoon almond extract, and the 2 tablespoons flour; beat until combined. Stir in pears, walnuts (if desired), and 1 teaspoon of the ginger. Spoon pear filling over batter in pan or dish. Spoon mounds of the remaining chocolate batter over pear filling. Using a table knife, swirl to marble.

4 Bake about 40 minutes or until set. Cool in pan or dish on a wire rack. Cover and store in the refrigerator within 2 hours.

5 To serve, in a small bowl stir together powdered sugar and the remaining ¼ teaspoon ginger. Sift mixture over brownies. Using the edges of the foil, lift the uncut brownies out of the pan or dish. Cut into bars.

Makes 24 brownies.

Nutrition Facts per brownie: 190 cal., 9 g total fat (5 g sat. fat), 50 mg chol., 90 mg sodium, 26 g carbo., 1 g fiber, 2 g pro.

373

To store: *Layer bars between waxed paper in an airtight container. Cover; seal. Store in the refrigerator for up to 1 week.*

MARMALADE-NUT BROWNIES

The tang of orange marmalade is a perfect complement to these light chocolate squares. A pinch of cayenne adds a hint of heat.

Prep: 20 minutes   **Bake:** 30 minutes   **Oven:** 350°F

1½ cups sugar

1 cup butter, melted

3 eggs

½ cup orange marmalade

1 teaspoon vanilla

1 cup all-purpose flour

¾ cup unsweetened cocoa powder

1 teaspoon baking powder

¼ teaspoon salt

¼ teaspoon cayenne pepper

1 cup semisweet or milk chocolate pieces

½ cup chopped walnuts, toasted

½ teaspoon shortening

1 Line a 9×13-inch baking pan or baking dish with foil, extending foil over the edges of the pan or dish. Grease foil; set aside. Preheat oven to 350°F. In a large bowl stir together sugar and melted butter. Add eggs, one at a time, beating well with a wooden spoon after each addition. Stir in marmalade and vanilla. Stir in flour, cocoa powder, baking powder, salt, and cayenne pepper until well mixed. Stir in ½ cup of the chocolate pieces and the walnuts.

2 Spread batter evenly in prepared pan or dish. Bake about 30 minutes or until center is set. Cool in pan or dish on a wire rack.

3 Using the edges of the foil, lift the uncut brownies out of the pan or dish. Cut into bars.

4 In a small saucepan combine the remaining ½ cup chocolate pieces and the shortening; cook and stir over low heat until melted. Cool slightly. Transfer melted chocolate mixture to a small resealable plastic bag. Snip off a small corner of the bag; drizzle chocolate mixture over brownies. Chill until chocolate sets.

Makes 32 or 36 brownies.

Nutrition Facts per brownie: 165 cal., 9 g total fat (5 g sat. fat), 35 mg chol., 76 mg sodium, 20 g carbo., 1 g fiber, 2 g pro.

To store: *Layer brownies between waxed paper in an airtight container. Cover; seal. Store at room temperature for up to 3 days. (Or layer undrizzled brownies between waxed paper in an airtight container. Cover; seal. Freeze for up to 3 months. Thaw brownies before serving; drizzle with chocolate mixture.)*

PUDDINGS, COBBLERS, CRISPS, AND MORE

There will come a time in your week when all you need is a sweet little ending to your meal to remind you how good something simple and uncomplicated can be. The joy in all these desserts is that they are easy to make and even easier to love. Don't be surprised if you come back to these again and again.

PEACH PINWHEEL DUMPLINGS

Peach filling is rolled into pastry dough then baked on top of more sweet peaches for these delectable, double-peach dumplings.

Prep: 40 minutes **Bake:** 45 minutes **Cool:** 30 minutes **Oven:** 350°F

- 2 cups sugar
- 2 cups water
- 1 teaspoon vanilla
- 2 cups self-rising flour*
- ½ cup shortening
- ½ cup milk
  Self-rising flour
- ½ cup butter or margarine, melted
- 5 cups chopped peeled peaches or frozen unsweetened peach slices, thawed and chopped
- ½ teaspoon ground cinnamon
- ¼ to ½ teaspoon ground nutmeg
  Vanilla ice cream

1 For syrup, in a medium saucepan combine sugar and the water. Cook and stir over medium heat until sugar is dissolved; bring to boiling and boil, uncovered, for 5 minutes. Remove saucepan from heat; stir in vanilla. Cover and keep warm.

2 For dough, place the 2 cups self-rising flour in a large bowl. Using a pastry blender, cut shortening into flour until pieces are the size of small peas. Make a well in center. Add milk all at once. Stir just until moistened. Turn out dough onto a lightly floured 12×14-inch piece of waxed paper; knead 10 to 12 strokes or until nearly smooth. Lightly sprinkle dough with additional self-rising flour. Cover dough with another 12×14-inch piece of waxed paper. Roll out dough to a 10×12-inch rectangle (about ¼ inch thick). Remove top sheet of waxed paper.

3 Preheat oven to 350°F. Pour melted butter into 9×13-inch baking pan or baking dish; set aside. For filling, in another large bowl combine peaches, cinnamon, and nutmeg. Spoon 3 cups of the peach mixture on top of the melted butter in pan or dish, spreading evenly to form a single layer. Spoon the remaining 2 cups peaches evenly over the dough rectangle. Starting from a long side, roll up dough into a spiral. Pinch seam to seal. Cut into twelve 1-inch-wide pieces. Arrange pieces, cut sides down, over the peaches in pan or dish. Pour syrup carefully around rolls. (This will look like too much syrup, but the rolls will absorb the liquid during baking.)

4 Bake, uncovered, for 45 to 50 minutes or until golden brown. Cool in pan or dish on a wire rack for 30 minutes. Serve warm in dishes with vanilla ice cream.

Makes 12 servings.

Nutrition Facts per serving: 378 cal., 17 g total fat (7 g sat. fat), 21 mg chol., 324 mg sodium, 56 g carbo., 2 g fiber, 3 g pro.

----

*Test Kitchen Tip: *If you can't find self-rising flour at your supermarket, substitute a mixture of 2 cups all-purpose flour, 2 teaspoons baking powder, 1 teaspoon salt, and ½ teaspoon baking soda.*

SAUCY APPLE DUMPLINGS

These pretty pastry packages have raisin-filled apples baked inside. Serve warm with the butter sauce for a special autumn dessert.

Prep: 45 minutes   **Bake:** 1 hour   **Oven:** 350°F

- 2 cups water
- 1¼ cups sugar
- ½ teaspoon ground cinnamon
- ¼ cup butter or margarine
- 2 cups all-purpose flour
- ½ teaspoon salt
- ⅔ cup shortening
- ⅓ to ½ cup half-and-half, light cream, or whole milk
- 2 tablespoons chopped golden raisins or raisins
- 2 tablespoons chopped walnuts
- 1 tablespoon honey
- 2 tablespoons sugar
- ½ teaspoon ground cinnamon
- 6 small cooking apples (such as Granny Smith or Rome Beauty) (about 1½ pounds)
- 1 tablespoon butter or margarine, cut up

1 For sauce, in a medium saucepan combine the water, the 1¼ cups sugar, and ½ teaspoon cinnamon. Bring to boiling; reduce heat. Simmer, uncovered, for 5 minutes. Stir in the ¼ cup butter. Set aside.

2 Meanwhile, for pastry, in a medium bowl combine flour and salt. Using a pastry blender, cut in shortening until pieces are the size of small peas. Sprinkle 1 tablespoon of the half-and-half over part of the mixture; gently toss with a fork. Push moistened dough to the side of the bowl. Repeat moistening dough, using 1 tablespoon of the half-and-half at a time, until all of the dough is moistened. Form dough into a ball. On a lightly floured surface, roll dough to an 12×18-inch rectangle.* Using a pastry wheel or sharp knife, cut into six 6-inch squares.

3 In a small bowl combine raisins, walnuts, and honey. In another small bowl stir together the 2 tablespoons sugar and ½ teaspoon cinnamon. Set aside.

4 Preheat oven to 350°F. Peel and core apples. Place an apple on each pastry square. Fill centers of apples with raisin mixture. Sprinkle with sugar-cinnamon mixture; dot with the 1 tablespoon butter. Moisten edges of each pastry square with water; fold corners to center over apple. Pinch to seal. Place dumplings in an ungreased 9×13-inch baking pan or baking dish. Reheat sauce to boiling and pour over dumplings.

5 Bake, uncovered, about 1 hour or until apples are tender and pastry is golden brown. To serve, spoon sauce from pan or dish over the dumplings.

Makes 6 servings.

Nutrition Facts per serving: 586 cal., 36 g total fat (18 g sat. fat), 32 mg chol., 306 mg sodium, 68 g carbo., 4 g fiber, 1 g pro.

*Test Kitchen Tip: *If desired, roll pastry slightly larger so you'll have excess pastry to make leaves for garnishing. Cut the 6-inch squares of pastry; then reroll scraps and cut into leaf shapes. Before baking dumplings, moisten underside of leaf shapes with water; place on top of dumplings, pressing slightly to adhere.*

WARM BANANA BREAD COBBLER

Here is the most luscious banana pudding of all. This one's made with a batter instead of bread. Served warm with vanilla ice cream, it's about as good as it gets.

Prep: 20 minutes **Bake:** 25 minutes **Cool:** 30 minutes **Oven:** 375°F

1 cup self-rising flour*
1 cup granulated sugar
¾ cup milk
½ cup butter, melted
1 teaspoon vanilla
4 medium bananas, peeled and sliced
1 cup rolled oats
¾ cup packed brown sugar
½ cup self-rising flour*
½ cup butter
½ cup chopped walnuts
Vanilla ice cream

1 Grease a 9×13-inch baking pan or baking dish; set aside. Preheat oven to 375°F.

2 In a medium bowl stir together the 1 cup self-rising flour and the granulated sugar; add milk, melted butter, and vanilla. Stir until smooth. Spread evenly in the prepared pan or dish. Top with sliced bananas.

3 In a large bowl combine oats, brown sugar, and the ½ cup self-rising flour. Using a pastry blender, cut in ½ cup butter until crumbly. Stir in walnuts. Sprinkle mixture over bananas. Bake, uncovered, for 25 to 30 minutes or until browned and set. Cool in pan or dish on a wire rack for 30 minutes. Serve warm with vanilla ice cream.

Makes 12 to 16 servings.

Nutrition Facts per serving: 560 cal., 28 g total fat (15 g sat. fat), 74 mg chol., 378 mg sodium, 75 g carbo., 3 g fiber, 7 g pro.

*Test Kitchen Tip: *If you can't find self-rising flour at your supermarket, substitute a mixture of 1½ cups all-purpose flour, 1½ teaspoons baking powder, ¾ teaspoon salt, and ⅜ teaspoon baking soda. Use 1 cup of the mixture for step 2 and the remaining ½ cup of the mixture for step 3.*

PEACH-PRALINE COBBLER

Treat your family to this summertime favorite when peaches are in their prime. Biscuits filled with pecan swirls make the perfect topping.

Prep: 40 minutes **Bake:** 25 minutes **Cool:** 30 minutes **Oven:** 400°F

- 8 cups sliced peeled fresh peaches or frozen unsweetened peach slices
- ¾ cup packed brown sugar
- ¼ cup butter, melted
- 1½ cups chopped pecans
- 1 cup granulated sugar
- 1 cup water
- 2 tablespoons cornstarch
- 1 teaspoon ground cinnamon
- ¾ cup milk
- 2 teaspoons lemon juice
- 2¼ cups all-purpose flour
- 2 teaspoons granulated sugar
- 2 teaspoons baking powder
- ½ teaspoon baking soda
- ½ teaspoon salt
- ½ cup shortening
- Half-and-half, light cream, or milk (optional)

1 Thaw frozen peach slices, if using; do not drain. For pecan filling, in a medium bowl stir together brown sugar and melted butter. Add pecans; toss to mix. Set aside.

2 Preheat oven to 400°F. In a Dutch oven combine peaches, the 1 cup granulated sugar, the water, cornstarch, and cinnamon. Cook and stir until thickened and bubbly. Cover and keep warm.

3 In a small bowl combine milk and lemon juice; set aside. For dough, in a large bowl stir together flour, the 2 teaspoons granulated sugar, the baking powder, baking soda, and salt. Using a pastry blender, cut in shortening until mixture resembles coarse crumbs. Make a well in the center; add milk mixture. Stir just until dough clings together.

4 Turn out dough onto a lightly floured surface. Knead gently for 10 to 12 strokes. Roll dough into an 8×12-inch rectangle; spread with pecan filling. Starting from one of the long sides, roll up dough into a spiral. Cut into twelve 1-inch-wide pieces.

5 Transfer hot peach mixture to an ungreased 9×13-inch baking pan or baking dish. Place filled dough pieces, cut sides down, on top of the hot peach mixture. Bake, uncovered, about 25 minutes or until golden brown. Cool in pan on dish on a wire rack for 30 minutes. Serve warm. If desired, serve with half-and-half.

Makes 12 servings.

Nutrition Facts per serving: 511 cal., 23 g total fat (6 g sat. fat), 12 mg chol., 272 mg sodium, 76 g carbo., 7 g fiber, 6 g pro.

CINNAMON PLUM COBBLER WITH CANDIED GINGER TOPPING

Using a variety of plums in this yummy cobbler only makes it more delicious. Look for crystallized ginger, which has a delightful spicy taste, in the baking aisle.

Prep: 30 minutes   **Bake:** 30 minutes   **Cool:** 45 minutes   **Oven:** 350°F

- 8   cups sliced pitted plums (about 8 plums)
- ⅓   cup granulated sugar
- ¼   cup orange juice or apple juice
- 1   tablespoon cornstarch
- 2   teaspoons ground cinnamon
- 1½   cups all-purpose flour
- ½   cup granulated sugar
- 2   teaspoons baking powder
- ¼   teaspoon salt
- 6   tablespoons butter, cut up
- 1   egg, slightly beaten
- ¾   cup milk
- 1   cup whipping cream
- ½   cup dairy sour cream
- 2   tablespoons packed brown sugar
- 3   tablespoons finely chopped crystallized ginger

1 Lightly grease a 9×13-inch baking pan or baking dish; set aside. Preheat oven to 350°F. In a large saucepan toss together plums, the ⅓ cup granulated sugar, the orange juice, and cornstarch. Cook and stir until boiling; stir in cinnamon. Pour into prepared pan or dish; set aside.

2 In a food processor combine flour, the ½ cup granulated sugar, the baking powder, and salt. Cover and process with several on/off turns until combined. Add butter; cover and process until mixture resembles coarse crumbs. Transfer mixture to a medium bowl. (Or combine flour mixture in a medium bowl. Using a pastry blender, cut in butter until pieces are size of coarse crumbs.) In a small bowl combine egg and milk; stir into flour mixture. Drop dough into 10 to 12 mounds on top of hot plum mixture.

3 Bake, uncovered, for 30 to 35 minutes or until a wooden toothpick inserted in topping comes out clean. Cool in pan or dish on a wire rack for 45 minutes.

4 Meanwhile, in a chilled medium bowl combine whipping cream, sour cream, and brown sugar. Beat with an electric mixer on low to medium speed until soft peaks form. Fold in crystallized ginger. Serve immediately with warm cobbler.

Makes 10 to 12 servings.

Nutrition Facts per serving: 396 cal., 20 g total fat (11 g sat. fat), 79 mg chol., 190 mg sodium, 53 g carbo., 3 g fiber, 5 g pro.

BLUEBERRY CRISP

There is no better way to utilize blueberries in the summer months than with blueberry crisp. Scoops of vanilla ice cream add to the dessert's perfection.

Prep: 20 minutes **Bake:** 30 minutes **Cool:** 45 minutes **Oven:** 375°F

- 3 tablespoons all-purpose flour
- 2 tablespoons granulated sugar
- 6 cups fresh blueberries
- ¼ cup lemon juice
- 1 cup packed brown sugar
- ¾ cup all-purpose flour
- ¾ cup quick-cooking rolled oats
- 1¼ teaspoons ground cinnamon
- ½ cup cold butter

1 Preheat oven to 375°F. In a large bowl combine the 3 tablespoons flour and the granulated sugar. Add fresh blueberries and lemon juice; toss gently to combine. Spread blueberry mixture evenly in an ungreased 9×13-inch baking pan or baking dish; set aside.

2 For topping, in a medium bowl combine brown sugar, the ¾ cup flour, the rolled oats, and cinnamon. Using a pastry blender, cut in butter until mixture resembles coarse crumbs. Sprinkle topping evenly over blueberry mixture.

3 Bake, uncovered, about 30 minutes or until topping is golden brown and edges are bubbly. Cool in pan or dish on a wire rack for 45 minutes. Serve warm.

Makes 8 servings.

Nutrition Facts per serving: 371 cal., 13 g total fat (8 g sat. fat), 33 mg chol., 142 mg sodium, 63 g carbo., 4 g fiber, 4 g pro.

RHUBARB-OATMEAL CRISP

This old-fashioned dessert stars one of early summer's favorite fruits. Rhubarb's slightly tart taste is complemented with a sweet crumb topping.

Prep: 30 minutes   **Bake:** 45 minutes   **Oven:** 325°F

- 2 pounds fresh rhubarb, cut into ½-inch-thick slices (8 cups) or 8 cups frozen unsweetened sliced rhubarb
- 1 cup packed brown sugar
- ¼ cup butter, cut into small pieces
- ¼ cup all-purpose flour
- 2 cups quick-cooking rolled oats
- 1¾ cups packed brown sugar
- 1 cup all-purpose flour
- 1 cup shortening

  Whipped cream or vanilla ice cream (optional)

1 Grease a 9×13-inch baking pan or baking dish; set aside. Preheat oven to 325°F. For filling, in a large bowl combine rhubarb, the 1 cup brown sugar, the butter, and the ¼ cup flour. Spread filling evenly in prepared pan or dish.

2 For topping, in a medium bowl combine oats, the 1¾ cups brown sugar, and the 1 cup flour. Using a pastry blender, cut in shortening until mixture resembles coarse crumbs. Sprinkle topping over filling.

3 Bake, uncovered, for 45 to 50 minutes or until fruit is tender and topping is golden brown. If desired, serve warm with whipped cream or ice cream.

Makes 12 servings.

Nutrition Facts per serving: 500 cal., 21 g total fat (7 g sat. fat), 11 mg chol., 65 mg sodium, 74 g carbo., 3 g fiber, 4 g pro.

APPLE PIE CRISP

A crunchy top bakes over the apple filling with delicious results. Pancake mix and crackers are surprise ingredients that make the preparation extra easy.

Prep: 30 minutes   **Bake:** 45 minutes   **Oven:** 350°F

8	cups sliced peeled cooking apples
½	cup packaged regular pancake mix
½	cup packed brown sugar
¼	cup granulated sugar
2	teaspoons apple pie spice
¾	cup milk
2	eggs
2	tablespoons butter, cut up
1	cup packaged regular pancake mix
¾	cup crushed rich round crackers
½	cup packed brown sugar
¼	cup cold butter
	Vanilla ice cream (optional)
	Caramel-flavor ice cream topping (optional)

1 Preheat oven to 350°F. In a very large bowl toss apples with the ½ cup pancake mix, ½ cup brown sugar, the granulated sugar, and apple pie spice. In a small bowl stir together milk and eggs; add to apple mixture and stir to coat. Transfer to an ungreased 9×13-inch baking pan or baking dish; dot apples with the 2 tablespoons butter. Set aside.

2 In a medium bowl stir together the 1 cup pancake mix, the rich round crackers, and ½ cup brown sugar. Using a pastry blender, cut in the ¼ cup butter until crumbly. Sprinkle over apples.

3 Bake, uncovered, for 45 to 50 minutes or until apples are soft and topping is golden brown. Cool in pan or dish on a wire rack. If desired, serve with vanilla ice cream and caramel topping.

Makes 16 servings.

Nutrition Facts per serving: 212 cal., 7 g total fat (3 g sat. fat), 41 mg chol., 232 mg sodium, 36 g carbo., 2 g fiber, 3 g pro.

APPLE-CRANBERRY DESSERT

Two of autumn's best fruits combine in this down-home dessert that's pretty enough for holiday tables and a favorite of all ages.

Prep: 30 minutes **Bake:** 1 hour **Cool:** 30 minutes **Oven:** 325°F

2 12-ounce packages fresh or frozen cranberries or two 16-ounce packages frozen unsweetened pitted tart red cherries*

2 cups chopped peeled cooking apples

2 tablespoons butter, cut up

1¼ cups sugar

¾ cup chopped walnuts or pecans

2 eggs, slightly beaten

¾ cup butter, melted

1 cup sugar

¾ cup all-purpose flour

Vanilla ice cream

1 Grease the bottom of a 9×13-inch baking pan or baking dish. Preheat oven to 325°F. Toss the cranberries and apples together in the pan or dish. Dot cranberry mixture with the 2 tablespoons butter. Sprinkle evenly with the 1¼ cups sugar and the chopped nuts.

2 In a medium bowl whisk together eggs, melted butter, the 1 cup sugar, and the flour until well mixed. Pour evenly over the top of the cranberry mixture.

3 Bake, uncovered, for 1 to 1¼ hours or until top is golden brown. Cool in pan or dish on a wire rack for 30 minutes and serve warm or serve at room temperature. Serve with vanilla ice cream.

Makes 15 servings.

Nutrition Facts per serving: 312 cal., 16 g total fat (6 g sat. fat), 58 mg chol., 91 mg sodium, 42 g carbo., 3 g fiber, 3 g pro.

*Test Kitchen Tip: *If using frozen cranberries, do not thaw before tossing with the apples. If using frozen cherries, let stand at room temperature for 30 minutes before tossing with the apples.*

BROWNIE PUDDING CAKE

Originally from a 1944 *Better Homes and Gardens*® magazine, this homey dessert is still winning people over. The batter separates while baking, creating cake on top and sauce on the bottom.

Prep: 20 minutes **Bake:** 30 minutes **Cool:** 30 minutes **Oven:** 350°F

- 1½ cups all-purpose flour
- 1¼ cups granulated sugar
- 3 tablespoons unsweetened cocoa powder
- 1 tablespoon baking powder
- ¼ teaspoon salt
- ⅔ cup milk
- 3 tablespoons cooking oil
- 1½ teaspoons vanilla
- ¾ cup chopped walnuts
- 1 cup packed brown sugar
- ⅓ cup unsweetened cocoa powder
- 2¼ cups boiling water
- Vanilla ice cream (optional)

1 Grease a 9×13-inch baking pan or baking dish; set aside. Preheat oven to 350°F. In a large bowl stir together flour, granulated sugar, the 3 tablespoons cocoa powder, the baking powder, and salt. Stir in milk, oil, and vanilla. Stir in walnuts.

2 Pour batter into prepared pan or dish. In a medium bowl stir together brown sugar and the ⅓ cup cocoa powder. Stir in the boiling water. Slowly pour brown sugar mixture evenly over batter in pan or dish.

3 Bake, uncovered, for 30 minutes. Cool in pan or dish on a wire rack for 30 to 45 minutes. Serve warm. Spoon cake into dessert bowls; spoon sauce from pan or dish over cake. If desired, serve with vanilla ice cream.

Makes 18 servings.

Nutrition Facts per serving: 201 cal., 6 g total fat (1 g sat. fat), 1 mg chol., 103 mg sodium, 36 g carbo., 1 g fiber, 2 g pro.

CHOCO BREAD PUDDING

Chocolate chips melt into the pudding as it bakes. A hint of cinnamon, pecans, and rich caramel sauce add to the goodness. Try this sure-to-please dessert warm.

Prep: 25 minutes **Bake:** 40 minutes **Cool:** 30 minutes **Oven:** 350°F

- 12 ounces challah bread, cut into 1-inch cubes (about 9 cups)
- 1½ cups miniature semisweet chocolate pieces
- 4 eggs, beaten
- 3 cups half-and-half or light cream
- 1 cup packed brown sugar
- ¾ teaspoon ground cinnamon
- Dash salt
- 1 cup chopped pecans
- ½ cup packed brown sugar
- 1 tablespoon cornstarch
- ⅓ cup half-and-half or light cream
- ¼ cup water
- 2 tablespoons light-color corn syrup
- 1 tablespoon butter
- ½ teaspoon vanilla

1 Lightly grease a 9×13-inch baking pan or baking dish. Preheat oven to 350°F. In a large bowl combine bread cubes and chocolate pieces. Transfer to prepared pan or dish; set aside.

2 In a medium bowl stir together eggs, the 3 cups half-and-half, the 1 cup brown sugar, the cinnamon, and salt. Slowly pour egg mixture evenly over bread. Press down lightly with a rubber spatula or the back of a large spoon to moisten all of the bread. Sprinkle with pecans.

3 Bake, uncovered, for 40 to 45 minutes or until mixture is set in center.

4 Meanwhile, for sauce, in a heavy small saucepan combine the ½ cup brown sugar and the cornstarch. Stir in the ⅓ cup half-and-half, the water, and corn syrup. Cook and stir until thickened and bubbly (mixture may appear curdled at first). Cook and stir for 2 minutes more. Remove saucepan from heat; stir in butter and vanilla. Pour the hot sauce over the hot bread pudding. Let cool in pan or dish on a wire rack for 30 minutes before serving.

Makes 16 servings.

Nutrition Facts per serving: 400 cal., 20 g total fat (9 g sat. fat), 86 mg chol., 90 mg sodium, 50 g carbo., 1 g fiber, 7 g pro.

Make-Ahead Directions: *Prepare as directed through step 2, except do not sprinkle with pecans. Cover and chill for at least 2 hours or up to 24 hours. Sprinkle with pecans. Bake and serve as directed in steps 3 and 4.*

BLACK FOREST BREAD PUDDING

Rye bread, dark sweet cherries, and chocolate come together in this untraditional and utterly delicious pudding. Serve it warm with whipped cream or vanilla ice cream.

Prep: 25 minutes   **Chill:** 2 to 24 hours   **Bake:** 70 minutes   **Cool:** 45 minutes   **Oven:** 325°F

⅓ cup butter, softened

12 ounces black rye bread, cut into ½-inch-thick slices

1 12- or 16-ounce package frozen pitted dark sweet cherries

2 12-ounce packages semisweet chocolate pieces

½ teaspoon ground cinnamon

3¼ cups whipping cream

¾ cup sugar

8 eggs

½ teaspoon almond extract

Whipped cream or vanilla ice cream (optional)

Sliced almonds, toasted (optional)

1 Butter a 9×13-inch baking pan or baking dish with some of the butter; spread the remaining butter on the bread slices. Place bread slices in prepared pan or dish, overlapping as necessary to fit. Sprinkle with frozen cherries, half of the chocolate pieces, and the cinnamon; set aside.

2 In a medium saucepan combine the remaining chocolate pieces, 1 cup of the whipping cream, and the sugar; heat and stir just until chocolate is melted. Gradually stir in the remaining 2¼ cups whipping cream. In a very large bowl beat eggs with a whisk or a rotary beater; stir in the melted chocolate mixture and the almond extract. Slowly pour over bread in pan or dish (pan or dish will be very full). Cover and chill for at least 2 hours or up to 24 hours.

3 Preheat oven to 325°F. Uncover bread pudding and place pan or dish on a foil-lined baking sheet. Bake for 70 to 80 minutes or until an instant-read thermometer inserted in the center registers 160°F. Cool in pan or dish on a wire rack for 45 minutes. Serve warm. If desired, top with whipped cream or vanilla ice cream and/or almonds.

Makes 16 to 20 servings.

Nutrition Facts per serving: 546 cal., 38 g total fat (22 g sat. fat), 183 mg chol., 229 mg sodium, 51 g carbo., 4 g fiber, 8 g pro.

ORANGE-CHOCOLATE BREAD PUDDING

Melted chocolate and bits of orange peel turn humble bread pudding into a dessert worthy of the finest company. Serve the warm pudding with whipped cream.

Prep: 25 minutes **Bake:** 45 minutes **Cool:** 30 minutes **Oven:** 325°F

Butter

8 cups French or Italian bread cubes (1-inch cubes)

4 cups milk

1 cup sugar

6 ounces bittersweet chocolate, coarsely chopped

8 eggs, slightly beaten

1 tablespoon finely shredded orange peel

1 teaspoon vanilla

⅛ teaspoon salt

Whipped cream (optional)

1 Butter a 9×13-inch baking pan or baking dish. Preheat oven to 325°F. Spread bread cubes evenly in prepared pan or dish; set aside.

2 In a medium saucepan combine milk, sugar, and chocolate. Cook over medium heat until the chocolate melts, whisking frequently. Remove from heat.

3 In a large bowl combine eggs, orange peel, vanilla, and salt. Gradually whisk in the chocolate mixture. Pour mixture evenly over bread in pan or dish. Press down lightly with a rubber spatula or the back of a large spoon to moisten all of the bread.

4 Bake, uncovered, for 45 to 50 minutes or until evenly puffed and set. Cool in pan or dish on a wire rack for 30 minutes; serve warm. If desired, serve with whipped cream.

Makes 8 servings.

Nutrition Facts per serving: 434 cal., 18 g total fat (9 g sat. fat), 226 mg chol., 351 mg sodium, 59 g carbo., 2 g fiber, 16 g pro.

Make-Ahead Directions: *Prepare as directed through step 3. Cover and chill for up to 24 hours. Uncover and bake as directed in step 4.*

CHOCOLATE-NUT BREAD PUDDING
WITH COFFEE AND CREAM SAUCE

You might want to skip dinner and go right for this dessert. The pudding is a wealth of riches that only gets better when topped with the Coffee and Cream Sauce.

Prep: 25 minutes   **Bake:** 50 minutes   **Cool:** 1 hour   **Oven:** 350°F

Butter

6 cups dry firm white bread cubes or French bread cubes*

1¼ cups semisweet chocolate pieces

1 cup coarsely chopped pecans, walnuts, or almonds

4 eggs

3 cups milk

1 cup sugar

1 tablespoon vanilla

1 recipe Coffee and Cream Sauce

1 Generously butter a 9×13-inch baking pan or baking dish. Preheat oven to 350°F. Place dry bread cubes in prepared pan or dish. Sprinkle chocolate pieces and nuts over bread; set aside.

2 In a large bowl beat together eggs, milk, sugar, and vanilla. Pour egg mixture evenly over bread, chocolate pieces, and nuts. Press lightly with a rubber spatula or the back of a large spoon to moisten all of the bread and cover chocolate pieces and nuts completely.

3 Bake, uncovered, for 50 to 60 minutes or until a knife inserted near the center comes out clean. If the top starts to overbrown, cover loosely with foil. Cool in pan or dish on a wire rack for 1 hour. Serve warm with Coffee and Cream Sauce.

Makes 12 servings.

Nutrition Facts per serving: 464 cal., 23 g total fat (10 g sat. fat), 104 mg chol., 183 mg sodium, 55 g carbo., 2 g fiber, 8 g pro.

Coffee and Cream Sauce: *In a medium saucepan stir together ½ cup sugar and 4 teaspoons cornstarch. Add 1 cup whipping cream, ½ cup freshly brewed strong coffee, and ½ cup coffee liqueur or water. Cook and stir over medium heat until thickened and bubbly. Cook and stir for 2 minutes more. Serve warm over bread pudding. Makes 2¼ cups.*

*Test Kitchen Tip: *To dry bread cubes, preheat oven to 300°F. Spread bread cubes in a shallow baking pan. Bake for 10 to 15 minutes or until bread cubes are dry, stirring twice; cool before using.*

APPLE BREAD PUDDING

This comforting, oven-warm dessert is studded with apples, apricots, raisins, and dates. Serve it with ice cream and butterscotch sauce.

Prep: 30 minutes   **Bake:** 1 hour 5 minutes   **Cool:** 15 minutes   **Oven:** 350°F

- 4 cups finely chopped tart apples*
- 1 cup packed brown sugar
- ½ cup apple juice or apple cider
- 8 cups dry brioche cubes, challah bread cubes, or other egg bread cubes (1-inch cubes)
- ½ cup 3raisins
- ½ cup snipped dried apricots
- ½ cup snipped pitted dates
- 6 eggs, beaten
- 4 cups half-and-half or light cream
- 1⅓ cups granulated sugar
- 2 tablespoons vanilla
  Cinnamon ice cream
- 1 recipe Butterscotch Sauce

1 Grease a 9×13-inch baking pan. Preheat oven to 350°F. In the prepared pan combine apples, brown sugar, and apple juice. Bake, uncovered, for 15 to 20 minutes or until apples are tender. Cool apple mixture in pan for 15 minutes.

2 Add bread cubes, raisins, apricots, and dates to the apple mixture in pan; toss. In a large bowl beat together eggs, half-and-half, granulated sugar, and vanilla. Pour egg mixture evenly over bread mixture in pan. Press down lightly with a rubber spatula or the back of a large spoon to moisten all of the bread.

3 Bake, uncovered, for 50 to 60 minutes or until a knife inserted near center comes out clean. Cool slightly in pan on a wire rack. To serve, cut bread pudding into squares and place in dessert bowls. Top individual servings with scoops of cinnamon ice cream and drizzle with Butterscotch Sauce.

Makes 16 servings.

Nutrition Facts per serving: 615 cal., 23 g total fat (12 g sat. fat), 176 mg chol., 266 mg sodium, 94 g carbo., 2 g fiber, 11 g pro.

Butterscotch Sauce: *In a 2-quart saucepan stir together 1 cup packed brown sugar and 2 tablespoons cornstarch. Add 1½ cups water. Cook and stir over medium-high heat for 4 to 5 minutes or until thickened and bubbly. Cook and stir for 2 minutes more. Stir in ¼ cup butter until melted. Makes 2¼ cups.*

*Test Kitchen Tip: *If desired, peel the apples before chopping.*

CHERRY-APPLE BREAD PUDDING

This makes a comforting dessert when served à la mode or a delicious brunch dish when served with warm maple syrup. Either way, it's a winner.

Prep: 25 minutes **Bake:** 45 minutes **Cool:** 30 minutes **Oven:** 350°F

- 3 tablespoons butter, softened
- 9 slices firm-textured white bread
- 3 medium Golden Delicious apples, peeled and very thinly sliced
- 2 tablespoons lemon juice
- ½ cup dried tart red cherries
- 6 eggs, beaten
- 3 cups milk
- ½ cup sugar

1 Preheat oven to 350°F. Lightly butter one side of each of the bread slices; cut bread slices into quarters. Arrange half of the bread pieces, buttered sides down, in an ungreased 9×13-inch baking pan or baking dish.

2 In a medium bowl toss together apples and lemon juice. Sprinkle apple-lemon juice mixture and dried cherries over bread in pan or dish. Top with the remaining bread pieces, buttered sides up. In a large bowl whisk together eggs, milk, and sugar. Pour egg mixture evenly over bread in pan or dish. Press down lightly with a rubber spatula or the back of a large spoon to moisten all of the bread.

3 Bake, uncovered, for 45 to 50 minutes or until a knife inserted near the center comes out clean. Cool in pan or dish on a wire rack for 30 minutes. Serve warm.

Makes 8 to 10 servings.

Nutrition Facts per serving: 315 cal., 11 g total fat (5 g sat. fat), 178 mg chol., 270 mg sodium, 45 g carbo., 2 g fiber, 10 g pro.

BISCUIT BREAD PUDDING
WITH LEMON SAUCE

Cinnamon, nutmeg, and vanilla infuse this delightful pudding with homey flavor. Lemon sauce is the perfect complement.

Prep: 25 minutes **Stand:** 10 minutes **Bake:** 45 minutes **Oven:** 350°F

- 6 eggs, slightly beaten
- 1 12-ounce can (1½ cups) evaporated milk
- 1 5-ounce can (⅔ cup) evaporated milk
- 2½ cups sugar
- ⅓ cup butter, melted
- 1½ teaspoons vanilla
- ¾ teaspoon ground cinnamon
- ¾ teaspoon ground nutmeg
- 9 cups coarsely crumbled buttermilk biscuits (12 to 15 biscuits)*
- 1 recipe Lemon Sauce

1. Grease a 9×13-inch baking pan or baking dish; set aside. Preheat oven to 350°F. In a large bowl stir together eggs, evaporated milk, sugar, melted butter, vanilla, cinnamon, and nutmeg. Place crumbled biscuits in prepared pan or dish. Pour egg mixture evenly over biscuits. Press down lightly with a rubber spatula or the back of a large spoon to moisten all of the biscuits. Let stand for 10 minutes to thoroughly moisten the biscuits.

2. Bake, uncovered, about 45 minutes or until a knife inserted near the center comes out clean. Serve warm with Lemon Sauce.

Makes 12 to 14 servings.

Nutrition Facts per serving: 577 cal., 26 g total fat (13 g sat. fat), 190 mg chol., 702 mg sodium, 80 g carbo., 0 g fiber, 10 g pro.

Lemon Sauce: *In a medium saucepan stir together 2 eggs, beaten; ¼ cup water; and ¼ cup lemon juice. Add 1 cup sugar and ½ cup butter, cut up. Cook and stir until thickened and just bubbly on edges. If desired, strain sauce. Serve warm. Makes about 2 cups.*

*Test Kitchen Tip: *Use homemade biscuits or 2 packages refrigerated large Southern-style biscuits, baked according to package directions.*

CRANBERRY-PUMPKIN BREAD PUDDING

> Two of the holiday season's favorite ingredients combine into one satisfying dessert. A rich brandy-butter sauce adds extra richness.

Prep: 20 minutes **Stand:** 15 minutes **Bake:** 55 minutes **Oven:** 350°F

- 4 **eggs**
- 2 **egg yolks**
- 4 **cups milk**
- 1 **15-ounce can pumpkin**
- 1 **cup sugar**
- ¼ **cup brandy**
- 1½ **teaspoons pumpkin pie spice**
- 9 **slices whole wheat bread, cut into ½-inch cubes (about 8 cups)**
- 1 **cup dried cranberries**
- 1 **recipe Brandy-Butter Sauce**

1 In a very large bowl whisk together eggs and egg yolks; stir in milk, pumpkin, sugar, brandy, and pumpkin pie spice. Add bread cubes and dried cranberries; mix well. Let stand for 15 minutes.

2 Meanwhile, lightly grease a 9×13-inch baking pan or baking dish. Preheat oven to 350°F. Spoon pumpkin mixture into prepared pan or dish.

3 Bake, uncovered, about 55 minutes or until a knife inserted in the center comes out clean. Cool slightly. Serve warm with Brandy-Butter Sauce.

Makes 15 servings.

Nutrition Facts per serving: 338 cal., 12 g total fat (6 g sat. fat), 136 mg chol., 216 mg sodium, 49 g carbo., 3 g fiber, 7 g pro.

Brandy-Butter Sauce: *In a small saucepan melt ½ cup butter over medium heat. Stir in 1½ cups powdered sugar until mixture is smooth. Stir in 2 egg yolks; cook and stir just until bubbly. Remove from heat. Stir in 1 to 2 tablespoons brandy. Serve warm.*

FRUIT-AND-NUT BAKLAVA

Not only nuts, but also a mix of dried fruits make this pastry scrumptious. Cut it into diamonds—the traditional shape for this Greek treat.

Prep: 35 minutes **Bake:** 45 minutes **Oven:** 325°F

- 1 cup butter, melted
- 32 sheets frozen phyllo dough (9×14-inch rectangles), thawed
- 1 recipe Fruit-and-Nut Filling
- 1¼ cups sugar
- ½ cup water
- 1 teaspoon finely shredded lemon peel or orange peel
- ¼ cup lemon juice or orange juice
- 3 tablespoons honey

1 Brush the bottom of a 9×13-inch baking pan or baking dish with some of the melted butter. Unfold phyllo dough; remove one sheet of the phyllo dough. (As you work, cover the remaining phyllo dough with plastic wrap to prevent it from drying out.) Brush phyllo sheet with some of the melted butter; arrange in prepared pan or dish. Layer seven more of the phyllo sheets in pan or dish, brushing each sheet with melted butter before layering. Sprinkle one-third of the Fruit-and-Nut Filling on top of the phyllo layers in pan or dish. Repeat layering phyllo and filling two more times. Layer remaining phyllo sheets atop layers in the pan or dish, brushing each sheet with melted butter before layering. Drizzle any remaining melted butter over the top.

2 Preheat oven to 325°F. Using a sharp knife, cut through all layers to make diamond-shape pieces, replacing any dough that pulls up while cutting.

3 Bake, uncovered, for 45 to 50 minutes or until golden brown. Place pan or dish on a wire rack.

4 Meanwhile, for syrup, in a medium saucepan stir together sugar, the water, lemon peel, lemon juice, and honey. Bring to boiling; reduce heat. Simmer, uncovered, for 20 minutes.

5 Pour hot syrup over baklava in pan or dish. Cool completely. Use a knife to separate pieces.

Makes about 32 pieces.

Nutrition Facts per piece: 190 cal., 11 g total fat (4 g sat. fat), 15 mg chol., 89 mg sodium, 22 g carbo., 1 g fiber, 2 g pro.

Fruit-and-Nut Filling: *Finely chop 2 cups walnuts, ⅔ cup dried cranberries, ½ cup dried apples, and ½ cup golden raisins. In a large bowl stir together finely chopped walnuts, dried cranberries, dried apples, golden raisins, ¼ cup sugar, and 1½ teaspoons ground cinnamon.*

CHOCLAVA

This version of baklava, the classic Greek pastry, adds chocolate to the heavenly mix of nuts, honey, citrus, and flaky phyllo.

Prep: 40 minutes   **Bake:** 45 minutes   **Oven:** 325°F

- 4 cups walnuts (1 pound), finely chopped
- 1 cup miniature semisweet chocolate pieces
- ¾ cup sugar
- 1½ teaspoons ground cinnamon
- ¾ cup butter, melted
- ½ of a 16-ounce package (20 sheets) frozen phyllo dough (9×14-inch rectangles), thawed
- ½ cup orange juice
- ⅓ cup sugar
- ⅓ cup water
- ⅓ cup honey
- 1 tablespoon lemon juice
- ⅓ cup miniature semisweet chocolate pieces (optional)
- 2 tablespoons water (optional)

1 Preheat oven to 325°F. For filling, in a large bowl stir together walnuts, the 1 cup chocolate pieces, the ¾ cup sugar, and the cinnamon; set aside.

2 Brush the bottom of a 9×13-inch baking pan or baking dish with some of the melted butter. Unfold phyllo dough; remove one sheet of the phyllo dough. (As you work, cover the remaining phyllo dough with plastic wrap to prevent it from drying out.) Brush phyllo sheet with melted butter; place in prepared pan or dish. Repeat with seven more of the phyllo sheets, brushing each sheet with melted butter before layering in pan or dish. Sprinkle about 2 cups of the nut mixture over phyllo in pan or dish.

3 Top with four more sheets of the phyllo, brushing each sheet with melted butter before layering. Sprinkle with 2 cups more of the nut mixture and top with four more phyllo sheets, brushing each sheet with melted butter before layering. Top with the remaining nut mixture and the remaining four phyllo sheets, brushing each sheet with melted butter before layering. Drizzle any remaining melted butter over top. Using a sharp knife, cut into diamond- or triangle-shape pieces, cutting to but not through the bottom layer.

4 Bake, uncovered, for 45 to 50 minutes or until golden brown. Immediately finish cutting diamonds or triangles. Cool slightly in pan or dish on a wire rack.

5 Meanwhile, in a small saucepan combine orange juice, the ⅓ cup sugar, the ⅓ cup water, the honey, and lemon juice. Bring to boiling; reduce heat. Simmer, uncovered, for 20 minutes. Pour over warm choclava in pan or dish. Cool completely.

6 To serve, if desired, in a heavy small saucepan heat and stir the ⅓ cup chocolate pieces and the 2 tablespoons water over low heat until smooth; drizzle chocolate mixture over choclava. Store leftovers in the refrigerator.

Makes about 45 pieces.

Nutrition Facts per piece: 156 cal., 11 g total fat (3 g sat. fat), 9 mg chol., 58 mg sodium, 14 g carbo., 1 g fiber, 2 g pro.

PRALINE CHEESECAKE SQUARES

A candylike pecan topping adds extra richness to creamy cheesecake. For parties, cut into bite-size pieces and serve on dessert trays.

Prep: 30 minutes **Bake:** 50 minutes **Cook:** 10 minutes **Chill:** 2 to 24 hours **Oven:** 350°F

- 2½ cups all-purpose flour
- 1 cup butter, melted
- ⅔ cup finely chopped pecans
- 2 tablespoons powdered sugar
- 3 8-ounce packages cream cheese, softened
- 4 eggs
- 1 14-ounce can sweetened condensed milk
- ⅔ cup granulated sugar
- 2 teaspoons vanilla
- 1 cup packed brown sugar
- 1 cup whipping cream
- 1 cup chopped pecans
- 1½ teaspoons vanilla

1 Preheat oven to 350°F. For crust, in a large bowl combine flour, melted butter, the ⅔ cup pecans, and the powdered sugar; mix well. Press mixture into an ungreased 9×13-inch baking pan. Bake for 15 to 20 minutes or until crust is set and light golden brown around the edges.

2 Meanwhile, for filling, in a large bowl beat cream cheese with an electric mixer on low to medium speed until smooth. Add eggs; beat well. Beat in sweetened condensed milk, granulated sugar, and the 2 teaspoons vanilla. Pour filling over baked crust. Bake, uncovered, in the 350°F oven for 35 to 40 minutes or until set in center. Cool in pan on a wire rack.

3 For topping, in a medium saucepan combine brown sugar and whipping cream. Cook and stir over medium heat until mixture boils; reduce heat. Simmer, uncovered, for 10 minutes. Remove from heat. Stir in the 1 cup chopped pecans and the 1½ teaspoons vanilla. Pour topping over cheesecake. Cover and chill for at least 2 hours or up to 24 hours before serving. Store in the refrigerator.

Makes 48 servings.

Nutrition Facts per serving: 214 cal., 15 g total fat (8 g sat. fat), 54 mg chol., 103 mg sodium, 18 g carbo., 1 g fiber, 3 g pro.

BERRY-GLAZED CHEESECAKE DESSERT

Glazed fresh strawberries decorate the top of creamy cheesecake for this springtime favorite. Make the cake ahead and add the topping before serving.

Prep: 25 minutes **Bake:** 30 minutes **Chill:** 4 to 24 hours **Oven:** 350°F

- 1 cup all-purpose flour
- ¼ cup sugar
- 2 teaspoons finely shredded lemon peel
- 1 teaspoon baking powder
- ½ cup butter
- 1 egg, beaten
- ¼ cup milk
- ½ teaspoon vanilla
- 2 8-ounce packages cream cheese, softened
- 1 3-ounce package cream cheese, softened
- 1¼ cups sugar
- 1 egg
- 1 tablespoon lemon juice
- 2 teaspoons vanilla
- 4 cups fresh strawberries, sliced
- ½ cup currant jelly
- ¼ cup sliced almonds, toasted

1 Lightly grease a 9×13-inch baking pan or baking dish; set aside. Preheat oven to 350°F. For bottom layer, in a medium bowl stir together flour, the ¼ cup sugar, the lemon peel, and baking powder. Using a pastry blender, cut in butter until mixture resembles coarse crumbs. Make a well in the center.

2 In a small bowl combine beaten egg, the milk, and the ½ teaspoon vanilla; add all at once to flour mixture. Stir just until dough clings together. Spread dough into prepared pan or dish; set aside.

3 For cheesecake layer, in a medium bowl combine cream cheese, the 1¼ cups sugar, 1 egg, the lemon juice, and the 2 teaspoons vanilla. Beat with an electric mixer on high speed until smooth and creamy. Spread over dough in pan or dish.

4 Bake, uncovered, for 30 to 35 minutes or until top is golden brown. Cool in pan or dish on a wire rack. Cover and chill for at least 4 hours or up to 24 hours.

5 Not more than 3 hours before serving, arrange sliced strawberries over cake. Stir currant jelly to soften; brush over the strawberries. Sprinkle with toasted almonds. Cover and chill until serving.

Makes 12 servings.

Nutrition Facts per serving: 441 cal., 25 g total fat (15 g sat. fat), 105 mg chol., 226 mg sodium, 49 g carbo., 2 g fiber, 6 g pro.

PUMPKIN PIE DESSERT

The crunchy topping is a terrific contrast to the texture and flavor of the creamy pumpkin filling.

Prep: 20 minutes **Bake:** 50 minutes **Chill:** 2 hours **Oven:** 350°F

- 1 29-ounce can pumpkin
- 1 cup sugar
- 1 teaspoon ground cinnamon
- ½ teaspoon salt
- ½ teaspoon ground nutmeg
- ½ teaspoon ground ginger
- 4 eggs, beaten
- 1 12-ounce can evaporated milk
- 1 package 2-layer-size yellow cake mix
- 1 cup chopped nuts
- ¾ cup butter or margarine, melted
  Frozen whipped dessert topping, thawed (optional)

1 Grease a 9×13-inch baking pan or baking dish; set aside. Preheat oven to 350°F. In a large bowl combine pumpkin, sugar, cinnamon, salt, nutmeg, and ginger; add eggs. Beat lightly with a wooden spoon just until combined. Gradually stir in evaporated milk; mix well. Pour into prepared pan or dish. Sprinkle dry cake mix evenly over pumpkin mixture; sprinkle evenly with nuts. Drizzle with melted butter.

2 Bake, uncovered, about 50 minutes or until edges are firm and top is golden brown. Cool in pan or dish on a wire rack. Cover and chill for at least 2 hours before serving. If desired, serve with whipped dessert topping. Store in the refrigerator.

Makes 18 servings.

Nutrition Facts per serving: 328 cal., 17 g total fat (7 g sat. fat), 75 mg chol., 364 mg sodium, 41 g carbo., 2 g fiber, 5 g pro.

CREAMY STRAWBERRY SQUARES

These berry delicious gems are a favorite with guests. A pecan crust is topped with a creamy cheese layer, then strawberries and a gelatin glaze.

Prep: 30 minutes **Bake:** 20 minutes **Chill:** 4½ hours **Oven:** 350°F

- 1½ cups all-purpose flour
- ¾ cup butter, melted
- ¾ cup chopped pecans
- 1 cup granulated sugar
- ¼ cup all-purpose flour
- 3 tablespoons strawberry-flavor gelatin
- 1 cup water
- 2 cups powdered sugar
- 1 8-ounce package cream cheese, softened
- 1 8-ounce container frozen whipped dessert topping, thawed
- 3 cups sliced fresh strawberries

1 Preheat oven to 350°F. For crust, combine the 1½ cups flour and the melted butter; stir in pecans. Pat evenly in an ungreased 9×13-inch baking pan or baking dish. Bake, uncovered, about 20 minutes or until golden brown around the edges. Cool in pan or dish on a wire rack.

2 Meanwhile, in a medium saucepan combine the granulated sugar, the ¼ cup flour, and the strawberry-flavor gelatin; stir in the water. Cook and stir until thickened and bubbly. Cook and stir for 1 minute more. Remove from heat. Cover surface and chill about about 30 minutes or until partially set (consistency of unbeaten egg whites).

3 In a large bowl gradually add powdered sugar to cream cheese, beating with an electric mixer on medium speed until combined. Add whipped topping by spoonfuls, beating until smooth. Spread cream cheese mixture over cooled crust. Arrange sliced strawberries on top.

4 Spoon partially set gelatin mixture over strawberries. Cover and chill for at least 4 hours or up to 24 hours.

Makes 15 servings.

Nutrition Facts per serving: 389 cal., 22 g total fat (11 g sat. fat), 42 mg chol., 127 mg sodium, 46 g carbo., 2 g fiber, 4 g pro.

COOKIES AND CREAM DESSERT

Here's the dessert you'll be asked to make again and again. It's easy to do, with a chocolate cookie crust and a vanilla cream cheese topping.

Prep: 20 minutes **Chill:** 8 to 24 hours

½ cup butter or margarine, melted

1 1-pound package chocolate sandwich cookies with white filling, crushed

3 cups milk

2 4-serving-size packages instant vanilla pudding mix

1 8-ounce package cream cheese, softened

1 8-ounce container frozen whipped dessert topping, thawed

1 In a large bowl drizzle the melted butter over crushed cookies; toss to coat evenly. Set aside ½ cup of the crumb mixture. Sprinkle the remaining crumb mixture into an ungreased 9×13-inch baking pan or baking dish; set aside.

2 In a medium bowl combine milk and dry pudding mix. Set aside.

3 In a large bowl beat cream cheese with an electric mixer on low to medium speed until smooth. Add milk-pudding mixture. Beat until combined. Fold in dessert topping.

4 Pour the pudding mixture over the crumb mixture in pan or dish. Sprinkle the reserved ½ cup crumb mixture over the pudding mixture. Cover and chill for at least 8 hours or up to 24 hours.

Makes 12 to 14 servings.

Nutrition Facts per serving: 458 cal., 27 g total fat (15 g sat. fat), 46 mg chol., 587 mg sodium, 51 g carbo., 1 g fiber, 6 g pro.

FROZEN CHOCOLATE-PEANUT DESSERT

Chocoholics will be in heaven when they taste this fudge sundae concoction. Ice cream and chocolate cookies are topped with nuts, fudge topping, banana, and cherries.

Prep: 20 minutes **Freeze:** 4¼ to 24¼ hours **Stand:** 10 minutes

- 30 chocolate sandwich cookies with white filling, coarsely crushed
- ¼ cup butter, melted
- ½ gallon vanilla ice cream or chocolate ice cream
- 1 cup salted peanuts
- 1 12-ounce jar (about 1 cup) chocolate fudge ice cream topping
- 1 banana, sliced (optional)
  Maraschino cherries (optional)

1 Freeze a large bowl and a 9×13-inch baking pan or baking dish about 15 minutes or until very cold. Meanwhile, in a medium bowl combine crushed cookies and melted butter; set aside.

2 Place ice cream in the cold bowl; slightly soften ice cream by using a wooden spoon to press it against side of bowl. Spoon ice cream into chilled pan or dish; press ice cream into even layer in pan or dish. Sprinkle cookie mixture over ice cream. Top with peanuts. Place ice cream topping in a resealable plastic bag; cut a small hole in one corner of the bag. Drizzle topping over layers in pan or dish. Cover and freeze for at least 4 hours or up to 24 hours or until firm.

3 To serve, let stand at room temperature for 10 minutes to soften slightly. If desired, top with banana slices and maraschino cherries. Cut and serve immediately.

Makes 15 servings.

Nutrition Facts per serving: 412 cal., 23 g total fat (10 g sat. fat), 41 mg chol., 388 mg sodium, 46 g carbo., 2 g fiber, 8 g pro.

FRUIT AND ICE CREAM SANDWICH BARS

Good ol' ice cream bars never tasted so refreshing.
Peach sorbet and a whipped cream topping make a
hot-weather treat the ultimate in cool.

Prep: 20 minutes **Freeze:** 4¼ to 24¼ hours **Stand:** 10 minutes

10 to 14 rectangular ice cream sandwiches, unwrapped

2 pints peach sorbet or mango sorbet, softened

1 8-ounce carton dairy sour cream

1 cup whipping cream

¾ cup powdered sugar

2 cups fresh blueberries or raspberries

1 Place ice cream sandwiches in an ungreased 9×13-inch baking pan or baking dish, cutting to fit as necessary. Spread sorbet on top of ice cream sandwiches. Freeze about 15 minutes or until sorbet is firm.

2 Meanwhile, in a medium bowl combine sour cream, whipping cream, and powdered sugar. Beat with electric mixer on medium speed until mixture thickens and soft peaks form. Spread over sorbet.

3 Cover and freeze for at least 4 hours or up to 24 hours or until firm. Let stand at room temperature for 10 minutes before serving. Sprinkle fresh berries over sour cream mixture.

Makes 12 servings.

Nutrition Facts per serving: 354 cal., 16 g total fat (10 g sat. fat), 52 mg chol., 49 mg sodium, 51 g carbo., 1 g fiber, 3 g pro.

INDEX

Note: Boldfaced page references indicate recipe photographs.

410

Q-R

ROASTING MEAT

Place meat, fat side up, on a roasting rack in a 9×13-inch baking pan or baking dish. (Roasts with a bone do not need a rack.) Insert an oven-going meat thermometer into meat so that the stem end is at least 2 inches into the center of the largest muscle or thickest portion of the meat. The thermometer should not touch fat, bone, or the baking pan or baking dish. Do not add water or liquid and do not cover. Roast in a 325°F oven (unless chart says otherwise) for the time given and until the thermometer registers the "final roasting temperature." (This will be 5°F to 10°F below the "final doneness temperature.") Remove the roast from the oven; cover with foil and let it stand for 15 minutes before carving. The meat's temperature will rise 5°F to 10°F during the time it stands.

Cut	Weight	Approximate Roasting Time	Final Roasting Temperature (when to remove from oven)	Final Doneness Temperature (after standing 15 minutes)
BEEF				
Boneless tri-tip roast (bottom sirloin) Roast at 425°F	1½ to 2 pounds	30 to 35 minutes 40 to 45 minutes	135°F 150°F	145°F medium rare 160°F medium
Eye round roast Roasting past medium rare is not recommended.	2 to 3 pounds	1½ to 1¾ hours	135°F	145°F medium rare
Ribeye roast Roast at 350°F	3 to 4 pounds 4 to 6 pounds	1½ to 1¾ hours 1¾ hours to 2 hours 1¾ hours to 2 hours 2 to 2½ hours	135°F 150°F 135°F 150°F	145°F medium rare 160°F medium 145°F medium rare 160°F medium
Rib roast (chine bone removed) Roast at 350°F	4 to 6 pounds	1¾ to 2¼ hours 2¼ to 2¾ hours	135°F 150°F	145°F medium rare 160°F medium
Round tip roast	3 to 4 pounds 4 to 6 pounds 6 to 8 pounds	1¾ to 2 hours 2¼ to 2½ hours 2 to 2½ hours 2½ to 3 hours 2½ to 3 hours 3 to 3½ hours	135°F 150°F 135°F 150°F 135°F 150°F	145°F medium rare 160°F medium 145°F medium rare 160°F medium 145°F medium rare 160°F medium
Tenderloin roast Roast at 425°F	2 to 3 pounds 4 to 5 pounds	35 to 40 minutes 45 to 50 minutes 50 to 60 minutes 60 to 70 minutes	135°F 150°F 135°F 150°F	145°F medium rare 160°F medium 145°F medium rare 160°F medium
Top round roast Roasting past medium rare is not recommended.	4 to 6 pounds 6 to 8 pounds	1¾ to 2½ hours 2½ to 3 hours	135°F 135°F	145°F medium rare 145°F medium rare
PORK				
Boneless sirloin roast	1½ to 2 pounds	¾ to 1¼ hours	150°F	160°F medium
Boneless top loin roast (double loin)	3 to 4 pounds 4 to 5 pounds	1½ to 2¼ hours 2 to 2½ hours	150°F 150°F	160°F medium 160°F medium
Boneless top loin roast (single loin)	2 to 3 pounds	1¼ to 1¾ hours	150°F	160°F medium
Loin center rib roast (backbone loosened)	3 to 4 pounds 4 to 6 pounds	1¼ to 1¾ hours 1¾ to 2½ hours	150°F 150°F	160°F medium 160°F medium
Tenderloin Roast at 425°F	¾ to 1 pound	25 to 35 minutes	155°F	160°F medium
Ham, cooked (boneless)	1½ to 3 pounds 3 to 5 pounds 6 to 8 pounds 8 to 10 pounds*	¾ to 1¼ hours 1 to 1¾ hours 1¾ to 2½ hours 2¼ to 2¾ hours	140°F 140°F 140°F 140°F	No standing time No standing time No standing time No standing time
Ham, cook before eating (with bone)	3 to 5 pounds	1¾ to 3 hours	150°F	160°F medium
Smoked shoulder picnic, cooked (with bone)	4 to 6 pounds	1¼ to 2 hours	140°F	No standing time

All roasting times are based on meat removed directly from refrigerator.

ROASTING POULTRY

To prepare a bird for roasting, follow the steps below. Because birds vary in size and shape, use the times as general guides.

1. If desired, thoroughly rinse a whole bird's body and neck cavities. Pat dry with paper towels. If desired, sprinkle the body cavity with salt.

2. For an unstuffed bird, if desired, place quartered onions and celery in body cavity. To stuff a bird (do not stuff a duckling), just before roasting loosely spoon some stuffing into the neck and body cavities. For both a stuffed and unstuffed bird, pull neck skin to the back and fasten with a short skewer. If a band of skin crosses tail, tuck drumsticks under band. If there is no band, tie drumsticks to tail with 100%-cotton kitchen string. Twist wing tips under back.

3. Place bird, breast side up, on a roasting rack in a 9×13-inch baking pan or baking dish; brush with cooking oil or melted butter and, if desired, sprinkle with a crushed dried herb, such as thyme or oregano. (When cooking a domestic duckling, use a fork to prick skin generously all over and omit cooking oil or butter.) For whole birds, insert an oven-going thermometer into center of one of the inside thigh muscles. The thermometer should not touch the bone.

4. Cover Cornish game hen, pheasant, and squab with foil, leaving air space between bird and foil. Lightly press the foil to the ends of drumsticks and neck to enclose bird. Leave all other types of poultry uncovered.

5. Two-thirds through roasting time, cut the band of skin or string between drumsticks. Uncover small birds the last 30 minutes of roasting. Continue roasting until the meat thermometer registers 180°F in thigh muscle (check temperature of thigh in several places) or until drumsticks move easily in their sockets and juices run clear. (For a turkey breast, the thermometer should register 170°F.) Center of stuffing should register 165°F. Remove bird from oven; cover. Allow whole birds and turkey portions to stand for 15 minutes before carving.

Type of Bird	Weight	Oven Temperature	Roasting Time
CHICKEN			
Capon	5 to 7 pounds	325°F	1¾ to 2½ hours
Meaty pieces (breast halves, drumsticks, and thighs with bone)	2½ to 3 pounds	375°F	45 to 55 minutes
Whole	2½ to 3 pounds 3½ to 4 pounds 4½ to 5 pounds	375°F 375°F 375°F	1 to 1¼ hours 1¼ to 1¾ hours 1½ to 2 hours
GAME			
Cornish game hen	1¼ to 1½ pounds	375°F	1 to 1¼ hours
Duckling, domestic	4 to 6 pounds	350°F	1½ to 2 hours
Pheasant	2 to 3 pounds	350°F	1¼ to 1½ hours
Squab, domestic	12 to 16 ounces	375°F	45 to 60 minutes
TURKEY			
Boneless whole	2½ to 3½ pounds	325°F	2 to 2½ hours
Breast, whole	4 to 6 pounds 6 to 8 pounds	325°F 325°F	1½ to 2¼ hours 2¼ to 3¼ hours
Drumstick	1 to 1½ pounds	325°F	1¼ to 1¾ hours
Thigh	1½ to 1¾ pounds	325°F	1½ to 1¾ hours

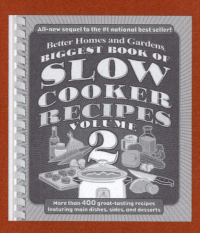

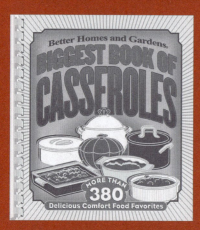

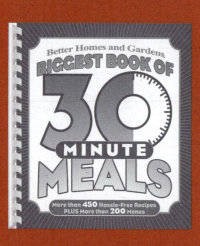

Dinnertime just got easier,
thanks to hundreds of quick and easy mealtime solutions.

Biggest Book of Slow Cooker Recipes Volume 2
Come home to a great-tasting dinner at the end of the day! Find 400 recipes for main dishes that will please every palate—from beef, pork, and lamb entrées to poultry, fish, and meatless recipes. Plus you'll find bonus chapters with light and healthful recipes and five-ingredient fixes.

Biggest Book of Casseroles
Few dishes say "comfort food" more than timeless favorites such as Upside-Down Pizza Casserole and Easy Beef Pot Pie. Along with the beloved classics are casseroles starring fabulous ethnic flavors. There are also breakfast dishes and potluck favorites. Anything you make is sure to disappear fast.

Biggest Book of 30 Minute Meals
No matter how tight your schedule, you'll be amazed at how easy preparing these satisfying meals can be. As a bonus, we've included a chapter of supereasy party foods that take advantage of quick-cooking ingredients.

Available where all great books are sold.

ADT1013_0408